Guide to the National Parks

West

Crevasse climbing, Mount Rainier NP

D1417121

NATIONAL GEOGRAPHIC

Guide to the National Parks
West

National Geographic
Washington, D.C.

4

Gulf Islands
San Juan
Islands
Deception Pass S.P.
Dungeness N.W.R.
OLYMPIC
NATIONAL
PARK
Grays Harbor N.W.R. Olympia
Mount
Baker
NORTH
CASCADES
N.P.
Seattle
Nisqually
N.W.R.

CANADA
U.S.

Pasayten
Wilderness
Lake Wenatchee
Area
Alpine Lakes
Wilderness

W A S H I N G T O N
MT. RAINIER
NATIONAL PARK

Mount Saint Helens
National Volcanic
Monument

Columbia

Kootenai
N.W.R.

GLACIER
N.P.
Jewel Basin
Hiking Area
Flathead
Lake
Flathead Lake
State Park

National
Bison Range

Snake

Portland

Columbia

Salem

Williamette
National
Forest

Newberry National
Volcanic Monument

O R E G O N

I D A H O

Oregon Dunes
N.R.A.

Cape Arago S.P.

CRATER LAKE
NATIONAL
PARK

Klamath Marsh N.W.R.

Boise

Samuel H.
Boardman
State Scenic
Corridor

Oregon
Caves
Nat.
Mon.

Bear
Valley
N.W.R.

Upper Klamath N.W.R.

Lower Klamath N.W.R.

Redwood
State Parks
REDWOOD N.P.

Klamath

Six Rivers
N.F.

Tule Lake N.W.R.

Humboldt Bay
N.W.R.
Headwaters
Forest Reserve

Castle Crags
S.P.

Mount
Shasta
Drive

Humboldt
Redwoods
S.P.

Trinity
Alps
Wild.

Ahjumawi
Lava Springs S.P.

LASSEN VOLCANIC
NATIOMAL PARK

N E V A D A

Sacramento

Plumas-
Eureka
S.P.

Lake
Tahoe

Carson City

Lake Tahoe Basin

C A L I F O R N I A

Sacramento

Calaveras
Big Trees S.P.

Mono Basin National Forest Scenic Area

SAN FRANCISCO Oakland

SAN JOSE

Tuolumne

Mono Lake

YOSEMITE
NATIONAL
PARK

Devils Postpile Nat. Mon.
Mammoth Lakes Area

Ancient Bristlecone Pine Forest

San Joaquin

KINGS CANYON
NATIONAL PARK

MAP KEY

National Park

Excursion Site

SEQUOIA
NATIONAL PARK

Kern
N.W. & S.R.

0   miles   300

0   kilometers   400

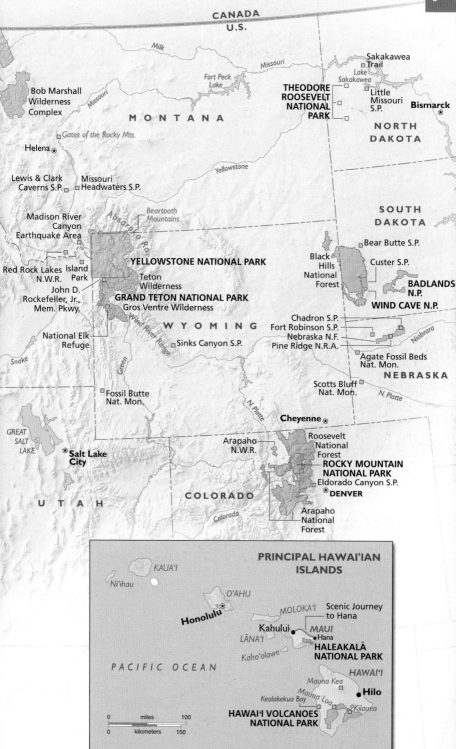

CANADA
U.S.

Milk

Missouri

Fort Peck
Lake

Sakakawea
Trail

Lake
Sakakawea

Little
Missouri
S.P.

**THEODORE
ROOSEVELT
NATIONAL
PARK**

Bismarck

Bob Marshall
Wilderness
Complex

Missouri

M O N T A N A

**N O R T H
D A K O T A**

Gates of the Rocky Mts.

Helena

Yellowstone

Lewis & Clark
Caverns S.P.

Missouri
Headwaters S.P.

**S O U T H
D A K O T A**

Beartooth
Mountains

Bear Butte S.P.

Madison River
Canyon
Earthquake Area

Absaroka Rg.

YELLOWSTONE NATIONAL PARK

Black
Hills
National
Forest

Custer S.P.

Red Rock Lakes
N.W.R.

Island
Park

Teton
Wilderness

**BADLANDS
N.P.**

John D.
Rockefeller, Jr.,
Mem. Pkwy.

GRAND TETON NATIONAL PARK

Gros Ventre Wilderness

WIND CAVE N.P.

W Y O M I N G

Chadron S.P.

National Elk
Refuge

Wind River Range

Sinks Canyon S.P.

Fort Robinson S.P.

Nebraska N.F.

Pine Ridge N.R.A.

Niobrara

Snake

Green

Agate Fossil Beds
Nat. Mon.

N E B R A S K A

Fossil Butte
Nat. Mon.

Scotts Bluff
Nat. Mon.

N. Platte

GREAT
SALT
LAKE

N. Platte

Cheyenne

Arapaho
N.W.R.

Roosevelt
National
Forest

**Salt Lake
City**

**ROCKY MOUNTAIN
NATIONAL
PARK**

Eldorado Canyon S.P.

DENVER

U T A H

C O L O R A D O

Colorado

Arapaho
National
Forest

**PRINCIPAL HAWAI'IAN
ISLANDS**

KAUA'I

Ni'ihau

O'AHU

MOLOKA'I

Scenic Journey
to Hana

Honolulu

Kahului

LĀNA'I

MAUI

Hana

PACIFIC OCEAN

Kaho'olawe

**HALEAKALĀ
NATIONAL PARK**

HAWAI'I

Mauna Kea

Hilo

Mauna Loa

Kealakekua Bay

Kilauea

0   miles   100

0   kilometers   150

**HAWAI'I VOLCANOES
NATIONAL PARK**

Contents

Photos: Cover, El Capitan, Yosemite NP;
pp. 2-3, Olympic Mountains, Olympic NP;
opposite, Haleakala NP

Mountain Paradises

THE NATIONAL PARKS OF THE WEST—far flung and stunningly diverse—dwell in a vast geographic area extending east from the Hawaiian Islands to the Great Plains, and south from the Olympic Peninsula to central California. As is fitting for such an enormous area, the parks preserve an abundance of extremely varied terrain. There are tropical beaches, misty rain forests, ice-clad summits, prairie flatlands, strangely eroded badlands, and treeless expanses of alpine tundra.

As different and as distant from one another as they are, virtually all of these parks have one thing in common: mountains. The Hawaiian Islands are themselves mountains—the tallest peaks in the world, if measured from their base on the ocean floor. Some parks, such as Grand Teton and Glacier, contain entire mountain ranges. Others, such as Yosemite, Redwoods, and Rocky Mountain, take in a section of a range or, in the case of Mount Rainier, encompass a single grand peak.

Even the mountainless parks have been profoundly influenced by their relative proximity to mountains. For example, the semiarid climate of Badlands and Theodore Roosevelt is largely determined by the fact that both lie within the rain shadow of the Rocky Mountains.

A joy to gaze upon, a thrill to travel through, the mountains of these parks also tell some astounding geologic stories. This is particularly true of the volcanic parks, which make up nearly half of this book's roster. Yellowstone literally detonated several hundred thousand years ago, leaving a gigantic, still steaming caldera some 30 to 40 miles in diameter. Mount Rainier, a giant stratovolcano, exploded just 5,700 years ago and blew away 1,000 vertical feet of its own summit. A similar eruption of Mount Mazama 7,700 years ago gave us Crater Lake.

The Hawaiian national parks, Haleakala and Hawaii Volcanoes, represent a gentler, far less explosive form of volcanism. These lie atop colossal shield volcanoes that were built up slowly by successive eruptions of fluid basaltic lava. We tend to think of geology as a record of the far distant past, but in these Hawaiian parks you can see geology being made as lava continues to flow.

Cataclysmic eruptions and the flow of molten rock certainly grab our attention, but there are other, slower moving stories in the rocks of these parks. The Tetons, composed of some of the oldest rocks on the continent, are among North America's youngest mountains, heaved upward some 30,000 feet in past ten million years or so. Glacier, also composed of ancient rocks, slid eastward some 40 miles as an immense overthrust slab. The Olympic Peninsula was literally scraped off the floor of the Pacific Ocean by the nearly unfathomable power of a tectonic plate collision.

Some parks recall the great Ice Age. Yosemite, Rocky Mountain, and

American bighorn sheep

Glacier were all touched by the benevolent vandalism of glaciation. They are Pleistocene landmarks, endowed with broad U-shaped valleys, horns, hanging valleys, waterfalls and morainal lakes.

Height, of course, is a mountain's most salient feature. It provides us with a visual treat, but also accounts for a splendid diversity of plants and animals. Generally speaking, the higher you go the colder it gets and the more difficult it becomes for plants and animals to survive. In Rocky Mountain, the rule of thumb is that for every 1,000 feet you gain in elevation, you lose at least three degrees of average temperature. Drive from Estes Park to the top of Trail Ridge Road in a T-shirt and a pair of shorts and you'll be grateful you packed your sweater and a windbreaker—even on a sunny July day.

Because of these abrupt differences, mountains tend to compress within a relatively small area an extremely broad cross section of plants and animals. In Glacier, a 20-mile drive takes you from the grasslands of the Great Plains through two major forest types and up into a climate more challenging than that of the Arctic. In Olympic, you can start barefoot on a beach, crouched beside a tide pool, then wend your way upward through four distinct forest types to an alpine realm cloaked by 60 active glaciers.

These mountain parks, laced with scenic highways and trails, call out to us as never before. City life may have become the norm, but we do not shed our instincts so easily. We still need places where we can amble down a dirt path and wonder what left that hoof print in the mud. We need room to breathe, birdsong on the wind, and a rock to sit on in a starlit meadow. —*Thomas Schmidt*

HOW TO USE THIS GUIDE

Using the Guide

Welcome to the 18 scenic national parks of the West. Whether you are a regular visitor or a first-timer, you have a great treat in store. Each of the parks offers you fun, adventure, and—usually—enthralling splendor. What you experience will depend on where you go and what you do.

Our coverage of each park begins with a portrait of its natural wonders, ecological setting, history, and, often, its struggles against such environmental threats as pollution, erosion, and development. Each park entry includes the following sections containing practical information on how to visit the park and make the most of your visit:

How to Get There You may be able to include more than one park in your trip. The regional map in the front of the book shows them in relation to one another. Base your itinerary not so much on mileage as on time, remembering that parks do not lie alongside interstates; park roads are usually rugged—and, in summer, crowded.

When to Go The parks of the West are mostly year-round parks, though, of course, the activities change according to the season. Instead of going in midsummer, when the parks are often crowded, schedule your trip for spring or fall (or for July or late August) and time your arrival early on a weekday. Fall is a glorious time to visit, when trees are ablaze with color and visitors are relatively scarce. Many of the parks bloom with fields of wildflowers in spring. Winter often brings snow that lasts into late spring—a time of skiing, snowboarding, and cozy evenings beside a cabin fireplace. Consult this heading in each park chapter for details about the best times to visit.

How to Visit Don't rush through a park. Give yourself time to savor the beauty. Incredibly, the average time the typical visitor spends in a park is half a day. Often, that blur of time flashes past a windshield. No matter how long you decide to stay, spend at least part of that time in the park, not in your car. Each park's **How to Visit** section recommends a plan for visits of half, 1, 2, or more days. Guide writers devised the plans and trekked every tour, but don't be afraid to explore on your own.

Other Features of the Guide

Information & Activities This section, which follows each park entry, offers detailed visitor information. Call or write the park, or visit the park's website for further details. Brochures are usually available free of charge from the parks. For a small fee you can buy a copy of the "National Park System Map and Guide" by writing to the Consumer Information Center, P.O. Box 100,

Pueblo, CO 81002; or calling 719-948-3334. Visit the Park Service website at: www.nps.gov.

Entrance Fees The entrance fees listed in this book reflect fees at press time. In addition to daily or weekly fees, most parks also offer a yearly fee, with unlimited entries.

For $50 you can buy a National Parks Pass, which is good for a year and admits all occupants of a private vehicle to all national parks with a vehicle entrance fee. The pass does not cover parking fees where applicable.

For an additional $15 you can purchase a Golden Eagle hologram to affix to the pass for unlimited admission to U.S. Fish and Wildlife Service, Forest Service, and Bureau of Land Management sites.

People over 62 can obtain a lifetime Golden Age Passport for $10, and blind and disabled people are entitled to a lifetime Golden Access Passport for free, both of which admit all occupants of a private vehicle to all national parks and other federal sites and a discount on usage fees. These documents are available at any Park Service facility that charges entrance fees.

For further information on purchasing park passes, call 888-467-2757 or visit www.national parks.org.

Pets Generally they're not allowed on trails, in buildings, or in the backcountry. Elsewhere, they must be leashed. Specific rules are noted.

Facilities for Disabled This section explains which parts of each park, including visitor centers and trails, are accessible to visitors with disabilities.

Special Advisories

■ Do not take chances. People are killed or badly injured every year in national parks. Most casualties are caused by recklessness or inattention to clearly posted warnings.
■ Stay away from wild animals. Do not feed them. Do not try to touch them, not even raccoons or chipmunks (which can transmit diseases). Try not to surprise a bear and do not let one approach you. If one does, scare it off by yelling, clapping your hands, or banging pots. Store all your food in bear-proof containers (often available at parks); keep it out of sight in your vehicle, with windows closed and doors locked. Or suspend it at least 15 feet above ground, and 10 feet out from a post or tree trunk.
■ Guard your health. If you are not fit, don't overtax your body. Boil water that doesn't come from a park's drinking-water tap. Chemical treatment of water will not kill *Giardia,* a protozoan that causes severe diarrhea and lurks even in crystal clear streams. Heed park warnings about hypothermia and Lyme disease, which is carried by ticks. Take precautions to prevent Hantavirus pulmonary syndrome, a potentially fatal airborne virus transmitted by deer mice.

■ Expect RV detours. Check road regulations as you enter a park. Along some stretches of many roads you will not be able to maneuver a large vehicle, especially a trailer.

Campgrounds The National Parks Reservation System (NRPS) handles advance reservations for campgrounds at the following Western parks: Glacier, Mount Rainier, Olympic, Rocky Mountain, Sequoia & Kings Canyon, and Yosemite. For a single campsite, reserve up to five months in advance by calling 800-365-2267 (800-436-7275 for Yosemite), or visiting http://reservations.nps.gov. Pay by credit card over the phone or Internet, or by check or money order within 21 days. Or, write to NPRS, 3 Commerce Dr., Cumberland, MD 21502. Likewise, the National Recreation Reservation Service accepts reservations for Crater Lake, Lassen, Mount Rainier, North Cascades, Olympic, Redwood, Sequoia & Kings Canyon, Yellowstone, and Yosemite, as well as numerous Forest Service and BLM campsites. They can be reached at 877-444-6777, 877-833-6777 (TDD), or 518-885-3639 (international callers); or by visiting www.ReserveUSA.com.

Hotels, Motels, & Inns The guide lists accommodations as a service to its readers. The lists are by no means comprehensive, and listing does not imply endorsement by the National Geographic Society. The information can change without notice. Many parks keep full lists of accommodations in their areas, which they will send you on request. You can also contact local chambers of commerce and tourist offices for accommodations suggestions.

Excursions The excursions at the end of the park entries take you to other natural areas in the region. If time allows, be sure to explore some of these as well. Many of the sites are much less known than the national parks and often much less crowded. The distances noted from the parks are approximate and intended for planning purposes only.

Resources The back of this guide lists additional resources that can be helpful: federal and state agencies, general lodgings numbers, fishing and hunting divisions, and other helpful phone numbers and websites.

Maps The park maps and regional map were prepared as an aid in planning your trip. For more detail, contact the Park Service, phone the park itself, or visit the website. Contact the individual excursions sites for more information about them. Always use a road map when traveling and detailed hiking maps when walking into the backcountry.

The maps note specially designated areas within park borders: Wilderness areas are managed to retain their primeval quality.

MAP KEY and ABBREVIATIONS

☐ National Park Service system	U.S. Interstate **5**	U.S. Federal or State Highway **50 33**
☐ National Forest Service system		Other Road **J59**
☐ National Wildlife Refuge system	Unpaved Road	Trail	Scenic Byway
☐ National Grassland system			Continental Divide
☐ State or Provincial Park system	Railroad / Tram	Ferry	
☐ Indian Reservation	Wilderness Area	National Marine Sanctuary	National Wild & Scenic River
	National boundary	State boundary	

POPULATION

- **DENVER** above 500,000
- **Sacramento** 50,000 to 500,000
- Helena 10,000 to 50,000
- Morton under 10,000

SYMBOLS

- ⊛ State/Provincial capital
- ⌂ Ranger Station/ Visitor Center/ Park Headquarters
- ☐ Point of interest
- △ Campground
- ⊟ Picnic area
- ↙ Overlook / Viewpoint
- + Elevation
- ⤳ Pass
- ⊣⊢ Falls
- ○ Geyser
- ⤙ Dam
- Glacier
-)-(Tunnel
- Swamp

ABBREVIATIONS

Admin...Administrative
AVE..Avenue
Cr..Creek
DR..Drive
Hdqrs...Headquarters
HWY...Highway
I.-s..Island-s
I.R...Indian Reservation
L...Lake
Mt.-s..Mount-ain-s
NAT...National
N.F..National Forest
N.M.S...........................National Marine Sanctuary
Nat. Mon......................................National Monument
N.P...National Park
N.H.P..............................National Historical Park
N.S.T................................National Scenic Trail
N.W. & S.R..................National Wild and Scenic River
N.W.R.............................National Wildlife Refuge
Pk..Peak
PKWY..Parkway
P.P...Provincial Park
Pres...Preserve
Pt..Point
R..River
RD...Road
Rec..Recreation
Res...Reservoir
S.F...State Forest
S.P..State Park
ST...Street
TR...Trail
WILD...Wilderness

Roads, buildings, and vehicles are not allowed in them. National preserves may allow hunting.

The following abbreviations are used in this book:

NP National Park
NRA National Recreation Area
NF National Forest
NM National Monument
NWR National Wildlife Refuge
BLM Bureau of Land Management
SP State Park

Treading Lightly

As you head into the nation's marvelous national parks, keep in mind that a single step off a trail can harm fragile plants. Many parks have already suffered from the impact of tourism. Be sure to leave all items—plants, rocks, artifacts—where you find them. The parks are not just for people; they conserve ecosystems that sustain plants and animals.

Enjoy your explorations!

Badlands

They call it The Wall. It extends for 100 miles through the dry plains of South Dakota—a huge natural barrier ridging the landscape, sculpted into fantastic pinnacles and tortuous gullies by the forces of water. Those who pass through the upper prairie a few miles north might not even know it exists. Those who traverse the lower prairie to the south, however, can't miss it; it rises above them like a city skyline in ruins, petrified.

The Badlands Wall, much of which is preserved within the boundaries of Badlands National Park, may not conform to everyone's idea of beauty, but nobody can deny its theatricality. It's been compared to an enormous stage set—colorful, dramatic, and not quite real. Water, the main player on this stage, has been carving away at the cliffs for the past half million years or so, and it carves away an entire inch or more of mudstone in some places every year—and more like 6 inches in areas where loosely consolidated ash makes up the surface of the ground. But there have been other players, too. Beasts with names like *Titanothere* and *Archaeotherium* once roamed here; their fossilized bones can be found by the hundreds. In fact, the park preserves one of the world's richest Oligocene fossil beds, an irreplaceable window on vertebrate life from 23 million to 35 million years ago. Today, The Wall serves as a backdrop for bison, pronghorn, and bighorn sheep, as well as the million human visitors who pass through the park every year.

A national monument since 1939, Badlands acquired the Stronghold Unit in 1976, adding yet another dimension to the drama. This large stretch of land belongs to the Oglala, and one of their most sacred places is now preserved within it. It was here, on Stronghold Table, that the final Ghost Dance took place in 1890, just a few weeks before more than 150 Lakota were massacred by Army troops at Wounded Knee, 25 miles to the south.

- Southwest corner of South Dakota
- 244,300 acres
- Established 1978
- Best seasons spring—fall
- Camping, hiking, bird-watching, wildlife viewing, paleontology, history programs
- Information: 605-433-5361 www.nps.gov/badl

Isolated buttes and rock fragments near Cedar Pass, Badlands National Park

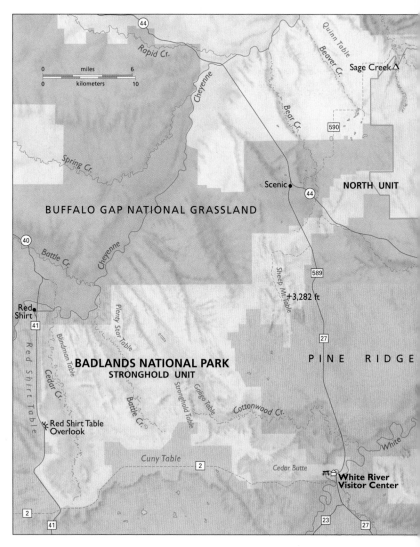

How to Get There

From Rapid City, take I-90 east 53 miles, then go south on S. Dak. 240 to the Pinnacles Entrance. From Kadoka, take I-90 west 19 miles, then S. Dak. 240 to the Northeast Entrance. Nearest airport: Rapid City.

When to Go

All-year park. Summer is the most popular season, though daytime temperatures may top 100° F. Spring and fall are usually pleasant, with moderate temperatures and fewer crowds. Winters can be bitter cold, but

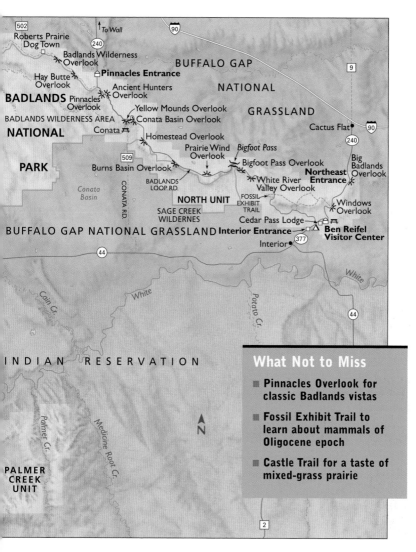

What Not to Miss

- **Pinnacles Overlook** for classic Badlands vistas

- **Fossil Exhibit Trail** to learn about mammals of Oligocene epoch

- **Castle Trail** for a taste of mixed-grass prairie

snow accumulations are rarely a problem in this arid climate.

How to Visit

The 30-mile **Badlands Loop** provides a rich eyeful of classic badlands for a 1-day **North Unit** visit. Make sure to take advantage of the informative nature trails. For those with a second day and a pioneering spirit, a trip to the park's undeveloped **Stronghold Unit** can be rewarding; make sure to check with rangers about road conditions before going.

EXPLORING THE PARK

North Unit: Badlands Loop: 32 or 89 miles; a half or full day

Enter the park at the Northeast Entrance on S. Dak. 240 and stop at the **Big Badlands Overlook** for your first, but by no means best, view of **The Wall** from above. Before you are the characteristic tiered cliffs of the badlands, dropping precipitously to the lower prairie, where the White River meanders between a fringe of cottonwood trees.

Stop next at the **Windows Overlook,** which serves as the trailhead for three short nature trails—each of which is highlighted by exhibits and/or wayfinding markers. While these trails may sound like the components of an architectural tour, they are actually brief forays into the Badlands Wall. The **Door Trail** *(0.75-mile round-trip, boardwalk)* passes through a narrow opening in The Wall into a jumble of barren, eroded hills reminiscent of the lunar surface. The **Window Trail** *(quarter-mile round-trip, paved)* leads to a natural window overlooking a deeply cut canyon. And the **Notch Trail** *(1.5-mile round-trip, very rough)* leads up a ladder and along the side of a gully to a break in The Wall, where you can look out over prairie and badlands, the White River, and the Pine Ridge Reservation on the plain down below.

If a longer walk interests you, consider hiking all or part of the 5-mile **Castle Trail,** which begins along the west side of the road between the Door Trail and the Window Trail and ends along the Badlands Loop Road adjacent to the Fossil Exhibit Trail. Mostly level, the Castle Trail skirts the badlands and wanders across a section of the park's mixed-grass prairie. This is special ground, supporting 56 species of grass and a wealth of prairie wildflowers which, in turn, support black-tailed prairie dogs, deer, pronghorn, bison, coyotes, bighorn sheep, and birds of prey. It is a precious remnant of the sort of grassland that once covered a roughly a third of North America.

Back in the car, a short drive brings you to the head of the **Cliff Shelf Nature Trail** *(trail guide available at trailhead).* This half-mile, steep loop takes you through a fascinating microenvironment in the badlands. Many years ago, a giant block of stone fell from the surrounding cliffs, creating this relatively flat shelf. The impact of the fall compacted the stone, making it less porous and allowing water to collect here. The resulting vegetation makes this place a delightful oasis in the otherwise barren wall. You can see mule deer browsing at dawn or dusk, and flamboyant magpies careening across the sky anytime.

Stop next at the **Ben Reifel Visitor Center,** where a video and various exhibits provide a good introduction to the park's history and geology. From this point, the road descends to the lower prairie for a brief stretch and then begins a gradual, stunning climb back up the Badlands Wall.

The **Fossil Exhibit Trail** takes you on a quarter-mile paved walk through an area dense with fossils. Copies of some are displayed at trailside under clear plastic domes. Though the park's rock strata includes an abundance of marine invertebrate species from roughly 75 million years ago, its most notable fossils are of Oligocene mammals that lived here 23 million to 35 million years ago. Some lived in subtropical forests. Later, after the climate changed, others lived among savannas and grasslands. They included *Leptomeryx,* a small, deerlike animal; *Archaeotherium,* a distant relative of the pig; and *Hoplophoneus,* a leopard-sized animal and one of the first to be described as a saber-toothed cat.

The road then continues level for 15 miles, punctuated by a dozen or so pullouts; each offers a slightly different perspective on

Western painted turtle in the parched Badlands landscape

the knife-sharp ridges, twisted canyons, and multicolored hills that characterize this broken terrain. Particularly spectacular among these are the **Yellow Mounds** and **Pinnacles Overlooks**.

If you're short of time, exit the park at this point and rejoin the interstate at the town of Wall. Otherwise make a left turn onto Sage Creek Rim Road and continue along the **Sage Creek Wilderness,** the largest prairie wilderness within the National Park System. This is excellent wildlife country; bison and pronghorn are numerous, and the road passes a town of those always entertaining prairie dogs. Longer hikes into the wilderness area start at the Sage Creek Campground, which lies about a mile off Co. Rd. 590 near the park's western boundary.

Beyond the campground turnoff, the road leaves the park. To complete the loop, continue along unpaved Co. Rd. 590 and make a left (south) onto S. Dak. 44 *(see sidebar opposite)*. If you're heading toward Rapid City, turn right; this stretch takes you through beautiful **Cheyenne River Valley** prairie and gives you views of the Black Hills. The highway goes through Scenic, the turnoff for the S Unit, if you want to continue directly there.

Stronghold Unit Drive: About 55 miles; at least a half day

The Stronghold Unit, administered jointly by the Park Service and the Oglala Tribe, is almost entirely undeveloped. Exploring it by car involves backtracking, driving on rough dirt roads, and generally putting a lot of wear and tear on your vehicle. For your safety, be sure to check with a ranger before setting out.

Begin at the town of **Scenic,** with its automobile graveyard and shanty-like saloon, and head south on Co. Rd. 589 for 4 miles. The turnoff for **Sheep Mountain Table** is marked. Follow the road across the flats and up a seemingly impregnable cliff to a grass-topped table dotted with yuccas. If you go on to the juniper grove at the road's end, you can stand on a finger of high land and be almost surrounded by a stunning assortment of spires and pinnacles— perhaps the park's best view. This is sacred ground for the Lakota; visitors must not disturb any religious artifacts or disturb people participating in religious activities.

Return to the paved road and continue south for 16 miles until you arrive at the **White River Visitor Center** *(open in summer only)*. It offers exhibits on Native American culture and a videotape on the Oglala. Here you can also get detailed directions to the many other sites worth visiting in the Stronghold Unit.

A visit to the **Stronghold Table** will either be a disappointment or the emotional culmination of your visit, depending on your perspective and imagination. Getting there involves driving some extremely rutted tracks through lonely grasslands, where you will probably get lost *(bring along a topographical map)*. It also involves opening and closing many gates. The reward for this effort? An unspectacular view, but the chance to stand in the place where, in December 1890, a group of Lakota danced the Ghost Dance for the last time. In this impassioned ritual, converts fell into hypnotic trances, "died," and envisioned the paradise soon to come, sweeping the white man from the land and repopulating it with bison, elk, and pronghorn. This, too, is sacred Lakota ground.

Backroad to Badlands

Weary of the interstate? A pleasant backroad alternative, S. Dak 44 runs for 65 lonely miles between the Black Hills near Rapid City and Badlands National Park, passing Wild West towns, ranches and farms, and open prairies.

Going east from Rapid City, the route follows Rapid Creek, with its verdant ribbon of elms and cottonwoods snaking across prairielands. It passes through the small ranching communities of Caputa and Farmingdale and then descends to the valley of the Cheyenne River.

Soon, you'll find yourself engulfed in a shallow bowl of long, rolling, brown-carpeted prairie creased with gullies. To a non-native, the sheer immensity of space can seem almost overwhelming. Here, you can see buttes and tablelands 30 miles away, with no sign of civilization anywhere.

Stretching throughout this area are broad expanses of **Buffalo Gap National Grassland** *(605-279-2125)*, one of 20 such areas on the Great Plains restored from "dust bowl" conditions after the Great Depression. Today, cattle ranchers graze livestock here by permit, and anyone can hike or camp for free anywhere on Buffalo Gap's 591,000 acres.

This is also Lakota country. To hear the language and music of this division of the Sioux, tune your radio to 90.1 FM.

As you approach Badlands, its magnificent saw-toothed wall of stone pyramids and castles rises to your left.

INFORMATION & ACTIVITIES

Headquarters
P.O. Box 6
Interior, SD 57750
605-433-5361
www.nps.gov/badl

Visitor & Information Centers
Ben Reifel Visitor Center, in the **North Unit,** open daily all year. White River Visitor Center, in the **Stronghold Unit,** open only in summer.

Seasons & Accessibility
Park open year-round. Snowstorms may block roads temporarily in winter. Call park headquarters to check current road and weather conditions and accessibility to the undeveloped Stronghold Unit.

Entrance Fees
$10 per car; $20 annual.

Pets
Permitted on leashes anywhere in the park except in the Sage Creek Wilderness.

Facilities for Disabled
Visitor centers and some trails are wheelchair accessible. Free brochure available.

Things to Do
Free naturalist-led activities during summer: nature walks and hikes, evening programs, night walks, fossil demonstrations. Also available: interpretive exhibits and audiovisual programs, hiking, biking, and wildlife viewing.

Special Advisories
■ Prairie rattlesnakes and cactuses live here; watch where you step when walking.
■ Bison are unpredictable and can be dangerous; keep your distance.
■ Be prepared for sudden changes in weather and severe thunderstorms in summer. Check weather conditions by contacting headquarters or a visitor center before you hike.
■ No permit required for overnight camping in the backcountry; consulting a ranger for advisories is recommended.

Campgrounds
Two campgrounds, both with a 14-day limit. Cedar Pass and Sage Creek rarely fill up and are open all year, first come, first served. (*Heavy snows may close them in winter.*) Cedar Pass is $10 in summer, with water; $8 in winter, without water. Sage Creek is free year-round, without water. No showers. Tent and RV sites; no hookups. Cedar Pass Group Campground, reservations accepted

Echinacea

Memorial Day to Labor Day; campsites $2 per person, $20 minimum; contact park head-quarters. Food service available in park.

Hotels, Motels, & Inns
(Unless otherwise noted, rates are for two persons in a double room, high season.)

INSIDE THE PARK:
■ **Cedar Pass Lodge** (on S. Dak. 240 near visitor center) P.O. Box 5, Interior, SD 57750. 605-433-5460. 22 cabins. $63. AC, restaurant. Open mid-April through October.

OUTSIDE THE PARK
In Interior, SD 57750:
■ **Badlands Inn** (half mile from park entrance) P.O. Box 103. 605-433-5401. 18 units. $70.

AC, pool. Open mid-May to Labor Day.
■ **Badlands Ranch & Resort** HCR 53, P.O. Box 3. 605-433-5599. 4 units $52; 7 cabins $60-$100; 35 RV hookups $16. AC, pool.

In Wall, SD 57790:
■ **Best Western Plains Motel** (1 block off I-90) 712 Glenn St., P.O. Box 393. 605-279-2145 or 800-528-1234. 74 units. $75-$95. AC, pool. Open March through November.
■ **Knights Inn** South Blvd., P.O. Box 424. 605-279-2127 or 800-782-9402. 47 units. $56. AC, pool.
■ **Motel 6** Tenth Ave., P.O. Box 76. 605-279-2133 or 888-279-2233. 41 units. From $40. AC, pool.
■ **Sunshine Inn** 608 Main St. 605-279-2178 or 800-782-2613. 26 units. $50-$59. AC.
■ **Walls Econolodge** 804 Glenn St., P.O. Box 426. 605-279-2121 or 800-341-8000. 49 units. $90-$160. AC, pool. Open May through October.

For additional accommodations contact the Wall Chamber of Commerce, P.O. Box 527, Wall, SD 57790. 605-279-2665. www.gwtc.net/~wallchamber

Excursions from Badlands

Nebraska's Pine Ridge Parks

65 miles southwest of Badlands The northwestern corner of Nebraska is one of the best kept secrets of America's great outdoors. Here, uniform prairie gives way to the rugged Pine Ridge, an area of buttes, breaks, and timbered ridges roughly 100 miles long and up to 20 miles wide. Chadron and Fort Robinson State Parks are the crown jewels of the Pine Ridge, but nearby public lands on the **Nebraska National Forest** add thousands of acres and miles of trails. Among these is the heralded **Pine Ridge Trail**, which traverses wide tracts of the **Pine Ridge National Recreation Area.**

Travel south from Chadron on US 385 for 8.5 miles to **Chadron State Park,** where you can overnight in a well-shaded campground or a fully equipped housekeeping cabin *(available April–Nov., reservations accepted up to a year in advance for minimum 2-night stay),* swim, ride horses, and take a paddleboat ride.

For an outstanding 5-mile loop hike or mountain bike ride, start in the campground near the walk-in campsites and follow the brown posts with white diamonds up the wide drainage through

Red Cloud Buttes, overlooking Fort Robinson State Park

ponderosa pine forest. After about half a mile, bear right at the first junction, passing through and beneath lofty rock outcrops. At 1.25 miles, you reach the crest of a ridge overlooking an extremely steep, timbered slope and a maze of eroded dry land. At about 2 miles you arrive at the **Black Hills Overlook.** The trail widens beyond, leading to a parking area and a gravel road. Follow the road through the prairie for a little over a mile, then turn left near a windmill and follow the trail markers down into ponderosa pine forest. Sharp-shinned and Cooper's hawks, northern saw-whet owls, and Clark's nutcrackers are among the birds you might glimpse here. In the 4-mile range you'll walk directly in the bottom of a lush draw, with big sediment blocks above on both sides, and banks that seem too steep to hold the grasses that they do. You'll close the loop after 4.5 miles and return to the trailhead.

To reach **Fort Robinson State Park,** travel west on US 20 from Chadron. The park lies a couple of miles beyond Crawford. A former military post, Fort Robinson played an important role as a base of Army operations during the Plains Indian Wars. It was here that the Oglala warrior chief Crazy Horse was murdered in 1877 while being held captive. The fort remained in operation until the end of World War II, during which it served as a POW camp.

Officers quarters, barracks, and other military buildings now house the park's visitor center, the **University of Nebraska's Trailside Museum of Natural History** *(308-665-2929. Adm. fee),* and overnight lodgings *(available April–Nov., reservations accepted up to a year in advance for minimum 2-night stay).* The historic area is well worth exploring; consider doing so on the guided **Tour Train** *(inquire at visitor center).*

If it's solitude and a wilder experience you seek, head west on **Soldier Creek Road,** which turns to gravel after exiting the military grounds. At just over 6 miles you'll leave the state park and enter a Nebraska National Forest primitive campground.

To investigate the encouraging aftermath of a 1989 wildfire, consider taking all or part of a 4-mile **loop trail** that begins in the campground. Start by fording the stream and bearing right through the lower camping area; walk through the gate and follow the two-track road across the Middle Fork of Soldier Creek.

The lightning-caused Fort Robinson fire of July 1989 burned across 48,000 acres, including the entire 7,794-acre Soldier Creek Wilderness, formerly part of the Fort Robinson Military Preserve.

The fire raged across both ridges visible from the trail, but left the creek bottoms fairly unscathed. After half a mile, veer right onto a less distinct two track and head up away from the creek. Once you're on top you'll see that the next ridge to the right also burned extensively, but today lots of younger trees have taken root.

Pass the foundations of the **Officers' Club** at 1.25 miles, then turn right onto the **Boots and Saddle Trail,** then follow the brown posts up toward a hilltop windmill and a captivating view of the burned area. Along the way, you are likely to flirt with semiwild, open-range cattle.

After crossing a saddle at 1.5 miles, you'll come into another big, fire-scorched drainage. The trail appears to be a single track worn down the middle of an old roadbed, whose meanderings you'll follow up and around the heads of several subdrainages. Watch for a coyote or two as you climb toward the top, gained at 2.5 miles. At this point you'll begin skirting the fence line marking the wilderness boundary, surrounded by a proliferation of yucca and the sweet aroma of sagebrush. As you gaze out over this rough, seemingly untamed landscape, you might wonder whether you are still in Nebraska.

By 3.75 miles you reach a creek bottom timbered in green ash, boxelder, chokecherry, and other trees and shrubs. In summer, the trail might lie ankle deep in dust churned up by cattle and horses. Watch and listen for wild turkeys. You'll cross the creek at just under 4 miles, then turn right to stay low as you head downstream. After another couple of creek crossings in the shade of huge cottonwoods trees, return to the beginning at about 4 miles.

Another outstanding badlands site worth investigating before bidding the Nebraska panhandle goodbye: **Toadstool Geologic Park** *(308-432-4475. Adm. fee)*, located 19 miles northwest of Crawford, 15 of them over improved gravel. Located within the **Ogalala National Grasslands** *(see sidebar opposite),* the remote park includes hiking trails and a six-site campground.

■ 23,000 acres ■ Northwestern Nebraska, outside Chadron and Crawford ■ Year-round ■ Hiking, backpacking, mountain biking, horseback riding, swimming, fishing, cross-country skiing ■ Adm. fee ■ Contact Chadron State Park, 15951 Hwy. 385, Chadron, NE 69337, 308-432-6167; or Fort Robinson State Park, P.O. Box 392, Crawford, NE 69339, 308-665-2900. www.ngpc.state.ne.us/parks/

Agate Fossil Beds National Monument

100 miles southwest of Badlands

As you descend Nebr. 29 into the Niobrara River Valley, you see before you a classic western landscape of rolling prairie and low, broken buttes. The latter marks the general level of the surface of an ancient landscape and one of the world's preeminent fossil beds, now preserved within Agate Fossil Beds National Monument.

Here, thousands of now extinct animals perished in and around a few isolated water holes about 20 million years ago. All were subsequently buried by waterborne sediments. Some might seem familiar to modern eyes, while others appear unbelievably grotesque and bizarre. Among the fossilized animals uncovered here are the *Daphoenodon,* a wolf-sized creature whose family is now extinct; *Stenomylus,* a fast-moving, camel-gazelle-like animal just 2 feet tall; and *Parahippus,* a distant relative of the horse.

Just inside the monument entrance, look left for the 1-mile

More Than Just a Drugstore

Almost everyone in America has heard of Wall Drug. Bumper stickers and billboards advertising the business proliferate throughout the West and elsewhere. Far fewer people realize that the town of Wall, whose name derives from The Wall of the Big Badlands, is also home to the outstanding **National Grasslands Visitor Center** *(708 Main St. 605-279-2125. Open year-round).* The facility celebrates our under-appreciated national grasslands, created largely in response to the devastating soil erosion that was taking place on intensively farmed private lands during the Great Depression. The center features exhibits on geology, as well as displays explaining the four main components of a typical grassland: uplands, wetlands, woody draws, and prairie dog towns. The center's video presentations include the 24-minute *Return of the Bison* and the 48-minute *Wind Country,* focusing on the wheres, whys, and hows of the national grasslands. There are plenty of hands-on displays and games for kids, too, along with an outlet of the Badlands Natural History Association. Here they offer for sale a good selection of books, maps, and items such as stuffed toy grassland animals and prairie seed packets.

Daemonelix Trail, which leads past giant sandstone spirals once thought to be fossilized roots. They are actually casts of burrows dug by a giant, dryland beaver known as *Paleocastor.* Many native and non-native prairie plants are also identified along the trail.

Next, drop by the **visitor center** for an orientation film and to have a look at fossil displays and the Native-American-goods collection of James H. Cook, who owned Agate Springs Ranch and hosted pioneer paleontologists studying the fossil beds.

From the visitor center, take the 2-mile round-trip hike to **University Hill** and **Carnegie Hill.** The hard-surfaced trail includes a 200-yard boardwalk spanning river backwaters rich with sandbar willow, the bamboo-like smooth scouring rush, cattails, and sedges. Watch for great blue herons, belted kingfishers, red-winged blackbirds, and blue-winged teal.

■ **2,762 acres** ■ **Northwestern Nebraska, 22 miles south of Harrison on Nebr. 29** ■ **Year-round** ■ **Hiking, fishing, fossil beds** ■ **Adm. fee** ■ **Contact the monument, 301 River Rd., Harrison, NE 69346; 308-668-2211. www.nps.gov/agfo**

Scotts Bluff National Monument

135 miles southwest of Badlands

For thousands of 19th-century emigrants traveling the Oregon Trail, Scotts Bluff marked the end of the monotonous, 600-mile crossing of the plains. Here they celebrated finding spring water, ample firewood, and good campsites. For the truly aware among today's westbound travelers, Scotts Bluff is not much less significant: A symbol that the Midwest has been left behind for the real West, the bluff offers the student of nature a chance to explore something truly different from the ocean of mixed-grass prairie in which it stands.

After entering the monument on Nebr. 92, stop at the **visitor center** to learn about Scotts Bluff's history and natural history. In front of the center is a small prairie restoration plot, a segment of the Oregon Trail you can set foot on, and a short but sweet **bicycle path** running about a mile to the monument's eastern boundary.

The best way to become intimate with Scotts Bluff and its microenvironments is to hike the hard-surfaced **Saddle Rock Trail,** leading 1.5 miles from the base to the top.

After skirting drainages teeming with rabbitbrush and other

Scotts Bluff

shrubs for half a mile, the trail climbs in earnest. Up and to the left, at the south end of the bluff, there is an immense natural amphitheater, framed with cliffs on both sides. Soon the trail leads into dispersed groves of ponderosa pines, then switchbacks at 0.75 mile to open an impressive view of the **Mitchell Pass** area. In the distance, separated by many miles of prairie and farmlands, are the pine-clad **Wildcat Hills.**

A short tunnel runs to the opposite side of the bluff; then, in less than a quarter mile, you'll pass back over and walk along a 12-foot-wide shelf of volcanic ash. The top of the butte, elevation 4,649, is surprisingly big and well-wooded. Here a trail leads north to a vista of the **North Platte River** and the badlands that forced most pioneers to travel south, far away from the river. A second trail leads to a south-rim overlook: Below, emigrants would have seen unbroken prairie populated by bison and pronghorn.

Heading back down, look for black-billed magpies, loud, mocking flashes of black and white against a cerulean backdrop. If it's autumn, listen for the far-off, crazy calling of sandhill cranes, flying so high on migration that you can't even see them.

■ **3,000 acres** ■ **Northwestern Nebraska, 5 miles southwest of Scotts Bluff** ■ **Year-round** ■ **Hiking, biking** ■ **Contact the monument, P.O. Box 27, Gering, NE 69341; 308-436-4340. www.nps.gov/scbl**

Crater Lake

Few forget their first glimpse of Crater Lake on a clear summer's day—21 square miles of water so intensely blue it looks like ink, ringed by cliffs that tower up to 2,000 feet above its surface. The mountain bluebird, Native American legend says, was gray before dipping into Crater Lake's waters. The tranquil Gem of the Cascades is set in a dormant volcano called Mount Mazama, one in the chain of volcanoes that includes Mount St. Helens. Mount Mazama's biggest eruption occurred about 5700 B.C. The explosion, which was 42 times as severe as the 1980 Mount St. Helens blast, catapulted volcanic ash miles into the sky. It expelled so much pumice and ash that soon Mount Mazama's summit collapsed, creating a huge, smoldering caldera up to 6 miles in diameter and and 4,000 feet deep.

Over the centuries, rain and snowmelt accumulated in this caldera, forming a lake more than 1,900 feet deep, the deepest lake in the United States. Wildflowers, along with hemlock, fir, and pine, recolonized the lava-covered surroundings. Black bears and bobcats, deer and marmots, eagles and hawks returned.

Scientists have yet to understand completely Crater Lake's ecology. In 1988 and 1989, using a manned submarine, they discovered evidence that proves hydrothermal venting exists on the lake's bottom and may play a role in the lake's character.

Crater Lake forms a superb setting for day hikes. Thanks to some of the cleanest air in the nation, you can see more than 100 miles from points along many of the park's 140 miles of trails. Forests of mountain hemlock and Shasta red fir predominate near the caldera rim. Ponderosa pine, the park's largest tree, and lodgepole pine are common farther down from the rim. At high points along the rim, twisted, whitebark pine testify to the harshness of the long winter, during which, on average, 44 feet of snow fall. Despite severe winter conditions, the lake itself rarely freezes over—thanks to its great depth.

- Southwest Oregon
- 183,224 acres
- Established 1902
- Best seasons summer–fall
- Camping, hiking, biking, scenic drive, boat tours
- Information: 541-594-3000 www.nps.gov/crla

Crater Lake, along Rim Drive near Inspiration Point

UMPQUA NATIONAL FOREST

230

DESERT RIDGE

North Entrance
Station

Cascade
Mountain Pass
5,925 ft

Boundary
Springs

Gaywas Peak
6,781 ft

miles   4
N
0
0   kilometers   6

Timber Crater
7,424 ft

Bald Crater
6,478 ft

PUMICE DESERT

Crescent Ridge

Desert Cone
6,672 ft

ROGUE
RIVER
NATIONAL
FOREST

Oasis Butte

PACIFIC CREST N.S.T.

CRATER LAKE NATIONAL PARK

Crater Creek

Sphagnum
Bog

Red Cone
Spring

Grouse Hill
7,412 ft

RIM DRIVE

Llao Rock
8,049 ft

Steel
Bay

Palisade
Point

Merriam Point

Llao Bay

Wineglass

Hollman Peak
815 ft

Devils Backbone

Grotto
Cove

Bybee Creek

The Watchman
8,013 ft

Wizard
Island

Crater Lake

Cloudcap
Overlook

Lightning
Spring

RIM DRIVE

Discovery Point

Sentinel Rock

Castle Creek

Phantom Ship
Overlook

Rim Village Visitor
Center (summer only)

Cafeteria and Gift Shop

Crater Lake Lodge

62

Sun Notch

Dutton Ridge

Kerr Valley

Steel Information Center
Park Headquarters

Union Creek

Thousand
Springs

Castle Point
6,276 ft

Annie
Spring

Annie
Creek
Canyon

Vidae
Falls

GRAYBACK RIDGE

Annie Spring
Entrance Station

Mazama Village

Duwee Falls

Sun Creek

Arant Point
6,800 ft

Crater Peak
7,263 ft

ROGUE
RIVER
NATIONAL
FOREST

Union Peak
7,709 ft

62

Annie Creek

PUMICE
FLAT

Scoria Cone
6,648 ft

Baldtop
6,200 ft

Red Blanket Creek

Stuart
Falls

PACIFIC CREST N.S.T.

Goose Nest
7,249 ft

WINEMA

SKY LAKES
WILDERNESS

NATIONAL

Jerry Mountain

Goose Egg
7,124 ft

FOREST

What Not to Miss

- Sinnott Memorial Overlook for classic vista of Crater Lake setting
- Rim Drive, which circles Crater Lake's caldera
- Cleetwood Cove Trail, only route down to lake
- Wizard Island boat cruise
- Pinnacles Overlook for view of volcanic spires
- Castle Crest Wildflower Trail, for colorful blossoms
- Phantom Ship Overlook

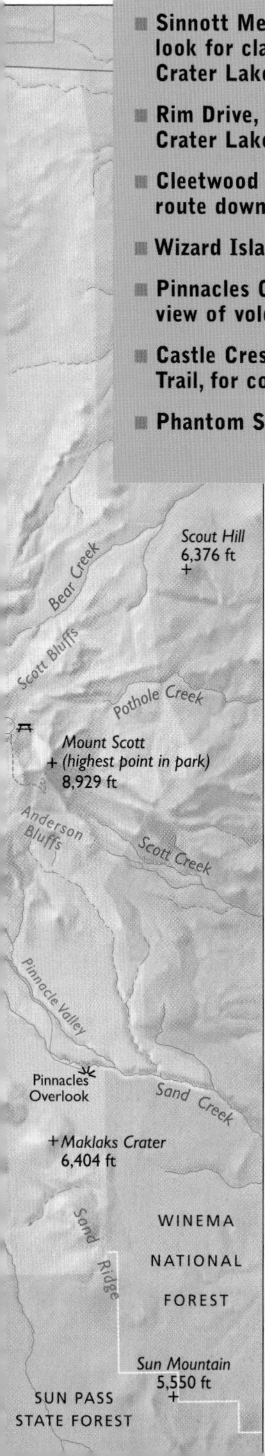

Bear Creek

Scott Bluffs

Scout Hill
6,376 ft
+

Pothole Creek

Mount Scott
+ (highest point in park)
8,929 ft

Anderson Bluffs

Scott Creek

Pinnacle Valley

Pinnacles Overlook

Sand Creek

+ Maklaks Crater
6,404 ft

Sand Ridge

WINEMA

NATIONAL

FOREST

Sun Mountain
5,550 ft
+

SUN PASS
STATE FOREST

How to Get There

Enter the park from the west (Medford, about 75 miles away) or the south (Klamath Falls, about 55 miles away) on Oreg. 62, or from the north on Oreg. 138. Airports: Medford and Klamath Falls.

When to Go

The lake looks best in summer. Oreg. 62 and the access road leading to Rim Village remain open during daylight in winter, and cross-country skiing is becoming increasingly popular. The scenic drive around the lake usually closes in October because of snow; in some years, the drive may not reopen completely until as late as mid-July.

How to Visit

Spend at least a half day touring the 33-mile **Rim Drive,** enjoying its many overlooks. Also plan to spend some time hiking one or more of several trails, perhaps to the fire lookout atop **The Watchman,** the **Godfrey Glen Trail,** or the **Castle Crest Wildflower Trail.** On a second day, consider hiking down to the shore for the narrated **boat tour** of the lake. The boat stops at **Wizard Island;** if time and weather permit, climb to the top of it and catch a later boat back.

EXPLORING THE PARK

Rim Village Area: 1 hour to a half day

Most visitors simply want to see the lake. If that's all they accomplish, they'll miss peaks, creeks, canyons, desert, hiking trails, and more in their rush to check it off their list of things to do. It's much better to take your time. If you arrive from the south, as most do, enhance your understanding of the park and its surroundings by making a quick stop at the **Steel Information Center** to watch the 18-minute orientation film. Then drive the last 3 miles to the lake, turn right into **Rim Village** and hustle over to **Sinnott Memorial.**

From the viewing point atop the 900-foot cliff, that first unobstructed vista of Crater Lake's shocking blueness and its magnificent caldera setting is a moment to be relished, like seeing your first grizzly bear or shooting star. It's also a good time to remember this caution: Much of the rock near the crater's rim is crumbly, so stay back from the edge unless you are at an established viewpoint.

It is the lake's depth and clarity that creates the storied shade of blue. In 1997 scientists conducted a standard measurement of water clarity by lowering an 8-inch disk into the lake and watching to see when it would disappear. It remained visible from the surface for an incredible 142 feet. Scientists also found green algae growing at a record 725 feet below the surface, indicating that sunlight may penetrate deeper in Crater Lake than in any other body of water in the world.

As light passes through water, different colors of the spectrum are absorbed. Red is absorbed first, then orange, then yellow, and, at about 350 feet, green vanishes, too. Only the blues remain unabsorbed, and at depths greater than 350 feet they constitute the only illumination, which is what scatters back to the admiring eyes of visitors along the rim.

From the Sinnott Memorial vista, a moderate 7.5-mile pathway leads along the rim in either direction. In Rim Village itself, you'll find a restaurant, gift shop, the Rim Village Visitor Center and the grand **Crater Lake Lodge** *(541-830-8700)*, with its outstanding views of the caldera.

Outside the lodge, you can pick up the rather steep 1.7-mile **Garfield Peak Trail,** which leads east to the top of Garfield Peak (8,054 feet). The elevation gain of 1,000 feet will leave you panting, but so will the view from the summit. Along the way stop to appreciate the Indian paintbrush, phlox, and penstemon.

Rim Drive: **33 miles; a half to a full day**

This marvelous drive along the calderic rim of Mount Mazama offers more than 25 scenic overlooks, several good picnic areas, a promising side road, and plenty of opportunities for hikes and strolls *(trailers and other oversize vehicles not recommended on east Rim Drive)*. To begin, set your car's odometer at zero (or note the setting) as you leave Rim Village. Head west or clockwise around the lake, and be careful: The road is narrow and has sharp curves. Watch out for pedestrians and bicyclists.

The first stop *(Milepost 1.3)* brings you near **Discovery Point,** where, on June 12, 1853, a group of prospectors searching for a gold mine happened upon the lake, which they named Deep Blue Lake. Native Americans, believing the lake sacred, had told no outsiders about it. **Hillman Peak,** to the far left on the rim, is named for

Wizard Island, Crater Lake

one of the prospectors. The peak is a 70,000-year-old volcano—one of the compact cluster of overlapping volcanic cones that formed Mount Mazama. It was cleaved in half when the summit collapsed. At 1,978 feet above the water, it forms the highest point on the rim and makes a convenient measuring device: The distance from the lake surface to the summit is roughly the same as the maximum depth of the lake (1,932 feet).

The overlook at Mile 4 offers a good view of **Wizard Island,** named for its resemblance to a sorcerer's hat. Rising 767 feet above the surface of the lake, the island is a classic cinder cone—built of red-hot cinders ejected from the caldera floor sometime after Mount Mazama collapsed. A Native American legend portrays the island as the head of Llao, chief of the Below World. Skell, chief of the Above World, killed and dismembered Llao in the final, literally earth-shattering battle waged on the mountain top.

Time, weather, and stamina permitting, you'll enjoy superb views in every direction if you take the steep, 0.8-mile trail that leads from the overlook to a fire tower atop the 8,013-foot peak called **The Watchman.** The trail switchbacks 650 feet up to the summit, which nearly hangs over the lake. The peak earned its name when it was used as a reference point for sounding the lake in 1886 and lived up to it as the site of a fire lookout during the 1930s. The sturdy lava-boulder-and-wood-beam structure is still standing. Note the old wooden stool with glass insulators on the ends of its legs; in bygone days that is where the fire spotter would sit, probably a bit uneasily, during lightning storms.

Back in your car, turn away from the lake at the **Mount Thielsen Overview** on the left. A plaque identifies the major landmarks of the countryside. When the road forks at **North Junction** (Mile 6.1), you could make a short but rewarding side trip on the **North Entrance Road:** Drive 15 minutes north for a look at **Pumice Desert,** where Mount Mazama dumped more than 50 feet of ash, creating a porous soil that holds little water.

Back on Rim Drive, heading east, you'll skirt **Steel Bay** (Mile 8.8), which commemorates William Gladstone Steel, who dedicated his fortune and career to making Crater Lake a national park. Steel became fascinated by the lake when he read about it in a newspaper used to wrap his school lunch. Seventeen years of lobbying, culminating in a personal appeal to President Theodore Roosevelt, succeeded in making it the country's sixth national park in 1902.

The tireless Steel stocked the lake with fish and led the efforts to build Rim Drive and the Crater Lake Lodge.

Six miles farther on, pull off the road at **Skell Head** for another excellent view of the entire lake. **Mount Scott,** highest point in the park at an elevation of 8,929 feet, looms ahead as you drive on toward Cloudcap. Bear right at Mile 17.4 for the short spur road to **Cloudcap Overlook,** Rim Drive's highest, at 7,960 feet. **Phantom Ship,** an island to the southwest, consists of 400,000-year-old lava flows from the extinct Phantom cone. Dwarfed by the surrounding cliffs, it nevertheless stands 160 feet above the water.

Circle back to Rim Drive and turn right. For a closer look at Phantom Ship, which in some lights seems to vanish and reappear, stop at **Kerr Notch** *(Mile 23.2),* one of the U-shaped valleys carved by a glacier before Mount Mazama exploded. A road here leads to **The Pinnacles,** spires of hardened volcanic ash. Just after Kerr Notch, bear right to stay on Rim Drive.

At Mile 31.2 you can stretch your legs on the **Castle Crest Wild-flower Trail.** This nearly flat, 0.4-mile loop features a classic babbling brook and plenty of the wildflowers promised by the trail's name. It begins in a forest of mountain hemlock and red fir, then enters a meadow run riot with flowers, including Lewis monkey flower and scarlet paintbrush. Plaques identify many of the species. Remember, in this snow-ridden realm—the area receives an average of about 44 feet of snow a year—spring doesn't come until the summer months, so flowers are blooming in late July and early August. Watch your step: The wet rocks can be slippery.

From here you can either proceed back to Rim Village or, if time permits, turn left toward Oreg. 62 and, after 2.3 miles, park on the left for a stroll on the 1-mile **Godfrey Glen Trail,** a nearly level

Winter at the Lake

For nearly nine months of the year snow covers Crater Lake National Park. The road from the south entrance to the rim is cleared, however, and from Rim Village you can tour established lookout sites. At unofficial stops, stay back from the rim; snow can obscure the edge, and ice makes slipping all too easy. On weekend days interpreters lead winter ecology walks; they even provide snowshoes.

Hiking on Wizard Island

loop accessible to wheelchairs. The path winds through an old-growth forest that developed on a flow of pumice and ash 250 feet thick, and in a few places it overlooks **Annie Creek Canyon.** The fluted pinnacles on the walls of the gorges began as the same material, but hot gases seeped up from within the Earth and hardened these areas. They defied erosion as the creeks formed canyons.

Boat Tour & Other Hikes

The 1.1-mile **Cleetwood Cove Trail,** starts along the north side of the rim, and descends 750 feet to the water, inflicting a relentless 11 percent grade on hikers and offering little or nothing of note by way of scenery or wildlife. But it is popular because it is the only trail in the park that leads to the lake and to the landing for the park's ranger-led **boat tour** (*purchase tickets in parking lot on Rim Drive*). The tours run from July through Labor Day and last 1 hour and 45 minutes.

The water-level perspective justifies the steep climb that awaits at the end of the boat tour. Gaze down into the lucid water or look up at the cliffs as the ranger explains the horizontal striping that defines the different layers of lava that have been deposited there. Sometimes boat tours encounter the **Old Man of the Lake,** a 35-foot barkless tree that has been bobbing about the lake since at least 1929. Perhaps you'll cruise through one of the yellow swirls that can be seen from the rim. The ranger will explain that it's not pollution but pine pollen that has blown in from the surrounding forests. By dating pollen grains found in sediments at the bottom of the lake, scientists have determined that Crater Lake began filling immediately after the collapse of Mount Mazama and that it took 300 years for the water to reach its present level.

If you have timed it right, you can get off the boat for the 2 p.m. **Wizard Island tour** *(weather permitting; check schedule for next boat to pick you up).* The relatively steep **Wizard Island Summit Trail** (0.9 mile one way) begins at the island's dock and winds through mountain hemlock, Shasta red fir, and wildflowers to the crater at the top. Awaiting you are superb views of bleached, contorted whitebark pines against the blue water, as well as a wonderful panorama of the inside of the cinder cone's own crater, which measures 90 feet deep.

The **Mount Scott Trail,** considered by many to be the most spectacular in the park, starts from the left side of Rim Drive along the east side of the caldera. It ascends 2.5 miles to the park's highest point and offers panoramic views of the lake, the east side of the park, and Klamath Basin. On this trail you might see falcons, hawks, and eagles, particularly in spring and fall.

Another good park hike is on the **Annie Creek Canyon Trail,** a 1.7-mile self-guided loop that winds through beds of wildflowers to the bottom of a deep, stream-cut canyon and back. It begins behind the amphitheater at the Mazama Campground. At the trailhead, pick up one of the excellent interpretive brochures. The path winds along the canyon rim and then descends 200 feet to Annie Creek. This canyon used to be a broad, U-shaped glacial valley, but the big eruption of Mount Mazama filled it with pumice and other rock fragments, which the creek later carved into a V-shaped canyon. In places along the trail you'll see contorted pumice spires fashioned by rain and wind, reminders of the eruption. Most of the canyon, however, is lushly vegetated by old-growth red firs and mountain hemlocks and a verdant understory, sprinkled with occasional meadows full of buttercups, Indian paintbrush, and monkey flowers. Watch for animals, too, such as marmots, Steller's jays, and chipmunks. When the huckleberries ripen, you might even encounter a black bear with a purple-stained mouth.

INFORMATION & ACTIVITIES

Headquarters
P.O. Box 7
Crater Lake, OR 97604
541-594-3000
www.nps.gov/crla

Visitor & Information Centers
Rim Village Visitor Center, on
rim overlooking lake, 7 miles
off Oreg. 62, open daily from
early June to end of September,
closed rest of year. Steel Information Center at park headquarters, open daily all year.

Seasons & Accessibility
South and West Entrances open
year-round. North Entrance
open mid-June to mid-October,
snow permitting. East side of
Rim Drive, from Cleetwood
Cove to park headquarters, may
remain closed by snow until
mid-July. Call headquarters for
current conditions.

Entrance Fees
$10 per car per week; $20 for
annual pass.

Pets
Pets must be leashed at all
times and are not permitted on
any of the trails.

Facilities for Disabled
Most viewpoints are accessible
to wheelchairs, as are the visitor
centers, Mazama Village
Campground, the cafeteria and
gift shop at Rim Village, the
Crater Lake Lodge, and the
1-mile Godfrey Glen Trail.

Things to Do
Free naturalist-led activities:
nature walks, children's programs, campfire programs. Fees
for the ranger-narrated boat
tours. Also available: hiking,
bicycling, fishing *(license
required)*, snowshoeing, and
cross-country skiing.

Special Advisories
■ Hiking inside the caldera rim
permitted only on the Cleetwood Cove Trail. Volcanic rock
and soil are unstable and dangerous to climb on.
■ Biking permitted only on
open paved roads; mountain
biking allowed on unpaved
Grayback Drive.
■ Permits required for camping
in the backcountry. They are
free and can be obtained at the
Steel Information Center, the
Rim Village Visitor Center, and
on the Pacific Crest Trail where
it enters the park.

Campgrounds
Two campgrounds, both with
14-day limit. Lost Creek open
mid-July to late September.
Mazama Village open late-June
to mid-October. Both first

come, first served. $18-$23.
Showers at Mazama Village.
Both tent and RV sites at
Mazama. Tent sites only at Lost
Creek. Food services at Rim
Village.

Hotels, Motels, & Inns
(Unless otherwise noted, rates are
for two persons in a double room,
high season.)

INSIDE THE PARK:
■ **Mazama Village Motor Inn**
541-830-8700. 40 units. $107.
Open early June tomid-October.
■ **Rim Village/Crater Lake Lodge**
1211 Ave. C, White City, OR
97503. 541-830-8700. 71 units.
$126-$241. Restaurant. Open
late May to mid-October.

OUTSIDE THE PARK
In Canyonville, OR 97417:
■ **Riverside Lodge** 1786 Stanton
Park Rd. 541-839-4557. 12
units. $35-$75. AC.
■ **Seven Feathers Hotel & Casino
Resort** 146 Chief Miwaleta Ln.
800-548-8461. 146 units $89
and up; 32 RV hookups $14-
$16. AC, restaurant.

In Chiloquin, OR 97624:
■ **Melita's Motel**
39500 Hwy. 97. 541-783-2401.
14 units $33-$58; 20 RV
hookups $22. AC, restaurant.
■ **Rapid River Bend Motel**
33551 Hwy. 97 N. 541-783-
2271. 10 units. $47-$57.

■ **Spring Creek Ranch Motel**
47600 Hwy. 97 N. 541-783-
2775. 10 units, 7 with kitchenettes. $42-$55.

In Diamond Lake, OR 97731:
■ **Diamond Lake Resort**
350 Resort Dr. 541-793-3333.
92 units, 42 with kitchenettes.
Rooms $75; cabins $139-$195;
studios $88.

In Prospect, OR 97536:
■ **Prospect Historical Hotel**
P.O. Box 50. 541-560-3664 or
800-944-6490. 24 units. $95-
$150. Restaurant. www.prospect
hotel.com
■ **Union Creek Resort**
56484 Hwy. 62. 541-560-3565.
14 cabins, 8 with kitchenettes;
9 rooms with shared baths.
Cabins $65-$160; rooms $50-
$55. Restaurant. www.union
creekoregon.com

In Shady Cove, OR 97539:
■ **Royal Coachman Motel** 21906
Hwy. 62. 541-878-2481.
21 units, some with kitchenettes. $49-$64. Riverfront.
www.royalcoachmanmotel.com

Contact the park for a complete list of accommodations
within a 1-hour drive.

Excursions from Crater Lake

Klamath Basin National Wildlife Refuges

50 miles south of Crater Lake Renowned for the amazing numbers of waterfowl that migrate through, the six Klamath Basin wildlife refuges straddle the Oregon-California border, on the southeast edge of the Cascades. Twice a year, one million to two million birds move through these refuges, including three-quarters of all the geese, ducks, and swans that migrate up and down the Pacific flyway. That's the largest concentration in North America.

Two of the refuges are closed to the public most of the year, but the other four welcome visitors and offer a variety of ways to explore their rich assortment of grasslands, conifer forests, meadows, rocky cliffs, farmlands, marshes, lakes, and ponds. You can drive through some areas using your car as a bird blind, hike in others, or enjoy a day trip in a canoe.

Start at the northernmost unit, **Klamath Marsh NWR** *(off US 97, near Crater Lake NP)*, which takes in the finest and most extensive natural marshes in the Klamath Basin. A 10-mile **loop trail** makes this one refuge that can be explored in part on foot. **Silver Lake Road** leads across the main marsh, and in summer you can canoe on **Wocus Bay,** a marshy area in the extreme southeast portion of the refuge. The basin's ubiquitous waterfowl show up here, of course, along with herons, pelicans, snipes, muskrat, phalaropes, ospreys, avocets, mule deer, and hundreds of other species that thrive in this relatively undisturbed wetland complex. The pine forests of the refuge even harbor elk.

Working south, the **Upper Klamath NWR** is of special interest to paddlers, since the only way into these 15,000 acres of marsh and open water is via the **canoe trail.** If you don't have your own craft, you can rent a canoe at the start of the route *(call 541-356-2287)*. Paddle quietly and you'll likely encounter all manner of wildlife, including American white pelicans, snakes, and river otters. Ospreys and bald eagles also fish the refuge waters.

Except for early fall deer hunters, the general public may not enter **Bear Valley NWR,** located 15 miles south of Klamath Falls on US 97. Yet this is one of the most popular places among wildlife-watchers because of the huge concentration of bald eagles that gather here from December to mid-March. To see them, start before dawn and drive out on the short dirt road that comes within about half a mile of the southeast corner of the refuge.

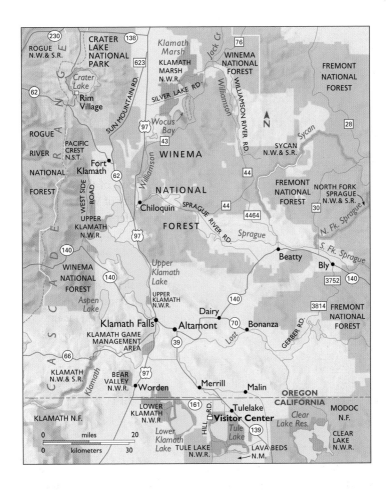

To the southeast on Calif. 161 lies the largest of the six refuges, **Lower Klamath NWR,** the country's first waterfowl refuge, established in 1908. Lower Klamath hosts the highest numbers of migrating waterfowl in the basin. If you want to overwhelm your senses with masses of geese and ducks flapping, honking, feeding, and quacking, take a spring or fall drive on the 10-mile **auto tour route,** which loops right through the middle of the refuge. In the spring you'll also spot stately sandhill cranes stalking about the refuge like wise elders lost in thought. For a summer treat take in the nesting white-faced ibis—more than 4000 pairs in 2003.

Just to the east you'll find **Tule Lake NWR** off Calif. 161. Stop at the visitor center for brochures, wildlife lists, and interpretive

Great egret flying over Klamath Basin refuge complex

guides for the refuge auto tour routes, hiking trails, and canoe trips. There are two short interpretive trails near the center: a short, level path into **Discovery Marsh;** and a quarter-mile climb to a fine vista of the basin.

Next, drive south 5 miles on Hill Road to the start of the **Wildlife Tour Route**. Along the way pause beside the shallow lake. From fall through spring look for geese, ducks, and tundra swans. Once you've turned east onto the gravel auto tour route, drive between Sump 1-A and the Southwest Sump and enjoy the sight of preening white-fronted geese or yellow-headed blackbirds hanging from the cattails. Your car serves as a wildlife blind; getting out will likely spook the animals. In winter, you can watch in comfort the spectacle that occurs when the lakes freeze over, except for those areas kept open by huge flocks of ducks. Bald eagles and hawks, sometimes by the hundreds, come to feed on the vulnerable waterfowl.

As you pass from Sump 1-A to Sump 1-B, you'll drive along the west bank of the **English Channel**. In spring watch for western grebes, famed for their courtship ritual, which includes the so-called rushing display: The courting pair runs across the water flapping madly. Another member of this bird family, the eared grebe, usually forms summer colonies in Sump 1-B. They construct floating nests out of algae and reeds, anchored to rooted plants. Look at the grebes' backs and you may spot a little fluff ball with a bill—grebe chicks hitching a ride on the adults.

■ 185,000 acres ■ South-central Oregon, north-central California, off US 97 ■ Best seasons vary with wildlife; check with NWR headquarters ■ Hiking, canoeing, bird-watching, wildlife viewing, auto tours ■ Contact the refuges, Route 1, Box 74, Tulelake, CA 96143; 530-667-2231. www.klamathnwr.org

Oregon Caves National Monument

90 miles southwest of Crater Lake

A cavern is sometimes little more than a big hole in the ground. Not so with Oregon Caves. What draws people here are the elaborate dripstone formations that decorate the cavern's marble walls. The monument's **guided cave tour** takes about 1 hour and 15 minutes, includes 500 stairs, and slithers for about 1.5 miles through the dimly lit subterranean corridor. *(Children must be at least 42 inches tall and able to climb a set of test stairs unassisted in order to tour cavern.)*

Some formations immediately grab the eye, such as **Paradise Lost,** a big cluster of tan-and-white marble shapes that look like jellyfish. Other cave features require closer observation, such as moonmilk, which is a mass of minuscule calcite crystals that looks like cottage cheese. It was used as a folk medicine to treat cuts on livestock. You'll likely see cave popcorn, too. It's a residue created when water evaporates as air flowing into the cave passes over it; the translucent, large white bumps look more like eyeballs than like popcorn. If it's creatures you're looking for, lucky visitors may spot some of a handful that are native to the cave—perhaps pallid bats or a flea-size albino springtail, which feeds on the bacteria in little pools of water.

After returning to the surface, you can explore the outer world of the monument via half a dozen trails. They all start in the monument proper, but most extend into the surrounding lands of the **Siskiyou National Forest** *(541-858-2200),* which features some fine old growth. For the best vistas, take the **Lake Mountain Trail,** which climbs 2.5 miles to the highest point in the area (it requires much

Serpentine Treasures

A significant portion of the Siskiyous' exceptional floral diversity stems from the presence of serpentine. This uncommon rock came to the surface all the way from the Earth's mantle (the upper edge of the planet's molten interior). Serpentine is very brittle and shattered and has trouble retaining water; it contains chrome, nickel, and other elements that inhibit plant growth; and it produces nutrient-poor soils. Needless to say, one doesn't find pansies growing in serpentine outcrops. A suite of rare and hardy plants grows in these impoverished patches, often including plants typically found in deserts. A small exposure of serpentine can be found on the monument, and larger outcrops can be observed a few miles north of Cave Junction at **Eight Dollar Mountain** or a few miles south at the **Rough & Ready Botanical Wayside.**

up-hill huffing and puffing). Along the way, you will likely see mule deer and the occasional black bear. The 3.3-mile loop called **Big Tree Trail** winds amid many enormous trees, including white fir and pine, before culminating at the base of the thickest Douglas-fir in Oregon. This behemoth is between 1,200 and 1,500 years old, and its trunk measures an astonishing 12.5 feet in diameter. The trail also offers options to visit Bigelow Lakes.

■ 480 acres ■ Southwest Oregon, 20 miles southeast of Cave Junction ■ Best season summer; road to monument covered with snow or ice Nov.–April; cave is cold and somewhat dim ■ Hiking, bird-watching, wildlife viewing, cave tours ■ Fee for tours; to avoid long waits for cave tours, take early or late tours and get in line early to sign up ■ Contact the monument, P.O. Box 128, Cave Junction, OR, 97523; 541-592-3400. www.nps.gov/orca

Samuel H. Boardman State Scenic Corridor

110 miles southwest of Crater Lake

This scenic corridor along Oregon's southern coast gives landlubbers the chance to go "gunkholing." This isn't as distasteful as it sounds—the term is nautical slang for boating along a coastline in a leisurely fashion, frequently putting into this cove or that bay. This route provides motorists with a similar opportunity: About a dozen well-marked viewpoints and trailheads allow US 101 travelers to dip into this skinny, 13-mile-long coastal park as the spirit moves them. The **Oregon Coast Trail** also strings the viewpoints together, so hikers can troop from one end of the park to the other.

Cape Ferrelo, located near the park's southern border, is an excellent starting point for exploring Boardman. A trail at the south end of the parking lot winds through wind-stunted conifers and within minutes emerges into the treeless meadows that carpet the cape's seaward portion. A quarter-mile stroll through the open grasslands brings you to the tip of this stubby finger of land, from which you can see well down into California.

A couple of miles north of Cape Ferrelo lies **Whalehead Beach,** a vital stop for visitors who yearn to feel sand between their toes. Travelers who see the sign for **Natural Bridges Cove** and pull off will find an unprepossessing parking area without views. But a 1-mile trail from the south end of the parking lot leads to a cliff-rim view of the cove. On a foggy morning, ghostly mist curls through branches of scattered spruce and fir trees that jut from the cliffs and sea stacks. Two rock bridges, created by the collapse of an ancient sea cave, arch across the water, giving the cove its name.

Goat, Samuel H. Boardman SSC

■ **1,471 acres** ■ **Southern Oregon coast, 4 miles north of Brooking**
■ **Year-round** ■ **Hiking, beachcombing, swimming** ■ **Some informal trails may be steep, slippery, or unstable** ■ **Contact Harris Beach State Park, 1655 US 101 N, Brookings, OR 97415; 541-469-2021. www.prd.state.or.us**

Cape Arago State Park

100 miles northwest of Crater Lake

At just 134 acres, Cape Arago is a pocket park, but it leverages its location to achieve a grandeur far beyond its size. Atop the 150-foot bluff at the tip of the cape, the park's **main overlook** serves as a crow's nest from which you can see thousands of square miles of the Pacific. You can look for the green flash that sometimes flares in the wake of the setting sun, spot migrating gray whales, and thrill to the crash of monstrous waves during winter storms.

Another spectacle awaits just a few hundred yards northwest of the cape at **Shell Island** and **Simpson Reef.** Pinnipeds, which are fin-footed mammals, favor these rocky sanctuaries. At various times of the year, you'll see elephant seals, California sea lions, harbor seals, and Steller sea lions, sometimes by the hundreds, and occasionally by the thousands. Steep trails lead from the main overlook to three coves that lie within the park. **North Cove** provides a ground-level

Alien Invader

By the middle of the 21st century, the open waves of sand that define Oregon Dunes NRA may have vanished beneath a shroud of vegetation. The culprit is an alien plant called European beachgrass.

Worried that the ever shifting dunes would roll over waterways, roads, railroad tracks, and other development, people in the late 1920s began planting beachgrass on some of the dunes near Florence in an effort to stabilize them. It worked. Native plant-eaters don't like beachgrass, and this invasive species thrives when repeatedly buried by sand. From these and other plantings, beachgrass spread rapidly along the Pacific coast.

Beachgrass isn't overrunning the vast expanses of open sand, however; its effect has been more that of a long siege than an overwhelming attack. As existing inland dunes migrate east, there are no freshly supplied waves of sand coming behind them to take their place. European beachgrass is starving the dune system to death. Native vegetation now encroaches on areas where shifting sands once prevent plants from growing. If a removal program doesn't eradicate large amounts of beachgrass, the dunes area will shrink until it disappears.

view of the pinniped parade; the seals and sea lions often swim in the surf and sometimes come ashore *(keep your distance)*. All three coves offer excellent opportunities for tide-pooling.

■ 134 acres ■ Southern Oregon coast, 14 miles southwest of Coos Bay, at the end of Cape Arago Hwy. ■ Tide-pooling, wildlife viewing ■ Contact Sunset Bay State Park, 89814 Cape Arago Hwy., Coos Bay, OR 97420; 541-888-3778, ext. 2. www.prd.state.or.us

Oregon Dunes National Recreation Area

110 miles northwest of Crater Lake

Encompassing what is widely regarded as the foremost coastal dune system on the West Coast, this recreation area averages only 1 or 2 miles in width and stretches for some 40 miles north to south along Oregon's southern coast. The individual sand dunes, too, are of impressive size; some reach to 200 feet and range up to a mile in length.

Start from the southern end of Oregon Dunes, at North Bend/Coos Bay, and drive 4 miles north on US 101. Turn off on Horsfall Road and head west to **Horsfall Dune and Beach.** About a quarter mile short of the beach, pull into the parking lot for the **Bluebill Trail,** a 1-mile loop around Bluebill Lake, an old lake bed that becomes a wetland during the rainy season. You'll pass through western hemlock and shore pine forest and walk along boardwalks above the marsh. Birds love this area.

About 10 miles north of the Horsfall turnoff, you'll come to the parking lot for the **Umpqua Dunes Trail.** This 5-mile loop leads to the most stunning dunes in the whole recreation area. After a nice half-mile

Animal tracks in the sand, Oregon Dunes NRA

stroll through the coastal evergreen forest, you'll suddenly emerge into the **Umpqua Dunes**—several square miles of open sand. Many frolic for a while in that first series of high dunes and then loop back to their cars, but you can hike on another mile to the beach.

About 10 miles north of the Umpqua Dunes Trail parking lot is the town of Reedsport, home of the **Oregon Dunes Visitor Center**. It's small, but a few displays and a short introductory video effectively describe the area's natural, cultural, and geological history.

The finest hiking in Oregon Dunes awaits 7 miles north of the visitor center, on the **Tahkenitch Dunes Trail,** which starts from the south end of the Tahkenitch Campground and runs 2 miles to the beach. To extend this hike, you can branch off north onto the **Tahkenitch Creek Trail** or south for 1.5 miles along the beach or along the eastern edge of the deflation plain to join the **Threemile Lake Trail** and loop back to your car.

A 2-mile drive north from the Tahkenitch Campground brings travelers to the **Oregon Dunes Overlook,** the most accessible site from which to see a representative sample of the dunes ecosystem. From a couple of viewing structures and from the walkway that runs next to the parking lot, you can sweep your gaze across open sand dunes, forest, tree islands, deflation plain, foredune, and beach.

The **Siltcoos Recreation Area,** about 3 miles north of the dunes overlook, offers two appealing trails: the Lagoon Trail and the Waxmyrtle Trail. Park at the lot labeled Stagecoach Trailhead—there is no Stagecoach Trail—and walk a quarter mile east, back to the bridge across the Siltcoos River and the entrance to Waxmyrtle Campground. The **Waxmyrtle Trail** crosses the bridge, then turns west and follows the south bank of the Siltcoos to the beach, about 1.5 miles. The river soon widens into a lush estuary, home to herons, egrets, bitterns, and ospreys, which often nest in the tall conifers along the riverbanks. At the mouth of the Siltcoos, you'll encounter more wildlife in marshes and along the driftwood-littered beach. The **Lagoon Trail,** a 1-mile loop, strikes north from the bridge. Move quietly along the boardwalk and be on the lookout for kingfishers, ospreys, wood ducks, frogs, and herons.

■ **40 coastal miles** ■ **Southern Oregon coast, between Coos Bay and Florence off US 101** ■ **Year-round** ■ **Camping, hiking, walking, beach-combing, swimming, bird-watching, wildlife viewing** ■ **Day-use fee, camping fee** ■ **Contact the recreation area, 855 Highway Ave., Reedsport, OR 97467; 541-271-3611. www.fs.fed.us/r6/siuslaw/odnra**

Tracking Dune Beetles

Sand dunes, particularly when slightly damp, register the tracks of even the lightest animals. Explore away from the tramplings of human visitors, and you'll encounter the traces of many critters. Among them, you'll often see a curving, circling line that looks as if it were left behind by a wayward strand of cooked spaghetti. This odd track marks the slow passage of a ciliated sand beetle. These quarter-inch dwellers of the dunes spend the day under the sand and make those tracks at night as they crawl about in search of food. Another little track you may find looks like the herringbone marks left by a skier walking up a slope, with a dashed line running down the middle. Follow this trail and you may catch up to the shiny, black, 1-inch-long insect known as a stink beetle. Beware, if it tilts its hind end in your direction it may be about to demonstrate the aptness of its name.

Newberry National Volcanic Monument

80 miles northeast of Crater Lake

Newberry Volcano covers more than 500 square miles, making it one of the largest recent shield-type volcanoes in the United States. Yet you can drive right past it without even noticing it's there. Unlike the tall, proud cone of a classic composite volcano, a shield volcano is a nondescript, flattened dome. But looks can be deceiving. Newberry has erupted powerfully and often during the last million years, leaving volcanic features over a section of central Oregon informally referred to as the "Lava Lands." Despite its slumped form, it is an active volcano, having erupted as recently as 1,300 years ago.

Newberry Volcano and many of the geologic features it spawned make up the Newberry National Volcanic Monument, established by Congress in 1990. The monument includes lava tubes, cinder cones, mountain-size obsidian flows, an eerie forest of lava casts, and vast fields of stubbly lava. Visitors also will enjoy many non-volcanic attractions within the monument's 55,000 acres, which are squeezed between the Cascade Range to the west and the high desert to the east and share elements of each.

Start at **Lava Lands Visitor Center** (off US 97 about 15 min. S of Bend) for an introduction to the area's wildlife, archaeology, and, especially, geology. From the back patio, you'll see **Lava Butte,** a 500-foot cinder cone looming just a few hundred yards north. It formed 7,000 years ago when gas-charged magma blew up through the ground and spewed ash and cinders high into the sky. Liquid lava gushed from its base, eventually hardening into more than 9 square miles of jagged lava. You can explore the lava flow on the easy **Trail of the Molten Lands,** a paved, 0.75-mile loop dotted with interpretive signs. To see the view from above, walk, drive (only during off-season), or take the shuttle bus (fare) up the 1.75-mile road to the summit of Lava Butte. There, a quarter-mile interpretive loop guides you through the cinder cone, which is about 180 feet deep in places.

For a refreshing hike to a waterfall, take FR 9702 west 4 miles from the visitor center to the **Benham Falls Trail,** which follows the Deschutes River 0.75 mile to a series of cascading rapids.

If it's a hot summer day, you might cool off in **Lava River Cave** (1 mile S of visitor center on US 97), a 1-mile-long lava tube where the temperature is a constant 42° F deep inside. Aside from the comforting chill, the tube offers an interesting creation story

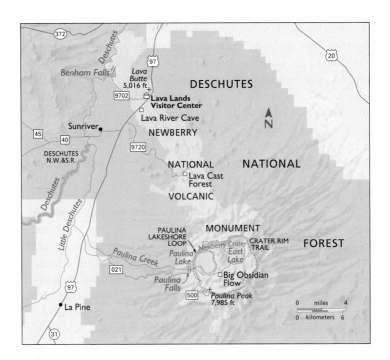

and several engaging formations, including figures of water-sculpted sand.

At **Lava Cast Forest** (SE of Lava River Cave via US 97 and FR 9720) you'll find a 5-square-mile pahoehoe (PA-hoy-hoy) lava field containing an abundance of lava casts of trees that burned during an eruption 6,000 years ago. An easy, 1-mile interpretive trail loops through this fascinating ghost forest.

Back on US 97, head south about 9 miles, then head east on FR 021 (Paulina Lake Road) about 12 miles to reach **Newberry Crater,** the centerpiece of Lava Lands. Take the half-mile loop trail to **Paulina Falls,** drop by the **Paulina Visitor Center,** then continue east on FR 021 to the 4-mile spur road that climbs to the summit of **Paulina Peak.** Views of the crater and surrounding lands are outstanding. Hikers can reach the same point from the visitor center via the **Paulina Peak Trail,** which climbs 1,600 feet in 3.5 miles. Other trails include **Crater Rim Trail,** a 20-mile loop around the whole basin; and the **Paulina Lakeshore Loop,** a 7.5-mile circuit that passes an obsidian flow and a beach where the icy lake water is warmed by an underwater hot springs.

Arguably the most fascinating feature of the caldera is the **Big Obsidian Flow,** off FR 021 between Paulina and East Lakes. A mere 1,300 years ago, a vent in the side of Newberry Volcano disgorged tens of millions of cubic yards of molten glass, which hardened into this mountain of obsidian. The **Big Obsidian Flow Trail,** a 0.3-mile loop, guides you up and around a small section of this massive flow, which is stained black by a small amount of iron mixed with the molten glass.

The early inhabitants of the Northwest prized obsidian as a material for making arrowheads, knives, and other tools. High-quality Newberry obsidian was traded throughout the Pacific Northwest. A 1994 dig near Paulina Visitor Center unearthed an obsidian spearpoint 9,000 years old.

■ 55,000 acres ■ Central Oregon, just south of Bend on US 97 ■ Best months mid-June–Sept. ■ Camping, hiking, boating (hand-powered only), fishing, wildlife viewing, lava tube cave ■ Adm. fee ■ Contact Lava Lands Center, 58201 S. Hwy. 97, Bend, OR 97707, 541-593-2421; or Deschutes National Forest, 1645 Hwy. 20 E, Bend, OR 97701, 541-388-2715. www.fs.fed.us/r6/deschutes/monument/monument.html

Willamette National Forest

90 miles north of Crater Lake

Most Americans have never set foot in an old-growth forest, but some of the finest stands of these old monarchs remain in the 1.7 million-acre Willamette National Forest in the central Oregon Cascades, near the junction of US 20 and Oreg. 126, west of Santiam Pass.

Start with the **Hackleman Creek Trail,** on US 20 just over 5 miles west of the junction with Oreg. 126. The main 1.2-mile loop *(wheelchair accessible)* among 400-year-old Douglas firs and western hemlocks is keyed to an interpretive brochure that you can obtain from Sweet Home Ranger District *(541-367-5168).* You can add another half mile to your hike by taking the spur trail that swings down by the creek. This trail is not wheelchair accessible.

A quarter mile east of the Hackleman Creek Trailhead, turn north on FR 055 and wind north a couple of miles to the **Echo Basin Trail,** also called the Echo Mountain Old Growth Trail. This 2.5-mile loop starts at around 3,700 feet and leads up, but not steeply, through a high-elevation old-growth forest that is distinctly

Man dwarfed by tree, Willamette NF

different from the mid-elevation community found at Hackleman Creek. You'll see snow-resistant Pacific silver fir trees and towering Alaska cedars, a species uncommon in Oregon that have trunk diameters up to 6 feet.

To see a low-elevation old-growth forest, go to the junction of US 20 and Oreg. 126 and head south on Oreg 126. Go just over 2 miles and turn left at the sign for the **McKenzie River Trail.** Take the rutted dirt road about 100 yards to a parking area, where you'll pick up the trail. Hike south across a narrow foot-bridge and amble through a lush forest of king-size Douglas-fir.

After about a mile you'll come to a second footbridge and a fork in the trail; you've intersected the northern end of the 5-mile **Clear Lake Trail,** which circles the lake. If you don't have time for the whole loop, at least cross the footbridge and walk the short distance to **Clear Lake.** Look closely into the clear, blue-green water of this mountain lake, and you can see the bleached skeletons of dead trees on the bottom. These are relics from the forest that stood here 3,000 years ago, before a lava flow dammed the river and created the lake. Farther along the trail skirts a partly overgrown lava field with trees 5 and 6 feet in diameter.

■ **1.7 million acres** ■ **North-central Oregon, 30 miles west of Sisters, near US 20 and Oreg. 126** ■ **Best season summer** ■ **Camping, hiking** ■ **Contact the national forest, Federal Building, 211 E. Seventh Ave., Eugene, OR 97440; 541-465-6521. www.fs.fed.us/r6/willamette/index.htm**

Glacier

Waterton-Glacier International Peace Park World Heritage site contains 2,000 square miles of what naturalist John Muir called "the best care-killing scenery on the continent." Many-hued summits—whittled by ancient glaciers into walls and horns—rise abruptly from gently rolling plains. Some 650 lakes, dozens of glaciers, and innumerable waterfalls glisten in forested valleys. A scenic highway crosses the park, making much of its beauty accessible to the casual visitor. More than 700 miles of trails await hikers and horseback riders.

In 1932 Canada and the United States declared Waterton Lakes National Park (founded in 1895) and neighboring Glacier National Park (founded in 1910) the world's first International Peace Park. While administered separately, the park's two sections cooperate in wildlife management, scientific research, and some visitor services.

The tremendous range of topography in Waterton-Glacier supports a rich variety of plants and wildlife. More than 1,800 plant species provide food and haven for 63 native species of mammals and more than 270 species of birds. In the 1980s the gray wolf settled into Glacier for the first time since the 1950s.

But now strip-mining and oil, gas, housing, and logging projects proposed or underway near the park's borders threaten the habitats of both water and land animals, including elk, bighorn sheep, and the threatened grizzly. Park officials and conservation groups are working with the Forest Service, the Canadian government, the Blackfeet Indian Reservation, and private companies to try to protect critical habitats.

Sheltered valleys and bountiful food have lured people here for nearly 10,000 years. Ancient cultures tracked bison across the plains, fished the lakes, and traversed the mountain passes. The Blackfeet controlled this land during the 18th and much of the 19th centuries, fiercely defending the rich bison country from other tribes.

- Alberta, Canada, and northern Montana

- Glacier, 1 million acres; Waterton Lakes, 73,800 acres

- Established 1910

- Best seasons summer–fall

- Camping, hiking, wildlife viewing, scenic drives

- Information: 406-888-7800 www.nps.gov/glac

St. Mary Lake, Glacier National Park

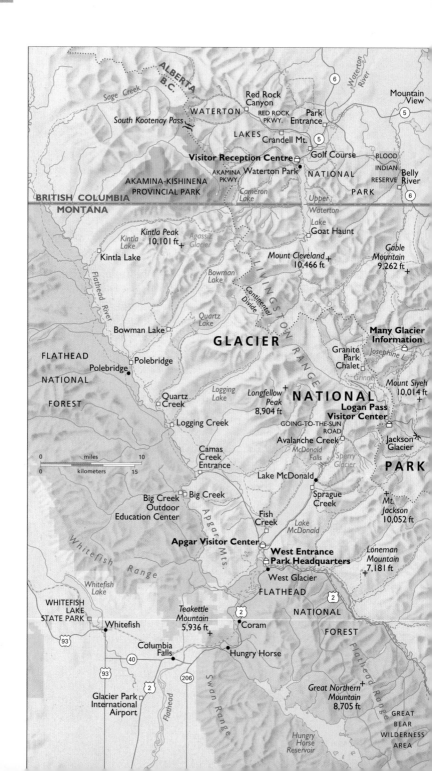

ALBERTA
B.C.

Sage Creek

WATERTON

Red Rock
Canyon

RED ROCK
PKWY.

Park
Entrance

6

Waterton River

Mountain
View

5

South Kootenay Pass

LAKES

Crandell Mt.

5

Visitor Reception Centre

AKAMINA
PKWY.

Waterton Park

Golf Course

NATIONAL

BLOOD
INDIAN
RESERVE

Belly
River

AKAMINA-KISHINENA
PROVINCIAL PARK

Cameron
Lake

PARK

6

BRITISH COLUMBIA

Upper

MONTANA

Waterton
Lake

Goat Haunt

Kintla Peak
10,101 ft

Kintla
Lake

Agassiz
Glacier

Mount Cleveland
10,466 ft

Gable
Mountain
9,262 ft

Kintla Lake

Bowman
Lake

Flathead River

Bowman Lake

Quartz
Lake

Continental Divide

GLACIER

LIVINGSTON RANGE

Many Glacier
Information

Josephine L.

Granite
Park
Chalet

Grinnell

FLATHEAD

Polebridge

Polebridge

NATIONAL

FOREST

Quartz
Creek

Logging
Lake

Logging Creek

Longfellow
Peak
8,904 ft

NATIONAL

Mount Siyeh
10,014 ft

Logan Pass
Visitor Center

GOING-TO-THE-SUN
ROAD

Jackson
Glacier

miles   10

0

kilometers   15

0

Camas
Creek
Entrance

Avalanche Creek

McDonald
Falls

Sperry
Glacier

PARK

Lake McDonald

Big Creek

Sprague
Creek

Mt.
Jackson
10,052 ft

Big Creek
Outdoor
Education Center

Apgar Mts.

Fish
Creek

Lake
McDonald

Apgar Visitor Center

West Entrance
Park Headquarters

Loneman
Mountain
7,181 ft

Whitefish Range

West Glacier

FLATHEAD

Whitefish
Lake

WHITEFISH
LAKE
STATE PARK

Teakettle
Mountain
5,936 ft

2

NATIONAL

2

Whitefish

Coram

FOREST

Flathead Range

93

Columbia
Falls

40

93

Glacier Park
International
Airport

2

206

Flathead

Hungry Horse

Swan Range

Great Northern
Mountain
8,705 ft

GREAT
BEAR
WILDERNESS
AREA

Hungry
Horse
Reservoir

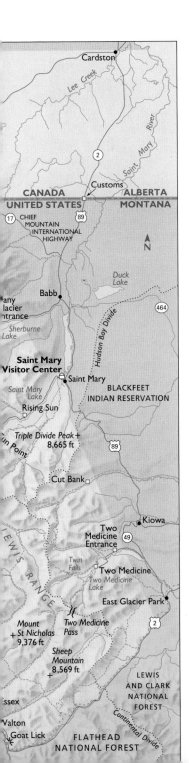

What Not to Miss

- Skipping rocks at a pebble beach on Lake McDonald

- Driving historic Going-to-the-Sun Road

- Strolling Trail of the Cedars

- Visiting Logan Pass and looking for mountain goats along Hidden Lake Trail

- Stopping at Siyeh Bend and scoping slopes for bears

- Visiting Sun Point for view of St. Mary Lake, peaks

- Mountain vista from Many Glacier Hotel

How to Get There

Approach West Glacier (from Kalispell, Montana, about 35 miles) and East Glacier Park from US 2, which wraps around the southern lobe of the park. US 89 leads to Many Glacier and St. Mary in the east; US 89 and Mont. 17 (Chief Mountain International Hwy.) form the shortest connection between Glacier and Waterton Lakes. Coming from Canada, follow Alta. 2, 5, or 6. Amtrak trains from Chicago and Seattle stop year-round just outside the park at West Glacier (Belton), Essex, Browning, and East Glacier Park; by prior arrangement, buses take travelers into the park. Airports: Kalispell and Great Falls, Mont.; and Lethbridge, Alta.

Glacier's woodlands

When to Go

Summer through early fall. All of Going-to-the-Sun Road open about mid-June to mid-October; Chief Mountain International Highway, mid-May to late September.

Trails at lower elevations usually clear of snow by mid-June; higher trails can remain snowed in until mid-July. Cross-country skiing popular late December to April in many areas of the park.

How to Visit

Spend your first day on and around **Going-to-the-Sun Road,** considered by many one of the world's most spectacular highways. On a second day, travel the Chief Mountain International Highway north to **Waterton Lakes,** enjoying the contrast of peak and prairie. Drive Waterton's **Akamina Parkway** and **Red Rock Canyon Parkway.** Stay at least another day to visit Glacier's **Many Glacier.** For a longer visit, drive to **Two Medicine** for a boat ride and walk to an exquisite lake, then continue on to the **Walton Goat Lick Overlook,** both also in Glacier.

If you have the stamina and the reservations, consider an overnight trip into **Sperry Chalet,** one of two remaining backcountry chalets built for well-heeled guests early in the 20th century by the Great Northern Railway.

EXPLORING THE PARK

Going-to-the-Sun Road: **50 miles; a full day**

Begin early at Apgar on Glacier's west side. At the visitor center pick up details about trails and, since this is grizzly and black bear country, cautionary advice on avoiding encounters. Take time to admire **Lake McDonald** from the vantage point a little farther down the road. The park's largest lake, McDonald is 10 miles long and 472 feet deep; a glacier more than 2,000 feet thick gouged out its basin. Kootenai Indians, who performed lakeshore ceremonies, called the waters Sacred Dancing Lake.

Continue driving the Apgar loop, turn left at Going-to-the-Sun Road *(vehicles longer than 21 feet and wider than 8 feet prohibited on most of this road)*, and drive the length of the lake. At **McDonald Falls,** stroll down to the viewpoint and note the layered rock. Waterton-Glacier's mountains are built mainly of sedimentary rock formed from mud and sand at the bottom of a sea that existed here for nearly a billion years. Over the eons, pressures in the Earth uplifted, thrusted, and folded the seabed into mountains. The rock exposed at McDonald Falls is among the oldest in the park.

Pull over near the campground at Avalanche Creek and start the self-guided **Trail of the Cedars** from the right side of the road. This wheelchair-accessible trail is on a boardwalk. The easy, quite popular, 0.75-mile nature stroll acquaints you with the cedar-hemlock

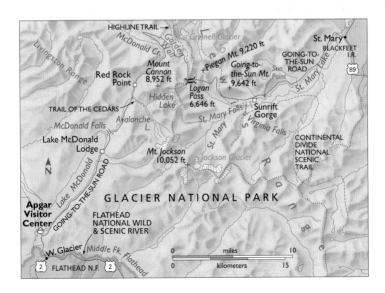

The Grizzly

Blackfeet Indians called it Real Bear, this huge, intelligent, unpredictable animal we call the grizzly. An adult male may weigh 400 to 600 pounds, twice as much as a black bear, yet it can sprint up to 35 miles per hour.

Tens of thousands of grizzlies roamed western North America in 1850; by 1975, the guns of settlers, hunters, and livestock owners, coupled with loss of habitat, had driven the bears close to extinction in the lower 48 states. While some 50,000 grizzlies may remain in Alaska and Canada, fewer than a thousand now inhabit the rest of the United States. Perhaps 300 of them live in Waterton-Glacier and in wilderness areas adjoining the parks.

Though mythologized as a ruthless predator, the grizzly eats mostly grass, berries, and roots. It will also consume insects and rodents and even larger animals if easy prey. Unless accustomed to human scent and food, most grizzlies will move on when they hear a human coming.

In Glacier it's said that 90 percent of grizzly management is people management. And people management has changed greatly since 1967,

Grizzly bear

when two Glacier campers were killed by grizzlies accustomed to eating garbage. Today rangers carefully instruct visitors on how to share the wilderness with bears. Precautions include: Always have bear deterrent pepper spray ready for immediate use; be alert where recent bear activity has been documented; make plenty of noise on the trail; leave the area immediately if you come across bear cubs; and always travel in groups.

forest through which you've been driving. Along the trail, Avalanche Creek tumbles through contoured walls of surprisingly red stone, formed during a period when the sea here retreated. In contact with oxygen, iron-bearing minerals in the mud formed the bright red mineral hematite that colors the rock. Extend your walk, if you wish, by taking the **Avalanche Lake Trail** from near the gorge up to glacier-fed Avalanche Lake. The trail climbs gently for about 2 miles to the lakeshore, offering fine views of creek, lake, and several waterfalls plunging from the cliffs.

Return to your car. Directly ahead, in about 2 miles, you'll see the **Garden Wall,** part of the Continental Divide. West of the divide, waters flow to the Pacific; east of it, to the Arctic or Atlantic. Two glaciers ground down opposite sides of a ridge to form the knife-edged Garden Wall. At the **Bird Woman Falls** viewpoint *(about 10 miles from campground at Avalanche Creek),* an exhibit illustrates how glaciers also carved this spectacular U-shaped valley. Glacier National Park takes its name from the huge rivers of ice that sculpted the landscape during ice ages of the last two million years. Today's glaciers are not remnants of the ice age glaciers.

At **Logan Pass,** atop the Continental Divide, the peaks crowd around as if nearly close enough to touch. Park and walk up the hill past the visitor center to take the **Hidden Lake Nature Trail** *(see map p. 64).* Be sure to buy or borrow a self-guiding pamphlet at the trailhead. The 3-mile round-trip is perhaps the most popular in the park. It begins on the asphalt paths behind the visitor center and continues up the long boardwalk, climbing 460 feet to a drop-away vista of Hidden Lake. Along the way, you're likely to see mountain goats, often within a dozen yards or so. Bighorn sheep are also seen, and there is always the chance you might spot a distant grizzly bear.

As you start out, you'll pass through an island of stunted sub-alpine fir. These are not saplings, but old growth. Some trees just a few inches in diameter can be hundreds of years old. Their size reflects the harsh environment, with its short growing season, cold temperatures even in summer, bitter winds, intense sunlight, high evaporative rates, and gravelly soils.

Soon you step onto a boardwalk built to protect the fragile alpine meadows from foot traffic. Directly ahead is 8,760-foot **Clements Mountain.** The similar peak to the left is 9,125-foot **Reynolds Mountain.** Both are "horns," which form when three or more glaciers gnaw away at a mountain from different directions and eventually hew the rock into a sharp point. The tiny wildflowers, sedges, and grasses around you have adapted to the ferocious climate in remarkable ways. Their compact size conserves moisture and requires fewer nutrients. Many contain chemicals that turn sunlight into heat, and some can grow through a layer of snow.

Few animals live all year in Glacier's high country, but one of them, the Columbian ground squirrel, teems in these meadows during summer. True hibernators, the squirrels pass the winters in their burrows, where their body temperatures can drop to 37° F.

Once off the boardwalk, start looking for mountain goats among the tree islands and rocky outcroppings below Clements Mountain. Soon you reach the overlook, with **Hidden Lake** nestled 750 feet below in its glacially carved basin.

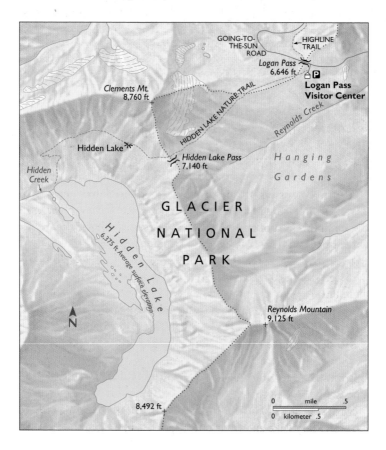

McDonald Creek

Also from Logan Pass, the **Highline Trail,** which starts across the road from the parking area, offers splendid panoramic views as it traverses the Garden Wall and leads 7.6 miles to **Granite Park Chalet.** Part of the trail is cut into the cliff face, so it is not for the faint of heart.

Return to your car and turn right onto the main road. Soon you'll be approaching **Going-to-the-Sun Mountain**—at 9,642 feet, the highest in this area of the park. The name comes, depending on which story you believe, from a Blackfeet legend or an early explorer. The legend says that Napi, the creator, came to help the Blackfeet, then climbed this mountain to return to the sun.

Pull over again to view **Jackson Glacier,** one of the few glaciers visible from the road, about 4.5 miles after Logan Pass. Near the head end of St. Mary Lake, look for the 1-mile trail to **St. Mary Falls,** a fierce double-stranded cascade that boils through a tight chasm. A half-mile walk beyond St. Mary Falls leads to **Virginia Falls,** which drops a full 100 feet through the forest and thunders concussively during spring runoff.

Next, stop at **Sun Point,** where you'll find picnic tables, fine vistas of St. Mary Lake and its attendant peaks, and a nature trail that introduces the ecology of the drier eastern portion of the park. Continue along the lake to **Wild Goose Island Overlook,** for its fine vista, and the **Triple Divide Peak** exhibit, less than 3 miles beyond. The road now crosses grasslands punctuated by groves of aspen and conifers. Going-to-the-Sun Road ends at Divide Creek, the border of the Blackfeet Indian Reservation.

Chief Mountain to Waterton Lakes: 75 miles; a full day

Chief Mountain International Highway begins north of Babb off US 89, and its namesake peak soon dominates the horizon to your left. This solitary peak is sacred ground. Blackfeet seeking spiritual guidance often tie a traditional offering of colored cloth to trees at its base. The mountain also represents the easternmost extension of the Lewis Overthrust, a major geological feature. About 8.5 miles after the U.S.-Canada customs station, an exhibit explains the over-thrust. Pull over again in 1.5 miles for a superb view of **Waterton Valley** and a display that identifies the summits.

Follow the signs for **Waterton Lakes National Park.** The park's main information center will be on your right, about 4 miles beyond the park entrance, just before Waterton Park townsite. On your left stands the **Prince of Wales Hotel,** which commands a first-rate view of **Upper Waterton Lake** from its lobby. This is the best-kept of the old park hotels built by the Great Northern Railroad in the early 20th century. For a loftier panorama of the lakes, climb the steep but gratifying **Bears Hump Trail,** 2 miles round-trip. The path starts from the information center.

At road's end awaits Waterton Park townsite, a village of about a

West Side Forest

On Glacier's warmer, moister west side, a deep forest of hemlock, cedar, larch, white pine, and birch surrounds Lake McDonald and spreads over the lower slopes of the mountains. Like most forests, it divides into layers. At the top, a dense canopy of branches forms a protective roof over the forest community. Below it grows an understory of young trees, then a shrub layer of plants that grow to head height. Next comes the herb layer of wildflowers, grasses, and ferns. Finally, on the forest floor, you'll find various types of mosses, fungi, and vines.

hundred year-round residents. It blossoms in summer with eateries and gift shops. Wildlife is often on hand: Bighorn sheep and deer may be hiding in the shadows; you'll less likely spot the rare mountain lion or bear. On the lakeshore, near the end of the road, a pavilion reviews the park's history.

Back in your car, turn onto **Akamina Parkway,** which traces Cameron Valley 10 miles to **Cameron Lake.** At the lake, which lies in a large glacier-carved basin, rent a boat, fish for trout, or stroll the 2-mile round-trip **Cameron Lakeshore Trail** through the forest of Englemann spruce and subalpine fir. Do not continue past the end of the trail—grizzlies are often sighted there.

Onward, return to Alta. 5; turn left, then left again onto 10-mile-long **Red Rock Canyon Parkway.** The prairie here brims with flowers in May, June, and early July. Native Americans hunted bison along Blakiston Creek, driving them over the cliff to your left. In about 3 miles, near Crandell Mountain Campground, stop at the exhibit on ancient Native American life. Drive on to the road's end at **Red Rock Canyon,** where archaeologists found a camp dating from 8,400 years ago. Don't miss the half-mile **Red Rock Canyon Loop Trail.** Bighorn sheep frequent the area.

Back at the townsite, a visit to the **Heritage Centre** *(Waterton Ave. 403-859-2224)* will catch you up on the park's natural history. Or, consider a cruise *(403-859-2362. Fare)* along the length of Upper Waterton Lake to **Goat Haunt,** in Glacier, where an easy 1-mile trail leads to **Rainbow Falls.** The cruise and stroll make for one of the nicest day trips in the area.

Many Glacier Area: 13 miles from Babb; at least a half day

Many Glacier, named for the glaciers on surrounding mountains, is a hiker's Eden and a good place to see wildlife. A dam a few miles outside the park created **Lake Sherburne,** on your left as you enter the park. The lake submerged much of Altyn, a boomtown built during the mining frenzy that started and fizzled out here at the turn of the 20th century.

Anchored by the historic **Many Glacier Hotel** *(602-207-6000),* a Swiss-style lodge built in 1914–15 by the Great Northern Railway, the area forms the hub of a large trail network that offers everything from an hour's stroll to week-long treks. It is also one of the most dependable sites in the park for seeing black bears and grizzlies, mountain goats and bighorn sheep.

Hiker in the Rockies, Glacier National Park

As you make your way along the flank of Altyn Peak, the road suddenly tops a band of cliffs and you come face to face with the Many Glacier area's dramatic span of mountain peaks. Straight ahead lies **Swiftcurrent Lake,** nestled beneath the great promontory of Grinnell Point, which separates two glacial valleys—each of which leads back to a section of the knife-edged Garden Wall.

To your left is the **Many Glacier Hotel,** a bit threadbare after years of deferred maintenance, but still commanding a premier vista of its extraordinary surroundings. It's worth a stop just to take in the view and admire its interior. This is one of four gracious hotels built in Glacier and Waterton by the Great Northern Railway. The company also built more than a dozen backcountry tent camps and chalets. Early tourists rode horses between the railway stations, hotels, and chalets.

From the hotel, take the **Swiftcurrent Nature Trail,** an easy 2.6-mile loop around the lake that offers a fine introduction to the area's plants, animals, peaks, and glaciers. The trail traverses both 400-year-old spruce-fir forest and 60-year-old lodgepole pine forest, planted in the aftermath of a great fire in 1936. The trail connects with another short trail that leads to **Josephine Lake,** another alpine gem on the south side of Grinnell Point. If you'd rather not walk so much, you might opt for the **boat tour,** which cruises both lakes with a short stroll between docks.

With more time and plenty of stamina, take the 5.5-mile hike from Swiftcurrent Lake to the edge of **Grinnell Glacier,** one of the largest in the park. The route skirts Swiftcurrent and Josephine Lakes, then climbs steeply for a few miles to **Upper Grinnell Lake.** The trip takes most of a day. Park naturalists often lead this hike. Check departure times in the park newspaper.

Other promising hikes in the Many Glacier area include the **Iceberg Lake Trail,** which leads you among wide panoramas to an iceberg-studded turquoise lake, a 10-mile round-trip. **Cracker Lake Trail,** 12.3 miles round-trip, parallels boulder-strewn **Canyon Creek** partway to a glacier-fed lake and the remains of **Cracker Mine.**

Two Medicine Valley: 9 miles; at least 2 hours

Just a shade less dramatic than Many Glacier but much less crowded, Two Medicine Valley is located off Mont. 49 south of Kiowa. This lovely, high-country valley was plowed out by glaciers that carved the surrounding peaks into interesting shapes and left behind chains of lakes and waterfalls. It's a great spot for hiking and a likely one for seeing bighorn sheep, mountain goats, and bears. Have a quick look at **Two Medicine Lake,** then double back on the entrance road to the trail for **Running Eagle Falls,** an easy, half-mile round-trip walk. This curious, double-channeled waterfall, formerly known as Trick Falls, spills both over the edge and through the face of a beautiful limestone cliff. Or, take the **boat tour** *(fare)* to the upper end of Two Medicine Lake and walk an easy mile to **Twin Falls,** where two strands of cascading water tumble from a shaded cliff and pool over a bed of red mudstone.

More ambitious day hikes include trails to **Upper Two Medicine Lake** (10 miles round-trip, easy); **Oldman Lake** at the foot of Pitamakan Pass (11 miles round-trip, moderate); and **Scenic Point** (6.2 miles round-trip, difficult), which offers a commanding view of the Two Medicine Valley.

A short drive south of Two Medicine on Mont. 49 brings you to East Glacier Park, worth a stop just to see **Glacier Park Lodge** *(602-207-6000),* another elegant legacy of the Great Northern Railway.

INFORMATION & ACTIVITIES

Headquarters
Glacier: P.O. Box 128
West Glacier, MT 59936
406-888-7800
www.nps.gov/glac
Waterton: Waterton Park
Alberta, T0K 2M0
403-859-2224
www.parkscanada.gc.ca/
waterton

Visitor & Information Centers
Glacier: Visitor centers at Apgar,
Logan Pass, and St. Mary.
Waterton: Waterton Information Centre in Waterton Park.

Seasons & Accessibility
Parks open year-round; Going-to-the-Sun Road usually open
mid-June to mid-October.

Entrance Fees
Glacier: $20 per car valid for 7
days; $25 annual.
Waterton: Rates are complex;
call or write for information.

Facilities for Disabled
Glacier: Most visitor center
facilities; Trail of the Cedars,
Running Eagle Falls Trail, and
Apgar Bike Path.
Waterton: International Peace
Park Pavilion, Heritage Centre,
Cameron Lake exhibit building;
also several camping facilities,
most rest rooms, and the Lake
Linnet Trail.

Things to Do
Glacier: Free naturalist-led
activities: walks and hikes, slide
talks, campfire programs. Also,
hiking, horseback rides, boating, bicycling, fishing, boat
tours, nature courses.
Waterton: Naturalist-led activities: walks and hikes, slide
shows, campfire programs.
Also, swimming, fishing *(license
required)*, boating, nature
courses, horseback rides, golf.

Overnight Backpacking
Permits required. Call in
advance about reservations and
fees: Glacier, 406-888-7857;
Waterton, 403-859-5133.

Campgrounds
Glacier: Thirteen campgrounds,
limit 7 days July through
August, otherwise 14 days.
Reservations for Fish Creek and
St. Mary *(800-365-2267)*. Others, first come, first served. $12-
$17. Tent and RV sites; no
hookups. Apgar Group Campground first come, first
served.
Waterton: Three campgrounds,
14-day limit. First come, first
served. Canadian $10-$23. Tent
and RV sites; hookups at
Waterton Park. Reservations
required at Belly River Group
Campgrounds; contact the
park's headquarters.

Sperry Glacier

Hotels, Motels, & Inns
(Unless otherwise noted, rates are for two persons in a double room, high season.)

Inside Glacier NP:
The lodgings that follow are open from June to mid-September. Contact Glacier Park, Inc., P.O. Box 2025, 774 Railroad St., Columbia Falls, MT 59912. 406-756-2444.

■ **Glacier Park Lodge** 161 units. $135-$500. Pool, restaurant.
■ **Lake McDonald Lodge** 100 units. $92-$142. Restaurant.

■ **Many Glacier Hotel** 216 units. $111-$219. Restaurant.
■ **Rising Sun Motor Inn** 72 units. $90-$98. Restaurant.
■ **Swiftcurrent Motor Inn** 88 units. Cabins $43-$73; rooms $88. Restaurant nearby.
■ **The Village Inn** 36 units. $100-$165. Restaurant nearby.

Backcountry Chalets
■ **Granite Park Chalet** 406-387-5555 or 800-521-7238. 12 rooms, $132-$152.
■ **Sperry Chalet** 406-387-5654. 17 rooms, $300, full-service lodge, includes meals.

In Waterton, T0K 2M0:
■ **Aspen Village Inn** P.O. Box 100. 403-859-2255. 52 units. Can. $139-$245. Open mid-May to mid-October.
■ **Bayshore Inn** 111 Waterton Ave. Summer 403-859-2211; winter 403-238-4847. 70 units. Can. $129-$199. Restaurant. Open April to October.
■ **Crandell Mt. Lodge** 102 Mt. View Rd. 403-859-2288. 17 units, 8 with kitchenettes. Can. $129-$149. Open March to October.
■ **Prince of Wales Hotel** (overlooking Waterton Park townsite) Reservations: Glacier Park, Inc., P.O. Box 2025, 774 Railroad St., Columbia Falls, MT 59912. 406-756-2444. 86 units. Can. $259-$799. Restaurant. Open May to September.

Excursions from Glacier

Jewel Basin Hiking Area

40 miles south of Glacier

Set aside for foot travelers, this glaciated tract of sub-alpine forest, meadow, lake, and stream lies in the northern crest of the Swan Range. It's a small area, ideal for day hikes, with 35 miles of trails that link more than two dozen lakes and lead to panoramic vistas of the Flathead Valley.

You can reach trailheads for Jewel Basin from both sides of the range, but perhaps the convenient access is from Kalispell along FR 5392 *(take Mont. 83 E, turn N on Echo Lake Rd., follow signs)*, which switchbacks high into the west-facing slopes.

Many hikes are possible, but you can make a pleasant loop of 5 miles by following **Trail No. 8** north over the dividing crest. It then drops to **Twin Lakes** before heading back south on **Trail No. 7**, with possible tangents into Jewel Basin proper, Black Lake, and Picnic Lakes *(excellent topographic map available at ranger stations in Hungry Horse or Bigfork)*.

■ **16,000 acres** ■ **Northwest Montana, east of Kalispell off Mont. 83**
■ **Best months June–Sept.** ■ **Hiking, fishing, bird-watching, wildlife viewing, wildflower viewing** ■ **Contact Flathead National Forest, 1935 Third Ave., East Kalispell, MT 59901; 406-755-5401. www.fs.fed.us/r1/flathead**

Flathead Lake State Park

55 miles southwest of Glacier

Deep, clean, and inviting, Flathead Lake is the largest natural freshwater lake west of the Mississippi. It occupies a glacially formed basin south of Kalispell and stretches for 28 irresistible miles beneath the steep, densely wooded flank of the Mission Range, which looms nearly 3,500 feet above the eastern shore. Among the bays, coves, points, and peninsulas that compose the lake's shoreline, the state park lies scattered in six small units. Most lie along the west and east shores. Compact, shaded, always pleasant, they generally encompass just enough room for a campground, picnic area, boat ramp, beach, and perhaps some casual walking trails.

Along the west shore, look for **Big Arm,** with its canopy of ponderosa pines. It makes a convenient launching point for **Wild Horse Island,** the largest unit but most difficult to reach as you need your own boat (or rent one from a private marina). Farther north, you

Flathead Lake

can stroll through the larch and fir forest of **West Shore** and pause atop a set of glacially carved cliffs that face the Mission and Swan Mountains. Three more units dot the eastern shore. The southernmost, **Finley Point,** lies on a narrow, curving peninsula and caters to RV owners with large boats.

■ **2,620 acres** ■ **Northwest Montana, south of Kalispell on US 93** ■ **Closed Oct.–May; Wayfarers Unit open year-round** ■ **Camping, hiking, boating, swimming, wildlife viewing** ■ **Adm. fee** ■ **Contact the park, 4901 N. Meridian St., Kalispell, MT 59901; 406-752-5501. www.fcvb.org/html/ sparks.html**

Ponderosa Pines

Most of the evergreens you see along Flathead Lake are ponderosa pines. These pines with long needles can grow as high as 150 feet with trunk diameters of 3 to 4 feet. They prefer a hot, dry climate and collect water through a taproot and a wide radius of lateral roots. A thick, platy bark protects them from quick-burning grass fires. Put your nose to the creases in the bark of older trees and you will often smell hints of vanilla, butterscotch, or pineapple.

Classic Backcountry Trips

Y ou can spend a contented lifetime skimming along the fringe of the northern Rockies' wildest lands by taking day trips along the region's trails and pristine rivers. But nothing can compare with spending some time safely out of reach of the nearest internal combustion engine. Here is a very brief list of classic hiking and boating trips that lead into the heart of the backcountry, where nothing will come between you and the night sky but a scrim of ripstop nylon.

Teton Crest: Grand Teton National Park and environs. Trails along the crest of this jagged mountain range allow strong backpackers to traverse the entire length of the Tetons from Teton Pass to the northern tip of Jackson Lake. But most opt for the shorter trek from Phillips Canyon to Leigh Lake, which winds through the craggy upper reaches of the range and descends to Jackson Hole through Paintbrush Canyon. 3 to 4 days. Contact Grand Teton National Park at 307-739-3300.

Highline Trail: Glacier National Park. This trip starts at Logan Pass and crosses Glacier's high country for 43.6 miles to Waterton townsite, following the slopes of the Garden Wall, a razor-backed arête, between McDonald Valley and the Many Glacier area. Consider a night at Granite Park Chalet, posh by backpacking standards. Connecting trails from Swiftcurrent Pass make a loop possible through the Many Glacier area.

Or you can continue north on the Highline Trail to link up with trails leading to Upper Waterton Lake. 4 to 6 days. Contact Glacier National Park at 406-888-7800.

Wind River High Country: Elkhart Park to Titcomb Valley, Wind River Range, Wyoming. The hike starts at Elkhart Park trailhead at the end of Fremont Road northeast of Pinedale. It climbs through deep evergreen forests to expansive, boulder-strewn wildflower meadows and stunning alpine lakes at the foot of Fremont Peak. Connecting trails lead north to Green River Lakes and south to the awesome Cirque of the Towers area. 5 to 14 days. Contact Pinedale Ranger District, Bridger-Teton National Forest at 307-367-4326.

Beartooth Traverse: East Rosebud Trail, Alpine to Cooke City, Beartooth Range, Montana. The trail makes an arduous climb along steep stream beds, then bowls along the glaciated back of the Beartooth Plateau, pass-

Mount Moran, Grand Teton National Park

ing within sight of Granite Peak, Montana's highest mountain. Prime grizzly habitat; be careful with food odors. 3 to 4 days, one way. Contact Beartooth Ranger District, Custer National Forest at 406-446-2103.

Upper Missouri Wild and Scenic River: North-central Montana.

This 149-mile stretch of the Missouri extends from Fort Benton to US 191 and passes through a classic, high plains valley of badlands, prairie hills, and sandstone cliffs described rapturously by Meriwether Lewis in 1805. 7 to 8 days. Contact Lewiston Field Office, BLM at 406-538-7461.

National Bison Range

110 miles south of Glacier

Established in 1908 to help save North America's largest land mammal from extinction, the National Bison Range lies among the rumpled Palouse prairie hills south of Flathead Lake and faces the crags and yawning glacial canyons of the Mission Range. Within this spectacular setting, some 350 to 500 bison roam in large groups—grazing, dozing, competing for mates, bearing their young, and tolerating carloads of people toting binoculars, spotting scopes, and cameras.

Excellent exhibits at the **visitor center** tell the sad tale of the bison's near extinction and chronicle the range's efforts to save the species. To see bison on the hoof, pick up a map at the visitor center and follow **Red Sleep Mountain Drive** *(allow at least 2 hours).* This 19-mile loop road climbs 2,000 feet over a rumpled mountain covered with grass and pockets of evergreen forest. It offers knock-out vistas of the Mission Range and the Flathead Valley as well as the range's best chances for seeing not only bison, but also prong-horn, elk, deer, bighorn sheep, and mountain goats. Near the crest of the mountain, stretch your legs on two trails: the easy, half-mile **Bitterroot Trail** and the moderate, 1-mile **High Point Trail.**

Near the visitor center, a picnic area is tucked into the luscious riparian corridor of Mission Creek. Cool off in the shade, and consider a jaunt along the 1-mile **Nature Trail** beside the creek.

■ **18,564 acres** ■ **Northwest Montana, west of Ravalli via Mont. 200**
■ **Best months mid-May–Sept.** ■ **Hiking, bird-watching, wildlife viewing, wildflower viewing, auto tour** ■ **Adm. fee** ■ **Contact the range, 132 Bison Range Rd., Moiese, MT 59824; 406-644-2211. http://bisonrange.fws.gov/nbr**

Bison Facts

Weighing up to a ton and standing as high as 6 feet, the bison is North America's heaviest land animal. Well-adapted to the environment of the Great Plains, where water sources are widely scattered, these giants can store huge amounts of water. Bison have had a profound effect on the prairie ecosystem. By cropping, digesting, and excreting grasses and other plants, they played a major role in building up the very soil they thundered across.

Bob Marshall Wilderness Complex

70 miles south of Glacier

Extending southeast from Glacier National Park for nearly 125 miles, this vast and precious tract of open land is composed of three contiguous wilderness areas—the Bob Marshall, Great Bear, and Scapegoat. Taken together, they encompass roughly 1.5 million acres of high, glaciated peaks, plunging canyons, pristine rivers, deep evergreen forests, and boundless, high-country wildflower meadows. Toss in the million or so acres of national forest lands that surround them, and you're looking at an ecosystem larger than Delaware and Rhode Island combined.

The **Bob Marshall,** largest of the three wilderness areas, was named for the founder of the Wilderness Society, a potent voice for the preservation of wildlands during the 1930s and a legendary long-distance hiker *(see sidebar p. 79).* The **Great Bear** lies to the north, the **Scapegoat** to the south.

Access to the heart of this magnificent landscape is by foot or horseback only, which is as it should be. Still, there are several areas along the east slope of the Rocky Mountain Front where, without much trouble, you can get a sense of what lies beyond.

A good place for a casual day hike, the **Blackleaf Wildlife Management Area** *(14 miles W of Bynum on Blackleaf Rd.)* lies tight against the base of the mountains and offers a lovely mix of rolling prairie grasslands, marsh, forest, and canyon. Grizzlies and black bears frequent it in the spring, elk winter here, and mountain goats live here all year. Start at **Antelope Butte** *(turn S at fork in Blackleaf Rd.),* a prominent sandstone escarpment and the most promising spot on the preserve for wildlife viewing. Marshes and ponds at the butte's south end are especially rewarding for bird-watchers. Don't miss a walk up **Blackleaf Canyon** *(trail begins where Blackleaf Rd. dead-ends),* which penetrates the dizzying, 1,000-foot cliffs of Volcano Reef. A stroll of less than a mile takes you to where various hawks, eagles, and falcons nest in the rocks and a herd of 75 mountain goats amble among the crags.

For a taste of the high country and a glimpse of "The Bob," head for **Our Lake** *(trailhead 24 miles NW of Choteau via US 89 and Teton Canyon Rd.),* a tiny gem of bone-chilling water. The moderate 3.5-mile hike climbs beyond tree line into vibrant wildflower meadows. Mountain goats are commonly seen among the cliffs, and from the saddle overlooking the lake you can gaze west into the mountainous heart of the wilderness area and see a portion of the **Chinese Wall,** a 12-mile line of 1,000-foot limestone cliffs.

The road to the trailhead for Our Lake also passes **Pine Butte Swamp Preserve** *(entrance 15 miles NW of Choteau along Teton Canyon Rd.),* another springtime haven for grizzly bears where a vast swamp stretches along the base of a high, sandstone butte. A short trail leads from the parking area to an overlook.

For a good chance of seeing bighorn sheep, consider a trip to the **Sun River Canyon Wildlife Viewing Area** *(22 miles NW of Augusta via Willow Creek and Sun River Rds. 406-466-5341),* home to one of the largest herds in North America. The road into the canyon is spectacular, following Sun River through a sheer limestone wall and then cutting through row upon row of high, steep-sided mountain ridges all the way to Gibson Reservoir. The mix of cliff, rushing water, forest, and broad fields of grass provides excellent habitat for elk, deer, and bighorns. Some 800 to 1,000 sheep graze among the hillsides and talus fields of the canyon. In late autumn, you can watch the rams square off and knock heads for mating rights with the ewes.

Serious backcountry routes through the wilderness are legion, but the classic traverse starts at **Holland Lake** *(E of Mont. 83 in*

Fall ride in the Bob Marshall Wilderness

Walkin' Bob

By the time Bob Marshall was 36, he had logged upward of 250 day hikes of 30 miles, 51 hikes of more than 40 miles, and several day hikes of up to 70 miles. He wrote that pushing oneself to such extremes develops "a body distinguished by a soundness, stamina and elan unknown amid normal surroundings." But some of his longer hikes took a heavy toll. At the end of one 50-miler, he was so tired that he repeatedly stumbled, fell, and then lay on the ground for a while before hiking onward.

Swan River Valley), makes its way to the South Fork Flathead, then follows the White River (Trail 112) to Larch Hill Pass in the Chinese Wall. From there, the route then continues to the Sun River trailhead at Benchmark *(S of Gibson Reservoir)*.

■ **1.5 million acres** ■ **Northwest Montana** ■ **Best months June–Sept.**
■ **Camping, hiking, boating, bird-watching, wildlife viewing** ■ **Prime grizzly habitat; take precautions** ■ **Contact Hungry Horse Ranger District, Flathead National Forest, Box 190340, Hungry Horse, MT 59919; 406-387-3800.**

Gates of the Rocky Mountains

160 miles southeast of Glacier

Named by Meriwether Lewis in 1805 and easily visited today, this exceptionally narrow limestone chasm grips the Missouri River for roughly 6 miles, cutting between 1,000-foot cliffs and precipitous ridges black with evergreen forests. Eroded pinnacles, arches, and great brows of creamy white limestone rise directly from the water. Eagles and ospreys glide overhead, scanning for unwary fish, while bighorn sheep and mountain goats nibble at vegetation along the riverbanks.

For a quick, informative excursion through the gorge, take the 2-hour **Gates of the Mountains Boat Tour** *(18 miles N of Helena off I-15. 406-458-5241)*. Boat pilots are well versed in the canyon's natural history as well as in Lewis and Clark lore. They also point out Native American pictographs and recount the tragic story of the Mann Gulch fire, which killed 12 Forest Service smoke jumpers in 1949 *(see sidebar p. 80)*.

Mann Gulch Fire

On Aug. 5, 1949, 15 smoke jumpers parachuted into the head of Mann Gulch to fight what appeared to be a routine forest fire. After the men established a base camp, the fire suddenly accelerated. They tried to escape down the gulch toward the river, but then the firestorm surrounded them. The foreman set fire to a small area, intending to create a haven by burning out the light fuel. He urged the others to join him within the protective fire ring, but the rest of the crew plus one firefighter on the ground set off for the ridge-top. The foreman survived without a scorch. Two others outran the flames. The rest died.

The boats make a stop at the **Meriwether picnic area,** upstream from where most historians believe the Lewis and Clark expedition spent the night of July 19, 1805. There, you can jump off for a day of loafing, hiking, and swimming before catching the last boat home. You can also arrange longer stays. It is an easy 1-mile hike from the boat drop-off at Meriwether picnic area to **Colter Campground,** a primitive Forest Service camp where you can spend the night or several days. From that base camp, you can explore steep side canyons that climb away from the river and offer high vantage points of the Missouri's narrow, winding course. If you have your own boat, you can also paddle or motor through the gates at your own pace, camping along the way and emerging at Holter Lake.

East of the gorge, the **Gates of the Mountains Wilderness** protects about 28,500 acres of limestone cliff, rugged forest, and wildflower meadow in the **Big Belt Mountains.** It's not a large wilderness area, but it's lightly traveled and makes for a pleasant night in the backcountry—especially when combined with a day on the **Missouri River.** The easiest entry is by boat; road access is roundabout and confusing so make sure to take a good map.

■ 28,500 acres ■ Western Montana, 18 miles north of Helena off I-15 ■ Best months June–Sept. ■ Camping, hiking, boating, swimming, birdwatching, wildlife viewing ■ Contact Helena Ranger District, Helena National Forest, 2001 Poplar St., Helena, MT 59601; 406-449-5490. http://gatesofthemountains.com

Kootenai National Wildlife Refuge

130 miles west of Glacier

Located in northern Idaho along the Kootenai River's verdant floodplain, this expansive wildlife refuge doubles as a great bird-watching spot and a showcase of classic Idaho Panhandle terrain. It lies between the **Selkirk Mountains** to the west and the **Purcell Mountains** to the east, both of which are covered with deep evergreen forests and appear rather low, dark, broad backed, and smooth.

The refuge also lies within the great Purcell Trench, a major geologic structure that runs the length of the panhandle and extends far into Canada as a deep, roomy trough. This portion of the trench formed when a burgeoning mass of magma pushed through the Earth's surface to become the Selkirks. As the magma rose, the overlying rocks shifted eastward to become the Purcells. Ice age glaciers smoothed both ranges and flattened the floor of the trough by filling it with glacial debris.

Today, the refuge meadows, wetlands, forests, and grainfields attract at least 218 species of birds and 45 species of mammals. Tundra swans, Canada geese, and various ducks lay over during the migration seasons. Throughout the summer you can spot great blue herons, bald eagles, ospreys, owls, and ruffed grouse. Early in the day, or as dusk falls, you might also see deer and moose. Elk are occasionally present during the winter.

Drop by refuge headquarters for a map and a bird list. Nearby, a short footpath winds through a forest of ponderosa pine and Douglas-fir to **Myrtle Falls,** a lovely cascade that plunges from a narrow chasm. Also at headquarters you'll find the start of a 4.5-mile self-guided **auto tour** that rings the bottomlands and offers many opportunities for spotting some of the refuge's wildlife.

The road also leads to a turnout for the **Myrtle Pond Observation Blind,** an excellent vantage point where you can watch or photograph nesting mallard and geese dabbling among the weeds. If you're looking for a long walk, head for the easy, 2.2-mile (one way) **Deep Creek Nature Trail,** which follows a meandering creek along the refuge's southeast border.

■ **2,774 acres** ■ **Northern Idaho, 5 miles west of Bonners Ferry on Riverside Rd.** ■ **Open year-round, but snow closes some roads.** ■ **Hiking, bird-watching, wildlife viewing, auto tour** ■ **Contact the refuge, HCR 60, Box 283, Westside Rd., Bonners Ferry, ID 83805; 208-267-3888**

Grand Teton

The peaks of the Teton Range, regal and imposing as they stand nearly 7,000 feet above the valley floor, make one of the boldest geologic statements in the Rockies. Unencumbered by foothills, they rise through steep coniferous forest into alpine meadows strewn with wildflowers, past blue and white glaciers to naked granite pinnacles. The Grand, Middle, and South Tetons form the heart of the range. But their neighbors, especially Mount Owen, Teewinot Mountain, and Mount Moran, are no less spectacular.

A string of jewel-like lakes, fed by mountain streams, are set tightly against the steep foot of the mountains. Beyond them extends the broad valley called Jackson Hole, covered with sagebrush and punctuated by occasional forested buttes and groves of aspen trees—excellent habitats for pronghorn, deer, elk, and other animals. The Snake River, having begun its journey in southern Yellowstone National Park near the Teton Wilderness, winds leisurely past the Tetons on its way to Idaho. The braided sections of the river create wetlands that support moose, elk, deer, beavers, trumpeter swans, sandhill cranes, Canada geese, and lots of ducks.

The Tetons are normal fault-block mountains. About 13 million years ago, two blocks of the Earth's crust began to shift along a fault line, one tilting down while the other lifted up. So far, movement has measured some 30,000 vertical feet, most of it from the subsidence of Jackson Hole.

Before Europeans arrived, the Teton area was an important plant-gathering and hunting ground for Native Americans of various tribes. In the early 1800s, mountain men spent time here; it was they who called this flat valley ringed by mountains Jackson's Hole after the trapper Davey Jackson. (In recent times the name has lost its apostrophe *s*.) The first settlers were ranchers and farmers. Some of their buildings are historic sites today, although ranching is still practiced in the vicinity.

- Northwest Wyoming
- 309,994 acres
- Established 1929
- Best seasons summer–fall
- Camping, hiking, climbing, boating, bird-watching, wildlife viewing
- Information: 307-739-3300 www.nps.gov/grte

Mount Moran, Grand Teton National Park

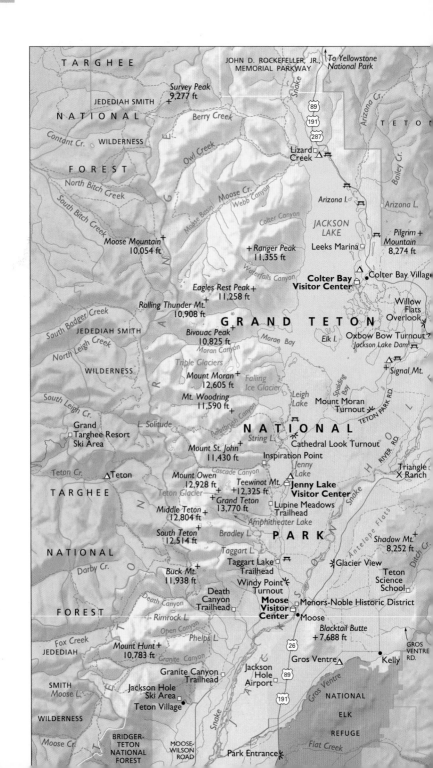

TARGHEE

JEDEDIAH SMITH

NATIONAL

Contant Cr. WILDERNESS

FOREST

North Bitch Creek

South Bitch Creek

Moose Mountain +
10,054 ft

JOHN D. ROCKEFELLER, JR.,
MEMORIAL PARKWAY

To Yellowstone
National Park

Survey Peak
9,277 ft
+

Berry Creek

Owl Creek

Moose Cr.

Moose Basin
Webb Canyon

Colter Canyon

Ranger Peak +
11,355 ft

Waterfalls Canyon

89
191
287

Lizard
Creek

Arizona I.

JACKSON
LAKE

Leeks Marina

TETON

Arizona Cr.

Bailey Cr.

Arizona L.

Pilgrim +
Mountain
8,274 ft

Eagles Rest Peak +
11,258 ft

Rolling Thunder Mt. +
10,908 ft

JEDEDIAH SMITH

South Badger Creek

North Leigh Creek

WILDERNESS

South Leigh Cr.

Bivouac Peak +
10,825 ft
Moran Canyon

Triple Glaciers

Mount Moran +
12,605 ft

Mt. Woodring +
11,590 ft

Moran Bay

Falling
Ice Glacier

Leigh
Lake

GRAND TETON

Elk I.

Spalding Bay

NATIONAL

Colter Bay
Visitor Center

Colter Bay Village

Willow
Flats
Overlook

Oxbow Bow Turnout
Jackson Lake Dam

Signal Mt.

Mount Moran
Turnout

TETON PARK RD.

Grand
Targhee Resort
Ski Area

Teton Cr.

Teton

TARGHEE

NATIONAL

Darby Cr.

FOREST

Fox Creek

JEDEDIAH

SMITH

Moose L.

WILDERNESS

Moose Cr.

L. Solitude

Patutbrugh Canyon

Mount St. John +
11,430 ft

Cascade Canyon

Mount Owen +
12,928 ft
Teton Glacier

Middle Teton +
12,804 ft

South Teton +
12,514 ft

String L.

Inspiration Point

Jenny
Lake

Teewinot Mt.
+12,325 ft

+ Grand Teton
13,770 ft

Amphitheater Lake

Bradley L.

Taggart L.

Buck Mt. +
11,938 ft

Death
Canyon
Trailhead

Death Canyon

Rimrock L.

Open Canyon

Phelps L.

Mount Hunt +
10,783 ft
Granite Canyon

Granite Canyon
Trailhead

Jackson Hole
Ski Area
Teton Village

BRIDGER-
TETON
NATIONAL
FOREST

MOOSE-
WILSON
ROAD

Cathedral Look Turnout

Jenny Lake
Visitor Center

Lupine Meadows
Trailhead

PARK

Taggart Lake
Trailhead

Windy Point
Turnout

Moose
Visitor
Center
Moose

SNAKE

RIVER RD.

Triangle
X Ranch

Antelope Flats

Shadow Mt. +
8,252 ft

Glacier View

Snake

Ditch Cr.

Teton
Science
School

Menors-Noble Historic District

Blacktail Butte
+ 7,688 ft

26

Jackson
Hole
Airport

89

191

Gros Ventre

Gros Ventre

NATIONAL

ELK

REFUGE

Flat Creek

Park Entrance

Kelly

GROS
VENTRE
RD.

What Not to Miss

- **Driving to summit of Signal Mountain for panoramic Teton vistas**

- **Jenny Lake boat shuttle and a hike up to Hidden Falls, Inspiration Point, and beyond**

- **Scenic raft trip on Snake River**

- **Driving Teton Park Road**

- **Hiking or paddling along String Lake to Leigh Lake**

- **In winter, sleigh ride through National Elk Refuge**

How to Get There

From Jackson, take US 26/89/191 north past the National Elk Refuge; entrance station and Moose Visitor Center are in Moose Junction. From Dubois, follow US 26/287 to Moran Junction and turn west to the Moran Entrance Station. From Yellowstone's South Entrance, the John D. Rockefeller, Jr., Memorial Parkway leads directly into the park. Airport: Jackson Hole, inside the park.

When to Go

Any time of year is a joy in the Tetons. Most people visit during July and August, when it's sunny and warm, after the snow has melted in the high country. In September and

Snake River Overlook at dawn

October, the days are pleasant, nights are brisk, the park is less crowded, and the animals are still active. You have a better chance of seeing elk during fall than in summer.

Winter, although spectacular, can be very demanding; snowshoeing and cross-country skiing are popular. The main park road, US 26/89/191, remains open all year, but snow closes Teton Park Road (the "inner road") north of Cottonwood Creek from November through April. The road from Moose to Wilson is also closed. At Teton Village, just south of the park, you'll find excellent downhill skiing.

How to Visit

On a 1-day visit take the **Teton Park Road** from Moose Junction to Jenny Lake for excellent views of the Tetons and short walks or longer hikes. On the second day, go farther north to **Signal Mountain** and **Jackson Lake.** For a longer stay, consider floating the **Snake River,** hiking, canoeing, climbing, or attending one of many activities led by the park's rangers.

EXPLORING THE PARK

Teton Park Road & Jenny Lake: 17 miles; a half day

From Moose Junction, cross the Snake River to the **Moose Visitor Center,** a good place to get your bearings and learn a bit about the park's plants, animals, and geology. It's also a place you'll want to stop at for permits if you plan to boat the park's waters or take an overnight backpacking trip.

The first right turn after the entrance station leads to **Menor-Noble Historic District,** where an old cable ferryboat and a cluster of buildings perch along the banks of the Snake River and recollect the valley's settlement era. It's also a peaceful spot to watch the river's quick, clean current wash over its bed of cobbles.

Back on the road, you soon climb out of the river bottoms; ahead, the Tetons burst straight off the sage-covered valley floor. You will see the mountains clearly throughout this drive from various changing angles; each viewpoint reveals striking perspectives different from the last.

From **Windy Point Turnout,** you get a good view east across the valley to the **Gros Ventre Slide,** a reddish scar on the flank of Sleeping Indian Mountain. The 1925 slide impounded the Gros Ventre River; two years later the dam gave way, unleashing a flash flood that destroyed the town of Kelly and killed six people.

If you look toward the Tetons from **Taggart parking area,** you can see the results of a 1985 forest fire. An easy 1.6-mile trail leads to **Taggart Lake** and offers a close-up view of forest regeneration. **Bradley Lake** lies half a mile to the north, just above Taggart.

Farther ahead, stop at **Teton Glacier Turnout** for a close-in view of the three Tetons. The **Grand Teton,** at 13,770 feet, is the highest point in the range. A major route used by climbers follows the left-hand, southern skyline; just as it appears, there is no easy way to the top. Looking to the left of the Grand, you see the **Middle Teton** and **South Teton.** The sharp pinnacle jutting up over the shoulder of the South Teton (actually in front of it) is the peak called **Nez Perce.** To the right of the Grand are the sharp peak of **Mount Owen** and, in the foreground, the craggy battlements of **Teewinot Mountain.**

Notice the steep, glacier-carved gulch coming straight down from the Grand Teton. At the head of the gulch, beneath the mountain's near-vertical northeast face, lies **Teton Glacier.** During an ancient ice age, glaciers covered Jackson Hole to a depth of

3,000 feet and carved the canyons in the Teton Range. The glaciers that exist now only at high elevations established themselves in more recent years.

If you can take your eyes off the mountains, scan the sage flats on both sides of the road for pronghorn, elk, deer, and coyotes, especially in the fall. Across Jackson Hole to the southeast is the **Gros Ventre Range,** where herds of elk and mule deer roam the deeply forested gorges and bighorn sheep the highest peaks.

Heading north, the **Lupine Meadows** spur road leads to a major trailhead. From here you can take a very rewarding but strenuous hike, which climbs 3,000 feet to **Amphitheater Lake** near timberline. Lupine Meadows itself is a good place to look for wildlife in the evening, especially elk during the autumn rut.

Back on the main road, the **South Jenny Lake** area is next, but unless you're planning to hike around the lake, or to take the boat across to Cascade Canyon at this point in your tour, you should drive past it for now.

Four miles ahead is the junction for **Jenny Lake Scenic Drive,** where a narrow 1-mile loop road provides the best approach to the area, which many consider to be the scenic heart of the Tetons. The road angles back to the southwest, offering stunning views of the central peaks. Stop at **Cathedral Group Turnout** to take it all in. The north face of the Grand is visible from here, flanked by Teewinot on the left and Owen on the right. North of them, in order, are precipitous **Cascade Canyon** (one of the park's best hikes), **Mount St. John, Mount Woodring,** and then the massive, flat-topped **Mount Moran.** Moran's **Falling Ice Glacier** is prominent. Notice also the obvious line of black rock rising above the glacier. Called the **Black Dike,** it was caused when molten rock intruded into a crack in the older metamorphic rock called gneiss, before the Tetons rose. The dike, now exposed by erosion of the gneiss, actually stands out from the mountain face near the summit. Similar dikes are on the Middle Teton (not visible from here) and Grand Teton.

Just ahead, a short road forks off the scenic drive and leads to tiny **String Lake,** which laps the bases of Mount St. John and Rockchuck Peak, and warms enough by late summer for swimming. An easy 2.2-mile trail leaves from the end of the road to follow the shoreline through open forest to sparkling **Leigh Lake,** named after a 19th-century mountain man, Richard "Beaver Dick" Leigh, who, it was said, could "trap beaver where there warn't any."

Field of arrowleaf and balsam root

The lake offers superb views of Mount Moran, and, like String Lake, warms enough in summer to accommodate hardy swimmers.

Continuing on, the scenic drive reaches **Jenny Lake** and becomes one way. For understandable reasons, this place is highly popular; the road in summer is crowded with vehicles. Even so, if you desire solitude amid the grandeur, you can generally find it. Leave your car in a parking area and walk down to the shore. Instantly you are isolated from the world of automobiles. Near the parking area you will find the Jenny Lake Visitor Center, rest rooms, ranger station, a store, and a campground for tents only.

If you have time for just one hike while you're in the Tetons, take the trail to Hidden Falls and Inspiration Point. This 2-mile classic outing starts with a boat ride *(fare)* across Jenny Lake, then climbs into the mouth of **Cascade Canyon** to a lovely waterfall and an overlook of the lake and the Jackson Hole Valley. Quite popular for good reason, the trip condenses into a leisurely 3-hour jaunt the essential elements of the Tetons—the morainal lake, cliffs soaring from the western shoreline, glaciers hanging among the peaks, cascading streams, a refreshing waterfall, deep forest, open meadows, wildlife, and a viewpoint overlooking the valley.

Arrive early at the Jenny Lake boat dock to avoid the crowds.

As you putter across the lake, the Cathedral Group of peaks (Teewinot, Mount Owen, and the Grand) rise to the left, Mount St. John to the right. From the dock it's a half mile walk through a forest of pine, spruce, and fir to **Hidden Falls,** where Cascade Creek tumbles for 200 feet down a ramp of boulders and rock ledges.

Just below the falls, the trail branches to the north and switch-backs for a steep half mile to **Inspiration Point,** a knob of bare rock with a great view of Jenny Lake and the terminal moraine that forms its eastern shore. The mountains across the valley are the Gros Ventres. From Inspiration Point, the trail climbs gradually into the mountains along one of the park's gentlest canyon ascents. It's a wonderful place to ramble—a wide open canyon floor car-peted with wildflower meadows and sheer rock walls rising more than 3,500 feet on either side. Go up the canyon as far as you like before turning around. It's a long walk to **Lake Solitude,** 7 miles from the west side boat dock, but the views keep getting better and tend to egg you along. On the way back, consider walking to the ranger station on the south shore rather than taking the boat; the easy trail is nearly 3 miles long.

Teton Park Road & Jackson Lake: About 30 miles; at least a half day

Start at North Jenny Lake Junction on the Teton Park Road. Drive north 2.5 miles through sage land and lodgepole pine to the **Mount**

Dogsledding beneath the Tetons

Moran Turnout. Mount Moran, at 12,605 feet, is more than a thousand feet lower than the Grand Teton, but you wouldn't know that looking up. On its summit, this massive peak bears a thin layer of sandstone that once covered the entire range before erosion stripped away the overlying rocks. A corresponding layer of sandstone lies an estimated 24,000 feet below the surface of the valley. Millions of years of movement on the Teton Fault has separated the layers by some 30,000 feet.

North of Mount Moran, **Bivouac Peak, Rolling Thunder Mountain,** and **Eagles Rest Peak** dominate the most remote section of the park, cut off from roads and easy trail access by the wide waters of Jackson Lake, just ahead. The natural lake was enlarged by a dam built before the park was established.

Before you get to the lake, take the right-hand turn to **Signal Mountain,** an unpretentious hump of forested rock that rises from the east shore of Jackson Lake and offers a staggering vista of the Tetons, Jackson Lake, and the entire length and breadth of the Jackson Hole Valley. No peak in the park is easier to ascend: A steady foot on the gas pedal does it. The road, on which trailers and RVs are not allowed, winds right to the summit. There's no better place than here to appreciate the unusual geology of the Teton area: the abrupt meeting of valley floor and the Teton Range; the meandering course of the Snake River through deposits of gravel and clay brought down by ice age glaciers; and the ranges to the east. From Signal Mountain, it is easy to see why the early trappers thought of mountain-ringed valleys like this one as holes.

Back on the Teton Park Road, you pass Signal Mountain Campground and cross the Snake River over the rebuilt dam. A mile farther, the road joins US 89/191/287. If you're headed north toward Yellowstone, it's worthwhile to turn right and take a short side trip (about a mile) to **Oxbow Bend,** a cut off meander of the Snake River frequented by moose, ospreys, swans, and bald eagles. When the water is calm, it reflects a classic view of the Tetons dominated by Mount Moran.

Going north once again, stop at **Willow Flats Overlook.** The willows are a likely place to see moose browsing among the shrubs. Failing that, watch the meadows below the bridge just to the north as you cross Christian Creek.

A few minutes north, **Colter Bay Visitor Center** has an excellent museum of Native American arts and crafts. Behind the building you'll find the start of the easy, 1.5-mile **Colter Bay Nature Trail,** which circles a small peninsula in Jackson Lake and offers terrific views of Mount Moran and Eagles Rest Peak. Self-guiding trail booklets can be had at the trailhead or at the visitor center.

North of Colter Bay, the main road stays close to the lake. Just before Lizard Creek Campground, you catch one last glimpse of the Tetons and Jackson Lake, then enter dense lodgepole forest. Ten miles farther, along the John D. Rockefeller, Jr., Memorial Parkway (see p. 96), is the South Entrance to Yellowstone.

More Hikes & Other Activities

The park has more than 200 miles of maintained trails; many lead up canyons separating the major peaks. All the trails have something to offer, but they vary in difficulty, and some are more scenic than others. Keep in mind that most trails begin at about 6,800 feet, so shortness of breath can come quickly.

From Lupine Meadows parking area, the **Amphitheater Lake Trail** climbs to 9,700 feet and rewards those who make this strenuous 9-mile round-trip with a breathtaking view of Jackson Hole. The lake itself is a beauty, nestling beneath high craggy peaks. Allow at least 8 hours for this vigorous hike.

Death Canyon Trailhead, off the Moose-Wilson Road, leads up to a nice view of **Phelps Lake;** from there, the trail climbs to join the **Teton Crest Trail,** a magnificent backcountry route that makes a classic traverse of the range *(see feature p. 74)*, descending Paintbrush Canyon near String Lake. The trip runs about 40 miles and takes about 3 days *(backcountry permit required)*.

In summer and early fall, park rangers lead a variety of highly recommended interpretive programs: walks and hikes, talks, demonstrations, and campfire chats. These programs enrich one's understanding of the region's geology, plants, animals, and history. A schedule is printed in the park publication *Teewinot.* Those hungry for more in-depth instruction might consider taking a course from the **Teton Science School** *(307-733-4765),* based in Kelly.

Boating in the Tetons

The park's large lakes and the Snake River are open to boating, with some restrictions. The Snake and all of the lakes except for Jackson, Jenny, and Phelps are closed to motors. All the lakes are gorgeous, but if you have time for just one head for **Leigh Lake,** accessible to paddlers via the short portage trail at String Lake's

Aspen and maples in autumn

north end. The lake offers marvelous views of Mount Moran, a sand beach, good fishing, and campsites *(permit required)*.

Perhaps the park's greatest boating joy is a trip on the **Snake River**. Several spur roads lead down to it from US 191, making possible a variety of partial-day or full-day float trips all the way from Jackson Lake Dam to Moose Junction. Though this is known as the scenic stretch of the Snake (as opposed to the white-water section that roars through the canyon south of Hoback Junction), it is easy to underestimate. Alert paddlers should have no problem, but snags and other flood debris tend to pile up at the bends and snare unwary boaters. Cautious maneuvering is required. Paddlers should not take this river casually—especially when traveling between the Pacific Creek landing and Moose.

Still, floating the Snake is an incomparable experience. Without much effort it carries you far from the bustle of the roads, opens up tremendous mountain vistas, and presents abundant opportunities for seeing moose, otters, herons, swans, elk, deer, and bison.

INFORMATION & ACTIVITIES

Headquarters
P.O. Drawer 170
Moose Junction, WY 83012
307-739-3300
www.nps.gov/grte

Visitor & Information Centers
Moose Visitor Center open
daily all year; visitor centers at
Colter Bay and Jenny Lake
open seasonally.

Seasons & Accessibility
All-year park: summer luscious,
rich in wildflowers; autumn
crisp, rich in bugling elk; winter exceptionally cold; spring
wet, cold, and nasty. Main road
into park, US 26/89/191, open
all year; inner road closes for
winter. Call headquarters for
current conditions.

Entrance Fees
$20 per car, good for one week
at both Grand Teton and Yellowstone. $40 annual for both.

Pets
Permitted on leashes except on
trails, at ranger-led activities, in
backcountry, and visitor centers; not permitted on boats on
the Snake River, or on lakes
other than Jackson Lake.

Facilities for Disabled
Visitor centers, Indian Arts
Museum, some rest rooms,
some ranger-led activities. Also,
some trails and the Menor-
Noble historic District.

Things to Do
Free ranger-led activities:
wildlife walks and talks, day
and twilight hikes, bicycle
tours, slide talks, illustrated
campfire programs, children's
programs, skill development
courses, tepee demonstration,
wildlife watches, snowshoe
walks. Also, boat cruise, natural
history seminars, wayside
exhibits, boating *(permit
required)*, river rafting, climbing, bicycling, horseback riding
(stables in park), fishing and ice
fishing *(license required)*, snowshoeing, cross-country skiing,
dogsledding, snowmobiling.

Special Advisories
■ If you set off on a trail in the
Tetons, never hike alone, always
carry a good map, and be prepared for sudden weather
changes. Snow has fallen here
in every month of the year.
■ Read and obey the park's
rules for safety around bears,
bison, and other wild animals.
■ Climbing is rewarding but
dangerous; prudence demands
training and experience.
■ Winter avalanches common;
backcountry skiers are advised
to prepare for the hazard.

Overnight Backpacking

Permits required for backcountry camping and boating; free, at visitor centers and Jenny Lake Ranger Station. One-third of permits can be reserved for a nonrefundable $15 fee; the rest of the permits are issued on a first-come, first-served basis.

Campgrounds

Five campgrounds, Jenny Lake has 7-day limit, others 14-day limit. Generally open late May to October, except Lizard Creek, which opens mid-June. All first come, first served. $12. Showers at Colter Bay. Tent sites only at Jenny Lake; all others have tent and trailer sites, no hookups. Two group campgrounds; reservations suggested; contact headquarters. RV sites only at Colter Bay RV Park. $22. For reservations contact Grand Teton Lodge Co., Box 250, Moran, WY 83013. 307-543-2855.

Hotels, Motels, & Inns

(Unless otherwise noted, rates for two persons in a double room, high season.)

INSIDE THE PARK:
■ **Signal Mountain Lodge** P.O. Box 50, Moran Junction, WY 83013. 307-543-2831 or 800-672-6012. 80 units. Cabins $101-$215. 2 restaurants. Open May to October.

■ **Triangle X Ranch** 2 Triangle X Rd., Moose Junction, WY 83012. 307-733-2183. 21 cabins. $1,145-$1,610 per person, per week, all inclusive. Open end of May through October; and late Dec. through March.

The following lodges and cabins are operated by Grand Teton Lodge Co., P.O. Box 250, Moran Junction, WY 83013. 307-543-2811 or 800-628-9988.
■ **Colter Bay Village and Marina** 166 cabins. $37-$135. Restaurant. Open mid-May to Oct.
■ **Jackson Lake Lodge** (1 mile north of Jackson Lake Jct.) 385 units. $120-$210. Pool, restaurant. Open May to mid-October.
■ **Jenny Lake Lodge** 37 cabins. $459-$654, includes 2 meals. Restaurant. Open May to October.

OUTSIDE THE PARK:
■ **Lost Creek Ranch** (8 miles north of Moose) P.O. Box 95, Moose, WY 83012. 307-733-3435. 10 cabins, 20 rooms. $5,395-$12,860 per week, all inclusive. Open June through October.

For a full list of accommodations, contact the Jackson Hole Chamber of Commerce, P.O. Box 550, Jackson Hole, WY 83001. 307-733-3316.

Excursions from Grand Teton

John D. Rockefeller, Jr., Memorial Parkway

Half mile north of Grand Teton Set aside as a scenic corridor in honor of John D. Rockefeller, Jr.'s contribution to the expansion of Grand Teton National Park, this 20-mile road leads through a small tract of gently rolling lodgepole pine forest between the northern end of Jackson Lake and Yellowstone's South Entrance. Though US 89 carries a steady stream of traffic between the parks, the lands beyond the road are left largely to the elk, moose, deer, and bears that live there.

When Grand Teton National Park was established in 1929, it included just the mountains and the morainal lakes at their base. During the 1930s, Rockefeller recognized the importance of preserving the area and bought up large amounts of private land in the valley. He donated it to the government in 1943, when President Roosevelt declared the valley floor a national monument. In 1950, Congress joined the monument to the park, creating a single national park comprising 485 square miles.

Traveling north from Grand Teton, the parkway leads through a lodgepole pine forest that was burned during the great Yellowstone fires of 1988 and is now clearly on the mend. Soon, the road crosses the Snake River and plunges back into lodgepoles unaffected by the fires. Notice the difference in the understories—the relatively open floor of the mature forest versus the lush tangle of shrubs, wildflowers, and lodgepole saplings of the new forest.

At the river crossing, you'll find the **Snake River picnic area,** a pleasant spot to relax or to launch a canoe for the 10-mile paddle down the Snake to Lizard Creek Campground on Jackson Lake. Totally unaffected by dams, the stretch above Jackson Lake is arguably the last truly wild section of the mighty **Snake River.**

Beyond the picnic area, a turnoff for Flagg Ranch leads to **Grassy Lake Road,** a 45-mile stretch of gravel that heads west into Idaho and makes for a pleasant day trip. It follows the Snake River for a few miles and then bounds through rolling lodgepole pine forests that open occasionally around large meadows—look for elk, moose, and deer.

■ **8 miles long** ■ **Northwest Wyoming, US 89 between Jackson Lake and Yellowstone National Park** ■ **Best months May–Oct.** ■ **Canoeing, wildlife viewing, scenic drive** ■ **Contact Grand Teton National Park, P.O. Drawer 170, Moose, WY 83012; 307-739-3300. www.nps.gov/jodr**

Teton Wilderness

30 miles northeast of Grand Teton   The Teton Wilderness protects the forests and mountains wrapped around Yellowstone's southeast corner. The Absaroka Crest forms its eastern boundary (shared with the adjacent Washakie Wilderness), while a length of the Continental Divide cuts across its middle and Grand Teton National Park abuts it to the west. Its high country gives rise to both the Yellowstone and Snake Rivers, but there's really no dominant drainage. Small streams and novice rivers run every which way. In the wilderness's western part, the mountains are a jumble of ridges and plateaus and isolated high points. The eastern section, up against the Absaroka Crest, is more rugged with narrow, steep-sided valleys and large areas above timberline. As in Yellowstone, a forest of mainly lodgepole pine blankets the wilderness, but it's broken up by frequent meadows and treeless ridges providing superb wildlife habitat.

The Continental Divide winds out of Yellowstone across country whose crest is so poorly defined that in one marshy area called **Two Ocean Plateau,** water comes together only to divide again, heading either to the west or east. When water is plentiful, it's possible that trout might swim up one side and down the other—surely one of the rarest phenomena in the Rockies.

Two Ocean Plateau, Teton Wilderness

If the wilderness has a heart, it must be the great wetlands of the Yellowstone River that run north into the park to Yellowstone Lake. That broad, mountain-rimmed marshland is called the **Thorofare,** and is reputed to be the most remote spot in the lower 48 states. The isolation appears to suit the many elk and grizzlies that summer in the valley and adjacent alpine meadows.

Because the distances are long and valleys are broad, the preferred way to see this wilderness is from the saddle. Backpackers need lots of time to go any distance, and should know that main trails can be horse highways while the side routes shown on maps sometimes do not exist. Also, the fires of 1988 burned large areas of the wilderness, and deadfall can make for tough going.

That's not to say don't go. There are magnificent opportunities here, but they demand some creativity and plenty of skill. Three popular access points include: **Pacific Creek** from Grand Teton National Park, **Turpin Meadows** in the Buffalo Valley, and **Brooks Lake** near Togwotee Pass. The last of these provides the easiest chance for getting a high northward view across the wilderness.

■ **585,468 acres** ■ **Northwest Wyoming, southeast of Yellowstone National Park** ■ **Best months mid-June–mid-Oct.** ■ **Camping, hiking, horseback riding, wildlife viewing** ■ **Bear-country precautions pertain while hiking and camping** ■ **Contact Bridger-Teton National Forest, Moran, WY 83013; 307-543-2386. www.fs.fed.us/r4/btnf/teton/wilderness**

National Elk Refuge

15 miles south of Grand Teton

Largely deserted during summer but crowded with thousands of squealing elk every winter, the National Elk Refuge occupies a spacious platter of grass that extends north from the town of Jackson to the boundary of Grand Teton National Park. The refuge, established in 1912, replaces crucial winter range denied to elk by ranching operations and the town of Jackson and its satellite communities.

Triggered by heavy snows, the annual migration of elk begins in late October or early November. Herds from Yellowstone and Grand Teton National Parks, as well as Bridger-Teton National Forest, filter down to the refuge for several weeks, eventually filling it with 7,000 to 10,000 elk. The animals forage for themselves for as long as possible, but elk in such numbers can not be sustained

Elk Talk

Of all the ungulates that inhabit the Rockies, elk are the most vocal. During the autumn rut, males emit especially long, squealing calls that rise in pitch before falling away in a series of hoarse grunts. Year-round, cows and calves communicate through a variety of mews, squeals, and grunts that carry long distances through forest or across mountain basins. The sounds can be heard during a winter sleigh tour of the herds on the National Elk Refuge.

even on nearly 25,000 acres of prime grazing land. So, the refuge also feeds them alfalfa, like domestic livestock. In April, the herds begin moving back to their summer ranges.

November to April, elk are visible in large numbers from US 191 north of Jackson. In midwinter, you can get a much closer look from **horse-drawn sleighs,** which glide slowly into the midst of the animals. Besides elk, you may see trumpeter swans and other waterfowl on the open water of **Flat Creek,** just north of town.

■ **24,700 acres** ■ **Northwest Wyoming** ■ **Best months Nov.–April**
■ **Wildlife viewing** ■ **Contact the refuge, P.O. Box 510, Jackson, WY 83001; 307-733-9212. http://nationalelkrefuge.fws.gov**

Gros Ventre Wilderness

25 miles southeast of Grand Teton

People hardly notice the Gros Ventre Range because it rises opposite the Tetons and looks relatively tame. That's an illusion. The Gros Ventres (pronounced GROW vahnts) may lack gravity-defying spires, but their 287,080-acre wilderness area is rich in pleasing, wildlife-rich high country well suited for rambling. Most of the summits are 10,000 feet and higher, with Doubletop Peak at 11,682 being the high point. You can get an easy sample by driving **Gros Ventre Road** (FR 30400). It starts 1 mile north of the town of Kelly and soon passes the impressive scar of the **Gros Ventre Slide.** In 1925 the side of the mountain collapsed, damming the Gros Ventre River and creating **Upper** and **Lower Slide Lakes.** The road continues some distance past trailheads and campgrounds through some of the sweetest summer landscapes you'll find anywhere in Wyoming.

Another popular access is **Granite Creek,** off US 189/191 about 15 miles east of Hoback Junction. FR 30500 leads 10 miles up the scenic valley of Granite Creek to a campground near the excellent **Granite Creek Hot Spring.** From the hot springs, hike to Bunker Creek on the **Granite Creek Trail,** a 10-mile round-trip that affords tremendous views of the glacial valley. Another good hike begins about a mile south of the hot springs on FR 30500; the **Shoal Falls Trail** leads 7 miles to the cascade and provides scenic views of the Gros Ventre Range.

■ **287,080 acres** ■ **Northern Wyoming, northeast of Jackson** ■ **Snow-free season July–Sept.** ■ **Camping, hiking, boating, fishing, wildlife viewing** ■ **In recent years, chances for bear encounters have increased; take all camping and hiking precautions** ■ **Contact Jackson Ranger District, Bridger-Teton National Forest, P.O. Box 1689, Jackson, WY 83001; 307-739-5400. www.fs.fed.us/r4/btnf/teton/wilderness**

Wind River Range

60 miles southeast of Grand Teton

A magnificent crest of bare rock peaks draped with glaciers and peppered with hundreds of lakes, the Wind River Range stretches southeast from the Jackson Hole area for roughly 100 miles and extends the Greater Yellowstone Ecosystem far into central Wyoming. Arguably the highest mountain range in the northern Rockies, it contains more than 20 peaks over 13,000 feet, including the region's highest summit: 13,804-foot Gannett Peak. It also harbors the largest glacial ice field in the lower 48 states.

Named for the river that drains its eastern slopes and protected by three wilderness areas, the range takes in an immense and sprawling landscape well suited for day hikes or extended backpacking trips. The most accessible portion lies east of Pinedale, where **Skyline Drive** (*S end of town*) climbs through steep morainal hills to two beautiful lakes and then continues on to forests, meadows, and trails leading into the scenic heart of the range.

Though it may be difficult to resist the emerald waters of Fremont Lake, it's best to drive right past the turnoff for now and head for the **Elkhart Park Overlook** (*follow FR 740 and FR 134*), which offers a smashing vista of the lake, the forested midriff of the Winds, and an arresting line of 13,000-foot peaks that form the crest of the range. Perched some 2,000 feet above the lake, the overlook peers down into the great maw of **Fremont Glacier Canyon,** a vast bowl of glacially polished cliffs that wrap around the head end of Fremont Lake. Far across the void, a ferocious ribbon of white water called Miller Creek cascades for nearly a mile down the face of the cliffs.

The road dead-ends at Trails End Campground, a good place for a picnic and a major staging area for backpacking and horse-back trips into the wilderness. From the Pine Creek Canyon parking lot, a steep but rewarding 2-mile trail descends to the shores of **Long Lake,** a veritable fjord glimmering beneath 2,000-foot cliffs. The same trail bends west around a lobe of magnificent cliffs and follows **Fremont** and **Pine Creeks** for 3.5 easy miles to the head end of **Fremont Lake** and Upper Fremont Lake Campground. It's a gorgeous place, with Miller Creek pouring down over the cliffs, but you'll have to share the hard-won shore with powerboaters.

On the return to Pinedale, a spur road descends to the southeast shore of Fremont Lake and dead-ends at a Forest Service campground and boat ramp, a lovely spot to camp or launch a canoe.

Farther north along the range, northeast of Cora, lie the **Green River Lakes,** a pair of large alpine lakes that nestle against the base

Hikers in Wind River Range

of high, bare rock peaks and form the headwaters of the Green River. **Squaretop Mountain,** one of the most distinctive peaks in the Winds, rises some 3,800 feet above the water as a grand, flat-topped stump of naked rock. The lakes make a fine car camping destination full of possibilities for day hikes, boating adventures, and a major jump-off for extended backcountry treks.

To reach the lakes, follow Wyo. 352 for 21 miles north from Cora, then bump along 17 miles of gravel and dirt roads to a forested campground and boat landing on the lower lake.

A pleasant day hike runs along the east shore of the lower lake for an easy 1.5 miles, then heads 4.5 miles up magnificent **Clear Creek Canyon** to **Clear Lake,** tucked between 2,500-foot walls of rock. If you prefer flatter terrain, turn right at the Clear Creek junction and take the **Highline Trail.**

■ **2.23 million acres** ■ **Western Wyoming, southeast Jackson** ■ **Best months May–Oct.** ■ **Camping, hiking, boating, fishing, bird-watching, wildlife viewing** ■ **Contact Bridger-Teton National Forest, P.O. Box 220, Pinedale, WY 82941; 307-367-4326. www.fs.fed.us/r4/btnf**

Sinks Canyon State Park

90 miles southeast of Grand Teton

Site of a peculiar disappearing river, Sinks Canyon bends through the eastern foothills of the Wind River Mountains southwest of Lander as a swerving, glacially carved trough lined with great brows of smooth limestone. Down its center flows the **Middle Popo Agie River,** a vigorous, crystal clear stream that rushes into the maw of a large cavern known as **The Sinks.** Little is known about what happens underground except that the water trickles back to the surface a quarter mile down the canyon in a springlike pool called **The Rise.**

Stop by the **visitor center** for a summary of the canyon's geology and wildlife, and an explanation of the river's vanishing act. Have a look at The Sinks, then drive down the canyon to The Rise, where you can toss fish food to lunker trout.

■ **600 acres** ■ **Central Wyoming, southwest of Lander on Wyo. 131** ■ **Visitor center closed Labor Day–Mem. Day** ■ **Camping, hiking, wildlife viewing** ■ **Contact the park, 3079 Sinks Canyon Rd., Lander, WY 82520; 307-332-6333. http://wyoparks.state.wy.us/sinks.htm**

Fossil Butte National Monument

110 miles south of Grand Teton   One of the world's great mother lodes of fossils, Fossil Butte preserves part of an ancient lake bed where the remains of a startling variety of fish, reptiles, birds, mammals, insects, and plants record one of the most exquisitely detailed views we have of an Eocene ecosystem. Fish fossils, for example, often retain not only skeletons and teeth, but also scales and skin. The delicately webbed veins of leaves, the wings of insects, even the feathers of birds remain visible.

Displays at the **visitor center** include a great slab of shale bearing the remains of dozens of fish, an immense crocodile, a stingray, North America's oldest known fossil bat, and the leaves, stems, and flowers of many plants. Films and exhibits explain how the fossils were formed, discovered, and prepared for display. Daily in summer, park staff offer guided hikes throughout the monument as well as engaging lectures that explain the site's geology, paleontology, biology, and history.

Two interpretive trails leave from the visitor center. The 2.5-mile **Historic Quarry Trail** meanders to an old fossil quarry on the face of Fossil Butte. The 1.5-mile **Fossil Lake Trail** winds through a high desert landscape to the bottom layers of the ancient lake bed.

Nearby, you can dig your own fossils at commercial quarries *(fee)*, or buy them. Ulrich's Fossil Gallery *(307-877-6466)* near the monument's entrance is worth the stop just to browse the exhibits.

■ 8,198 acres ■ Southwest Wyoming, 14 miles west of Kemmerer on US 30 ■ Hiking ■ Contact the monument, P.O. Box 592, Kemmerer, WY 83101; 307-877-4455. www.nps.gov/fobu

Fossilization

The animals and plants that now appear as fossils at Fossil Butte settled to the bed of an Eocene lake roughly 50 million years ago. There, the remains were quickly buried in moist sediments that prevented weathering and excluded the oxygen and bacteria that would otherwise have led to decay. Instead, successive sedimentary layers sealed the remains and applied an increasing amount of pressure. Over time, what was once living tissue became dark brown rock, pressed between thin layers of shale.

Haleakala

Haleakala, a giant shield volcano, forms the eastern bulwark of the island of Maui. According to legend, it was here, in the awe-inspiring basin at the mountain's summit, that the demigod Maui snared the sun, releasing it only after it promised to move more slowly across the sky. Haleakala means "house of the sun"; the park encompasses the basin and portions of the volcano's flanks.

A United Nations International Biosphere Reserve, the park comprises starkly contrasting worlds of mountain and coast. The road to the summit of Haleakala rises from near sea level to 10,000 feet in 38 miles—possibly the steepest such gradient for autos in the world. Visitors ascend through several climate and vegetation zones, from humid subtropical lowlands to subalpine desert. Striking plants and animals such as the Haleakala silversword and the nene goose may be seen in this mountain section. The summit-area depression, misnamed Haleakala Crater, formed as erosion ate away the mountain, joining two valleys. This 19-square-mile wilderness area, 2,720 feet deep, is the park's major draw.

East of the rim, the great rain forest valley of Kipahulu drops thousands of feet to the coast. The upper Kipahulu Valley is a protected wilderness, home to a profusion of flora and fauna, including some of the world's rarest birds, plants, and invertebrates.

Visitors reach the lower valley of Kipahulu via a sliver of parkland on Maui's southeastern coast. Dominated by intense hues— azure sea, black rock, silver waterfalls, green forest and meadow—the coastal area Kipahulu was first farmed in early Polynesian times, more than 1,200 years ago. Mark Twain, who traveled to Hawaii in 1866, may well have had this part of Maui in mind when he wrote: "For me its balmy airs are always blowing, its summer seas flashing in the sun; the pulsing of its surf-beat is in my ear; I can see its garlanded crags, its leaping cascades, its plumy palms drowsing by the shore."

- Maui, Hawaii
- 29,094 acres
- Established 1916
- Year-round
- Camping, hiking, backpacking, bird-watching, scenic drive
- Information: 808-877-5111 www.nps.gov/hale

Above the clouds at Haleakala National Park

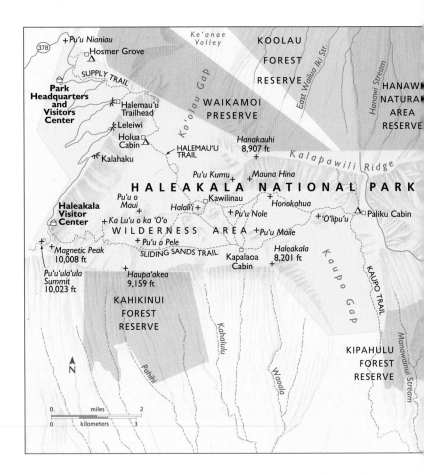

How to Get There

Fly to Kahului in central Maui; drive 38 miles to the summit of Haleakala via Hawaii 36, 37, 377, and 378; last chance for food and gas at Pukalani or Makawao. To reach Kipahulu, drive 62 miles via Hawaii 36, 360, and 31.

When to Go

Year-round park. Most rain comes in winter, although temperatures vary little month to month. To avoid crowds, visit the summit after 3 p.m. or arrive at Kipahulu early or camp overnight. Weather varies most at high elevations, and can change from very hot to rainy, cold, and windy in the same day. Temperatures can drop to freezing inside the wilderness area, although snow is rare. Coastal Kipahulu stays warm but receives considerable rain.

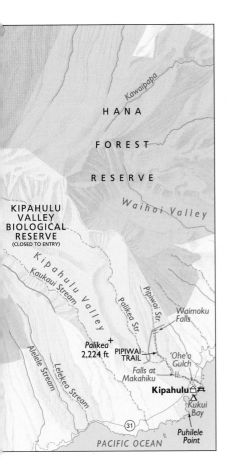

What Not to Miss

- **Puu Ulaula summit for vistas of Haleakala, Maui, and neighboring islands**

- **Kipahulu coast**

- **Pools of Oheo**

- **Pipiwai Trail to Falls at Makahiku and Waimoku Falls**

How to Visit

It's possible to tour both the **Haleakala summit** and the **Kipahulu coast** in 1 day, but you will spend much time in your car. Better to spend a day on the mountain, with a hike through the moonscape of the "crater," and a second day on the coast. Van and bus tours—some starting in predawn hours to take in a magical summit sunrise—can be arranged from most island hotels. Some companies will drive a group to the summit, then provide bicycles to ride down the mountain.

Consider taking a guided walk from **Hosmer Grove** into The Nature Conservancy's **Waikamoi Preserve,** home of living treasures including various species of honeycreepers, the premier family of native Hawaiian birds. Call ahead for the schedule.

EXPLORING THE PARK

Hosmer Grove to the Summit: 11 miles; at least a half day

A short distance above the park entrance lies **Hosmer Grove,** a cool, shady spot to picnic and camp. You may recognize some of the trees, which include Douglas-fir, California redwood, and eucalyptus—with its characteristic, green-and-red-striped bark. About 1910, forester Ralph Hosmer planted trees from all over the world to test their potential for watershed protection and timber here. A half-mile **loop trail** will refresh you after your drive. Guided nature walks are also available.

Back on the road, you reach **Park Headquarters Visitor Center** about a mile above the Hosmer turnoff. At this 7,000-foot elevation, you will see vegetation native to Hawaii. In front of headquarters, plantings of Haleakala geranium and silversword offer photo opportunities and biology lessons in adaptation and evolution. These two plants are endemic—found only on Haleakala volcano.

Leaving headquarters, drive up the mountain through subalpine heath of soft earthy hues. In spring, mamane, a dominant shrub, brightens these slopes with sprays of yellow blossoms. The small birds here are mainly native. With luck you may see some of the famous honeycreepers—brightly feathered birds that may be descendants of the first land birds to reach Hawaii.

From their original ancestors, the honeycreepers evolved at least 47 species, some adapted to only one island, some spread more widely. More than half of these species have become extinct. Driven from the lowlands by habitat change and disease, others are making their last stand high on the mountain. All told, 85 species of native Hawaiian birds have become extinct, and 32 species are on the federal endangered species list. Of the endangered species, seven may already be extinct or are on the brink of extinction.

Native species of plants and animals had just three ways to reach the Hawaiian archipelago: by wind, water, or wing. Before humans first arrived on the islands 1,500 years ago, new species arrived in these ways at the rate of just one every 10,000 to 100,000 years. Today, with ships and airliners bringing in people and cargos from all over the world, alien species arrive in Hawaii at the rate of 20 every year.

Summit hikers often start at the **Halemauu Trailhead,** 3 miles above the headquarters visitor center. This trail takes you through rolling country to the rim, then switchbacks as it steeply drops

Cinder cones dot the floor of 7-mile-long Haleakala crater

1,000 feet down the spectacular northwest wall of the wilderness area to Holua Cabin and the campground *(4 miles from trailhead)*. The wall is broken here by **Koolau Gap,** a wide, wet canyon that descends to the sea. In this corner, vegetation thrives on moisture carried by waves of clouds that slowly ebb and flow in the gap, and you will find the leathery amau fern and other unusual plants.

Motorists can get first views of the crater at **Leleiwi Overlook.** Drive approximately 2 more miles to the **Haleakala Visitor Center,** where rangers lead nature hikes partway into the center of the crater *(call ahead for schedules).*

An exhibit shelter crowns the highest point—**Puu Ulaula,** or "red hill"—where park naturalists give several interpretive talks daily. At 10,023 feet, Puu Ulaula offers the ultimate view: Often you can see the giant volcanoes of the Big Island, as well as Maui's neighboring islands of Lanai and Molokai and sometimes, at night, far to the northwest, the lights of Oahu. Nearby, but outside the park, are the

Haleakala Observatories, a cluster of buildings that are closed to the public.

The best way to experience the wilderness area is on a 2-day hike, spending the night at one of the three cabins or two campgrounds inside the crater. *(Reserve well in advance for cabins— see pp. 112–13.)* One popular overnight trip involves hiking the **Sliding Sands Trail** to Kapalaoa Cabin *(5.8 miles from visitor center).* This strenuous 7- to 10-hour hike loses and gains 3,000 feet on its descent and ascent through loose cinder. Many choose to exit via the Halemauu Trail, an easier 8-mile hike from the cabin back to the road. You'll need to arrange a ride between the two trailheads. Another challenging hike is to take the Sliding Sands Trail down to **Kaluu O Ka Oo,** the first big cinder cone; it is 5 miles round-trip.

Kipahulu: Pools of Oheo: A full day

In this strip of parkland along the gorge of **Pipiwai Stream,** visitors hike through lush rain forest and past breathtaking ocean overlooks. Perhaps the area's greatest draw, however, is Hawaii's cultural past. Archaeological evidence shows that large numbers of Hawaiians once lived in Kipahulu, from precontact inhabitants (before 1778) to those who worked as cattle ranchers at the turn of the 20th century and in the sugarcane industry from 1880 to 1925. Trails reveal traces of the past: stone-walled gardens, pictographs, evidence of taro and sweet potato patches, and temple and shelter sites. Please respect this legacy by staying on trails and reporting to park rangers anyone seen damaging cultural resources.

Camping is permitted on the oceanfront meadows south of the stream at the Kipahulu Campground. Bring your own drinking water, or boil stream water or treat it chemically. No permit is required, but there is a 3-night limit per month.

If you have 2 or 3 hours, take the **Pipiwai Trail,** one of the most memorable short hikes in the islands. This walk is easy for anyone in good health, but it is usually slippery with mud in spots, so wear sturdy footgear, and don't hike if the river is swollen.

Begin about 200 yards south of the Oheo bridge, near the Kipahulu Visitor Center. Walk up through gently sloping pasture about half a mile to overlook the **Falls at Makahiku,** 184 feet high. After another half mile, the trail enters the woods and crosses two bridges near a lovely double falls. Continue about a mile more through lush forest, including a stand of dense, 50-foot-high bam-

Silversward

boo, which on a breezy day clacks and creaks with a mysterious percussive music. Aromatic ginger and ti form the understory. Your destination looms above the forest as you get close: **Waimoku Falls,** more than 400 feet high, fills its jungle clearing with cool mists. Much of the year, mango, guava, and mountain apple provide additional refreshment.

Above the falls, the valley is closed to entry in order to prevent the spread of non-native plant species into one of the last intact native rain forest ecosystems that remains on the Hawaiian Islands: the **Kipahulu Valley Biological Reserve.** Within the park's rain forest, average annual rainfall ranges from 120 to 400 inches, supporting a wide diversity of trees and understory plants as well as many rare birds, insects, and spiders.

Swimming is a pleasant pastime in the Kipahulu sector of the park. Those who fancy a dip congregate around the big, cool pools and waterfalls below the highway bridge in **Oheo Gulch,** but less crowded spots await upstream. Some pools are deep, but beware of slippery or hidden rocks. Also, flash floods can follow heavy rains in the watershed above. There is no ocean access.

INFORMATION & ACTIVITIES

Headquarters
P.O. Box 369
Makawao, Maui, HI 96768
808-572-4400
www.nps.gov/hale

Visitor & Information Centers
Park Headquarters Visitor Center, 1 mile from park entrance. Haleakala Visitor Center, near the summit, 11 miles from park entrance, open daily all year.

Seasons & Accessibility
All-year park. Temperatures and weather conditions change abruptly with elevation. Call 808-871-5054 for weather forecast.

Entrance Fees
$10 per car per week, multiple entries; $20 for an annual pass. $5 per person per week.

Pets
Permitted on leashes in drive-in campgrounds only.

Facilities for Disabled
All visitor centers, park headquarters, and some campsites. A free brochure about visiting Maui is available from: Disability and Communication Access Board, 919 Ala Moana Blvd., Rm. 101, Honolulu, HI 96814. 808-586-8121. www.hawaii.gov/health/dcab.

Things to Do
Free naturalist-led activities: nature walks and hikes, interpretive talks, cultural demonstrations. Also available, hiking, horseback riding, swimming in Pools of Oheo.

Special Advisories
■ Wilderness area hikes are at high altitudes, with lower oxygen levels; take it easy. Be prepared for unpredictable weather that can change fast from hot to cold and rainy.
■ Wilderness area water supplies nonpotable; be prepared to purify water before drinking.
■ Bicycles restricted to paved roads and parking areas.
■ Driving can be hazardous due to narrow, winding roads, steep drop-offs and slippery pavement; take it slow.
■ Ocean swimming is hazardous and not recommended due to high surf and dangerous currents; swimming also dangerous in Kipahulu streams during high water, when levels can rise 4 feet in 10 minutes

Campgrounds
Two drive-in campgrounds, at Hosmer Grove and Kipahulu; open all year, first come, first served, 3-day limit, no fees, no showers, tent sites only, without hookups.

Two hike-in campgrounds, at Holua and Paliku; free permit required; issued first come, first served at headquarters on the day of the hike, limit of 2 consecutive nights, limit of 3 nights total per month.

Primitive hike-in cabins available at Holua, Kapalaoa, and Paliku; each with 12 bunks, minimal equipment. Reservations required by mail at headquarters before the first of the month three months prior to stay; give alternate dates; assignments made by lottery; limited to 2 consecutive nights, 3 nights total per month; $40 for 1 to 6 people, $80 for 7 to 12 people. Call headquarters for details.

Hotels, Motels, & Inns
(Unless otherwise noted, rates are for two persons in a double room, high season.)

In Hana, HI 96713:
■ **Aloha Cottages** 73 Keawa Pl., P.O. Box 205. 808-248-8420. 5 small cottages, with full kitchen, in residential areas of Hana. $65-$90.
■ **Hana Kai Maui Resort Condominiums** 1533 Uakea Rd., P.O. Box 38. 808-248-7506 or 800-346-2772. 16 units, kitchenettes. $125-$195. www.hanakaimaui.com
■ **Heavenly Hana Inn** 4155 Hana Hwy., P.O. Box 790. 808-248-

8442. 3 units. $190-$260. www.heavenlyhana.com
■ **Hotel Hana Maui** P.O. Box 9. 808-248-8211 or 800-321-4262. 66 units. $375-$845. Restaurant. www.hotelhanamaui.com
■ **Josie's Hana Hideaway** P.O. Box 265. 808-248-7727. 12 cottages with full kitchens, in various areas of Hana. $95-$185. www.josieshanahideaway.com

In Kahului, HI 96732:
■ **Maui Beach Hotel** 170 Kaahumanu Ave.; contact Hawaii Reservation Center, 3 Waterfront Plaza, 500 Ala Moana Blvd., Suite 555, Honolulu, HI 96826. 808-877-0051 or 888-649-3222. 145 units. $95-$550. AC, pool, restaurant. www.castleresorts.com/mbh
■ **Maui Seaside Hotel** 100 W. Kaahumanu Ave. 808-877-3311, or 800-367-7000. 186 units, 10 with kitchenettes. $140-$186. AC, pool, restaurant. www.sandseaside.com

In Kula, HI 96790:
■ **Kula Lodge** Rte. 377, 15200 Haleakala Hwy. 808-878-1535 or 800-233-1535. 5 units. $145-$195. Restaurant. www.kulalodge.com

Excursion from Haleakala

Scenic Journey to Hana

5 miles southwest of Haleakala

The scenic but twisty **Hana Highway** skirts the northeast coast of Maui and offers 53 slow miles of one-lane bridges, tight curves, waterfalls, rain forest, and rugged lava coastline: both paradise and "hell on wheels." The 6-hour route begins as Hawaii 36 at Kahului Airport, then passes sugarcane fields and the sandy sweep of Baldwin Beach Park. The first—and last—town of consequence is **Paia B,** which has the last gas station until Hana. This former plantation town went psychedelic in the sixties and has never quite gotten over it. Windsurfers congregate here since it's only 2 miles to **Hookipa,** a pilgrimage site for the sport.

At Milepost 16, the twists, turns, and bridges begin. Just beyond, Hawaii 36 becomes Hawaii 360 and the mileposts begin again at zero. In 2 miles you will pass three waterfalls: **Waikamoi, Puohokamoa,** and **Haipuaene.** There's a 30-minute nature walk at Waikamoi. Farther along, you can revisit movie sets for *Jurassic Park* at **Garden of Eden Arboretum and Botanical Garden** *(Mile 10. 808-572-9899).*

At Mile 11, **Puohokamoa Falls** plunges 30 feet into a good, icy swimming pool. Just past Mile 12, the size of the plants at **Kaumahina State Wayside Park** attest to the region's fecundity and rainfall—about 300 inches a year.

At the **Keanae Arboretum,** less than half a mile beyond Mile 16, you'll find Hawaiian ethnobotanical gardens, and you can picnic and swim in the pools. To have a look at Hawaii's traditional food crop, taro, growing in all its emerald glory, turn seaward at Mile 17 and drive down to **Keanae Peninsula** where you'll find fields

that are more than 500 years old. Between Wailua and Puaa Kaa State Wayside Park at Mile 22, you'll pass **Waikani Falls.** Gurgling streams and stillwater ponds make this a good picnic spot. Next stop is **Waianapanapa State Park** *(808-984-8109)*. Lava shoreline at its most dramatic is on show in black craggy cliffs, sea stacks, arches, lava caves and tubes, and a black-sand beach. Campsites and cabins are available by permit. The roads winds down into Hana.

■ **106 miles round-trip** ■ **Northeast coast of Maui, between towns of Kahului and Hana** ■ **Year-round** ■ **Camping, hiking, swimming, windsurfing, bird-watching** ■ **Contact State of Hawaii, Department of Land and Natural Resources, Kalanimoku Bldg., 1151 Punchbowl St., Honolulu, HI 96813; 808-587-0400. www.hawaii-guide.com/maui_guide**

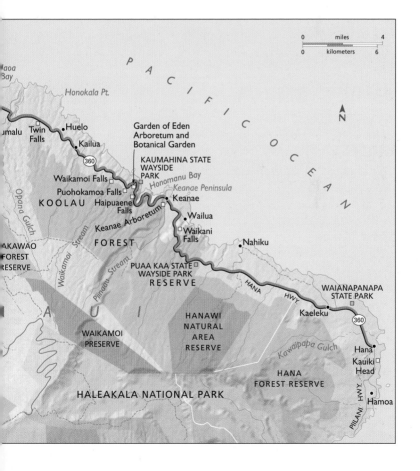

Hawaii Volcanoes

L ocated on the "Big Island" of Hawaii, Hawaii Volcanoes National Park offers the visitor a look at two of the world's most active volcanoes: Kilauea and Mauna Loa. More than 4,000 feet high and still growing, Kilauea abuts the southeastern slope of the older and much larger Mauna Loa, or "long mountain." Mauna Loa towers some 13,679 feet above the sea: Measured from its base 18,000 feet below sea level, it exceeds Mount Everest in height. Mauna Loa's gently sloping bulk—some 19,000 cubic miles in volume—makes it the planet's most massive single mountain.

The park stretches from sea level to Mauna Loa's summit. Beyond the end of the road lies Mauna Loa's wilderness area, where backpackers encounter freezing nights and rough lava trails amid volcanic wonders: barren lava twisted into nightmarish shapes, cinder cones, gaping pits. Kilauea, however, provides easy access to a greater variety of scenery and cultural sites.

On the slopes of Kilauea, whose name means "spreading, much spewing," lush green rain forest borders stark, recent lava flows. This natural laboratory of ecological change displays all stages of forest regeneration—from early regrowth of lichens and ferns to dense forest. The rain forest on the windward side of Kilauea's summit gives way to the stark, windswept Kau Desert on the hot, dry southwestern slope. At the shore, waves create lines of jagged cliffs; periodic eruptions send fresh lava flows down to meet the sea amid colossal clouds of steam.

Geological dynamism forms the park's primary natural theme, followed closely by evolutionary biology. Thousands of unique species have evolved on the isolated Hawaiian Islands, but many are now extinct or in peril as alien species invade. Cultural sites abound as well, reminders of the Polynesian pioneers who steered their great double-hulled canoes to Hawaii beginning some 1,500 years ago.

- Big Island, Hawaii
- 323,431 acres
- Established 1916
- Year-round; driest in early autumn
- Hiking, scenic drives, lava-flow viewing, volcanism workshops
- Information: 808-985-6000 www.nps.gov/havo

Backpacker ascending an old lava flow of ropy pahoehoe, Hawaii Volcanoes NP

How to Get There

Fly to the island of Hawaii, also called the Big Island. Airlines serve the Kona airport from the mainland and from other Hawaiian islands; only inter-island flights land in Hilo. From Kona, head south around the island on Hawaii 11 past Kealakekua Bay, where Captain Cook met his death, and continue on past Ka Lae, or South Point, southernmost point of land in the United States. You'll reach the Kilauea summit after a 95-mile drive on a good road.

From Hilo, Hawaii 11 climbs roughly 4,000 feet in 30 miles and passes along the way a series of small towns, orchards of macadamia trees, and sections of the rain forest before reaching Kilauea's summit.

What Not to Miss

- Volcano House for vista of Kilauea Caldera
- Crater Rim Drive, which circles Kilauea Caldera
- Thomas A. Jaggar Museum for volcano lore
- Mauna Loa Road
- Chain of Craters Road for descent over recent lava flows to the sea
- Kipuka Puaulu, remnant of ancient forest rich in native plants and birds
- Puu Loa Petroglyphs

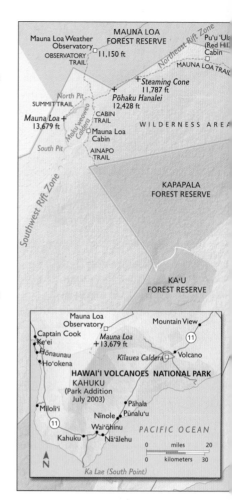

When to Go

All-year park. The weather is often driest in September and October. Climate ranges from warm and breezy on the coast, to cool and frequently wet at the summit of Kilauea to freezing and occasional snow atop Mauna Loa. Avoid most tour bus crowds by visiting major sights before 11 a.m. or after 3 p.m.

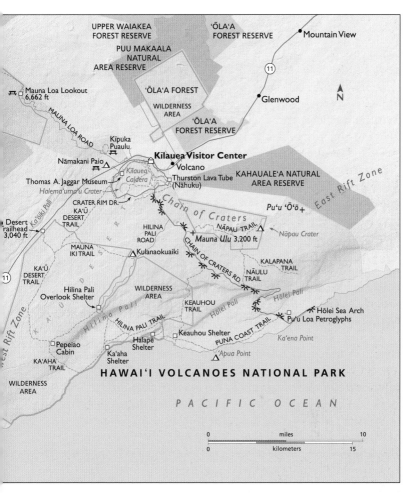

How to Visit

Intense 1-day visit encompasses highlights of Kilauea's summit via **Crater Rim Drive** and the coastal region via **Chain of Craters Road.** Regular tours by bus and small van operate daily from many Hilo and Kona hotels. Those with an interest in plants or birds will enjoy exploring **Mauna Loa Road** (*accessible from Hawaii 11*), which takes you through upland forest to the **Mauna Loa Lookout** at 6,662 feet. At **Kipuka Puaulu,** take the 1-mile loop trail through a 100-acre **Kipuka** (an island of vegetation surrounded by a more recent lava flow) containing one of Hawaii's richest concentrations of native plants and birdlife.

EXPLORING THE PARK

Crater Rim Drive: 11-mile loop; about a half day

Crater Rim Drive, the road encircling Kilauea's oval summit caldera is the main attraction of the park. On the drive you will pass through lush rain forests with tree ferns, and see raw, steaming craters and vast areas devastated by volcanoes. Well-marked trails and overlooks encourage you to get out of your car periodically and explore this strange landscape on foot. Since Kilauea's summit areas can be rainy and chilly at any time of the year, be prepared. Bring a windbreaker or jacket and wear long pants.

Begin at the **Kilauea Visitor Center,** where you can get the latest information on park roads and safety precautions. Don't miss the stunning film of recent volcanic eruptions. The rustic **Volcano House** and the **Volcano Art Center Gallery** are just a short stroll away. *(You can rent self-guided audiotour of Crater Rim Drive for nominal fee at art center.)* Walk through the lobby of the Volcano House to the rear of the hotel for a first dramatic view across **Kilauea Caldera,** a 3-mile-wide, 400-foot-deep depression that marks the volcanic summit.

After leaving the visitor center, proceed clockwise on Crater Rim Drive. For a time, the road traverses rain forest featuring Hawaiian tree ferns that lend the roadsides a prehistoric look. Scenic turnouts begin with a huge crater, **Kilauea Iki** ("little Kilauea") just east of the main caldera. The 1959 eruption that shaped so many of the park's features filled this crater with a lava lake and produced a lava fountain that shot 1,900 feet into the air—a record for Hawaiian volcanism. One of the park's most popular hiking trails ventures into this nuclear-looking wasteland.

Visit **Thurston Lava Tube** (Nahuku) by taking an easy 15-minute loop trail that descends quickly into a forest of tree ferns. Native birds have begun to nest in the area. With luck, you may see the scarlet iiwi or the chartreuse amakihi. You will cross a bridge over a small chasm and enter an electrically lit tunnel that once ran red with magma from the bowels of the Earth. It is 450 feet long and in places as high as 20 feet, all of it eerie and awesome. Ferns drape themselves over the entrance and exit.

From the lava tube parking area, the **Kilauea Iki Trail,** one of the park's most popular, descends 400 feet onto the wasteland floor of Kilauea Iki Crater. You can skirt the same area from above by following sections of the **Crater Rim Trail** (which makes an 11.6-mile loop around the entire Kilauea Caldera). Combine portions of the two trails to make a 4-mile loop that passes dramatic vistas of the caldera, vertical lava cliffs, rain forest, and steaming lava flows.

Continuing clockwise on Crater Rim Drive, look for koae kea, white-tailed tropicbirds. These ethereal-looking creatures nest on cliffside ledges, often soaring above Kilauea Caldera. With luck, you may spot a nene goose, an endemic Hawaiian bird probably descended from lost Canada geese that landed here. The state bird of Hawaii, the nene are a federally protected endangered species. Do not feed or approach any nene and take care to avoid hitting them when driving (you'll spot "nene crossing" road signs).

Devastation Trail is a half-mile, 15-minute, family-friendly stroll through hell. Here, the great lava fountains of 1959 gushed into the air, spilling ash and pumice, wiping out an ohia forest and leaving white tree skeletons standing in black cinders. Life has begun to proliferate again along the boardwalk, however, so that the name of the trail may have to be changed as it looks less and less devastated.

As the road descends along the southwestern side of Kilauea Caldera, you will notice the landscape becoming more arid. In the rain shadow of the summit, the **Kau Desert** receives about half as much rain as the 100 inches which fall annually at the Kilauea Visitor Center. It also bears the brunt of trade winds blowing sulfuric volcanic fumes and natural acid rain—which stunt plants—down from above.

At **Halemaumau Crater Overlook,** park and walk to the steamiest, most odorous area of the caldera. On some days the fumes are so toxic the site is closed. Halemaumau last erupted in 1974 but is obviously just napping. This is a favorite abode of Pele, goddess of the volcano. Many native Hawaiians still revere her; throughout the year they privately chant and dance at the crater's edge.

The **Hawaiian Volcano Observatory** of the U.S. Geological Survey *(closed to public),* and the small, excellent **Thomas A. Jaggar Museum** of volcano lore and research are next on your route. Nearing the visitor center once more, you'll pass fumaroles, or steam vents. Some produced the **Sulphur Banks.** Follow your nose to this steamy, smelly area where the rocks are mustard color from sulfur carried by volcanic fumes. From here you can opt for a short hike back toward the visitor center. Alternatively, a 1- to 2-mile walk along the caldera rim provides fine views.

Chain of Craters Road: 20 miles; 3 hours

From the Kilauea Visitor Center follow Crater Rim
Drive clockwise to the well-marked turnoff for
Chain of Craters Road. For about 4 miles as you
head toward the coast, your route follows the upper
part of the active **East Rift Zone** of Kilauea volcano.
Scenic turnouts and short walks bring you to the
rims of several impressive craters. If you have time,
hike the **Napau Trail** up Puu Huluhulu ("shaggy
hill") to the overlook at the top, just over 1 mile.
The overlook provides splendid views of the East
Rift Zone and **Mauna Ulu,** the large, steaming dome-
like hill directly to the south. Look for steam from
Puu Oo, a major vent of Kilauea's ongoing eruption,
far to the east.

Back on Chain of Craters Road, you will
drive over several miles of pahoehoe lava flows
produced when Mauna Ulu formed in the 1970s.
At the turnouts, you stand on some of the newest
ground on Earth. Pahoehoe (PA-hoy-hoy) lava
flows at more than 2000° F. It begins fluid then
chills to a smooth, ropy surface. This rock contrasts
with aa (ah-AH)—thicker, slow-moving lava
that has hardened into a chaotic jumble of rough
jagged cinders. As you descend toward the sea,
the climate becomes drier, and patches of forest
in various stages of recovery appear. Sulphur fumes
sweep down from active volcanic vents on the
rift to the east.

Turnouts along this section of the route offer sweeping views of
lava flows and white-capped waves pounding the black shoreline.
About 21 miles off this coast, a huge undersea volcano is building a
future Hawaiian island. Named Loihi, the volcano could breach the
ocean's surface in some 100,000 years.

A steep 800-foot descent marks **Holei Pali,** a cliff formed by vertical faulting; the huge coastal shelf is breaking away from the uplands
and sinking into the sea, albeit slowly on a human time scale. Down
on the lowlands, look for the **Puu Loa Petroglyphs** turnout; a modest
hike brings you to fine examples of ancient Hawaiian carvings, some
24,000 images and figures pecked into the lava. Visitors are asked to

A flautist pays homage to Pele, goddess of the volcano, at Halemaumau Crater.

stay on the boardwalk to help preserve these important carvings.

Hawaiians lived on this dry, rocky land for centuries. Your route along the coast takes you past several of their ancient settlements, though they are difficult to discern.

The road ends abruptly at a 1995 lava flow. Since 1986, an almost continuous flow of lava from Puu Oo has buried several miles of the road, as well as the Kamoamoa Campground and picnic site, and the Wahaula Visitor Center. Park rangers mark a path to a viewpoint close to current flows. Lava-flow viewing and access are unpredictable; obey all off-limit signs and heed the instructions of any park rangers on duty here. Ask at the visitor center for current lava-flow information.

INFORMATION & ACTIVITIES

Headquarters
P.O. Box 52
Hawaii NP, HI 96718
808-985-6000
www.nps.gov/havo

Visitor & Information Centers
Kilauea Visitor Center, located just off Hawaii 11 on Crater Rim Drive, a quarter mile from park entrance gate, and the Thomas A. Jaggar Museum on Crater Rim Drive, 3 miles from park entrance gate, are both open all year.

Seasons & Accessibility
Park open year-round. Chain of Craters Road is closed by lava flow at its eastern end. For eruption bulletins call the park headquarters.

Entrance Fee
$10 per car per week.

Pets
Not permitted on hiking trails or in backcountry; elsewhere must be leashed.

Facilities for Disabled
Kilauea Visitor Center, Jaggar Museum, Volcano House Hotel, Volcano Art Center Gallery all wheelchair accessible. Many paved trails and overlooks along Crater Rim Drive and Chain of Craters Road accessible with some assistance. Kulanaokuaiki Campground fully wheelchair accessible. Free brochure about visiting the Big Island from: Disability and Communication Access Board, 919 Ala Moana Blvd., Rm. 101, Honolulu, HI 96814. 808-586-8121. www.hawaii.gov/health/dcab

Things to Do
Free ranger-led activities: nature walks and talks, slide shows, films, museum exhibits on volcanism. Also, hiking, art center, workshops, seminars.

Special Advisories
■ Persons with heart or respiratory problems must beware of noxious sulfur fumes.
■ Stay on marked trails; vegetation may conceal deep cracks.
■ Coastline collapse can occur fast; do not go beyond barriers.
■ Strong winds and unpredictable surf along the coast make swimming dangerous; it is prohibited in places.
■ Do not enter any areas closed to the public.
■ Registration required for overnight backpacking; no fee.

Campgrounds
Two campgrounds, Namakani Paio and Kulanaokuaiki, both with a 7-day limit, open all year

first come, first served, no fees, no showers, tent sites only. Two patrol cabins on Mauna Loa Trail and 1 cabin at Kipuka Pepeiao may be used free, first come, first served. Must register at Kilauea Visitor Center. Food services in park.

Hotels, Motels, & Inns

(Unless otherwise noted, rates are for two persons in a double room, high season.)

INSIDE THE PARK:
The following are operated by the Volcano House, P.O. Box 53, Hawaii Volcanoes NP, HI 96718. 808-967-7321.

■ **Namakani Paio Cabins** (off Hawaii 11). 10 cabins with central bath. $50.

■ **Volcano House** (on Crater Rim Drive). 42 rooms. $95-$225. Restaurant.

OUTSIDE THE PARK
In Hilo, HI 96720:

■ **Country Club Apartment Hotel** 121 Banyan Dr. 808-935-7171. 148 units, 24 with kitchenettes. $65-$125. AC, restaurant. www.alakairealty.com

■ **Dolphin Bay Hotel** 333 Iliahi St. 808-935-1466. 18 units with kitchenettes. $79-$129. www.dolphinbayhotel.com

■ **Hawaii Naniloa Resorts** 93 Banyan Dr. 808-969-3333, or 800-367-5360. 325 units. $100-$140. AC, 2 pools

and 2 restaurants. www.naniloa.com

In Kailua-Kona, HI 96740:

■ **King Kamehameha Kona Beach Hotel** 75-5660 Palani Rd. 808-329-2911 or 800-367-2111. 460 units. $195-$250. AC, pool, restaurant. www.konabeachhotel.com

■ **Kona Seaside Hotel** 75-5646 Palani Rd. 808-329-2455 or 800-560-5558. 220 units. $60-$150. 2 pools, 2 restaurants.

In Pahala, HI 96777:

■ **Colony One at SeaMountain, Punaluu** (on Hawaii 11) P.O. Box 70. 808-928-6200 or 800-488-8301. 28 condominiums. $110-$145. Pool, tennis, golf.

■ **Pahala Plantation Cottages** P.O. Box 940. 808-928-9811. 5 units. $85-$500. AC.

For additional lodgings contact the Chambers of Commerce of Hilo, 106 Kamehameha Ave., Suite 208, Hilo, HI 96720. 808-935-7178; or Kailua-Kona, 75-5737 Kuakini Hwy., Kailua-Kona, HI 96740. 808-329-1758.

Excursions from Hawaii Volcanoes

Mauna Loa & Mauna Kea

15 miles NW of Hawaii Volcanoes Mauna Loa, the most massive mountain anywhere on Earth, is one hundred times the size of Mount Rainier, its volume so large that California's entire Sierra Nevada range could fit inside it. Nearby stands Mauna Kea, arguably the world's highest peak—32,796 feet, if you measure from the ocean floor. You can drive to the 6,662-foot level of **Mauna Loa** by taking the **Mauna Loa Road** from the park's **Crater Rim Drive.** Stop at **Kipuka Puaulu** for the 1.2-mile loop trail through an ancient forest; consider a picnic at road's end at **Mauna Loa Lookout.**

The road to the top of 13,796-foot **Mauna Kea** starts from Milepost 28 on Hawaii 200 and climbs 6 miles to 9,300 feet at the **Onizuka Center for International Astronomy** *(no children under 16, no pregnant women).* Stargazing is offered nightly from 6 to 10 p.m. Free summit tours, in your own vehicle *(4WD required),* depart from the center Saturdays and Sundays at 1 p.m. and offer access to one of several observatories housing immense telescopes. One, the **Keck Telescope,** is the largest in the world: eight stories high with a lens diameter of 33 feet.

■ **13.5 miles to Mauna Loa Lookout; 6 miles to Onizuka Center on Mauna Kea** ■ **Central Hawaii** ■ **Year-round** ■ **Hiking, bird-watching, stargazing, scenic drives** ■ **Contact the park, P.O. Box 52, Hawaii NP, HI 96718, 808-985-6000; or the observatory, 808-961-2180. http://hvo.wr.usgs.gov/ maunaloa and http://hvo.wr.usgs.gov/volcanoes/maunakea**

Kealakekua

80 miles NW of Hawaii Volcanoes In this picturesque bay on the west coast of Big Island, Hawaiians and Europeans had their first prolonged encounter when Capt. James Cook visited in 1779. During a month-long stay in this Hawaiian political and religious center, Cook's scientists and artists documented early Hawaiian culture. But local hospitality ran out during a dispute over a stolen boat, and Cook was killed in a fight on shore.

Motorists arrive at **Napoopoo.** Near the parking area is the stone platform of **Hikiau Heiau,** a temple that was once the scene of human sacrifices. Along the bay rises **Pali Kapu O Keoua,** a 600-foot-high sea cliff pocked with lava tubes where Hawaiian chiefs were buried. On the far side is **Kaawaloa,** a flat, lava peninsula home to top chiefs. Cook was killed here, and the white obelisk **Captain Cook's Monument** stands among kiawe trees. The best way to reach this side of the bay is by boat or kayak.

Kaawaloa Cove is popular with snorkelers because its shallow coral reef harbors many species of colorful fish. Kayakers often explore the pristine waters of the cove.

■ **Hawaii 12 miles south of Kailua, off Napoopoo Rd.** ■ **Year-round** ■ **No pets, no camping** ■ **Hiking, boating, kayaking, snorkeling, temple ruins** ■ **Contact Division of State Parks, P.O. Box 936, Hilo, HI 96721; 808-974-6200. www.state.hi.us/dlnr/dsp/dsp.html**

Mauna Kea observatory

Lassen Volcanic

On June 14, 1914, three men climbed Lassen Peak to see why a seemingly dormant volcano had started rumbling 16 days before. Now, peering into a newborn crater, they felt the ground tremble. As they turned and ran down the steep slope, the mountain erupted. Rocks hurtled through the ash-filled air. One struck a man, knocking him out. Ashes rained down on the men. They seemed doomed. But the eruption stopped as suddenly as it had begun, and the three men survived.

From 1914 to early 1915, Lassen spewed steam and ashes in more than 150 eruptions. Finally, on May 19, 1915, the mountain-top exploded. Lava crashed through the 1914 crater. A 20-foot-high wall of mud, ash, and melted snow roared down the mountain, snapping tree trunks. Three days later, a huge mass of ashes and gases shot out of the volcano, devastating a swath a mile wide and 3 miles long. Above the havoc a cloud of volcanic steam and ash rose 30,000 feet.

Since then, except for a small eruption in 1921, Lassen Peak has been quiet. But it is still a volcano, the centerpiece of a vast panorama, where volcanism displays its spectacular handiwork—wrecked mountains, devastated land, bubbling cauldrons of mud. Until Mount St. Helens blew in 1980, Lassen's eruption was the most recent volcanic explosion in the lower 48 states. Ecologists now study Lassen's regenerated landscape to see what the future may bring to the terrain around St. Helens.

Scientific interest in the volcano is undiminished, because it provides a useful 90-year model for what might be expected from other volcanoes in the Cascade Range. The park is especially interesting because it includes four different types of volcano: the big peak's plug volcano; an older, layered stratovolcano; shield volcanoes, where basalt forms low, smooth domes; and cinder cones.

- North-central California
- 106,000 acres
- Established 1916
- Best seasons spring–fall
- Hiking, boating, swimming, fishing, cross-country skiing
- Information: 520-638-7888. www.nps.gov/lavo

Snowshoeing, Lassen Volcanic National Park

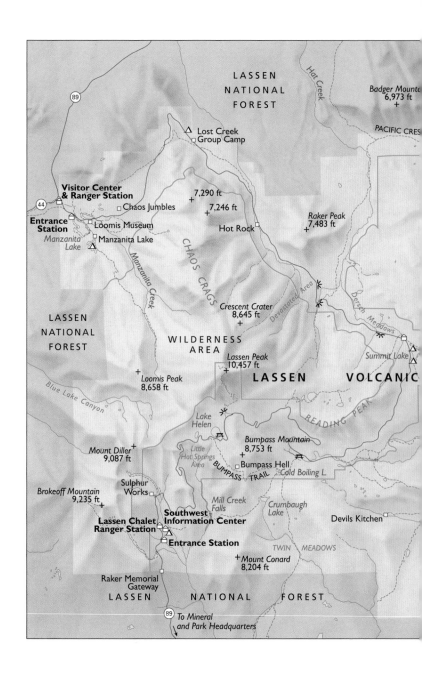

LASSEN
NATIONAL
FOREST

89

Hot Creek

Badger Mounta
6,973 ft
+

PACIFIC CRES

△ Lost Creek
□ Group Camp

**Visitor Center
& Ranger Station** □
Chaos Jumbles □

44

**Entrance
Station** ⌂
Loomis Museum □
Manzanita Lake △
*Manzanita
Lake* △

Manzanita Creek

CHAOS CRAGS

7,290 ft
+
7,246 ft
+

Hot Rock □

*Raker Peak
7,483 ft*
+

Crescent Crater
8,645 ft
+

Devastated Area

Bersch Meadows

LASSEN
NATIONAL
FOREST

WILDERNESS
AREA

Lassen Peak
10,457 ft
+

Summit Lake △
△

Loomis Peak
8,658 ft
+

LASSEN   VOLCANIC

Blue Lake Canyon

READING PEAK

Lake
Helen

Bumpass Mountain
8,753 ft
+

Mount Diller +
9,087 ft

*Little
Hot Springs
Area*

BUMPASS TRAIL

□ Bumpass Hell

Cold Boiling L.

Brokeoff Mountain
9,235 ft
+

Sulphur
Works □

*Mill Creek
Falls*

Crumbaugh
Lake

Devils Kitchen □

**Lassen Chalet
Ranger Station** △

**Southwest
Information Center**

□ **Entrance Station**

TWIN   MEADOWS

+ *Mount Conard
8,204 ft*

Raker Memorial
Gateway □

LASSEN   NATIONAL   FOREST

89
*To Mineral
and Park Headquarters*
↓

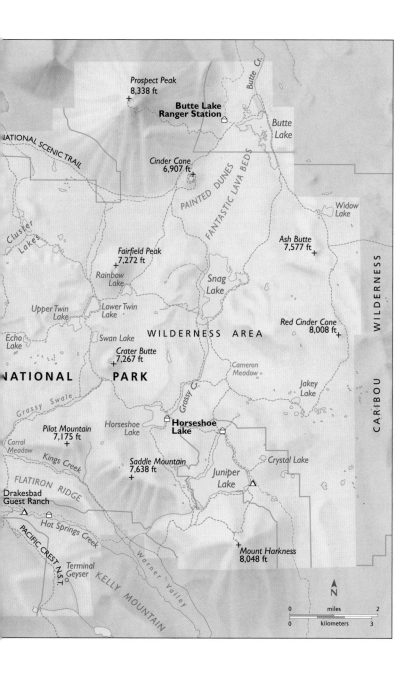

Prospect Peak
8,338 ft

Butte Cr.

**Butte Lake
Ranger Station**

Butte
Lake

NATIONAL SCENIC TRAIL

Cinder Cone
6,907 ft

PAINTED DUNES

FANTASTIC LAVA BEDS

Widow
Lake

Cluster
Lakes

Ash Butte
7,577 ft

Fairfield Peak
7,272 ft

Rainbow
Lake

Snag
Lake

Upper Twin
Lake

Lower Twin
Lake

WILDERNESS   AREA

Red Cinder Cone
8,008 ft

WILDERNESS

Echo
Lake

Swan Lake

Crater Butte
7,267 ft

Cameron
Meadow

NATIONAL   PARK

Grassy Cr.

Jakey
Lake

CARIBOU

Grassy Swale

Pilot Mountain
7,175 ft

Horseshoe
Lake

**Horseshoe
Lake**

Corral
Meadow

Kings Creek

Saddle Mountain
7,638 ft

Juniper
Lake

Crystal Lake

FLATIRON   RIDGE

Drakesbad
Guest Ranch

Hot Springs Creek

PACIFIC CREST N.S.T.

Terminal
Geyser

KELLY MOUNTAIN

Warner Valley

Mount Harkness
8,048 ft

N

0   miles   2

0   kilometers   3

How to Get There

From Redding (about 45 miles away), take Calif. 44 east then Calif. 89 south to Manzanita Lake Entrance; from Red Bluff, follow Calif. 36 east to Mineral, turn north on Calif. 89 to Southwest Entrance. The three other entrances—at Warner Valley, Butte Lake, and Juniper Lake—are reached via unpaved roads. Airports: Redding and Chico, Calif.; Reno, Nev.

When to Go

The volcanic areas are best visited in summer and fall. Heavy snows close most of the main road in winter. But small sections at the southern and

What Not to Miss

- Sulfur fumes and mud pots in Sulphur Works
- Hiking "Ring of Fire" Bumpass Hell Trail to Cold Boiling Lake
- Crags and canyons of 1915 eruption zone
- Day hike to Lassen Peak
- Crystal Lake
- Driving Warner Valley and visiting Devils Kitchen
- Hiking to Mill Creek Falls
- Scenic loop trail around Manzanita Lake

northern ends remain open for snowshoe hikes and cross-country skiing.

How to Visit

On a 1-day visit, drive the **main park road,** linking Calif. 89. The road, snaking across the western side of the park between the Southwest and Manzanita Lake Entrances, encompasses the major volcanic features. Explore **Bumpass Hell** and other sites along the way. If you can stay longer, climb **Cinder Cone,** an outstanding example of the results of volcanism, and, if you have the stamina for a more demanding trek, try **Lassen Peak,** a tough but rewarding high-altitude, 5-mile round-trip hike.

Bubbling Bumpass Hell, Lassen NP

EXPLORING THE PARK

Park Road & Bumpass Hell Trail: 30 miles; a half to full day

If you start at the Southwest Entrance, your first stop on this twisting, climbing road will be the **Sulphur Works.** At a roadside exhibit you walk through sulfur fumes and see hissing fumaroles, sputtering mud, and gurgling clay tinted in pastels by minerals. Here was the heart of ancestral Mount Tehama. The peaks around you once formed part of Tehama's rim, created by lava oozing from the inner Earth 600,000 to 200,000 years ago. Layer by layer, the lava built a mountain 11,500 feet high and 11 miles across.

Tehama gave birth to small volcanoes that emerged on its flanks. Repeated eruptions weakened the structure of the volcano, which collapsed, leaving behind a bowl-like caldera. Glaciers later scoured the caldera, wiping out the last remains of Tehama. **Lassen Peak,** born at least 27,000 years ago, was one of Tehama's offspring.

At **Bumpass Hell,** the road's next major stop, note a large balanced rock at the edge of the parking lot; it's a glacial erratic—a polished, glacierborne boulder. Nearby begins the **Bumpass Hell Trail,** a fairly easy 3-mile hike that takes about 3 hours. Go on it if you have time. The place is named after K.V. Bumpass, a local guide and promoter who, in the 1860s, plunged his leg through the thin crust covering a seething mud pot. Though badly burned, he wisecracked about his easy descent into hell.

As you walk along, you'll note (and smell) sulfurous vapors drifting over parts of the trail, which leads down to a railed boardwalk that winds past boiling mud pots, rumbling fumaroles, and hissing hot springs. At the springs' steamy pools look for floating golden flakes. They are crystals of iron pyrite—fool's gold—carried along in the superheated steam.

Resume driving on the road, which curves around Lassen Peak. Continue to the **Devastated Area,** wrecked by the massive May 1915 eruption. Amid the scarred and fallen trees you will notice the signs of renewal: Young trees and stubborn grasses are growing in a slow, natural comeback unaided by human hand. The road offers many turnoffs for viewing the crags and canyons that are Lassen's volcanic heritage.

You'll pass churned-up landscape dubbed **Chaos Crags** and **Chaos Jumbles;** if space along the road permits, stop and walk around. Here, about 300 years ago, a nearby volcanic dome suddenly collapsed, perhaps because of an Earth tremor. Millions of tons of rock, riding a cushion of trapped air, sped across 2 miles of flat land.

The horizontal avalanche smashed into a mountain and veered into a creek, damming it and forming **Manzanita Lake.**

Just beyond, the road ends its course through the park and enters Lassen National Forest.

Cinder Cone Nature Trail: **31-mile drive, 5-mile hike; a full day**

Leave the park via the Manzanita Lake Entrance. Head north on Calif. 44 toward the Butte Lake Entrance. From Calif. 44 take the marked dirt road 6 miles to the Butte Lake Campground, where the trail begins. **Cinder Cone,** a nearly symmetrical, 755-foot-high mound of lava surrounded by multicolored cinders, stands black and solitary above a pine forest. Why all the cinders? This type of cone volcano ejects light lava that shatters in the air and falls back as cinders, which pile up around the volcanic vent. Don't expect to hurry on the trail, a round-trip of about 5 miles. Walking on loose cinders is like walking through sand, your feet sinking with every step. At the top (6,907 feet), you will see the craters of recent eruptions; the last was in the mid-1600s.

Lassen Peak Trail: **5 miles round-trip; a half to full day**

The Lassen Peak Trail is a steep, arduous climb. The zigzagging trail begins at 8,463 feet, near the park road, and takes you to the 10,457-foot summit. The going can get tough for people used to breathing at sea level. Before you try the climb, be sure you are acclimatized to the park's high elevations. Carry water, wear a hat, and bring a jacket. Turn back if a storm threatens; the peak is a lightning attractor.

As you climb, you'll note that Lassen has scant vegetation. "A desert standing on end," one parched climber called it. But you can almost always spot a ground squirrel. And sometimes thousands of tortoiseshell butterflies suddenly flit by, their shadows cascading along the grayish volcanic rocks. At the summit, you can see the hardened vestige of the 1915 lava flow. And visible on a clear day, 75 miles away, is Mount Shasta.

Painted Dunes, at the base of Cinder Cone, Lassen Volcanic National Park

INFORMATION & ACTIVITIES

Headquarters
P.O. Box 100
Mineral, CA 96063
530-595-4444
www.nps.gov/lavo

Visitor & Information Centers
Both the visitor center on
Calif. 89 at Manzanita Lake and
the Southwest Information Sta-
tion are open daily from mid-
June to Labor Day. The
Headquarters Information
Desk & Book Nook is open
year-round on weekdays.
Contact the park headquarters
for current information.

Seasons & Accessibility
Park and both its entrances
open year-round. The main
park road can be closed by
snow from late October to late
June. For road conditions in
the park, phone 530-595-4444.

Entrance Fees
$10 per car; good for 7 days.
Those entering on foot or by
bicycle pay $5 for 7 days.

Facilities for Disabled
Park headquarters, Loomis
Museum, some rest rooms, the
Devastated Area Nature Trail,
and some picnic areas are
wheelchair accessible. Free
brochures available.

Things to Do
Among the free ranger-led
activities are nature walks and
hikes, talks, nature and history
demonstrations, children's programs, evening programs
(stargazing in summer), and
snowshoe walks. Other activities include hiking, swimming,
fishing, boating (no motors),
and cross-country skiing.

Overnight Backpacking
Permits required. They are free
and can be obtained at headquarters, visitor centers, and
ranger stations. No wood fires
permitted.

Campgrounds
Eight campgrounds, Summit
Lake-North and Summit Lake-
South have a 7-day limit; all
others have a 14-day limit.
Open late May through September, weather permitting.
    First come, first served. Fees
$10-$16 per night. Showers are
available at Manzanita Lake.
Roads to Warner Valley and
Juniper Lake not recommended
for RVs. Three group campgrounds; reservations required;
contact headquarters. Food services in park.

Ponderosa pines, Lassen Volcanic NP

Hotels, Motels, & Inns

(Unless otherwise noted, rates are for two persons in a double room, high season.)

INSIDE THE PARK:

■ **Drakesbad Guest Ranch** Chester, CA 96020. Call 530-529-1512; or call long-distance operator and ask for Drakesbad #2 in the 530 area code. 6 lodge rooms, 4 cabins $242; 6 bungalows $278. All meals included. Pool. Open June to early October.

OUTSIDE THE PARK
In Mineral, CA 96063:
■ **Lassen Mineral Lodge** (on Calif. 36, 8 miles from park gate) P.O. Box 160. 530-595-4422. 20 units, 2 with kitchenettes. $69-$85. Restaurant.

In Redding, CA 96002:
■ **Best Western Hilltop Inn** 2300 Hilltop Dr. 530-221-6100 or 800-336-4880. 114 units. $99. AC, pool, restaurant.
■ **Comfort Inn** 2059 Hilltop Dr. 530-221-6530 or 800-228-5150. 89 units. $77-$89. AC, pool.
■ **Red Lion Hotel** 1830 Hilltop Dr. 530-221-8700 or 800-547-8010. 192 units. $94-$114. AC, pool, restaurant.
■ **Vagabond Inn** 536 E. Cypress Ave. 530-223-1600 or 800-522-1555. 72 units. $69-$79. AC, pool, restaurant.

For more information on area accommodations, contact the park or the Redding Chamber of Commerce, 747 Auditorium Dr., Redding, CA 96001. 530-225-4433.

Excursions from Mount Lassen

Plumas-Eureka State Park

60 miles southeast of Lassen

Tucked away in a little-known corner of the Sierra Nevada, Plumas-Eureka State Park embraces an unsung realm of piney woods, glacier-gouged lakes, and jagged, snowcapped mountains.

The place wasn't so anonymous more than a century ago, when gold was discovered on **Eureka Peak.** In 1851 miners searching for a rumored "gold lake" climbed the massive mountain, where they stumbled across a quartz outcropping embedded with gold, silver, and lead. Soon the Sierra Buttes Mining Company moved in, digging 65 miles of tunnels; by the time operations ceased in the 1940s, they had extracted some eight million dollars worth of gold.

Hard-rock mining was tough work, but the miners managed to enjoy themselves during the long winters. Taking the lead from early pioneer "Snowshoe" Thompson, who delivered the mail over the Sierra Nevada on skis, the miners would strap on their own versions and race down the base of Eureka Peak. Catching a lift on the mining tram, ordinarily used to haul bucketfuls of ore down the slopes, they made Plumas-Eureka one of the nation's first (if unofficial) ski areas.

While Plumas-Eureka preserves the region's mining history, it's the park's location in the pristine **Lakes Basin** wilderness that makes it a supreme mountain escape, ideal for hiking, camping, fishing (*license required*)—and, of course, skiing.

Spend some time at the **visitor center** in the heart of the park. It contains a museum (*adm. fee*), chock full of assorted memorabilia: homemade tools, a miniature model of a stamp mill, pioneer household items, and early skis, including those belonging to local legend Snowshoe Thompson.

Across the street you'll see structures built by the Plumas-Eureka Mine, now in stages of restoration. Next, visit the nearby village of **Johnsville.** The rough-and-tumble buildings—some restored, others not—preserve the atmosphere of gold rush days.

The trail that best showcases the region's natural beauty is the 3-mile, moderately tough **Eureka Peak Loop** around 7,447-foot Eureka Peak. From picturesque **Eureka Lake,** you climb through the piney domain of coyote, bobcat, porcupine, long-tailed weasel, mountain lion, and black bear to a magnificent panoramic view of the surrounding peaks, including Sierra Buttes.

■ 5,500 acres ■ Northeastern California ■ Best seasons spring–fall
■ Hiking, camping, fishing, downhill skiing, historic sites ■ Contact the
park, 310 Johnsville Rd., Blairsden, CA 96103; 530-836-2380.
www.parks.ca.gov

Ahjumawi Lava Springs State Park

40 miles
north of
Lassen

Freshwater springs gush everywhere from the
volcanic rock that surrounds **Big Lake, Horr Pond,**
and the **Tule River.** Today this primeval landscape
survives, thanks largely to the absence of roads into beautiful
Ahjumawi Lava Springs State Park. That means few visitors
and little disturbance for the many species of birds that visit
or live here, including western grebe, marsh hawk, quail, and
bald eagle.

Plan to bring your own canoe, kayak, or small powerboat,
as there are no rentals in the area. From the launching area,
called the Rat Farm, paddle in a northwest direction across
Horr Pond, where the fly-fishing is excellent, to the park on
the north bank.

The park sits on lava flows that make up only a small portion
of the extensive volcanic activity that pushed up the peaks of
the Cascade Range over the last 20 million years. From here you
can see Mounts Shasta and Lassen to the west and south. Lava
tubes and fields of jagged black basalt cover much of the park.

But there are also fields of grass and sagebrush, forests of oak
and pine, and wetlands, all providing habitat for mule deer, black
bears, mountain lions, and yellow-bellied marmots. The Native
American word *ahjumawi* means "coming together of waters," and
the springs emerging from the lava beds constitute one of the
largest freshwater spring systems in the entire country. Meander
among the bubbling springs and you will marvel at the amazingly
clear water. In the deeper pools it takes on a rich cobalt or aqua-
marine color. Several trails traverse the park.

■ 6,000 acres ■ Northern California, 62 miles east of Redding off
Calif. 299 ■ Best season summer ■ Primitive camping, boating, fishing,
bird-watching ■ Access by boat only ■ Contact California State Parks,
24898 Hwy. 89, Burney, CA 96013; 530-335-2777. www.parks.ca.gov/north/
nobutes/alssp190.htm

Mount Shasta Drive 3 to 4 days

50 miles southwest of Lassen

This driving tour of 3 or 4 days, but lasting up to a leisurely week, will take you to the major attractions of remote and beautiful northern California. Depending on your schedule, you can treat it as a series of separate drives, or opt for a shorter circular route by omitting the section north of Mount Shasta. Each major stopping point has accommodations and places to eat.

Start in the small town of **Red Bluff** *(visitor information, 100 Main St. 530-225-4100 or 800-655-6225)*, reached from the south on I-5, or from the west on Calif. 36, which cuts across the scenic South Fork Trinity River. (If you are coming from the coast, the latter entails a full day's drive. Be sure to check your brakes before departing.) Red Bluff, set on the Sacramento River at the junction of several routes, has a long tradition of hosting travelers.

Take I-5 north and make a brief stop, about a mile north of Red Bluff, at the **William B. Ide State Historic Park** *(21659 Adobe Rd. 530-529-8599)*. Ide was an early settler, entrepreneur, and a leader of the 1846 Bear Flag Revolt in Sonoma. In early Red Bluff, he literally served as judge, clerk, prosecutor, and defense attorney in trials of horse thieves. After a jury found them guilty, he would invariably sentence them to be hanged. His home has been preserved here, along with some fascinating relics of early ranch culture.

Passing through the towns of **Anderson** *(visitor information, 1699 Hwy. 273. 530-365-7500)*, where the U.S. Fish and Wildlife Service runs the **Coleman National Fish Hatchery** *(530-365-8622)*, and Redding, I-5 now cuts through increasingly interesting terrain, crossing an arm of the scenic **Shasta Lake**, California's largest reservoir (29,740 acres).

At 14,162 feet **Mount Shasta** is almost permanently snow covered. A volcanic peak that last erupted more than 200 years ago, it is still considered an active volcano.

The mountain left John Muir with a less than pleasant memory—so bad was the frostbite he suffered there one winter that the great man walked with a limp for the rest of his life. Today, with some planning, the area is at least as comfortable—and every bit as scenic—as other ski country. A good place to stay, particularly when you are traveling in the summer, is the old lumber town of **McCloud** *(visitor information, 205 Quincy St.*

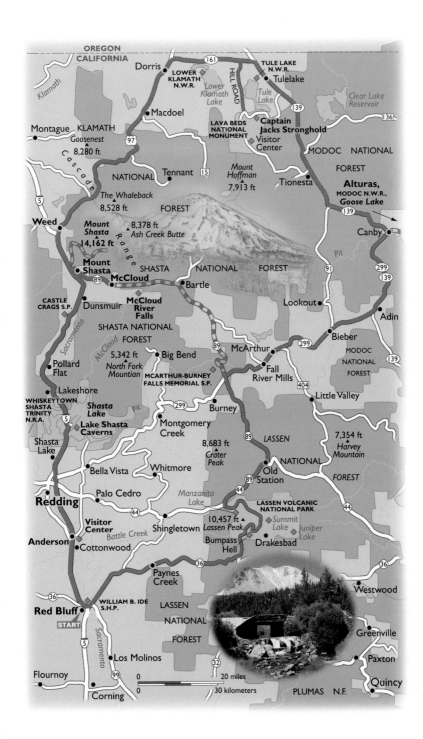

OREGON
CALIFORNIA

Dorris

161

TULE LAKE
N.W.R.

LOWER
KLAMATH
N.W.R.

Lower
Klamath
Lake

Tulelake

HILL ROAD

Tule
Lake

139

Klamath

Macdoel

Clear Lake
Reservoir

136

Montague   KLAMATH

LAVA BEDS
NATIONAL
MONUMENT

Captain
Jacks Stronghold

Goosenest
8,280 ft

97

Visitor
Center

MODOC   NATIONAL

Cascade

NATIONAL   Tennant   15

Mount
Hoffman
7,913 ft

Tionesta

FOREST

Alturas,
MODOC N.W.R.,
Goose Lake

The Whaleback
8,528 ft

FOREST

139

Weed

5

Mount
Shasta
14,162 ft

Range

8,378 ft
Ash Creek Butte

Canby

SHASTA   NATIONAL   FOREST

Pit

Mount
Shasta

89   McCloud

Bartle

91

299

139

CASTLE
CRAGS S.P.

Dunsmuir

McCloud
River
Falls

Sacramento

Lookout

Adin

SHASTA NATIONAL
FOREST

89

Bieber

MODOC

5,342 ft

McCloud

North Fork
Mountian

Big Bend

McArthur

299

NATIONAL

139

Pollard
Flat

MCARTHUR-BURNEY
FALLS MEMORIAL S.P.

89

Fall
River Mills

FOREST

Lakeshore

Pit

404

Little Valley

WHISKEYTOWN
SHASTA
TRINITY
N.R.A.

Shasta
Lake

299

Burney

Shasta
Lake

5

Lake Shasta
Caverns

Montgomery
Creek

89

LASSEN

7,354 ft
Harvey
Mountain

Bella Vista

Whitmore

8,683 ft
Crater
Peak

NATIONAL

Redding

Palo Cedro

Manzanita
Lake

89

Old
Station

FOREST

44

44

Visitor
Center

44

Battle Creek

Shingletown

10,457 ft
Lassen Peak

LASSEN VOLCANIC
NATIONAL PARK

Summit
Lake

Juniper
Lake

44

Anderson

Cottonwood

Bumpass
Hell

Drakesbad

Paynes
Creek

36

36

Westwood

Red Bluff

WILLIAM B. IDE
S.H.P.

LASSEN

START

5

Sacramento

NATIONAL

Greenville

Los Molinos

FOREST

32

Paxton

Flournoy

99

0   20 miles

0   30 kilometers

Quincy

Corning

PLUMAS N.F.

Mount Shasta at sunset

530-964-3113), a few miles east of I-5 on Calif. 89.

At this point, you can opt for an abbreviated version of this drive: Rather than heading into the northern section, proceed southeast from McCloud on Calif. 89 and rejoin the drive at McArthur-Burney Falls.

The main drive continues north on I-5 to the old lumber town of Weed, of which the tidy town actually has few. Bear northeast here on US 97 to cross the Cascade Range, a chain that extends into British Columbia. The Great Basin region is represented here by the Modoc Plateau—high, dry, laden with juniper and sage, and flat, flat, flat.

The Klamath Basin extends across the Oregon-California border and is home to some spectacular bird populations.

Just before the state border, don't miss the turnoff on Calif. 161. Head east, cutting across California's northernmost reaches. A worthwhile first stop is at the **Lower Klamath National Wildlife Refuge** *(see p. 43; 530-667-2231)*, part of a 180,000-acre wetland area under U.S. Fish and Wildlife Service protection. For bird-watchers, this refuge and the nearby **Tule Lake National Wildlife Refuge** *(see pp. 43–44; 530-667-2231)* are a dream come true. The vast basin of marshes and shallow lakes is a winter haven for bald eagles and for more than a million migrant ducks, geese, and swans. During the breeding season it is common to see herons and egrets, double-crested cormorants and cinnamon teal.

Just to the south of Tule Lake is **Lava Beds National Monument** *(off Calif. 161 on Hill Rd. S. 530-667-2282)*. Be prepared here for extremes: of heat during the day, cold in the evening. Clustered near the park's visitor center are the famous lava tubes. These 30,000-year-old signs of volcanic activity were formed when the exterior of long lava flows cooled and hardened before their centers. When the flow stopped and the remaining molten lava ran out of the other end, a tube resulted. Many of these tubes contain brightly colored lichens. Some are open for visitors to explore. To do so, you will need warm clothes, hard-soled shoes, a helmet, and a flashlight (visitor center provides flashlights).

Before leaving the park on Calif. 139, take the rare opportunity to visit a battleground most Americans do not even know about—that of the Modoc War. **Captain Jack's Stronghold,** at its center, is named for the ingenious Modoc warrior who, in 1872, startled the U.S. Army by beating them in a series of skirmishes over land policy. Two short walking trails take visitors around the captain's fortifications.

Follow Calif. 299 southwest, then head north on Calif. 89 for the entrance to **McArthur-Burney Falls Memorial State Park** *(530-335-2777)*. The 129-foot waterfall—Theodore Roosevelt proclaimed it the "eighth wonder of the world"—is easily reached by a well-maintained footpath. Flush with wildlife (the rare black swift nests here) and stands of fantastic incense cedar and ponderosa pine, the park is yet another of this region's undervisited gems. Small motels and inns just outside the park offer a restful natural getaway.

On the road once more, drive south on Calif. 89 to reach Lassen Volcanic National Park.

■ **431 miles long** ■ **Northern California** ■ **Best seasons summer–fall**
■ **Hiking, bird-watching, wildlife viewing, auto tour, historic towns and sites**

Castle Crags State Park

70 miles northwest of Lassen

The granite spires of **Castle Crags** emerge like a bundle of spear points from a quiver of forest along the Sacramento River. They form a dramatic skyline, an array of knobs, spires, and sheer faces. In geological terms the crags are a pluton, granite that hardened underground and then was pushed up through old seabed sediments. The crags were sculpted by glaciers and weather into the jagged shapes of today. They make a memorable sight for drivers along I-5, some 2,500 feet below.

The higher crags are part of **Castle Crags Wilderness,** which is in **Shasta-Trinity National Forest** *(530-964-2184)*. They are easily reached by trail through the state park, and provide some of the best hiking and climbing in the region. On the east side of I-5, the park includes a few miles of the upper Sacramento River. You can obtain maps and detailed information on trail conditions from a small visitor center at the ranger station near the park entrance.

From the visitor center, drive up to the Vista Point parking area to the trailhead for the 2.7-mile (one way) **Crags Trail.** It's not a long hike, but it's steep—2,200 feet elevation change. The reward at the end is 4,966-foot **Castle Dome,** and it is well worth the exertion. Many who make this hike will scramble about on the rocks around Castle Dome and then head back down the trail. Serious climbers will stick around for the face climbs on fairly solid rock.

If you're not going all the way to Castle Dome, at least get past **Bob's Hat Trail,** which is where you'll stop hearing traffic sounds from I-5. Views along the way are of the Trinity Mountains, the crags above, and the valleys and ridges stretching west and south. The trees thin out on top and the 360-degree views include Mount Shasta to the north.

The Flume Trail is a relatively level 2.5-mile (one way) hike that starts at the ranger station and passes through several different types of habitat, such as dry chaparral, pine forest, and oak woodland. From spring through the summer your path will be brightened by blossoming wildflowers, including many species of rare California orchids. Look for American kestrels and acorn woodpeckers as you saunter along the path.

■ **4,000 acres** ■ **Northern California** ■ **Best seasons spring–summer** ■ **Camping, hiking, backpacking, climbing, fishing** ■ **Adm. fee** ■ **Contact the park, P.O. Box 80, Castella, CA 96017; 530-235-2684. www.parks.ca.gov**

Trinity Alps Wilderness

90 miles northwest of Lassen

Pocket wilderness areas protect key habitat and natural wonders, but it's the big wilderness preserves that strike a primordial chord. Deep in the **Trinity Alps,** with no roadhead near and no shelter but the arbor of evergreens and the big slabs of granite, you can experience the sort of untethered wild experience that once was typical of California's northern forests. The Trinity Alps Wilderness is an exquisite collection of rivers, lakes, alpine meadows, and peaks over 8,000 feet.

To get a better understanding of the history and natural beauty of this region, take the 175-mile **scenic drive** that begins north of Yreka on Calif. 96. Following the Klamath River most of the way, the route goes through historic mining towns, over a series of passes, and down along the river bottom including sections of dry chaparral, dense forests of Douglas-fir, and occasional sprays of redbud in the early spring. At Willow Creek, head east on Calif. 299, which ambles along the Trinity River to Redding.

The most popular route in the wildness is along the **Canyon Creek Trail,** from a trailhead in Junction City on Canyon Creek Road.

■ **503,000 acres** ■ **Northern California** ■ **Best season summer** ■ **Camping, hiking, backpacking, white-water rafting and kayaking, swimming, fishing** ■ **Contact Big Bar Ranger Station, Shasta-Trinity National Forest, Star Rte. 1, Box 10, Big Bar, CA 96010; 530-623-6106. www.rs.fs.fed.us/shastatrinity**

Fording a tributary of Trinity River, Trinity Alps Wilderness

Mount Rainier

One of the world's most massive volcanoes, Mount Rainier can dominate the skyline for 100 miles before you reach the park named after it. At nearly 3 miles in height, Mount Rainier is the tallest peak in the Cascade Range; it dwarfs 6,000-foot surrounding summits, appearing to float alone among the clouds. Throughout history native peoples, pioneers, climbers, painters, and sightseers have been drawn to this towering volcano, which is visible from more than 200 miles away.

Mount Rainier may be the centerpiece of the park, but it is hardly the only attraction. Here, less than 3 hours' drive from Seattle, you can stroll through seemingly endless fields of wildflowers, listen to a glacier flow, wander among trees nearly a thousand years old. The park's convenient location, however, also leads to weekend traffic jams, both summer and winter, and guarantees you company on popular trails.

Mount Rainier is the offspring of fire and ice. Still active, it was probably born more than a half million years ago, on a base of lava spewed out by previous volcanoes. Lava and ash surged out of the young volcano's vent thousands of times, filling the neighboring canyons and building up a summit cone, layer by layer, to a height of some 16,000 feet.

Even while Mount Rainier was growing, glaciers carved valleys on and around the mountain. The 25 major glaciers here form the largest collection of permanent ice on a single U.S. peak south of Alaska.

Mount Rainier's summit deteriorated over time, but eruptions in the last 2,000 years rebuilt it to its current height of 14,410 feet. The mountain last erupted about a century ago. Today Mount Rainier is still a work in progress, prone to the occasional mudflow or exhalation of steam and ash. Scientists are certain it will erupt again, although they are unable to predict when that event might occur.

- Western Washington
- 236,000 acres
- Established 1899
- Best season summer
- Hiking, mountain climbing, fishing, cross-country skiing, snowshoeing
- Information: 360-569-2211 www.nps.gov/mora

Mount Rainier

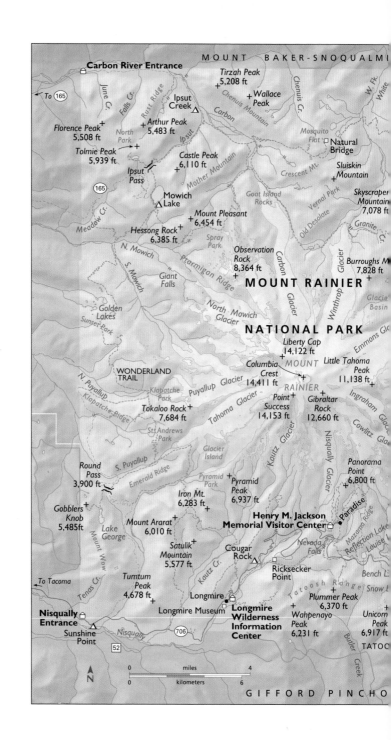

MOUNT BAKER-SNOQUALMI

Carbon River Entrance

Tirzah Peak
+5,208 ft

+Wallace
Peak

To (165)

June Cr.

Falls Cr.

Russ Ridge

Ipsut
Creek

Chenuis Mountain

Chenuis Cr.

W. Fk.
White

Carbon

Mosquito
Flat □ Natural
Bridge

Florence Peak+
5,508 ft

North
Park

+Arthur Peak
5,483 ft

Ipsut

Tolmie Peak+
5,939 ft

Castle Peak
+6,110 ft

Mother Mountain

Crescent Mt.

Sluiskin
Mountain

Ipsut
Pass

(165)

Mowich
△Lake

Goat Island
Rocks

Vernal Park

Old Desolate

Skyscraper
Mountain
7,078 ft

Granite

Meadow Cr.

Hessong Rock+
6,385 ft

Mount Pleasant
+6,454 ft

Spray
Park

N. Mowich

Observation
Rock
8,364 ft
+

Carbon

Glacier

Burroughs M
+7,828 ft

S. Mowich

Giant
Falls

Ptarmigan Ridge

MOUNT RAINIER +

Glacier
Basin

Golden
Lakes

Sunset Park

North Mowich
Glacier

NATIONAL PARK

Winthrop

Emmons Gla

Liberty Cap
14,122 ft
+

MOUNT

Little Tahoma
Peak
11,138 ft

N. Puyallup

WONDERLAND
TRAIL

Klapatche
Park

Puyallup Glacier

Columbia
Crest
14,411 ft

RAINIER

Point+
Success
14,153 ft

Gibraltar
Rock
12,660 ft

Ingraham

Klapatche Ridge

Tokaloo Rock+
7,684 ft

Tahoma Glacier

Cowlitz Gla

St. Andrews
Park

Glacier
Island

Kautz Glacier

Nisqually Glacier

Round
Pass
3,900 ft

S. Puyallup

Emerald Ridge

Pyramid
Park

Pyramid+
Peak
6,937 ft

Panorama
Point
+6,800 ft

Gobblers+
Knob
5,485ft

Lake
George

Mount Ararat
6,010 ft

Iron Mt.
6,283 ft
+

Paradise

Henry M. Jackson
Memorial Visitor Center

Mazama Ridge

Reflection Lake

To Tacoma

Mount Wow

Satulik+
Mountain
5,577 ft

Cougar
Rock
△

Nevada
Falls

Louise L

Ricksecker
Point

Bench L

Tenas Cr.

Tumtum
Peak
4,678 ft

Kautz Cr.

Tatoosh Range

Snow L

**Nisqually
Entrance**
△

Longmire

Longmire Museum

**Longmire
Wilderness
Information
Center**

Plummer Peak
+6,370 ft

Unicorn

Sunshine
Point

Nisqually

(706)

Wahpenayo
Peak
6,231 ft

Peak
6,917 ft

Butter Creek

(52)

TATOO

N

miles 4
0
0 kilometers 6

GIFFORD PINCHO

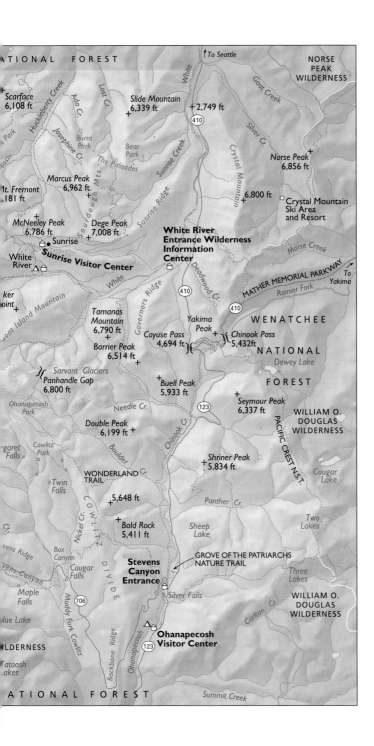

NATIONAL FOREST

NORSE PEAK WILDERNESS

To Seattle

White

Goat Creek

Scarface 6,108 ft

Lost Cr.

Ada Cr.

Huckleberry Creek

Josephine Cr.

Slide Mountain 6,339 ft

2,749 ft

410

Silver Cr.

Norse Peak 6,856 ft

Burnt Park

Bear Park

The Palisades

Sunrise Creek

Crystal Mountain

6,800 ft

Crystal Mountain Ski Area and Resort

Marcus Peak 6,962 ft

Mt. Fremont 7,181 ft

McNeeley Peak 6,786 ft

Dege Peak 7,008 ft

Sunrise

Sunrise Visitor Center

White River

Sunrise Ridge

Southough Mts.

White River Entrance Wilderness Information Center

Morse Creek

Deadwood Cr.

MATHER MEMORIAL PARKWAY

To Yakima

Rainier Fork

410

410

WENATCHEE

ker oint

White

Goat Island Mountain

Governors Ridge

Tamanos Mountain 6,790 ft

Cayuse Pass 4,694 ft

Yakima Peak

Chinook Pass 5,432ft

NATIONAL

Barrier Peak 6,514 ft

Dewey Lake

Sarvant Glaciers

Panhandle Gap 6,800 ft

Buell Peak 5,933 ft

FOREST

Ohanapecosh Park

Needle Cr.

123

Seymour Peak 6,337 ft

WILLIAM O. DOUGLAS WILDERNESS

argaret Falls

Double Peak 6,199 ft

Cowlitz Park

Chinook Cr.

Cougar Lake

Boulder Cr.

Shriner Peak 5,834 ft

PACIFIC CREST N.S.T.

Twin Falls

WONDERLAND TRAIL

5,648 ft

Panther Cr.

Two Lakes

vens Ridge

Cowlitz Cr.

Nickel Cr.

Bald Rock 5,411 ft

Sheep Lake

Box Canyon

Cougar Falls

DIVIDE

Stevens Canyon Entrance

GROVE OF THE PATRIARCHS NATURE TRAIL

Three Lakes

vens Canyon

Maple Falls

706

Silver Falls

Carlton Cr.

WILLIAM O. DOUGLAS WILDERNESS

Cr.

Muddy Fork Cowlitz

Backbone Ridge

Ohanapecosh

Ohanapecosh Visitor Center

lue Lake

123

ILDERNESS

atoosh akes

ATIONAL FOREST

Summit Creek

How to Get There

From Seattle (95 miles) or Tacoma (70 miles) to the Nisqually Entrance *(open year-round)*, take I-5 to Wash. 7, then follow Wash. 706. From Yakima, take Wash. 12 west to Wash. 123 or Wash. 410, and enter from the park's east side *(Stevens Canyon and White River Entrances closed in winter)*. For the northwest entrances (Carbon River and Mowich Lake), take Wash. 410 to Wash. 169 to Wash. 165, then follow the signs. Carbon River Road is subject to flooding in all seasons and may close at any time; contact the park. Airports: Seattle, Wash., and Portland, Oreg.

When to Go

All seasons. Wildflowers are at their best in July and August. High trails may remain snow covered until mid-July. Cross-country skiing and snowshoeing are popular in winter. Summer and winter, to miss the crowds; time your visit for midweek.

How to Visit

If you have only a day in summer, drive from the Nisqually Entrance in the southwest to the flowered fields of **Paradise,** then on to **Sunrise,** the highest point accessible by car, open

What Not to Miss

- **The short walk to 168-foot Narada Falls, off Nisqually-to-Paradise Rd.**
- **Hiking 5-mile Skyline Trail from Paradise to Panorama Point**
- **Ricksecker Point for great views of the Tatoosh Range and Nisqually River.**
- **Walking the 2.5-mile round-trip trail to Snow and Bench Lakes**
- **Grove of the Patriarchs nature trail to view 500- to 1000-year-old trees**

early July to early October. If you have 2 days, take the same route but do it more leisurely: Plan to explore as far as Paradise the first day, then tour **Stevens Canyon Road** and the route to Sunrise the next; arrive before 10 a.m. to catch the early morning light and wend your way back.

For a longer stay, drive out and reenter the lesser known northwest corner at **Carbon River** for a look at a rain forest and a hike to a dark, shiny glacier. Because Mount Rainier creates its own clouds and can hide for days or weeks at a time, come prepared to focus on delights close at hand: waterfalls, woods, and wildflowers. Be aware of the effects of high elevation.

EXPLORING THE PARK

Nisqually to Paradise: 18 miles; a half to full day

The pilgrimage to **Paradise** has been a classic for nearly a century. The first miles of your tour wind through a forest of giant Douglas-fir, western redcedar, and western hemlock. As you cross **Kautz Creek,** about 3 miles from the Nisqually Entrance, look for flood debris and dead trees amid the recovering forest. In 1947 the **Kautz Glacier** disgorged a flash flood of meltwater. The flood raged down the creek valley, carrying volcanic debris, trees, and boulders, and burying the road under 28 feet of mud. Similar, though mostly smaller, mudflows occur at least every few years at Mount Rainier.

Park at **Longmire Museum,** 6 miles from the entrance. Pioneer James Longmire discovered mineral springs here in 1883 and built Mount Rainier's first hotel; his ads for miraculous water cures helped generate early tourism and a constituency for the creation of the park. Take time for the easy half-mile **Trail of the Shadows** that starts on the opposite side of the main road. While in Longmire, also visit the **Wilderness Information Center** *(closed Oct.–late April)* for trail and weather information and backcountry permits.

A few other trails originate in Longmire, but they pale in comparison with those waiting farther along the road. Except, of course, for the aptly named **Wonderland Trail.** This route is a circle, so it doesn't exactly start at Longmire, but it is here that most visitors first cross its path. This 93-mile trail winds all the way around Mount Rainier, passing through deep forest, skirting along overgrown creeks and lakes, rising into alpine meadows, and edging so close to glaciers that you can feel their icy breath. Visitors who lack the time and the stamina for 93 miles can fashion shorter loops by combining the Wonderland with numerous access trails.

Back in your car, continue east for about 6.5 miles, then take the spur road to the right to **Ricksecker Point.** To the south loom the sawtoothed peaks of the Tatoosh Range, dramatic remains of lava flows that predated Mount Rainier by some 25 million to 35 million years. Glaciers that developed and receded during the last million years carved the sharp pinnacles and the steep-sided mountain side hollows called cirques. Below meanders the **Nisqually River,** originating at the snout of the **Nisqually Glacier,** which faces you on Mount Rainier. This glacier is about 4 miles long and flows downhill a foot every summer's day.

Rejoin the highway. Another 1.5 miles brings you to the **Narada Falls** pullover. The shimmering, 168-foot plunge of the Paradise River is well worth the steep but short walk down to the viewing area below the bridge. Climb back up to your car and proceed; in less than 3 miles you'll reach the most popular part of the park.

"It looks just like paradise!" exclaimed Martha Longmire in 1885 on first sighting the rolling hills swathed in wildflowers and framed by Mount Rainier's white dome. An average of 140 inches of precipitation falls here each year; as many as 40 species of flowers bloom on the thin, volcanic soil during July and August. Park near the **Henry M. Jackson Memorial Visitor Center,** or the **Paradise Inn,** built in 1917.

The center doubles as a museum, which spirals up through several levels of exhibits on Mount Rainier's geology, ecology, and wildlife; it also covers the history of climbing the mountain. At the

Climbers hiking up Mount Rainier

top, enormous windows afford expansive views of Mount Rainier and the surrounding landscape.

Begin your exploration of Paradise meadows on the **Nisqually Vista Trail** (1.2 miles), especially if time is short. This easy, self-guided nature walk starts at the staircase to the west of the visitor center. Its booklet acquaints you with the geology and meadow life of Mount Rainier. John Muir once called these meadows "the most luxuriant and the most extravagantly beautiful of all the alpine gardens I have beheld." In July and August, with the snow finally melted, these slopes are ablaze with flowering plants.

Make sure you stay on the path, no matter how tempting a meadow stroll. Trampling by just a few people can kill these fragile plants. Park staffers are still at work replanting old trails and other damaged areas. Only recently have the meadows recovered from the Camp of the Clouds, a tent city in operation here from 1898 to

1915. Not only people damage meadows, though. Elk, introduced in the first part of the century and now numbering some 2,000 inside the park, trample and graze the meadows. Researchers are seeking a solution to the problem.

If you're up to tackling some steep hills, try the 5-mile **Skyline Trail.** Start from the staircase west of the visitor center. The trail will take you to **Panorama Point** for some spectacular views.

Paradise to Sunrise: 50 miles; a half to full day

Leaving Paradise, turn left at the sign for Sunrise and Yakima. You'll soon pass the glacier-carved **Reflection Lakes** on your left; on a calm day, the reflection looks as solid as the mountain. Continue a mile past the lakes' pullover and park on the right for a 2.5-mile, hilly, round-trip walk to **Snow** and **Bench Lakes,** gems surrounded by the steep headwalls of the Tatoosh Range.

Drive on and stop after about 3 miles at an overlook of **Stevens Canyon.** Huge glaciers grating through this river gorge deepened

Debris Flows

Exploding peaks and lava rivers aren't the only geologic hazards spawned by Mount Rainier. Of more immediate concern to visitors are debris flows called lahars, which occur several times a decade on some streams. Though the causes of debris flows are poorly understood, they may stem from three major phenomena: the sudden drainage of meltwater from glacier cavities; flooding following intense rainfall; or rock avalanches. Any one of these conditions could trigger a flow of rock, soil, and water down stream channels.

The mass of rock and soil moves at about 10 to 20 miles per hour, but the occasional large flow roars like a freight train, generates strong winds and dust clouds, carries huge boulders, shakes the ground, and wipes out trees, roads, bridges, and almost anything else in its path. Debris flows most often occur during hot, sunny weather. Very few people have ever been caught in a flow and no one in recorded history has been killed by one. But in the unlikely event you hear the rumble of a flow, or if you're near a stream that starts to rise rapidly, move quickly to ground 160 feet or more above stream level.

and widened it into a classic U-shaped valley. Tributaries of **Stevens Creek** spill from the canyon's rim as waterfalls. Drive on another 3 miles, to **Box Canyon** (*just past picnic area*). Park and cross the road for the nearly level half-mile **Canyon Stroll** and you'll see a 100-foot-deep gorge whose straight walls were carved by the **Muddy Fork** of the **Cowlitz River**.

Continue another 9.5 miles, then park to walk the **Grove of the Patriarchs** nature trail. People often describe old-growth forests as majestic, but if ever there were a time to use that adjective, this is it. This grove of western redcedars and Douglas-firs comes right out of J.R.R. Tolkien's novel, *The Hobbit*. The easy 1.3-mile loop leads to an island in the **Ohanapecosh River** dominated by grand Douglas-fir, western redcedar, and western hemlock, many of them 500 to 1,000 years old. Touching a living thing that was ancient when Europe was still mired in the Middle Ages can induce a deep sense of calm. After rejoining the road, turn left on Wash. 123 for Sunrise. If time allows, take a short detour south on Wash. 123 to visit the Ohanapecosh Visitor Center, which has good information on the area.

At Cayuse Pass, continue north on Wash. 410, then make a sharp left toward the White River Entrance. The road ends at **Sunrise**. Spire-shaped subalpine fir and whitebark pine grow here. Near tree line, harsh temperatures and winds stunt the trees into twisted shrubs called krummholz, or elfin timber; trees only inches in diameter may be 250 years old. Fragile wildflowers bloom among grass and sedge in terrain inhospitable to trees.

At the visitor center, ask about snow conditions on the higher trails, and plan accordingly. If time is short, take the self-guided **Sourdough Ridge Nature Trail** for 1.5 miles, then the **Emmons Vista Trail** for half a mile. The Sourdough Ridge trail, which starts with a climb, introduces plants and animals of the subalpine region. The former flourish in this fertile but fragile volcanic soil. The Emmons Vista Trail offers an easy way to view **Emmons Glacier,** Mount Rainier's largest, covering more than 4 square miles.

If you have more time and energy, and the snow has melted (*snow on slopes can be dangerous if you're not equipped with an ice ax and trained to use it*), take the **Burroughs Mountain Trail** (5 miles to **First Burroughs,** or 7 miles to **Second Burroughs).** Begin as you did for the nature trail, but turn left about half way up the hill and follow the signs. You'll start amid those lush subalpine blooms and the scattered, stunted, high-elevation trees, but soon you'll leave the trees behind, and the plants will be shorter and hug the ground. This is true alpine, where the deep cold and furious winds of winter rule, where life hangs on rather than prospers. In this wide open high country you feel as if you're at the top of the world. Snow often stays on the ground up here well into July; so tread carefully, especially on steep slopes. The trail soon enters tundra. Compact little plants sport exquisite lilliputian blossoms and leaves that are a dull gray from the tiny hairs that protect them against drying winds. It is most important that you stay

Grove of the Patriarchs, Mount Rainier National Park

on the trail: If trod on, these delicate plants can take decades to heal. At Second Burroughs it feels as if you could almost touch Mount Rainier's imposing peak. Return to your car by way of the **Sunrise Rim Trail.**

The Northwest Corner: Carbon River: **5 miles inside park boundary; a half day**

To visit a rare inland temperate rain forest and peer at a glacier, take the **Carbon River Road** *(left fork off Wash. 165 about 6 miles past Wilkeson).* Unpaved inside the park, the road

may not be passable for ordinary cars. Stop at the entrance to take the self-guided **Carbon River Rain Forest Trail,** a half-mile loop among colossal Sitka spruce, Douglas-fir, and western red-cedar. If the road is passable, drive to the parking lot at Ipsut Creek Campground. If you're up to a 7-mile round-trip hike with a short, moderately steep climb, take the **Carbon Glacier Trail.** Bear right at first fork, left at second, then cross the swinging bridge over the river and continue on to the glistening glacier. Don't get close: Boulders continually tumble off the glacier's snout.

Snow often stays on the ground up here well into June and even July, so tread carefully. Carbon River is subject to flooding. Call the park's visitor center for status before attempting this drive.

INFORMATION & ACTIVITIES

Headquarters

Tahoma Woods, Star Route
Ashford, WA 98304
360-569-2211
www.nps.gov/mora

Visitor & Information Centers

Longmire Wilderness Information Center open daily mid-May through Sept. Longmire Museum open daily. Henry M. Jackson Memorial Visitor Center, at Paradise, open daily from early May to mid-Oct., weekends rest of year. Ohanapecosh Visitor Center, at park's southeast entrance, open daily Memorial Day to mid-October. Sunrise Visitor Center open daily, July to early Oct. Wilkeson Wilderness Information Center open year-round, Wed. to Sun.

Seasons & Accessibility

Park open year-round. Many roads closed by snow from late November through May or June. Call 360-569-2211 for recorded weather, road, and trail information; in the Nisqually area tune into 1610 AM.

Entrance Fees

$10 per car per week; $20 annual.

Pets

Permitted leashed on roads. Pets not allowed on trails or in the backcountry.

Facilities for Disabled

Most public buildings and some rest rooms are wheelchair accessible. Portions of some trails may be accessible (assistance may be needed). Inquire at park for details.

Things to Do

Free naturalist-led activities: nature and history walks, hikes, campfire and children's programs, talks, films, slide shows. Also available, hiking, mountain climbing, fishing, cross-country skiing, snowshoeing.

Special Advisories

■ Mount Rainier is an active volcano. While eruptions are usually preceded by an increase in earthquake activity, other hazards, such as mudflows, glacial outburst floods, or rockfalls can occur without warning.
■ Watch out for falling rocks, debris, and avalanches. Look up!
■ Some areas may be subject to flash floods, especially in late summer and fall. Inquire about current conditions before hiking.

Overnight Backpacking

Permit required; available from visitor centers, ranger stations, and wilderness centers. Contact the Longmire Wilderness Infor-

Tempting a gray jay, Mount Rainier National Park

mation Center in care of park headquarters, or call 360-569-2211. Make reservations through the National Parks Reservation Service at 800-365-2267.

Campgrounds

Five campgrounds, all with 14-day limit. Sunshine Point open all year. Others open late spring to early fall. Fees $10-$14 per night. Showers available in the visitor center at Paradise. Both tent and RV sites; no hookups. Advance reservations required at Cougar Rock and Ohanapecosh from late June to Labor Day. Call National Parks Reservation Service; 800-365-2267. All others, first come, first served. Food services in park.

Hotels, Motels, & Inns

(Unless otherwise noted, rates are for two persons in a double room, high season.)

INSIDE THE PARK:
The following are operated by Mt. Rainier Guest Services, P.O. Box 108, Ashford, WA 98304. 360-569-2275.

■ **National Park Inn** (at 2,700-foot level of Mount Rainier) 25 units, 18 with private baths. $78-$110. Restaurant.

■ **Paradise Inn** (at 5,400-foot level of Mount Rainier) 118 units, 86 with private baths. $77-$115. Restaurant. Open late May to early October.

For more information on area accommodations, contact the park's Guest Services *(see above)*.

Excursions from Mount Rainier

Alpine Lakes Wilderness

50 miles north of Mount Rainier

Think of this grand expanse of the Cascades as an endangered species. Designated wilderness areas are in short supply in our overdeveloped world. The size of Alpine Lakes Wilderness—about 400,000 acres—makes it uncommon indeed. And the fact that Alpine Lakes is located a mere 1 hour's drive east of Seattle and the Puget Sound metropolitan area by interstate highway makes it downright rare; seldom does one find a vast wilderness so close to a heavily urbanized region. But that proximity also accounts for the endangered status of Alpine Lakes. Wilderness-starved visitors flock to the area, and among the crowds are those who carelessly trample fragile vegetation, cause erosion by cutting trails, and corrupt the solitude in popular sections.

Old-growth Douglas-fir forest

It's easy to understand the popularity of Alpine Lakes. For one thing, some 500 lakes dot this wilderness. A sprawling network of rivers and creeks round out the aquatic riches of the area. Those waterways course down from peaks that range as high as 9,415 feet and slither through alpine meadows brimming with wildflowers.

Alpine Lakes hosts a tremendous variety of plants and animals thanks to its wide elevation range and extensive west-east breadth. The wilderness runs from the west side of the Cascades across the crest to the east side of the range. Western redcedar, western hemlock, and hulking Douglas-firs dominate westside forests while smaller Douglas-firs and an array of pines are more common on the east side. Most animals range on both sides of the crest, and include black bear, elk, Columbia black-tailed deer, mountain lion, beaver, and, at higher elevations, mountain goat.

In order to tour Alpine Lakes properly you must leave your car behind. More than 450 miles of trails provide both day hikes and backpacking opportunities, a few of which are mentioned below.

Many notable trails head south into the wilderness from US 2, on the north side of Alpine Lakes, or from spur roads that branch south from the highway. Located along FR 6412, **Dorothy Lake Trail** climbs a fairly steep 1.5 miles through dense forest to the north end of picturesque **Lake Dorothy.**

On the south side of the Alpine Lakes Wilderness, I-90 provides access to another complex of trails. The most popular is the 3.5-mile, moderately difficult hike to **Snow Lake.** It heads northwest from the ski area at Snoqualmie Pass and climbs along rocky slopes above the headwaters of the South Fork Snoqualmie River. Enjoy the surrounding peaks before descending to Snow Lake. Or pitch your tent on one of the primitive designated campsites.

Enchantment Lakes

On the east side of Alpine Lakes, the road along Icicle Creek reaches deep into the wilderness. Numerous trails heading north and south from the creek quickly lead into the wilds, though it takes long, hard hours to reach the area's most renowned destination: the Enchantment Lakes. But many people make the trek, drawn by the profusion of alpine lakes and lakelets and the views of granite spires and high mountains. These alpine lakes can be reached using the **Snow Lake Trail** (8.5 miles one way) or the **Stuart Lake Trail** via Colchuck Lake (5.5 miles one way). Both trails are located off Icicle Creek Road and are extremely steep. The trip is best done in 2 days. The **Enchantment Basin** is a limited-use area; for maps, reservations, and permits, inquire at the Lake Wenatchee Ranger District (*22976 Hwy. 207, Leavenworth. 509-763-3103*).

■ **400,000 acres** ■ **Southeast Washington, 35 miles east of Seattle**
■ **Year-round; best season summer** ■ **Camping, hiking, backpacking**
■ **Parking permit required at most trailheads** ■ **Contact Wenatchee National Forest, 215 Melody Ln., Wenatchee, WA 98801, 509-662-4335; or Mount Baker-Snoqualmie National Forest, 21905 64th Ave. W., Mountlake Terrace, WA 98043, 425-775-9702. www.fs.fed.us/r6/mbs /wilderness/alakes.htm**

Lake Wenatchee Area

75 miles northeast of Mount Rainier

The Lake Wenatchee area doesn't offer any scene-stealing attractions, yet the charms of the place add up. Groves of massive cedars; a scenic drive along a wild river; ospreys diving into a lake; meadows fragrant with wildflowers; river otters approaching your canoe. These and many other features form an appealing mosaic.

Five miles long and a mile wide, ringed by forest and marsh, **Lake Wenatchee** is a beauty. Such a setting has drawn the attention of many people over the years, but **Lake Wenatchee State Park** *(21588A Hwy. 207, Leavenworth. 509-763-3101)* on the southeast tip of the lake, still offers a semblance of wildness. So do two trails leaving from the Glacier View Campground at the end of Cedar Brae Road. One half-mile hike leads to **Hidden Lake** while another easy trail skirts part of the lake's shore for 1.2 miles.

Smaller but wilder **Fish Lake** is located about a mile northeast of Lake Wenatchee State Park. Informal trails and a rough road provide access to some of the shoreline. But the best vantage point from which to enjoy Fish Lake is in a small boat or canoe, which can be rented from Cove Resort *(509-763-3130)* on the south shore or at Cascade Hideaway *(509-763-5104)* on the north shore.

Auto Tour

Beginning just south of Fish Lake, the Chiwawa Valley auto tour heads north 24 miles up the **Chiwawa River.** The road was cut in the early 1900s as a wagon route to provide access to upriver mining camps. Today the **Chiwawa Valley Road** (FR 6200, mostly unpaved) takes motorists to 15 campgrounds and 22 hiking trails, and provides a scenic drive for those who prefer to experience the area from their cars.

■ **381,490 acres** ■ **North-central Washington** ■ **Best season summer** ■ **Camping, hiking, boating, canoeing, snowmobiling, cross-country skiing, snowshoeing, dogsledding, bird-watching, wildlife viewing, wildflower viewing, auto tour** ■ **Trailhead parking permit required in summer; ski parking permit required in winter** ■ **Contact Lake Wenatchee Ranger District, Wenatchee National Forest, 22976 State Hwy. 207, Leavenworth, WA 98826; 509-763-3103. www.fs.fed.us/r6/wenatchee**

Mount St. Helens National Volcanic Monument

45 miles southwest of Mount Rainier

For people in the Northwest, complacency about the natural order of their world evaporated with the explosion of Mount St. Helens on May 18, 1980. No doubt most people in the area got out of bed that Sunday morning assuming that the top 1,300 feet of this beloved Cascade peak would still be there when they went to bed that night.

At 8:30 a.m. a pilot and two geologists were flying in a small plane above Mount St. Helens. For months the volcano had been giving signs of an impending event, so the watch was on. But no one had anticipated what happened next. At 8:32 a.m. the excited pilot radioed that the whole north side of the mountain "just went." Its collapse released a pent-up brew of steam, ash, and hot gas in a lateral, 300-mile-per-hour blast that leveled everything in its path. People as far away as Canada and Montana heard the explosion. Climbers on Mount Adams, 34 miles east, saw the eruption; ten minutes later a heat wave washed over them, raising

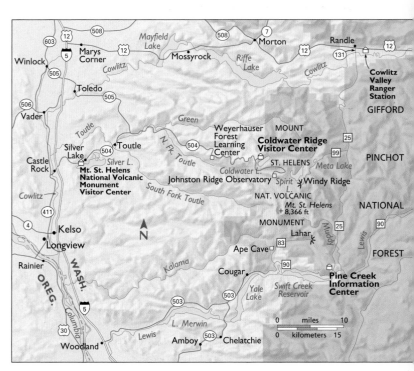

Lava dome, Mount St. Helens

the air temperature by an astounding 30 to 40 degrees. Flows surged down rivers and creeks, smashing bridges, leveling forests, and flooding the surrounding landscape. A mushroom cloud of ash billowed more than a dozen miles into the sky, turning day into twilight over thousands of square miles and laying a blanket of gray ash over vast expanses of eastern Washington. The lives of 57 people ended in an instant.

But devastation is no more permanent than tranquillity; life soon began returning to the area. Animals that burrow underground, including pocket gophers, peeked out; fish in nearby lakes survived; elk eventually returned; and within weeks flowers resprouted and hummingbirds returned. Now, 25 years later, you can see the beginnings of a future forest.

Most visitors approach Mount St. Helens from the west on Wash. 504. Five miles from the town of Castle Rock you'll come to the **Mount St. Helens National Volcanic Monument Visitor Center** on the shores of Silver Lake. Under the center's glass-walled, 50-foot ceiling you'll find a museumlike range of exhibits. One walk-through exhibit allows you to enter the interior of a simulated volcano and see how the Earth's forces produce an eruption.

From the Mount St. Helens Visitor Center, Wash. 504 continues about 40 miles east through private forestlands before it skirts along the northwest border of the monument. Stop at the **Weyerhauser Forest Learning Center** (*Milepost 42. 360-414-3439*) for a view onto the **North Fork Toutle River,** where evidence of the debris avalanche and massive mudflows can be seen. Look, too, for a large herd of elk that roams this valley.

Westside Crater

Soon after reaching the monument's border, the road turns south into the monument itself; about 1 mile ahead is the **Coldwater Ridge Visitor Center,** overlooking Coldwater Lake. From the center you have a good view of the mountain. You may even see a little steam rising from vents inside the crater. This visitor center focuses on the rebirth of the mountain after the eruption. Continue to the end of the road, just 5 miles from the crater. There you'll come to the newest of the monument's facilities: **Johnston Ridge Observatory.** From here you get a fantastic view of the gaping crater that was left when the north side of peak collapsed.

Southside Crater

The prime attraction on the south side is **Ape Cave,** a 2,000-year-old lava tube that you can explore on a 45-minute walk on your own or with a monument guide. The temperatures in the cave hover around 40° F so bring warm clothes. Seven miles farther up FR 83 you'll come to **Lahar Viewpoint.** Looming behind the lahar—a broad floodplain formed by a river of hot mud, water, and ash—is the mountain responsible for that mud and ash. Half a mile east of the view point is **Lava Canyon,** where 1980 mudflows scoured off all the vegetation, revealing old lava flows that speak of geologic events 2,000 year ago.

- ■ 110,000 acres ■ Southern Washington ■ Best months May–Oct.
- ■ Hiking, fishing, wildlife viewing ■ Visitors pass required for most sites
- ■ Contact the monument, 44218 N.E. Yale Bridge Rd., Amboy, WA 98601; 360-247-3900. www.fs.fed.US/gpnf/wshnvm/

Will It Blow Again?

Will Mount St. Helens erupt again? Yes. The only question is when, and that's difficult to predict. An eruption will occur when molten rock gushes up from the magma chamber that lies between 1 and 4 miles beneath the volcano. In 1998, increased seismic activity once more got the attention of volcano watchers. In 2004, scientists detected tremors again, and visitors saw plumes of steam and ash, indicating that new magma continues to move up in Mount St. Helens. A full-blown eruption had not yet occurred as of press time.

North Cascades

With glacier-clad peaks rising almost vertically from thickly forested valleys, the North Cascades are often called the American Alps. The national park forms two units, North and South, of the North Cascades National Park Service Complex. The two other units—Lake Chelan National Recreation Area and Ross Lake National Recreation Area—contain most visitor facilities and permit private land ownership and commercial activity.

The park complex preserves virgin forests, fragile subalpine meadows, and hundreds of glaciers. Mule deer and black-tailed deer graze the high meadows, where black bears gorge on berries and hoary marmots sunbathe. Mountain goats clamber on rock faces. Mountain lions and bobcats, seldom seen, help keep other wildlife populations in balance.

The wildness and ruggedness of the park especially lure hikers, backpackers, and mountaineers. "A more difficult route to travel never fell to man's lot," complained trapper Alexander Ross, who came here in 1814. But today the main road (through Ross Lake National Recreation Area) and easy access into the park—on some of its 360 miles of trails—also allow more casual visitors to experience the peaceful forests and the drama of the mountains.

The region forms part of the Cascade Range, named for its innumerable waterfalls. The range extends from British Columbia to northern California. A geological theory proposes that the mountains began as a microcontinent several hundred miles out in the Pacific Ocean. Over the eons a series of islands floated on their plate toward North America. About a hundred million years ago, the plate smashed into the North American continent, folding and crumpling into a mountain range as it lodged against the landmass. Those mountains eroded; the Cascades you see today rose only five million or six million years ago.

- North-central Washington

- 684,000 acres

- Established 1968

- Best seasons summer–fall

- Hiking, mountain climbing, boating, mountain biking

- Information: 509-682-3503 www.nps.gov/noca

Glaciers of Forbidden Peak, North Cascades National Park

How to Get There

From Seattle (115 miles from the park), take I-5 to Wash. 20. From the east, get on Wash. 20 south of Mazama. Airports: Seattle and Bellingham.

When to Go

Summer gives the best access, though snow can block high trails into July. The North Cascades Highway, from Ross Dam to beyond Washington Pass, closes in winter. The year-round community of Stehekin offers winter cross-country skiing.

How to Visit

On a day trip, take the **North Cascades Highway** through the **Ross Lake National Recreation Area** for an overview of the area's lakes and dams, mountains, and the glacier-fed **Skagit River.** If you have 2 days, drive up the unpaved **Cascade River Road** and hike among the park's peaks.

What Not to Miss

- **Drive North Cascades Highway**
- **Washington Pass Overlook**
- **Historic town of Diablo and boat tour of Diablo Lake**
- **Gorge Creek Falls**
- **Sauk Mountain Trail at Rockport**

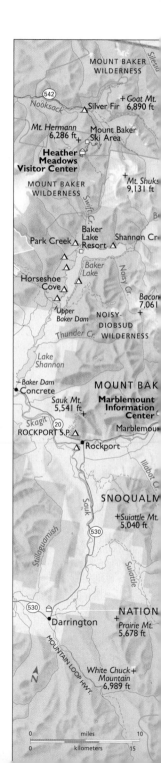

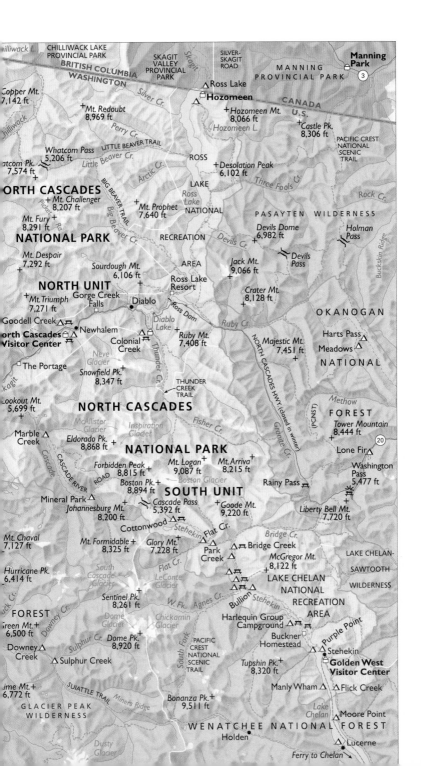

Chilliwack L.

CHILLIWACK LAKE
PROVINCIAL PARK

SKAGIT
VALLEY
PROVINCIAL
PARK

SILVER-
SKAGIT
ROAD

MANNING
PROVINCIAL PARK

Manning
Park

3

BRITISH COLUMBIA
WASHINGTON

Skagit

Silver Cr.

Ross Lake

Hozomeen

CANADA
U.S.

Copper Mt.
7,142 ft

Mt. Redoubt
8,969 ft

Perry Cr.

Hozomeen Mt.
8,066 ft

Hozomeen L.

Castle Pk.
8,306 ft

PACIFIC CREST
NATIONAL
SCENIC
TRAIL

Chilliwack

Whatcom Pass
5,206 ft

LITTLE BEAVER TRAIL

Little Beaver Cr.

ROSS

Desolation Peak
6,102 ft

Three Fools Cr.

Rock Cr.

atcom Pk.
7,574 ft

Arctic Cr.

LAKE

Ross
Lake

PASAYTEN WILDERNESS

Buckskin Ridge

ORTH CASCADES

Mt. Challenger
8,207 ft

BIG BEAVER TRAIL

Mt. Prophet
7,640 ft

NATIONAL

Devils Dome
6,982 ft

Holman
Pass

Mt. Fury
8,291 ft

NATIONAL PARK

Big Beaver Cr.

Pasayten R.

RECREATION

Devils Cr.

Devils
Pass

Mt. Despair
7,292 ft

Sourdough Mt.
6,106 ft

AREA

Jack Mt.
9,066 ft

NORTH UNIT

Ross Lake
Resort

Crater Mt.
8,128 ft

OKANOGAN

Mt. Triumph
7,271 ft

Gorge Creek
Falls

Diablo

Diablo
Lake

Ross Cr.

Ruby Cr.

Goodell Creek

Newhalem

Diablo Dam

Ruby Mt.
7,408 ft

Majestic Mt.
7,451 ft

Harts Pass

orth Cascades
Visitor Center

Colonial
Creek

Meadows

NATIONAL

The Portage

Neve
Glacier

Snowfield Pk.
8,347 ft

Thunder Cr.

NORTH CASCADES HWY. (closed in winter)

Skagit

Lookout Mt.
5,699 ft

THUNDER
CREEK
TRAIL

Methow

FOREST

NORTH CASCADES

Granite Cr.

Tower Mountain
8,444 ft

McAllister
Glacier

Inspiration
Glacier

Fisher Cr.

(PCNST)

Lone Fir

20

Marble
Creek

Eldorado Pk.
8,868 ft

NATIONAL PARK

Washington
Pass
5,477 ft

Cascade

CASCADE RIVER ROAD

Forbidden Peak
8,815 ft

Mt. Logan
9,087 ft

Mt. Arriva
8,215 ft

Rainy Pass

Mineral Park

Boston Pk.
8,894 ft

Boston Glacier

SOUTH UNIT

Liberty Bell Mt.
7,720 ft

Johannesburg Mt.
8,200 ft

Cascade Pass
5,392 ft

Goode Mt.
9,220 ft

Cottonwood

Stehekin

Flat Cr.

Bridge Cr.

Mt. Chaval
7,127 ft

Mt. Formidable
8,325 ft

Glory Mt.
7,228 ft

Park
Creek

Bridge Creek

McGregor Mt.
8,122 ft

LAKE CHELAN-

Hurricane Pk.
6,414 ft

South
Cascade
Glacier

Flat Cr.

LeConte
Glacier

LAKE CHELAN

NATIONAL

SAWTOOTH

WILDERNESS

FOREST

Downey Cr.

Sentinel Pk.
8,261 ft

W. Fk. Agnes Cr.

Bullion

Stehekin

RECREATION

AREA

Green Mt.
6,500 ft

Dome
Glacier

Chickamin
Glacier

Harlequin Group
Campground

Purple Point

Downey
Creek

Sulphur Cr.

Dome Pk.
8,920 ft

PACIFIC
CREST
NATIONAL
SCENIC
TRAIL

Buckner
Homestead

Stehekin

Sulphur Creek

South Fork

Tupshin Pk.
8,320 ft

Golden West
Visitor Center

ime Mt.
6,772 ft

SUIATTLE TRAIL

Miners Ridge

Manly Wham

Flick Creek

GLACIER PEAK
WILDERNESS

Bonanza Pk.
9,511 ft

Lake
Chelan

Moore Point

WENATCHEE NATIONAL FOREST

Holden

Lucerne

Dusty
Glacier

Ferry to Chelan

EXPLORING THE PARK

North Cascades Highway: Marblemount to Washington Pass: 60 miles; a half to full day

The ease of driving the North Cascades Highway belies the terrain's ruggedness, although names supplied by explorers and climbers attest to it: Mount Terror, Mount Despair, Damnation Peak, Mount Fury, Mount Challenger. This transmountain road was completed only in 1972.

Enter the **Ross Lake National Recreation Area** after crossing **Bacon Creek,** 6.5 miles beyond the Wilderness Information Center at Marblemount. Parallel to the road, the **Skagit River** appears emerald in summer—evidence of the park's many glaciers. As they move, glaciers grind bedrock into a fine "flour." Water carrying a high concentration of glacial flour reflects the green part of the light spectrum. In winter bald eagles feast on salmon running the Skagit.

At **Goodell Creek Bridge** *(Milepost 119),* look left to catch a rare glimpse of the high, sawtoothed peaks of the Picket Range. Discover the natural and human history of these mountains along trails or at the **North Cascades Visitor Center.** The visitor center features slide and film programs about the North Cascade wilderness. Nearby is an accessible viewpoint trail.

Farther east on Wash. 20, turn right onto Main Street at **Newhalem** *(Mile 121),* a town of Seattle City Light. The company's dams—Gorge, Diablo, and Ross—generate about a quarter of Seattle's peak-time electricity. The dams created **Diablo, Ross,** and **Gorge Lakes.** To haul men and materials for construction, the company built a railway from Rockport to Diablo in the 1920s.

Drive on to **Diablo,** another City Light settlement, by turning left at Mile 126. Near here in 1901, pioneer Lucinda Davis and her three children cleared land and put up a roadhouse to feed and house the miners who still trudged the mountains in the wake of two abortive gold rushes. The Davis family built the first hydroelectric project on the Skagit—a waterwheel that generated enough electricity to light three light bulbs. A reproduction of the waterwheel stands next to the modern Diablo powerhouse; the **Davis Museum** *(206-684-3030)* preserves mementos of the era.

Call the Seattle City Light information center *(see p. 178)* to see if there is room on City Light's 2.5-hour tour of Diablo Lake. If you are without a boat, this is the only way to actually get on the

Riding through Hannegan Pass

water. (Or board a City Light ferry traveling between **Diablo** and **Ross.** This enjoyable 1-hour round-trip begins across Diablo Dam Road, near the parking for the Ross Lake Resort.)

Drive back to the highway and, if you are looking for an invigorating climb, turn right after about 4 miles at Colonial Creek Campground. Behind the amphitheater the **Thunder Woods Nature Trail** begins. This moderately steep 1-mile loop rises among giant, fragrant cedar trees, some of them more than three centuries old. The redcedar—characterized by ropy, cinnamon-colored bark and flat, fernlike foliage—provided Native Americans with wood for canoes and houses and fiber for mats, clothing, and baskets. To extend your walk, continue along the 19-mile **Thunder Creek Trail** for a while; the views are good and the hiking relatively easy at first. (Eventually it ascends 6,100 feet.)

When you're back in the car, don't miss the **Diablo Lake Overlook** (1,600 feet), at Mile 132. Amid the splendid scenery are exhibits that honor Senator Henry M. Jackson, who helped create the park and to whom Congress dedicated it in 1987. The highest mountain visible here is **Colonial Peak** (7,771 feet) to the southwest; note the glacial cirque, or bowl-shaped depression, carved out of its side. North is **Sourdough Mountain,** site of a fire lookout.

Near Mile 134 you'll find an informative 0.3-mile boardwalk nature trail, the **Happy Creek Forest Walk.** A few miles farther on, the highway leaves the park complex and enters the **Okanogan National Forest** *(Mile 139)*. For a superb overview of Cascade peaks, follow the road about 20 miles to **Washington Pass Overlook** (5,477 feet), the highest point on the North Cascades Highway. Exit to the left at Mile 162, and walk to the overlook. Directly to the south is massive **Liberty Bell Mountain** (7,720 feet), south of that the **Early Winter Spires** (7,807 feet). With binoculars you might spot climbers and mountain goats on the solid granite faces.

North of the Highway

Many visitors to North Cascades never venture beyond the highway corridor, except perhaps to hike one or two of the shorter trails that branch out from the road. Though the corridor is undeniably marvelous, you'll miss out on the full North Cascades experience if you limit yourself to this narrow strip. For example, the section of the complex north of Wash. 20 is a vast wilderness that sprawls all the way up to Canada. No roads and few trails brave these 500 square miles of imposing mountains, glaciers, rivers, and forests. Expert backpackers and climbers will find many challenges and rewards in this section's backcountry.

Novices won't find many opportunities to explore the north, but there are a few, nearly all of which are tied to Ross Lake. This long, skinny body of water runs some 25 miles along the east side of the north section, from the North Cascades Highway to just beyond the Canadian border. If you happen to be in Hope, British Columbia, you can drive a 40-mile gravel road to the Hozomeen area on northern tip of the lake and boat or hike into the wilds. From the

Lichens

You'll see lichens, a composite life-form that consists of an alga and a fungus, all over North Cascades forests; some dangle from tree limbs like green hair, some blanket rocks, and some that look like rubbery lettuce blow down from the canopy and litter the trails below. Lichens provide nesting material for birds and they chemically alter nitrogen from the atmosphere to create a form plants and animals can use. During the winter, when food is scarce in most Northwest forests, lichens make up a key element in the diets of some deer and elk.

North Cascades Highway, you can only enter by foot, horseback, or boat.

The Ross Lake Resort *(206-386-4437)* runs a water taxi that will take hikers and campers to various campsites and trailheads on the lakeshore. For instance, you might motor a few miles uplake to the mouth of **Big Beaver Creek,** where a trail heads northwest for 17 miles into the heart of the north section and meets the **Little Beaver Trail,** which leads east, back to Ross Lake. This path tunnels through a barely touched forest that is home to black bear, lynx, and deer. The Big Beaver Creek riparian zone harbors numerous marshes and ponds. If you're quiet and patient, around dusk you may spot some of the beavers that created those ponds. In the same area during the day, look for river otters, ducks, and a variety of marsh birds, such as common yellowthroats, red-winged black-birds, and tree swallows. About 3 miles from the lake, the trail enters one of the largest stands of old-growth western redcedar in the contiguous 48 states. Some of these trees are more than a thou-sand years old and a mind-boggling 15 feet in diameter. How far you choose to follow the trail depends on your legs and where you want to spend the night.

Cascade River Road: 45 miles round-trip; a half day

The Cascade River Road, the only road to enter the park proper from the west, passes through national forest for most of its length. The road starts in front of the Log House Inn in Marblemount. Before departing, pick up maps and check road conditions at Mar-blemount's Wilderness Information Center. The road becomes pro-gressively narrower, steeper, and bumpier, though high-clearance cars can travel it in an hour without difficulty *(trailers should not attempt last few miles).* The drive ends at a parking lot and picnic area (3,660 feet) between the glacier-studded summits of **Johannes-burg Mountain** (8,200 feet) to the west and **Boston Peak** (8,894 feet) to the east.

Hikers will enjoy the 3.75-mile trail to **Cascade Pass** (5,384 feet). The Skagit and Chelan Indians used the pass to and from Lake Chelan for hunting and trading. As soon as you get out of your car, keep your ears open. While you go about preparing your gear and head up the first part of the trail, you may hear a sharp crack, like a rifle shot, echoing through the North Fork gorge and off the stone walls of the encircling mountains. Usually that crisp report is

Ross Lake

followed by a deep-throated rumbling, tumbling landsliding noise that reverberates in the canyon and may go on for a minute or more. You're listening to the sound of geology in action, as great chunks of ice split off the north face of 8,200-foot Johannesburg Mountain, a mile away across the gorge.

The trail proceeds via moderate switchbacks through the tall trees for a couple of miles, occasionally delivering views to the west and south. Then the forest begins thinning out and the trees are much shorter as the terrain grades into open parkland. Pikas scurry about the rock-jumbled slopes and plump marmots whistle if they're not snoozing in the sun. Meadows of grasses and wildflowers appear between the rock piles along with the occasional stunted subalpine tree. Look for glacier lilies, arnica, yarrow, bluebells, and monkshood.

By the time you reach the pass, nearly all the trees have melted away and you mount the crest amid that dizzying openness of the alpine. Mountains and glaciers lean close on the side. Behind stretches the green of the meadows and forests you've just left and ahead and below spreads the head of the verdant **Stehekin Valley.**

Park employees grow native plants in a greenhouse in Marblemount, then backpack or airlift them in for planting in summer to revegetate the pass. The greenhouse *(near Wilderness Information Center in Marblemount)* is open for visits.

Stehekin Valley: An overnight or 2

Stehekin has been a tourist hideaway since hotels first opened here at the turn of the 20th century and miners spread tales of magical scenery. On the northern shores of glacier-carved Lake Chelan and inaccessible by road, **Stehekin** is a community of hardy contemporary homesteaders, complete with a one-room schoolhouse in use from 1921 to 1988. The valley offers many lodging alternatives as well as backcountry camping without backpacking: Simply fill out a backcountry permit after you get there, take a shuttle bus to any of 12 backcountry camps, and stake your claim.

Even if you don't plan to camp, head for the Golden West Visitor Center when you arrive at Stehekin Landing to pick up hiking maps and schedules of tours and buses. Be sure to ask about trail conditions; high trails—and the last stretch of the shuttle bus route—can be closed by snow or flood damage.

After lunch, take a tour of the **Buckner Homestead.** Home of the Buckner family from 1911 to 1970, it offers a look at the challenges of frontier life.

Next morning follow the nature trails near the landing. The informative 0.75-mile **Imus Creek Nature Trail** starts near the visitor center, and the **McKellar Cabin Historical Trail** begins just past the post office. Or catch the early shuttle bus upvalley. The buses currently run 20 winding miles on the old mine-to-market road. *(Ask ranger for latest bus schedule; reservations may be required.)* The scenic round-trip to the terminus at Glory Mountain takes 4 hours and can be wearing. If you have the time, it may be better to get off at a trailhead, hike, and catch the later bus back. Another good bet is the **Horseshoe Basin Trail** (off the **Cascade Pass Trail),** a moderately steep 5.75-mile trail that passes more than 15 waterfalls among spectacular glacial and mountain views.

For an easier hike try the **Agnes Gorge Trail,** 5 miles round-trip and level. Get off the bus at High Bridge near the intersection with the Pacific Crest Trail and walk across the bridge, past the sign for Agnes Creek, to the trailhead for Agnes Gorge. The trail provides excellent views of the 210-foot gorge and **Agnes Mountain** (8,115 feet). Be sure to keep a bus schedule with you at all times to avoid being stranded.

Lake Chelan National Recreation Area: **1 to 2 days**

Improbably, the final major port of entry to North Cascades lies 50 miles southeast, in the small town of **Chelan,** on the edge of the eastern Washington desert. The town cozies up to one tip of the almost 55-mile-long, 2-mile-wide **Lake Chelan.** The other tip of the lake extends a few miles into the national park complex's south section, and the Lake Chelan Boat Company *(P.O. Box 186, Chelan, WA 98816. 509-682-2224 or 509-682-4584)* takes advantage of this connection. Throughout the year the company runs one passenger boat up and down the lake, and during the warm months two other vessels are added to the fleet, including a high-speed catamaran. The slowest boat takes 4 hours to reach the dock in the south section; the catamaran zooms there in just over an hour. You can also get there in 30 minutes via a scenic floatplane flight *(Chelan Airways 509-682-5065)* out of Chelan.

But faster isn't necessarily better for visitors who aren't short on time. Lake Chelan invites leisurely cruising. A natural lake raised 21

Mule deer

Don't Build It & They Will Come Back

Wolves don't like people. More accurately, they don't like the development that so often comes with us. They aren't likely to move into a landscape littered with logging operations, ski resorts, vacation homes, mines, and the other signs of industrial civilization. But wolves have moved into the North Cascades—a tribute to its wildness.

Actually, it's more correct to say that wolves moved back to the North Cascades. This area once supported plenty of wolves, but by the end of the 19th century they had been shot, poisoned, trapped, or driven away, as was the case throughout nearly the entire contiguous United States. During the following century, lone wolves occasionally passed through, but it wasn't until 1991 that a gray wolf began showing up regularly in the Ross Lake National Recreation Area, marking the return of wolves to the North Cascades from Canada. The numbers seem to be increasing, but it remains to be seen whether these icons of the wilderness will establish a breeding population in the area.

feet by a dam, it occupies a trough gouged out by glaciers. It is one of the country's deepest lakes, reaching down almost 1,500 feet, the last 400 below sea level.

Cruising Lake Chelan

The trip starts amid the high-desert hills around Chelan, many of them dotted with houses and orchards. The development soon is left behind as the boat enters national forest lands and the arid hills give way to low mountains and conifer forest. With each mile the mountains get higher and the forest thicker, and by the time you cross into North Cascades, 4 miles from the end of the lake, the peaks soar more than 8,000 feet and the forest is lush and deep. The only reason to rush up this lake is to spend more time in the area at the end of the line before your boat goes back to Chelan.

One way to have it all is to travel fast in one direction or to stay overnight at one of the lodges and campgrounds in Stehekin, the village in which the dock is located. No roads go to this back-of-beyond municipality of some one hundred residents.

INFORMATION & ACTIVITIES

Headquarters
810 State Rte. 20
Sedro Woolley, WA 98284
360-856-5700
www.nps.gov/noca

Visitor & Information Centers
North Cascades Visitor Center
(near Newhalem) open daily
mid-April to mid-November,
weekends only rest of year. Call
206-386-4495. Information
center on Wash. 20 (North Cascades Hwy.), in Sedro Woolley,
open daily late May to mid-
October, weekdays rest of year.
Wilderness Information Center in Marblemount *(just W
of park boundary off North
Cascades Hwy.)* open daily
summer only.
Lake Chelan NRA: Golden West
Visitor Center *(in Stehekin)*,
access by ferry, floatplane, or
foot, open mid-May to mid-
October. Ranger station open
week-days all year. For information call 509-682-2549.

Seasons & Accessibility
Park open year-round, but snow
prevents access to much of it
from mid-October to April.

Entrance Fees
No entrance fee, but $5 for
1-day vehicle pass to park at
some trailheads. $30 for annual
Northwest Forest pass.

Pets
Prohibited in national park
except in front country and on
Pacific Crest Trail, if leashed.
Permitted on leashes in NRAs.

Facilities for Disabled
Information facilities and
numerous short trails near
North Cascades Highway are
wheelchair accessible.

Things to Do
Free naturalist-led activities:
Ross Lake NRA: guided nature
walks, evening campfire programs. **Lake Chelan NRA:**
nature and Buckner Orchard
walks, evening programs. Also
available, hiking, boating, fishing, hunting *(NRAs only, in season)*, horseback riding, rafting
on upper Skagit, cross-country
skiing. In summer, Seattle City
Light sponsors tours of Diablo
Lake and Ross Lake. Reserve at
least a month in advance
through Seattle City Light's
Skagit Tour Desk, 500
Newhalem St., Rockport, WA
98283. 206-684-3030.

Overnight Backpacking
Permits required; available free
at Wilderness Information
Center in Marblemount and
Golden West Visitor Center.

Campgrounds

Ross Lake NRA: Three campgrounds, 14-day limit. Colonial Creek open midspring to mid-fall. Newhalem Creek open mid-May to early October. Goodell Creek open all year. All first come, first served.

Fees: None to $12 per night. No showers. Tent and RV sites; no hookups. Goodell Creek and Newhalem Creek Group Campground, reservations required; contact the park 206-386-4495.

Lake Chelan NRA: Three campgrounds, Harlequin, Bullion, and Purple Point, 14-day limit. Open mid-spring to mid-fall. First come, first served. No fees. Showers are located near Purple Point. Tent sites only. Reservations required at Harlequin Group Campground (see above); contact the park. Limited food service is available in Lake Chelan NRA.

Hotels, Motels, & Inns

(Unless otherwise noted, rates are for two persons in a double room, high season.)

In Ross Lake NRA:
■ **Ross Lake Resort** (access by boat or foot) 503 Diablo St., Rockport, WA 98283. 206-386-4437. 15 units floating on lake, kitchens. $116. Open mid-June to late October.

In Lake Chelan NRA:
■ **North Cascades Stehekin Lodge** P.O. Box 457, Chelan, WA 98816. 509-682-4494. 28 units. $100-$125. Restaurant.
■ **Silver Bay Inn** P.O. Box 85, Stehekin, WA 98852. 509-682-2212. 4 cabins, 3 kitchenettes, $145-$295.
■ **Stehekin Valley Ranch** P.O. Box 36, Stehekin, WA 98852. 509-682-4677. 12 tent cabins some with showers. $65-$85 per person, meals. Open June through September.

In Concrete, WA 98237:
■ **Cascade Mountain Inn** 40418 Pioneer Ln., Birdsview. 360-826-4333. 6 units. $120, includes breakfast.
■ **Ovenell's Heritage Inn** 46276 Concrete Sauk Valley Rd. 360-853-8494 or 866-464-3414. 8 units $95-$120; 5 cabins $105-$120. AC, restaurant.

For information on accommodations in Chelan, contact the Chamber of Commerce, P.O. Box 216, Chelan, WA 98816. 509-682-3503 or 800-424-3526.

Excursions from North Cascades

Mount Baker

20 miles west of Cascades

At 10,781 feet high and mantled by snow and 14 glaciers, Mount Baker rises above nearby peaks like a colossus. You won't be surprised to learn that this commanding volcanic peak lends its name to the major elements of what is referred to as the Mount Baker area. These elements include the Mount Baker National Recreation Area (where the mountain itself resides), the Mount Baker Scenic Byway, and the Mount Baker-Snoqualmie National Forest.

The Mount Baker area is rugged territory cut by rivers and forested by Douglas-fir, cedar, mountain hemlock, and other conifers, though much of the old-growth outside the wilderness has been logged. Located in extreme northwest Washington, touching the border with Canada and only 30 miles from the Strait of Georgia, the Mount Baker area receives prodigious amounts of precipitation. In the winter of 1998–99, a record 95 feet of snow fell. The snowpack may keep subalpine meadows covered until into July or August, but those flowers and grasses are unquestionably well watered when they emerge.

Mount Baker Scenic Byway

The Mount Baker Scenic Byway, which approaches the area from Bellingham to the west, consists of the last 24 miles of Wash. 542 (during winter the first 21 miles of the byway are plowed to provide access to the Mount Baker Ski Area). Start at the **Glacier Public Service Center** *(360-599-2714. Mid-May–mid-Oct.),* located in the little town of Glacier. It's a joint operation of the National Park Service and the Forest Service, and its staff will give you lots of information about the Mount Baker area. Shortly after you drive east from the center, you'll see **Glacier Creek Road** (FR 039) branching south. Take this spur 9 miles to its end and you'll come to **Mount Baker Vista,** which provides superb views of the **Coleman Glacier** and **Mount Baker,** just a mile or so away. From the junction with FR 039, the byway leads through a blend of old-growth forest and big second-growth forest along the **North Fork Nooksack River.** This wild river starts life in the snow and glaciers of Mount Shuksan, northeast of Mount Baker, and cuts deep into the land on its way to the sea, in places carving a gorge several hundred feet deep.

About 2 miles from Glacier, adjacent to the Douglas-fir Campground, you'll see the start of the **Horseshoe Bend Trail.** It's the first of nearly 20 trails that branch off the byway or its spur roads. This 1.5-mile trail follows the bank above the North Fork Nooksack then loops back to the trailhead. During the fall watch the shallows for spawning chinook salmon (also known as king salmon). This, the largest of all salmon species, was recently placed on the federal endangered species list, but its condition seems to be improving. To see a lot of salmon, visit during the big pink salmon runs, which take place during odd-numbered years in **Gallup Creek,** right in the town of **Glacier,** or in **Thompson Creek,** a mile south of the highway on Glacier Creek Road. All year, but especially in fall and winter, more salmon run through the creeks in northwest Washington than in any of the lower 48 states.

Another 5 miles along the byway takes motorists to **Nooksack Falls,** where the river plunges more than 100 feet over rocky outcrops. Past the falls the road slips through some fine old-growth western hemlock, Douglas-fir, and western redcedar. Some specimens of these trees are preserved in the **North Fork Nooksack Research Natural Area,** which gives scientists baseline information and offers passersby glimpses of some of the plant world's giants.

Now comes the good part. Sure, those first 14 miles of roaring river and towering trees are great, but the last 10 miles of the byway are one of the most dramatically beautiful drives in the

Where the Glaciers Are

Glaciers still move ponderously down the mountain slopes, sculpting the land, adding minerals to the food web, and pouring meltwater into creeks. You can hike to a glacier on one of several trails. On Mount Baker's south side, the **Park Butte Trail** leads up to Park Butte, which commands grand views of Easton Glacier. The **Railroad Grade Trail** branches off the Park Butte Trail and takes you right to the glacier. On Mount Baker's northwest side, the **Heliotrope Ridge Trail** provides up-close views of the Coleman Glacier; a branch, the **Hogsback Route,** ascends to the glacier. From the Heather Meadows area, the **Picture Lake Trail** yields views of several of Mount Shuksan's glaciers; the **Artist Ridge Trail** does likewise for Mount Baker's glaciers.

Northwest. Just past the Silver Fir Campground, the road turns south, leaves the North Fork Nooksack, and starts climbing. Soon you emerge from the forest into open, sparsely treed subalpine terrain. Switchbacking several miles up mountainsides steep enough to induce vertigo, you'll cross into the storied **Heather Meadows** area. Here the trees have shrunk to cowering knots of stunted evergreens and the slopes belong to sweeping blankets of heather, huckleberries, blueberries, and wildflowers. Tarns—little alpine lakes—wink in the sunlight and slender creeks wriggle down the mountainsides, sometimes leaping down small waterfalls.

A couple miles into Heather Meadows you should stop and stroll around **Picture Lake.** The lake itself certainly warrants a photo, but that's not how it got its name. Stand on the lake's northwest rim and look southeast and you'll get the picture. The reflection of **Mount Shuksan** in the still water, with the 9,127-foot peak itself in the background—it's about 3 miles away—is reputed to be one of the most photographed mountain scenes on the continent. As you continue you'll pass several trails that will take you into this ethereal realm.

■ **1.7 million acres** ■ **Central Washington** ■ **Best season summer**
■ **Hiking, boating, downhill skiing, wildflower viewing** ■ **Parking fee at Heather Meadows** ■ **Contact Mount Baker Ranger District, Mount Baker-Snoqualmie National Forest, 2105 State Rte. 20, Sedro Woolley, WA 98284; 360-856-5700; www.fs.fed.us/rb/mbs**

Pasayten Wilderness

20 miles NE of North Cascades

To put it simply, the Pasayten is big and wild. This designated wilderness encompasses more than half a million acres. Straddling the Cascades divide and abutting the Canadian border, the Pasayten sprawls more than 50 miles west to east, which results in a tremendous breadth of climate and habitat. The west side average 100 inches of precipitation, the east about 30. Throughout the wilderness you'll encounter tall peaks; 58 summits surpass 7,500 feet. You'll also find a lot of water, including more than a hundred lakes, scores of rivers and creeks, and water locked up in mountain glaciers. Wildlife thrives in this unspoiled place. Moose, black bear, mountain lion, wolf, grizzly, bighorn sheep, and wolverine can all be found here, as well as the largest population of lynx in the lower 48 states.

Mount Baker

For the experienced backcountry traveler, the options are dazzling. More than 600 miles of trails snake through the wilderness,
the longest a leg-straining 73 miles. On the east side, you might try
the 18-mile (one way) **Chewach Trail** to **Remmel Lake.** It shadows
the banks of the **Chewach River,** passes **Chewach Falls,** continues
through river-bottom forest and emerges into meadows colored by
lupine and Indian paintbrush before reaching the lake. Another 18-
miler, the **Devils Ridge Trail,** leaves **Ross Lake** on the east side and
heads deep into the western Pasayten Wilderness, climbing through
forest to Dry Creek Pass and ascending the 6,982-foot **Devils Dome**
for a fine view of glacier-clad **Jack Mountain,** the Pasayten's highest
point at 9,065 feet.

■ **530,000 acres** ■ **North-central Washington** ■ **Best season summer**
■ **Hiking, boating, bird-watching, wildlife viewing** ■ **Contact Methow Valley**
Ranger District, Okanogan National Forest, 502 Glover, Twisp, WA 98856;
509-997-2131. www.fs.fed.us/r6/oka

Olympic

Encompassing 1,441 square miles of the Olympic Peninsula, Olympic National Park invites visitors to explore three distinct ecosystems: subalpine forest and wildflower meadow; temperate forest; and the rugged Pacific shore. Because of the park's relatively unspoiled condition and outstanding scenery, the United Nations has declared Olympic both an International Biosphere Reserve and a World Heritage site.

Inside the park, the Olympic mountain range is nearly circular, contoured by 13 rivers that radiate out like the spokes of a wheel. No road traverses the park, but a dozen spur roads lead into it from US 101, making it easily accessible from outside the park.

Residents of the Olympic Peninsula refer to it as a gift from the sea, and its features were indeed shaped by water and ice. The rock of which the mountains are made developed under the ocean; marine fossils are embedded in the mountain summits. Another component, basalt, originated from undersea lava vents. About 30 million years ago, the plate carrying the Pacific Ocean floor collided with the plate supporting the North American continent. As the heavy oceanic plate slid beneath the lighter continental plate, the upper layers of seabed jammed against the coastline, crumpling into what would become the Olympic Mountains. Glaciers and streams sculptured the mountains into their current profiles.

Thick glaciers gouged out Puget Sound and Hood Canal to the east, and the Strait of Juan de Fuca to the north, almost cutting the peninsula off from the mainland.

In the Ice Age, this isolation led to the evolution of 15 animals and 8 plants that are not found anywhere else on Earth, such as the flowering Olympic Mountain milkvetch, Olympic marmot, and Olympic mudminnow. The list of other creatures here includes brown bears, bobcats, and mountain lions. Salmon spawn in the clear mountain streams, and sea otters swim along the coast.

- Western Washington

- 922,651 acres

- Established 1938

- Best seasons summer and winter

- Hiking, backpacking, fishing, bird-watching, biking, skiing

- Information: 360-565-3130 www.nps.gov/olym

Deer grazing in alpine meadow, Hurricane Ridge, Olympic National Park

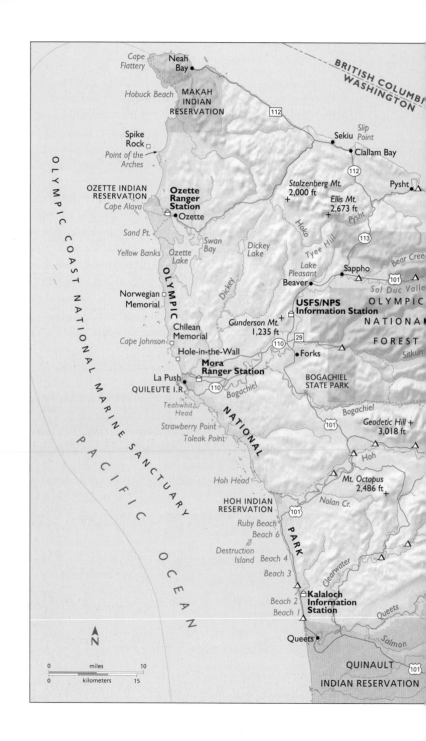

Cape Flattery
Neah Bay
Hobuck Beach
MAKAH INDIAN RESERVATION
112
Spike Rock
Point of the Arches
Sekiu
Slip Point
Clallam Bay
112
OLYMPIC COAST NATIONAL
OZETTE INDIAN RESERVATION
Cape Alava
Ozette Ranger Station
Ozette
Stolzenberg Mt. 2,000 ft
Ellis Mt. 2,673 ft
Pysht
Pysht
113
Sand Pt.
Swan Bay
Dickey Lake
Hoko
Tyee Hill
Bear Creek
Yellow Banks
Ozette Lake
Lake Pleasant
Beaver
Sappho
Sol Duc Valley
101
OLYMPIC
OLYMPIC COAST NATIONAL MARINE SANCTUARY
Dickey
Norwegian Memorial
Gunderson Mt. 1,235 ft
USFS/NPS Information Station
NATIONAL
FOREST
Chilean Memorial
29
Sitkum
Cape Johnson
Hole-in-the-Wall
110
Forks
La Push
QUILEUTE I.R.
Mora Ranger Station
110
Bogachiel
BOGACHIEL STATE PARK
Bogachiel
Geodetic Hill + 3,018 ft
Teahwhit Head
Strawberry Point
Toleak Point
NATIONAL
101
Hoh
Hoh Head
Mt. Octopus 2,486 ft
PACIFIC
HOH INDIAN RESERVATION
PARK
Nolan Cr.
Ruby Beach
Beach 6
Destruction Island
Beach 4
Beach 3
Clearwater
OCEAN
Beach 2
Beach 1
Kalaloch Information Station
Queets
N
Queets
Salmon
QUINAULT
INDIAN RESERVATION
101

BRITISH COLUMBIA
WASHINGTON

0 miles 10
0 kilometers 15

Vancouver Island
14

Strait of
Juan de Fuca

Ferry
CANADA
U.S.

LOWER ELWHA
KLALLAM
INDIAN RESERVATION

DUNGENESS
N.W.R.

Tongue
Point

Freshwater
Bay

Ediz Hook

Dungeness
Recreation Area

112
Joyce
112
Port Angeles
Harbour
Port Angeles

Agnew
Dungeness
101

Mt. Muller
3,748 ft
Lake
Sutherland

Park
Headquarters

Olympic National Park
Visitor Center

Lyre
Lake
Crescent
OLYMPIC N.F.
101

Heart O' the Hills
Ranger Station

Fairholm

Marymere Falls

Storm King
Information
Station

Elwha Ranger Station

Sol Duc
Eagle
Ranger Station
Observation
Point
Lake
Mills
Hurricane Hill
+ 5,757 ft

Blue Mt.
6,007 ft
Deer Park
Ranger
Station

Sol Duc
Hot Springs
Sol Duc Falls

Hurricane Ridge
Visitor Center
Obstruction Peak
+ 6,450 ft
OLYMPIC
N.F.

Sugarloaf Mt.
3,365 ft

OLYMPIC
GRAND VALLEY TRAIL

Hoh Rain Forest
Vistor Center
Hoh
Mt. Carrie
+ 6,995 ft
Elkhorn
Ranger
Station
Grand Pass

Gray Wolf
Gray Wolf Ridge

Olympus
Ranger Station
World's largest
subalpine fir
Cameron
Pass

Glacier Meadows
Ranger Station
Blue
Glacier
Hayes River
Ranger Station
Elwha
Hayden
Pass
Lost Peak
+ 6,515 ft

Dungeness

Mount Olympus +
7,965 ft
Constance
Pass

NATIONAL PARK
Silt Creek

+ Owl Mt.

MOUNTAINS

Mt. Anderson
7,321 ft
+

Dosewallips
Ranger Station

Kimta Peak
5,399 ft +
Queets
Low Divide
Ranger
Station
World's largest
western hemlock
Mt. La Crosse
+ 6,417 ft

Tshletshy Ridge

Park's Largest
Douglas-fir
Tshletshy Creek

O'Neil Peak
5,758 ft +
Enchanted Valley
Ranger Station
Mt. Lena
+ 5,995 ft

Sams Ridge
Sams

Park's largest
yellow cedar

Graves Creek
Ranger
Station
Hamma Hamma

OLYMPIC
NATIONAL
FOREST
Queets
North Fork
Ranger Station
Six Ridge
Pass
OLYMPIC
N.F.

Quinault Rain Forest
Ranger Station
Wynoochee
Pass
Six Ridge
Mt. Washington
6,255 ft

Quinault
Quinault
Lake
Staircase
Ranger Station

OLYMPIC NATIONAL FOREST
Lake
Cushman

LAKE
CUSHMAN
STATE
PARK

Quinault Ranger Station

How to Get There

Approach the park from US 101, which skirts three sides of the Olympic Peninsula. The main visitor center and entrance are in Port Angeles. From Seattle, take the Washington State Ferry to Bainbridge Island, then drive north to Wash. 104 to join US 101 west to Port Angeles, a drive of about 60 miles. Airports: Port Angeles, Seattle, Sequim, and Olympia.

When to Go

All-year park. Summer is the driest season, but be prepared for cool temperatures, fog, and rain at any time. Hurricane Ridge opens for skiing on winter weekends and holidays, weather permitting.

How to Visit

Plan to spend at least two days. On the first day, stroll sub-alpine meadows at **Hurricane Ridge** and admire the peaks and glaciers in the distance. Savor the **Lake Crescent** area and, if you're feeling energetic, wind up with a dip at **Sol Duc Hot Springs.**

On the second day, drive to the **Hoh Rain Forest** and sample its nature trails before heading west for the Pacific Ocean beaches and tide pools. If you have more time, consider a trip

What Not to Miss

- A visit to Hurricane Ridge and hike along Hurricane Hill Trail for stunning views of mountains
- Driving to Obstruction Peak for views of Mount Olympus and neighboring peaks
- Kayaking on azure waters of Lake Crescent
- Relaxing in hot springs at Sol Duc
- Hiking along a trail through lush Hoh Rain Forest

to **Ozette Lake,** a pretty 8-mile-long lake with trails nearby that lead to the beach. Or you can go to **Quinault Lake,** a lesser known part of the park. There's good fishing in the 250-foot-deep lake. At day's end, settle down at the grand **Lake Quinault Lodge.** Built in 1926, this is a peaceful place to stay; to guarantee solitude, there are no radios, televisions, or telephones in the rooms.

EXPLORING THE PARK

Port Angeles to Sol Duc: **76 miles; at least a day**

Plan to spend the night in the area to get an early start. At the Olympic National Park Visitor Center in Port Angeles, ask about the weather conditions on Hurricane Ridge and pick up a tide table for the next day.

On a clear day, the ridge offers spectacular views of the Olympic Mountains and northward as far as the Strait of Juan de Fuca and Canada's Vancouver Island. The 17-mile drive to **Hurricane Ridge**— so named for the force of its winter winds—takes you from lowland forest to tree line, nearly a mile above sea level, and reveals some of the remarkable geology of the peninsula.

After the tunnels, 9 miles in, stop at a pullover and look at the rock faces above the road. The bubbles of rock, called pillow basalt, are a clue that these mountains began under the ocean; when hot lava oozes into seawater, its surface cools and hardens quickly, often forming the globules you see here.

Drive on toward **Hurricane Ridge Visitor Center.** Plaques identify the peaks and glaciers of the inner Olympics. **Mount Olympus,** the tallest in the park at 7,965 feet, carries seven of Olympic's 60 major glaciers. Its Blue Glacier can receive up to 100 feet of snow a year and flows downhill as much as 5 inches a day.

Moist winds from the Pacific condense in the cool air of the Olympics and drop rain or snow, bestowing on the mountains' western slopes the wettest climate in the lower 48 states. Mount Olympus receives 200 inches of precipitation a year.

From your vantage point on

Olympic Mountains

Hurricane Ridge, you'll probably see black-tailed deer and possibly Olympic marmots that whistle when they're approached. Most of the trees are subalpine fir. Their distinctive steeple shape helps shed snow. Near tree line, a 3-foot-tall tree may be 100 years old; summer wildflowers thrive where no tree can take hold.

Fine picnic sites lie toward the end of the road, about a mile beyond Hurricane Ridge. Try the **Hurricane Hill Trail,** starting where the road ends, for 3 miles (round-trip) of wildflowers and stunning mountain views. The partly paved path begins a little above 5,000 feet and ascends about 700 feet up Hurricane Ridge to the summit. The first part ascends through a subalpine meadow—the riot of wildflowers makes resting a pleasure. The trees, mostly wind-stunted subalpine firs, get even sparser.

Tidal pool and sea stacks, Olympic National Park

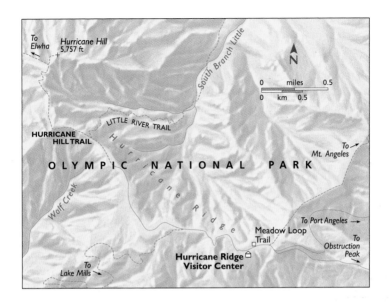

By the time you reach the saddle about halfway up, few trees obstruct the generous views. Scan the hillsides and you'll sometimes see deer or black bear. After dipping momentarily at the saddle, the trail rises fairly steeply through more superb meadows to the expansive, flat-top summit, which is laced with informal trails. *(Please don't make any new ones in this fragile habitat.)* Wildflowers and marmots compete for your attention, but you'll probably lose yourself in the views of the high country to the south, the islands in the Strait of Juan de Fuca.

If you prefer to continue driving—some of it is tricky—take the 8-mile, unpaved road to **Obstruction Peak** from the east end of the Hurricane Ridge parking lot for the park's best windshield view of Mount Olympus and some of Olympic's most diverse wildflower displays. The road generally opens by July 4. The **Grand Valley Trail** (3.5 miles one way) starts at the parking lot at road's end. Take at least a stroll on it for grand views from the top of the ridge. Then double back to Port Angeles and pick up US 101 west.

The highway passes **Lake Sutherland** before tracing the southern shore of **Lake Crescent.** Carved by a glacier, the two lakes began as one, but a great landslide created the dam that now divides them. A Native American legend says that Mount Storm King, angered at the fighting between the Quileute and Clallam Tribes, threw down a boulder, which killed the combatants and cut the the lake in two. Today, the 600-foot-deep lake is known for its trout.

Turn off at the Storm King Information Station to walk the **Marymere Falls Trail,** a 1.75-mile round-trip through lowland forest to a graceful, 90-foot waterfall. Fifty cents buys a booklet that identifies the trees, which are mostly Douglas-fir and western hemlock, with a few western redcedar.

Back in the car, if you have the time, turn left 1.5 miles west of Fairholm to take the 14-mile road to **Sol Duc.** Native Americans, who named the springs Sol Duc, or "sparkling water," probably used the hot springs for medicinal treatments. Travelers have soothed tired muscles in pools here since a resort was first established in 1912. In case you want to stroll before you soak, the **Sol Duc Falls Trail.** It start at the end of the road and leads through 0.75 of a mile of dense forest to a waterfall.

Hoh Rain Forest to the Pacific: 45 miles; a full day

The Hoh Rain Forest is located 2.5 hours from Port Angeles. To see it and the coast, continue skirting the park as you drive west and south on US 101. Check the schedule of guided tide-pool walks in your park newspaper and then decide whether to go first to the rain forest or to the beaches.

For the rain forest, take the **Hoh Road** inland 19 miles to the visitor center. You'll pass large areas on private, state, and national forest lands that once were entirely clear-cut. Logging is prohibited in the park, yet environmentalists cite evidence of damage done to park wildlife—some of whose living area extends outside the park—by shrinking habitat.

Two nature trails start behind the visitor center and are well worth taking: the **Hall of Mosses Trail** (0.75 mile) and the **Spruce Nature Trail** (1.25 miles). Both offer excellent jaunts through an enchanted land. Sitka spruce, western hemlock, and western redcedar, measuring up to 25 feet in circumference, tower 300 feet in the air. Club moss and licorice ferns drape the conifers and bigleaf maples, suffusing the air with green. Seedlings, unable to compete on the crowded forest floor, sprout luxuriantly on fallen trees, called nurse logs. Aged giants, lined up in colonnades, stand on huge roots called stilts where their nurse logs have rotted away. You might see some Roosevelt elk, which are members of the nation's largest herd, or hear their eerie bugle.

To see how the forest develops, take the Spruce Nature Trail. Where the Hoh River has shifted course in the last few decades, the first trees to move in needed full sunlight to grow—red alder, willow, and Douglas-fir. Later, shade-tolerant spruce and hemlock will succeed these pioneers to dominate the forest. As you stroll, see how the downed trees provide nutrients for emerging seedlings.

After your forest sojourn, rejoin US 101 south, stopping at **Ruby Beach.** Walk the trail down to the sand, and keep track of where you came out of the woods. It might be hard to find the trail again, and the oval-leaved shrubs off the trail are virtually impenetrable.

Olympic preserves more than 60 miles of coastal wilderness. To the north, the beaches tend to have more pebbles and rocks; to the south, the beaches are broader and sandier. Rock outcroppings called sea stacks, isolated from the shoreline by erosion, have caused many a shipwreck.

The driftwood you might have to climb over once grew where

Rain forest, Hoh River Valley

you just were: upriver in the forest. Toppled by a winter storm or undercut by a flooding creek, trees tumbled downstream to the sea. Beware: Picturesque at low tide, drift logs can suddenly roll with lethal force at high tide.

You may see harbor seals, the most common marine mammal on this coast, swimming or lounging on the rocks. In the spring and fall, California gray whales dive and spout near land on their migration between Alaska and Baja California. Gulls and crows drop clams from 50 feet in the air to crack them open on the rocks. Bald eagles soar from their forest perches to nab fish.

Continue south on US 101 and turn left at the sign for the big cedar tree, one of the world's largest. Standing at the end of a short spur road, the tree looks like something conjured up from the land of Oz. Monstrous in scale, its girth exceeds 66 feet.

The stretch of road from here to the park's southwest border is dotted with overlooks and short access trails to the beaches. If it's low tide (and you missed the guided tide-pool walk), try the trail at **Beach Four,** just north of Milepost 160. A short, steep hike brings you to the shoreline and the rocky tide pools. Alternately battered by waves and dried out by the sun, tide pools nevertheless teem

Juvenile northern saw-whet owl

Mountain Goats

Mountain goats have charisma to spare. Those comically somber faces made long by drooping beards. That thick, long-haired coat of pure white. Their acrobatic moves on treacherous mountain slopes.

But they don't belong in the park. Though mountain goats are native to other parts of Washington, they didn't penetrate the Olympic Peninsula until people introduced them back in the 1920s—before the park was established—so that they could be hunted.

As a result, since the ecosystem didn't evolve with goats as part of the mix, some plant species are suffering from the unaccustomed grazing.

As the problems associated with non-native species became better known, the park service started moving the goats to the Cascades and the Rockies. By the late 1980s, they had cut the goat population from more than a thousand to a few hundred.

This angered some animal lovers. In 1989, the Park Service stopped removing the goats. Since then they've tried other approaches, such as sterilizing goats, but with little success. So between 300 and 500 goats still roam the park, damaging some of the continent's rarest natural communities.

with life. An area a foot square may support 4,000 individual creatures that belong to more than 20 species. Look closely to spot gooseneck and acorn barnacles, periwinkle snails, and rocks with holes drilled by piddock clams. Brightly colored sea stars, or starfish, prowl the rocky pools, preying on the mussels and other mollusks. Green sea anemones stun their tiny prey with stinging cells on their tentacles.

If you still haven't had your fix of coastal hike, go to Ozette, a town near the northernmost realm of the park; take US 101 to Sappho, then head north to Wash. 112; follow this into Sekiu. From here, head southwest.

The **Ozette Lake-Cape Alava-Sand Point Trail** begins at the ranger station on the north end of Ozette Lake; you'll need to register at the station before you head out. The trail tunnels through coastal forest and over marshes until it reaches the ocean at Sand Point. Head north along the rocky beach to **Cape Alava,** the westernmost point of land in the contiguous United States.

INFORMATION & ACTIVITIES

Headquarters
600 E. Park Ave.
Port Angeles, WA 98362
360-565-3000
www.nps.gov/olym

Visitor & Information Centers
In Port Angeles, the Olympic
National Park Visitor Center,
3002 Mount Angeles Rd.; 360-
565-3132. On the western edge
of the park, the Hoh Rain Forest Visitor Center off
US 101, 360-374-6925. Both
open daily all year. Hurricane
Ridge Visitor Center also open,
weather permitting. In summer,
information stations open at
Storm King on Lake Crescent,
Kalaloch, and other locations.

For park information, tune
in to radio station 530 AM in
the Port Angeles and Lake
Crescent areas.

Seasons & Accessibility
Park open year-round. Some
roads closed in winter. For
weather and road information,
call 360-565-3131.

Entrance Fees
$10 per vehicle for 7-day pass
May to September. Some areas
charge entrance fee in winter.

Pets
Allowed on leashes except on
trails and in backcountry.

Facilities for Disabled
Visitor centers and some camp-
sites are accessible to wheel-
chairs. Also accessible are
Hurricane Ridge's paved trails,
a short loop trail into the Hoh
Rain Forest, the Madison Falls
Trail in the Elwha Valley, and
the Moments in Time Trail at
Lake Crescent.

Things to Do
Free naturalist-led activities:
meadow, forest, beach, and
tide-pool walks; campfire programs. Also available, hiking,
boating, fishing, climbing,
swimming, windsurfing, waterskiing, river rafting, cross-
country and alpine skiing,
snowshoeing.

Special Advisory
■ Be careful when hiking along
the coast; rocks and logs can be
slippery and unstable. Be aware
of incoming tides; current time
tables are posted at trailheads.
Surf logs can kill.

Overnight Backpacking
Call ahead for reservations.
Permits required; obtain at
Wilderness Information Center
that is directly behind Olympic
National Park Visitor Center
(360-565-3131), visitor centers,
ranger stations, or trailheads.

Campgrounds

Sixteen campgrounds, all with a 14-day limit. Deer Park, Dosewallips, North Fork, and Queets Campgrounds do not allow RVs. All first come, first served. Fees: $8-$16 per night. No showers. Three group campgrounds; reservations required; contact headquarters. Food services in park.

Hotels, Motels, & Inns

(Unless otherwise noted, rates are for two persons in a double room, high season.)

INSIDE THE PARK:

■ **Kalaloch Lodge** (on US 101, 36 miles south of Forks), 157151 Hwy. 101, Forks, WA 98331. 360-962-2271. 20 rooms; 44 cabins, 38 with kitchenettes. Rooms $139-$169; cabins $159-$269. Restaurant.

■ **Lake Crescent Lodge** (on US 101), 416 Lake Crescent Rd., Port Angeles, WA 98363. 360-928-3211. 52 units, 47 with private bath. $66-$195. Restaurant. Open late April through October.

■ **Log Cabin Resort** (on Lake Crescent), 3183 E. Beach Rd., Port Angeles, WA 98363. 360-928-3325 or 360-928-3245. 28 units, 3 with kitchenettes $55-$129; 10 tent sites $15; 23 RV hookups $30. Restaurant. Open April through September.

■ **Sol Duc Hot Springs Resort** (12 miles off US 101), P.O. Box 2169, Port Angeles, WA 98362. 360-327-3583. 32 cabins, 6 kitchens. $110-$130. Pool, restaurant. Open mid-May through September.

OUTSIDE THE PARK

In Forks, WA 98331:

■ **Olympic Suites Inn** 800 Olympic Dr. 800-262-3433. 33 units. $54-$110.

■ **Pacific Inn Motel** 352 South Forks Ave., P.O. Box 1997. 360-374-9400 or 800-235-7344. 34 units. $49 and up. AC.

In Port Angeles, WA 98362:

■ **Port Angeles Inn** 111 East Second St. 360-452-9285 or 800-421-0706. 24 units. $60-$140.

■ **Red Lion Hotel** 221 North Lincoln St. 877-333-2733. 187 units. $89-$99. AC, pool, restaurant.

For other lodgings, contact the Chambers of Commerce in Port Angeles, 121 E. Railroad, 98362. 360-452-2363; and Forks, P.O. Box 1249, 98331. 360-374-2531 or 800-443-6757.

Excursions from Olympic

Grays Harbor National Wildlife Refuge

45 miles southwest of Olympic

Bowerman Basin may not look like much to human eyes. To vast numbers of shorebirds, however, it means the difference between life and death. These few hundred acres of tidal mudflat and wetland in Grays Harbor provide food and shelter to hundreds of thousands of migrating shorebirds. It is one of only five key staging areas in North America, and the only one on the West Coast outside Alaska.

Shorebirds migrate between their nesting grounds in the Arctic and their wintering grounds in Central and South America. Flying

Black oystercatchers

hundreds of miles, often without stopping, drains these birds of energy. In order to complete their migration, they need abundant food resources to help them rapidly replenish their energy reserves.

Those hundreds of thousands of northbound shorebirds pack the basin during a short period each spring; check with the refuge for the best times to visit. The time of day also is critical. Plan to be there sometime during the period from an hour or two before high tide to an hour or two after; that's when the birds concentrate on the feeding grounds. During peak times the U.S. Fish and Wildlife Service asks people to call the refuge in advance for information on getting there.

Follow the 1-mile boardwalk on the **Sandpiper Trail;** it will keep you from wading through several inches of water and mud as you head for the tip of the Bowerman Peninsula. When you first arrive, pick out a bit of mudflat, train your binoculars on individual birds, and watch carefully.

■ **1,800 acres** ■ **North coast of Washington, 8 miles west of Aberdeen**
■ **Best months late April—early May** ■ **Bird-watching, boat trips**
■ **Contact Nisqually National Wildlife Refuge Complex, 100 Brown Farm Rd., Olympia, WA 98516; 360-753-9467. http://nisqually.fws.gov/**

Nisqually National Wildlife Refuge

45 miles southeast of Olympic

Nisqually National Wildlife Refuge is only 2.7 miles wide and 3.1 miles long, but plenty of wildlife seeks refuge in the Nisqually River Delta. One of the few undeveloped estuaries left in Puget Sound area, the delta serves as the home for some 300 species of animals and as a migratory stop for some 130 species of birds. The salt marshes and mudflats teem with invertebrates that feed hungry herons, killdeer, sandpipers, gulls, and ducks.

A third of the refuge's 3,000 acres is enclosed by the **Brown Farm Dike,** which keeps salt water out and creates the freshwater habitat favored by the 20,000 waterfowl here. Cattail-framed freshwater marshes shelter bitterns, frogs, and salamanders. Rodents throng the adjacent grasslands, attracting coyotes, hawks, and owls. Scan the bluffs and you may spot bald eagles, ospreys, and a great blue heron colony. You might also see salmon migrating upriver.

■ **3,000 acres** ■ **Northwest Washington, 8 miles east of Olympia**
■ **Best months May—Oct.** ■ **Hiking, bird-watching, wildlife viewing**
■ **Contact the refuge, 100 Brown Farm Rd., Olympia, WA 98516; 360-753-9467. http://nisqually.fws.gov/**

Dungeness National Wildlife Refuge

15 miles northeast of Olympic

This skinny, 5-mile crescent of mounded sediment piled up by waves and tidal currents is one of the longest natural sand spits in the world. Behind this barrier, animals and plants find shelter in quiet bays, beaches, eelgrass beds, ponds, and tidal mudflats.

Begin at the parking lot at the extreme southwest end of the refuge, immediately north of adjacent **Dungeness Recreation Area** (*Clallam County Parks 360-683-5847*). A trail runs 5.5 miles from the parking lot to the lighthouse near the tip of the spit. The first half mile winds through the mainland forest to the rim of the ocean bluff. From this point, you can see the spit and the strait beyond. There is also a platform deck equipped with a telescope for getting a detailed view of the refuge. Check out the trees for roosting bald eagles.

From the overlook, the trail descends to the spit and heads out along this narrow strip of land, bounded by the strait on one side and Dungeness Harbor on the southeastern side. As you walk the trail, scan the bay for the dark and stocky black brant, a small sea goose that drinks salt water and feeds on saltwater plants. About 1,500 winter in the refuge and up to 8,000 migrate through in the spring, peaking in late April.

The Dungeness refuge is one of the best places in Washington to see harlequin ducks, a species of concern in the state. These diving ducks get their names from the male's beautiful patchwork plumage of gray, white, russet, and black. You might see them loafing on gravel beaches, feeding in shallow water primarily on small crabs, or engaging in courting rituals.

In the protected waters and tidal flats, your binoculars also may pick up plover, common murres, buffleheads, and dunlins. You may also see tufted puffins, some of which nest on nearby **Protection Island National Wildlife Refuge** (*closed to the public to protect nesting seabirds and seals*).

■ **631 acres** ■ **Northwest Washington, northeast of Port Angeles**
■ **Best seasons spring and fall** ■ **Horseback riding, bird-watching, wildlife viewing** ■ **Contact the refuge, 33 S. Barr Rd., Port Angeles, WA 98362; 360-457-8451. www.dungeness.com/refuge**

A Place at the Table

To understand how different species of shorebirds manage to peacefully coexist, aim your binoculars on the mudflats in the Dungeness National Wildlife Refuge at low tide and note the relation between each species' bill and legs, and the feeding niche it occupies. Look in the algae-flocked mud near the tide line and you may spot a least sandpiper scooting around on its stocky legs, snatching up worms and snails with its short bill. You may see a marbled godwit nearby, probing deep burrows with its two-toned, upturned bill in search of juicy invertebrates that the sandpiper could never reach.

Farther out, in the shallow water of the receding tide, foraging dowitchers walk about on their long legs, their bodies safely above water that would swamp a stumpy sanderling.

Different bills and legs lead to different uses of resources, which allows dozens of different shorebird species to share the bounty of the mudflats.

Deception Pass State Park

45 miles northeast of Olympic

From sandy beaches to old-growth forest to freshwater marshes, Deception Pass State Park is a place of great natural abundance. For that reason, it's no surprise that it's the most popular state park in Washington, attracting about six million people a year. To avoid the crowds, try not to visit during the summer. If you are there then, explore the park either early in the morning or later in the evening.

The 4,128 acres of the park straddle two islands: Whidbey Island to the south and Fidalgo Island to the north. (Several ferries and a bridge service these islands.) You may enjoy starting in the middle, by walking out onto Deception Pass Bridge, the longer of the two spans that constitute the 1,487-foot link between the islands. You'll get a grand view of the rocky, forested islands and the blue-green sea 182 feet below. When the tide is running, the water squeezing through the narrow channel seems more river than ocean.

Just off the highway in the Whidbey unit of the park, you can get information at the park office. Try the **Caretakers of the Forest Trail** for a nice short jaunt through the woods. Across Cranberry Lake from Caretakers is the **Sand Dune Trail,** an 0.8-mile stroll along the lake's marsh and along the ocean beach.

The most popular trails lie to the north, across the bridge on Fidalgo Island. Two of these—the **Lighthouse Point** and **Canoe Pass Vista Trails**—can be combined into a nice, 2-mile route that passes through a forest of western redcedar and Douglas-fir, along the beach, and beside a marsh. Look for wildflowers in the spring and allow time to soak up great views of **Canoe Pass,** the narrower of the two passages that separate Fidalgo from Whidbey.

You'll be able to see some stirring views of the Pacific coastline more easily if you take the quarter-mile **Rosario Head Trail.** From the 100-foot bluffs, you can see a sizable expanse of the Strait of Juan de Fuca. During the spring and summer, excellent tidal pools emerge at low tide at the base of the bluffs at low tide. Take a moment to peer in them to see the tiny creatures in the water.

■ **4,128 acres** ■ **Northwest Washington, 60 miles north of Seattle on Whidbey and Fidalgo Islands** ■ **Best months May—Sept.** ■ **Camping, hiking, swimming, bird-watching, wildlife viewing** ■ **Contact the park, 5175 N. State Hwy., 20, Oak Harbor, WA 98277; 360-675-2417. www.parks.wa.gov/deceptn.htm**

San Juan & Gulf Islands

50 miles northeast of Olympic

Islands hold a special allure for many travelers. Their mountains, forests, and shorelines seem somehow more exotic than their mainland counterparts. Indeed, an island by definition is a place apart, not easily reached.

The San Juan Islands and the Gulf Islands are among those that can only be reached by boat (or small plane). Yet they are more easily reached than most islands because of the extensive ferry network that serves them *(see sidebar on opposite page.)* This ferry service has led to a compromise between isolation and accessibility; the islands regularly visited by the ferries have been developed to varying degrees, while the bypassed islands are largely if not entirely unpeopled; some are private islands and a few are provincial parks.

Even the most developed islands are lightly settled and blessed with natural beauty and pockets of wildness. **Friday Harbor,** by far the most populous town in the San Juans, has a population of less than 2,000. And the entire 74 square miles of **Salt Spring,** by far the most populous Gulf Island, is home to only about 10,000 people.

This archipelago of 786 islands straddles the border between the

Lime Kiln Lighthouse, San Juan Island

Planning Ahead

The ferries get very crowded during the summer weekends. Sometimes people wait for several hours to get aboard. Try to go early or late in the day or at a less popular time of year.

Hotels and inns can book up fast for the summer, too; so, make your reservations as early as possible.

For ferry reservations to the San Juan Islands, call Washington State Ferries at 206-464-6400; for the Gulf Islands, call BC Ferries at 250-386-3431.

United States and Canada. Those south and east of the sharp-angled international boundary are American, and those to the north and west are Canadian. They lie in the Strait of Georgia, bounded by the Washington mainland and Vancouver Island. Shielded from Pacific storms by Vancouver Island and the Olympic Mountains, the San Juan and Gulf Islands bask in some of the region's driest, sunniest weather.

San Juan Island anchors the U.S. chain and is the most developed. **American Camp,** a unit of **San Juan Island National Historical Park** *(350-378-2240)*, offers several trails that lead through woods and along an unspoiled stretch of southeastern shoreline. In the forest, look for the pileated woodpecker, the largest of its kind in North America, measuring some 16 to 17 inches long.

Drive east from American Camp and you'll come to **Cattle Point,** land's end for southern San Juan Island. Walk to the nearby high point and enjoy sweeping views of the islands and the Olympic Mountains, as well as Mount Baker and Mount Rainier, more than 75 miles away.

Residents of the San Juans dote on killer whales, also known as orcas. The creatures take center stage at the **Whale Museum** *(62 1st St. N., Friday Harbor. 360-378-4710 or 800-946-7227)*, an excellent place on the harbor. To see the orcas themselves, spend an hour or two at **Lime Kiln Point State Park** *(360-378-2044 or 800-233-0321)*; the resident pod spends much of May, June, and July preying on migrating salmon in Haro Strait. If you'd prefer to go out on the water to see them, contact the Whale Watching Operators Association of the Northwest *(P.O. Box 2404, Friday Harbor, WA 98250)* or ask at the museum about good operators.

Of the three other San Juan Islands served by the ferry—Lopez,

Orcas, and Shaw—**Orcas** has the most to offer. Its rugged, scenic topography is crowned by **Mount Constitution,** the high point of 5,000-acre **Moran State Park** *(360-376-2326).* You can hike or drive to the 2,409-foot summit and then ascend the old stone lookout tower for an even higher vantage point.

Just across the Canadian border from the San Juans lie the two major Gulf Islands, **North** and **South Pender Islands.** They're linked by a short wooden bridge. Seven parks and more than 20 beach access points provide plenty of opportunities to see the forest and seashore, especially on South Pender.

If you're up for a steep hike, take one of two trails to the 800-foot summit of **Mount Norman,** a few miles south of the bridge in **Mount Norman Regional Park** *(250-478-3344).* A wooden platform at the summit yields fine views of the islands and beyond.

The views are even better from the mountaintops on **Saltspring Island,** the largest of the Gulfs. The most accessible is 1,980-foot **Baynes Peak** in **Mount Maxwell Provincial Park** *(250-391-2300).*

The best hiking can be found in **Ruckle Provincial Park** *(250-*

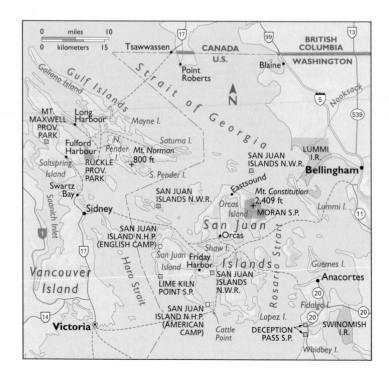

Look Who's Talking

Killer whales make a lot of noise. For one thing, they emit a rapid series of clicks to echolocate, sometimes transmitting as many as several hundred clicks a second.

But the sounds they use to talk to one another are much more elaborate, as befits these very social animals. According to the book *Killer Whales,* scientists divide these vocalizations into three categories: whistles, variable calls, and discrete calls. When members of a pod of orcas gather close together for an intimate chat, they seem to use the whistles and variable calls, which sound different from one time to the next. But the discrete calls sound exactly the same each time they're used.

Scientists who study orcas are particularly interested in discrete calls, which may serve to keep foraging pods together. Each pod has its own dialect consisting of anywhere from 5 to 15 discrete calls. Some pods share a few calls, but the repertoire of one pod never overlaps completely with that of another pod. Those pods that share some common calls are said to belong to the same clan.

Scientists can use these linguistic markers to identify orcas. Researchers have been able to figure out which whales held in captivity in aquariums belong to which pods by identifying their unique dialects.

391-2300. Adm. fee). Its 1,200 acres include interior second-growth forest and a long, dramatic stretch of Salt Spring's southeast coast.

Several concessionaires on Salt Springs give visitors the chance to explore tidal pools from a kayak, with or without a guide. You can glide along the shallow water close to the rocks, and see what goes on in the intertidal and subtidal communities. On longer kayak trips, you might venture farther out and explore the islands nearby, perhaps picnicking on your very own deserted island.

■ 786 islands ■ Northwest Washington, in the straits between Washington and Vancouver Island ■ Best season summer ■ Camping, hiking, kayaking, biking, bird-watching, whale-watching ■ Contact San Juan Islands Visitor Information Service, P.O. Box 65, Lopez Island, WA 98261, 360-468-3663. www.guidetosanjuans.com. Or contact Tourism Vancouver Island, 203-335 Wesley St., Nanaimo, BC V9R 2T5, 250-754-3500. www.islands.bc.ca/

Redwood

Sometimes, when the morning fog caresses the great trees, you can imagine the past flowing through the long, misty shadows … Vast redwood forests flourishing across a lush and humid North America … After the final ice age, a last stand here in the sustaining climate along the Pacific coast. Then, in a windswept moment, the past vanishes and you stand beside other visitors, gazing up at the Earth's tallest living things. That is the essence of Redwood National Park.

The park, near the northern limit of the coast redwood's narrow range, preserves the remnants of a forest that once covered two million acres and, at the turn of the 20th century, was badly threatened by logging. The state of California and the Save-the-Redwoods League came to the rescue by acquiring hundreds of groves and protecting them within 26 state parks. Three redwood state parks—Jedediah Smith, Del Norte Coast, and Prairie Creek—were encompassed by the national park when it was created in 1968.

Logging on surrounding private land, however, threatened the parks' redwoods. Soil and sediments from the logged-over tracts washed into the rivers and creeks, settling to the bottom downstream. Silt deposits can smother redwoods—the giants are amazingly vulnerable. And the waterlogged soil weakens the trees' resistance to wind. Their roots are shallow, often only 10 feet deep.

In 1978 Congress added 48,000 acres to the national park's 58,000, including about 36,000 that had been logged. The raw, clear-cut land, a park official wrote, had "the look of an active war zone." Today, in an epic earthmoving project, crews are beginning to reclaim vast stretches of logged-over lands. Hillsides are being restored; most of the 400 miles of roads are being erased. It will take at least 50 years for the scars of logging to disappear and another 250 years for the replanted redwood seedlings to grow to modest size.

- Northern California
- 113,000 acres
- Established 1928
- Best seasons spring–fall
- Hiking, canoeing, kayaking, horseback riding, swimming, fishing, whale-watching
- Information: 707-464-6101 www.nps.gov/redw

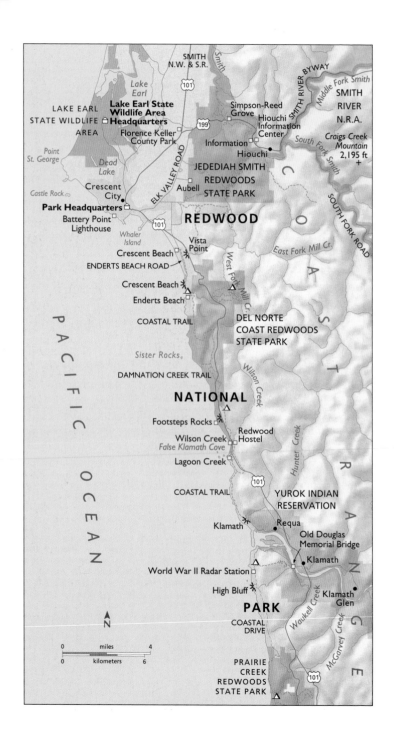

SMITH
N.W. & S.R.

Smith

101

Lake
Earl

LAKE EARL STATE WILDLIFE AREA

Lake Earl State
Wildlife Area
Headquarters

Florence Keller
County Park

199

Simpson-Reed
Grove

Hiouchi
Information
Center

SMITH RIVER BYWAY

Middle Fork Smith

SMITH
RIVER
N.R.A.

South Fork Smith

Craigs Creek
Mountain
2,195 ft
+

Point
St. George

Dead
Lake

Information

Aubell

Hiouchi

JEDEDIAH SMITH
REDWOODS
STATE PARK

C
O
A
S
T

SOUTH FORK ROAD

Castle Rock

Crescent
City

Park Headquarters

Battery Point
Lighthouse

101

REDWOOD

Whaler
Island

Vista
Point

Crescent Beach

ENDERTS BEACH ROAD

Crescent Beach

Enderts Beach

COASTAL TRAIL

West Fork Mill Cr.

East Fork Mill Cr.

DEL NORTE
COAST REDWOODS
STATE PARK

P
A
C
I
F
I
C

Sister Rocks

DAMNATION CREEK TRAIL

NATIONAL

Wilson Creek

Footsteps Rocks

Wilson Creek

False Klamath Cove

Lagoon Creek

Redwood
Hostel

O
C
E
A
N

COASTAL TRAIL

101

YUROK INDIAN
RESERVATION

Hunter Creek

Klamath

Requa

Old Douglas
Memorial Bridge

Klamath

World War II Radar Station

High Bluff

Klamath
Glen

R
A
N
G
E

PARK

COASTAL
DRIVE

N

Waukell Creek

McGarvey Creek

miles   4

kilometers   6

PRAIRIE
CREEK
REDWOODS
STATE PARK

101

ELK VALLEY ROAD

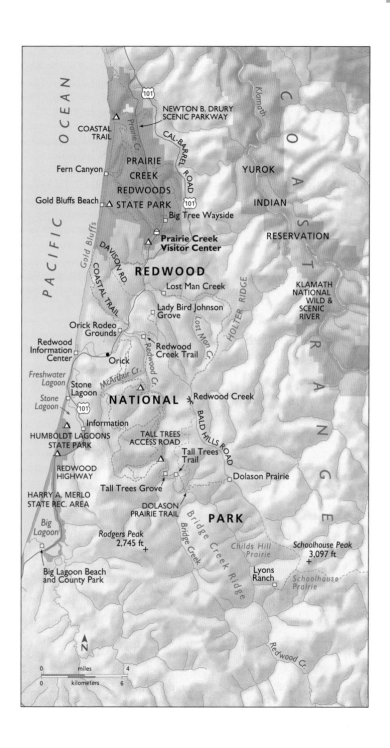

OCEAN

PACIFIC

101

NEWTON B. DRURY
SCENIC PARKWAY

COASTAL
TRAIL

CAL-BARREL ROAD

Prairie Cr.

PRAIRIE
CREEK

Fern Canyon

REDWOODS

YUROK

Gold Bluffs Beach

STATE PARK

101

Big Tree Wayside

INDIAN

Gold Bluffs

DAVISON RD.

Prairie Creek
Visitor Center

RESERVATION

COASTAL TRAIL

REDWOOD

Lost Man Creek

KLAMATH
NATIONAL
WILD &
SCENIC
RIVER

HOLTER RIDGE

Lady Bird Johnson
Grove

Orick Rodeo
Grounds

Lost Man Cr.

Redwood
Information
Center

Redwood
Creek Trail

Redwood Cr.

Orick

COAST

Freshwater
Lagoon

McArthur Cr.

Stone
Lagoon

Stone
Lagoon

NATIONAL

Redwood Creek

101

Information

BALD HILLS ROAD

RANGE

HUMBOLDT LAGOONS
STATE PARK

TALL TREES
ACCESS ROAD

Tall Trees
Trail

REDWOOD
HIGHWAY

Tall Trees
Grove

Dolason Prairie

HARRY A. MERLO
STATE REC. AREA

DOLASON
PRAIRIE TRAIL

PARK

Big
Lagoon

Rodgers Peak
2,745 ft

Bridge Creek

Bridge Creek Ridge

Childs Hill
Prairie

Schoolhouse Peak
3,097 ft

Lyons
Ranch

Schoolhouse
Prairie

Big Lagoon Beach
and County Park

N

Redwood Cr.

0   miles   4

0   kilometers   6

How to Get There

Tree-lined US 101, the Redwood Highway, runs the length of the park. From the south, take US 101 to the information center near Orick, about 40 miles north of Eureka. From the north, enter through Crescent City, also an information center site. From the east, take US 199, another redwood-flanked highway, to Hiouchi. Airports: Arcata and Crescent City.

When to Go

All-year park. Summer draws highway-clogging crowds, so think about a visit in spring or fall. In both seasons, bird migrations enhance the redwood groves. Rhododendrons burst forth in spring; deciduous trees add color in fall. Rains, welcome to the redwoods but not to visitors, drench the park in winter.

How to Visit

US 101, with its many redwood sentinels, gives you a windshield-framed panorama of the trees. But to appreciate the redwoods, you must walk among them. If you have only a day to visit this 50-mile-long park, stop and see the **Lady Bird Johnson Grove** and **Big Tree.** Hike or just stretch your legs (depending on your time)

What Not to Miss

- **Ladybird Johnson Grove Trail**
- **Big Tree at Prairie Creek Redwoods State Park**
- **Klamath Overlook**
- **Hiking Coastal Trail to Hidden Beach**
- **Tall Trees Grove**
- **Enderts Beach**
- **Paddling Lower Klamath River**
- **Hiking James Irvine Trail**

along the **Coastal Trail** and savor the Pacific prospect of the park. For a longer stay, visit the **Tall Trees Grove,** drive **Howland Hill Road,** and end your visit with a splash in a kayak on the **Klamath River** or a jouncy drive to **Fern Canyon** and **Gold Bluffs Beach.** If you are driving an RV or towing a trailer, some stretches of road may be closed to you; check at information centers throughout the park.

EXPLORING THE PARK

Lady Bird Johnson Grove & Big Tree: 13 miles; 2 hours

Just before Orick, stop at the **Redwood Information Center** (once the site of a redwood-slicing lumber mill) to see the exhibits, and then continue north on US 101 to the Bald Hills Road sign. Turn right and drive 2 miles to **Lady Bird Johnson Grove,** a jewel that gives you an understanding of the entire park treasure. On the grove's mile-long trail you feel the cool, moist air that redwoods need. You see a hollowed-out tree that still lives. Such redwoods—"goose-pen" trees—once sheltered settlers' fowl and livestock. You smell and touch the many plants that share the redwoods' domain. Most of all, you feel the peace; visitors speak quietly in this pillared place.

Return to US 101 and continue north about 4 miles. Near the entrance to **Prairie Creek Redwoods State Park,** pull into the turnout to watch the free-roaming Roosevelt elk that live in the park. A mile ahead on the right is a wayside sign for **Big Tree.** A short trail from the parking lot leads to the aptly named tree. It's 304 feet tall, 21.6 feet in diameter, 66 feet in circumference, and about 1,500 years old. Here the experience is singular: you and one great tree.

Coastal Trail: 4 miles one way; at least 2 hours

From Orick, drive north 20 miles on US 101, passing Klamath, and turn left onto Requa Road. Park and picnic at **Klamath Overlook,** a high hill. On a clear day you can see 65 miles down the bluff-guarded coast. The **Hidden Beach Section** of the **Coastal Trail** begins here, heads west, and then veers north along the wild, driftwood-decorated shore. Yurok Indians walked these shores, as did Jedediah Smith, the first white man to reach California's rugged northern coast by land.

The trail, often bowered by branches of spruce and alder, sometimes seals you from the sight—though not the sounds—of the ocean. But there are many spots where you can sit and gaze out to sea. In spring and fall you may see migrating gray whales. Almost any time you will see gulls, cormorants, and ospreys.

A short side path leads down to **Hidden Beach.** Even on a day when the park is crowded yours may be the only footprints on the sand. Look at the ocean but don't swim: The undertow is dangerous all along the park's coast. The beach walk ends at a wall of gnarled black rocks. Follow your footprints back to the path and return to the trail, which heads north along the wild shore, then veers inland.

The north trailhead is at **Lagoon Creek,** where fresh water and forest meet ocean and high bluff. If you don't want to trudge the 4 miles back, have someone drive up to meet you at the parking lot.

Tall Trees Grove: 2.6 miles; a half day

Obtain a permit to drive your vehicle to the Tall Trees Grove parking area, off Bald Hills Road *(permits available at any information center)*. From the parking area, the trail is a very steep 2.6-mile round-trip. The hike down to the grove, replete with ferns and rhododendrons, takes at least 30 minutes. Plan on another 30 to 45 minutes in the grove among the giant coast redwoods. The star is

Crescent Beach, Redwood National Park

the **Nugget Tree,** which was measured at 365.5 feet in 1995. This is one of the world's tallest known trees. It's estimated to be between 900 and 1,500 years old.

Howland Hill Road: **8 miles; about 2 hours**

Just south of Crescent City, take Elk Valley Road northeast. Keep a sharp watch on your right for the turnoff to Howland Hill Road, once a miners' supply road partially redwood-planked for oxcarts and horse-drawn wagons. The 6-mile road winds between redwoods that loom much closer than the ones along the highways. Mostly unpaved and often one lane, the road is not recommended for motor homes and trailers. Stop at **Stout Grove,** where you can see one of many preserves set aside, this one donated by the wife of

a logging company owner. Take time to enjoy the 1-mile trail among the redwoods. (In summer you can also reach the grove from the Hiouchi Information Center via a footbridge across the crystal-clear Smith River.)

Continue past the grove to Douglas Park Road, which ends at South Fork Road. Turn left to US 199 and drive west about 2.5 miles to the Hiouchi Information Center. Park here and sign up for an interpretive walk with a ranger. Or, continue west on US 199 to **Simpson-Reed Grove,** where you'll find a short pleasant self-guided trail among the giants.

Gold Bluffs Beach & Fern Canyon: 20 miles; a half day

From the Redwood Information Center, head north for 4.5 miles to Davison Road, on your left. Elk are often spotted along the first few hundred yards on this road. The rough dirt road bounces you for about 4 miles down to **Gold Bluffs,** named for the gold found here. The road continues for 4 miles along the beach, ending near **Fern Canyon,** where a 0.75-mile loop trail climbs to a prairie—site of a vanished mining camp. Back down the canyon, walk through elk-roamed grass to a beautiful, desolate beach sprinkled with driftwood and often shrouded in fog.

Return the way you came, pausing to admire the fern-covered, 30-foot-high walls. The more adventurous can make a longer hike by climbing to **Prairie Creek** and walking along its banks before heading back toward the ocean. Return to the parking area at Fern Canyon via the windswept southern stretch of the **Coastal Trail.** Be on the lookout for a variety of birds, including pelicans, terns, gulls, and wading birds. In the fall or spring scan the horizon for the telltale spouts of migrating gray whales, en route to or from their winter retreat in Baja California.

Redwood State Parks

The three state parks that were included within the boundaries of Redwood National Park make this jointly administered parkland unique in the National Park System. The state parks help protect what is left of the tallest forests in the country. What remains of the thick-barked coast redwoods today amounts to less than 5 percent of the two million acres that cloaked the area as recently as two centuries ago. From southern Oregon to south of California's Monterey Peninsula, these skyscraping conifers survive in a fairly narrow strip of habitat generally extending no more than 10 miles inland, but sometimes a little farther along streambeds. Redwoods need to be in the range of the year-round coastal fog—which collects on the needles and branches of the trees and keeps them well watered during the dry summer months. (You won't find redwoods right next to the ocean, however, because they can't tolerate too much salt.) Fallen needles and other litter from the trees are deep and wet beneath the shady canopy, providing fertile soil for ferns, mosses, and shade-loving plants such as redwood sorrel and pink-blooming huckleberry. Wildlife in the parks is both abundant and varied, including such animals as black bears, deer, coyotes, bobcats, mountain lions, skunks, foxes, beavers, squirrels, chipmunks, river otters, and Roosevelt elk. Bird-watchers have spied bald eagles and pileated woodpeckers, as well as two species dependent on old-growth forest, the spotted owl and the marbled murrelet.

To preserve and extend this habitat, federal and state park officials, along with the Forest Service managers of the adjacent **Smith River National Recreation Area** *(see pp. 220–222)*, are focusing on repairing the damage done in the watersheds by clear-cuts and logging roads. And the United Nations, recognizing the value of the parks, named each of them an International Biosphere Reserve and a World Heritage site.

The state parks offer visitors a lively mix of beaches and hiking trails, but the trees are the main attraction. People approach them like children in the presence of dignified elders, sentinels that novelist John Steinbeck called "ambassadors from another time."

There's a Difference

The redwoods in Sequoia and Kings Canyon National Parks *(see pp. 248–261)*, and the redwoods along the California coast are not the same tree. The coast redwood *(Sequoia sempervirens)* grows taller (up to 367 feet), lives up to 2,000 years, has bark about a foot thick, and can reproduce from seeds or a sprout. The giant sequoia *(Sequoiadendron giganteum)* grows thicker (up to 41 feet in diameter), can live more than 3,000 years, has bark up to 31 inches thick, and can reproduce only from seeds. A third member of this family, the smaller dawn redwood *(Metasequoia glyptostroboides)*, is found in central China.

Prairie Creek Redwoods State Park

On US 101 about 3 miles north of Bald Hills Road, you'll come to the **Newton B. Drury Scenic Parkway,** which leads you on an 8-mile journey through a lush strip of coastal redwoods. One mile after leaving US 101, you'll reach the visitor center for 14,000-acre Prairie Creek Redwoods State Park *(707-464-6101, ext. 5301),* the southernmost of the three state parks in the system. Right before the visitor center, you'll often see white-rumped, big antlered Roosevelt elk grazing in the meadow just west of the road.

From trailheads near the visitor center, you can take some of the best day and longer hikes in the park—up into the foothills, down into ferny canyons, and out onto the beach. One of the prettiest is a 4.5-mile ramble down the **James Irvine Trail** to Fern Canyon. From here an unmarked trail leads down to Gold Bluffs Beach. The jaunt becomes an 11-mile loop if you add the **Miner's Ridge Trail.**

Continuing north on the parkway, you'll pass out of Prairie Creek Redwoods State Park and back into the national park again. Here you can take the **Coastal Drive,** an 8-mile, alternately paved and unpaved road *(not for RVs or trailers)* that skirts the mouth of the Klamath River and takes you along wave-battered cliffs with great ocean views. Gray-whale-watching is one of the luresthat brings people to the coast in the spring and fall. To cross the Klamath River, which is bounded by Yurok reservation lands,you must turn inland to rejoin US 101. Once across the river, you can return to the north side of the Klamath estuary on Requa Road, about 3 miles north of the Klamath River Bridge. Again you'll have cliff-top views of the ocean and river mouth.

Del Norte Coast Redwoods State Park

Back on US 101 and continuing north, you'll come to 6,400-acre Del Norte Coast Redwoods State Park *(707-464-6101, ext. 5120),* with 8 miles of coastline and great ocean views. Steep cliffs make most of the rocky sea coast inaccessible except by **Damnation Creek Trail** *(trailhead on US 101 at Milepost 16).* The trail drops you down through a redwood forest where rhododendrons bloom in the spring. Just south of here is a half mile of sandy beach known as **False Klamath Cove.** The steep slope, rough seas, and cold water make the beach unsafe for swimming but at low tide the tide-pooling is excellent. *(Remember that marine organisms are easily destroyed; if you pick something up, replace it exactly the way you found it.)*

Jedediah Smith Redwoods SP

The northernmost park is 9,500-acre Jedediah Smith Redwoods State Park *(707-464-6101, ext. 5112 in season, ext. 5101 off-season).* Through it flows the emerald green **Smith River,** the last major undammed river in California and also the cleanest. The Smith slows down after spring runoff to provide good swimming and some beachfront.

Near the Jedediah Smith Campground, a 0.6-mile self-guided **nature trail** emphasizes the park's vegetation. Besides redwoods, you'll find western hem-lock, Sitka spruce, grand and

At Prairie Creek Redwoods SP

Douglas-fir, and the less common Port-Orford cedar, with tanoak, madrone, red alder, bigleaf maple, and California bay in the understory. A wide range of species and varieties of shrubs, flowers, ferns, lichens, and mosses make up the dense ground cover.

The park offers some horse and bicycle paths, as well as numer-ous hiking trails. For driving scenery, you can't beat the 33-mile **Smith River Byway** (Calif. 199), which begins at the junction of US 101 and Calif. 199 east of Crescent City and ends at the Collier Tunnel near the California-Oregon border. Deep green pools, waterfalls, and white-water rapids compete for your attention with the rhododendrons, azaleas, and ferns in the redwood forest. From November through April, you can fish for chinook salmon and steelhead. *(Steelhead are catch-and-release.)* Kayaking and rafting enthusiasts float the rivers, too, tackling some difficult white water

INFORMATION & ACTIVITIES

Headquarters
1111 Second St.
Crescent City, CA 95531
707-464-6101
www.nps.gov/redw

Visitor & Information Centers
Crescent City Park Headquarters Information Center, at north end of park, open daily all year. Redwood Information Center, at south end of park near Orick, also open all year. Hiouchi Information Center, at north end of park, open spring through summer.

Seasons & Accessibility
Open year-round.

Entrance Fee
None. $2 day-use fee for Jedediah Smith, Del Norte Coast, and Prairie Creek State Parks.

Pets
Permitted on leashes except on trails and in backcountry.

Facilities for Disabled
Information centers, Crescent Beach, Lagoon Creek picnic area, Klamath Overlook, and some trails are accessible to wheelchairs.

Things to Do
Free naturalist-led activities: tide-pool and seashore walks, evening programs. Also available, hiking, canoeing, guided kayak trips, horseback riding, freshwater and ocean fishing (license required), swimming (inland only), whale-watching.

Special Advisories
■ Be aware that ticks may transmit Lyme disease.
■ Ocean swimming is not advised because of extremely cold water and a treacherous undertow.

Overnight Backpacking
Permit required; can be obtained free at trailheads and at the national park information centers and state park visitor centers. The national park lands offer 3 backcountry campsites: DeMartin, Flint Ridge, and Nickel Creek; 14-day limit. Open all year, first come, first served. No fees. Tent sites only. No showers.

Butler Creek campsite in Prairie Creek Redwoods SP is available to bikers and hikers only (fee). Reserve at Prairie Creek Visitor Center.

Campgrounds
There are 4 state-run campgrounds inside the park: Gold Bluffs Beach, Jedediah Smith, Mill Creek, and Elk Prairie; 15-day limit. Mill Creek open

Exuberant surfer, Crescent Beach, Redwood National Park

April to October; others open all year; Gold Bluffs Beach may close in bad weather. Showers available nearby. Tent and RV sites; no hookups; large RVs not recommended and trailers prohibited at Gold Bluffs Beach. Fees $12 per night. Reservations recommended mid-May through August and available at www.reserveamerica.com. Reservations: 800-444-7275. No food services inside park.

Hotels, Motels, & Inns

(Unless otherwise noted, rates are for two persons in a double room, high season.)

In Crescent City, CA 95531:
- **Best Value Inn** 440 Hwy. 101 N. 707-464-4141. 61 units. $64-$79.
- **Curly Redwood Lodge** 701 Hwy. 101 S. 707-464-2137. 36 units. $61-$86.
- **Royal Inn Motel** 102 L St. 707-464-4113 or 800-752-9610. 35 units. $35-$55.

In Eureka, CA 95501:
- **Eureka Inn** 518 Seventh St. 707-442-6441 or 800-862-4906. 176 units. $109. Pool, 2 restaurants.
- **Hotel Carter** 301 L St. 707-444-8062 or 800-404-1390. 31 units. $135-$326, includes continental breakfast. Restaurant.

Excursions from Redwood

Six Rivers National Forest

20 miles northeast of Redwood

Six Rivers National Forest lies "behind the redwood curtain," very much in the shade of its neighbor to the west, Redwood National Park. Still, its many rivers, rich cultural heritage, and solitude offer visitors fine recreational opportunities. A narrow strip of inland forest stretching 140 miles south from the Oregon border, Six Rivers extends up to the 6,500-foot elevations of the Trinity Alps.

The forest encompasses a mix of topography, soils, and localized climates that produce an unusually rich and varied flora. Through it runs about 9 percent of California's total runoff, flowing in 1,500 streams, rivers, and waterways. Of its six rivers—the **Smith,** the **Klamath,** the **Trinity,** the **Eel,** the **Mad,** and the **Van Duzen**—the first four are designated Wild and Scenic Rivers. Three nationally designated scenic byways pass through Six Rivers National Forest, which also includes four wilderness areas.

At Six Rivers, you can plunk yourself down at a sandy beach on any of the rivers that cross the boundaries of the forest. One nice spot is **Hawkins Bar** on the Trinity River *(from Willow Creek, go E 6.5 miles on Calif. 299, turn N onto Hawkins Bar river access road),* where a trail leads to a small sandy beach for sunbathing and swimming. Rafters can put in from this day-use area, which also allows access to fishing.

Six designated botanical areas protect wildflower displays, conifer diversity, distinctive plant communities, and several species of rare plants, such as the California lady's slipper orchid and Bolander's lily.

If you happen to be heading toward the Central Valley, the **Trinity Scenic Byway** (Calif. 299) is a winding and picturesque route largely along the Trinity River that takes you from the junction of Calif. 299 and US 101 in Arcata east 150 miles through Bigfoot and historic mining country to Redding. You'll traverse coastal plains, steep granite cliffs, arid manzanita, and digger pine hillsides. Look out for digger pinecones in fall; these hard, heavy cones can be as dangerous as falling rocks. In the spring the redbuds are spectacular.

Smith River National Recreation Area

Tucked into the northwest corner of the state, Smith River National

A Primer on Salmon and Steelhead

Commercial and sport fishermen prize the Pacific salmon, which once swam up California streams as far south as the Ventura River, but now are found largely in the Northwest. The salmon and its cousin the steelhead trout are anadromous fish, which means they live in salt water most of their lives but are born in fresh water and return there to spawn. The three most significant species—the chinook or king salmon, the smaller silver or coho salmon, and the steelhead trout—have suffered declines over the last century. Among the arguable reasons: Dams that block migration routes, heavy commercial fishing at sea, silt in the rivers from logging and mining operations, water pollution, and drought. Even rivers that run clean and uninterrupted, such as the Smith, have seen lean runs.

The big king salmon born in the rivers migrate down to the ocean, where they live for five or more years before returning to spawn. Most of them make the upstream journey in the fall. Once they've made their run, they die. Silver salmon follow a similar pattern but use smaller streams and sometimes survive in fresh water for a year or two. Steelhead survive parenthood to make several trips to the ocean and back. Scientists believe these fish find their spawning stream by odor. There's no smell like home.

Steelhead caught in net, Smith River

Recreation Area's 300,000 acres encompass the largest undammed wild and scenic river watershed in the country. Dropping steeply from their headwaters (mostly in the Siskyou Mountains), the three forks of the Smith pass through a thick forest of firs and madrones, and their waters deepen the jade hue of rock that lines their beds.

All three forks of the Smith have navigable stretches, depending on your paddling skill and the time of year. Because no engineer is controlling a spigot on a dam, the Smith's steep runs can rev up to Class V white water in early spring, then subside to a bottom-scraping trickle by midsummer. All three forks of the Smith pass through rugged country, with rough roads and unmapped trails.

■ **980,000 acres** ■ **Northern California** ■ **Year-round** ■ **Camping, hiking, backpacking, walking, orienteering, boating, white-water rafting and kayaking, canoeing, swimming, scuba diving, tubing, fishing, mountain biking, horseback riding, cross-country skiing, snowshoeing, bird-watching, wildlife viewing, wildflower viewing** ■ **Contact the national forest, 1330 Bayshore Way, Eureka, CA 95501; 707-442-1721. www.r5.fs.fed.us/sixrivers**

White-water kayaking, Middle Fork Smith River

Headwaters Forest Reserve

45 miles south of Redwood

A 15-year battle over the fate of northern California's last large unprotected stand of old-growth redwoods was resolved in 1999 when the federal government and the state of California bought these forested lands in the Coast Ranges from the Pacific Lumber Company. Public protests over plans to log the property, and concerns over spawning streams and birdlife in the area, led to the 380-million-dollar purchase, a price that some conservation groups labeled extortion by the timber company's Texas owner, Charles Hurwitz.

More than half of the reserve's acreage is old-growth redwood, which provides shelter for the endangered marbled murrelet, a chubby black-and-white seabird that nests inland in trees. The reserve also protects sections of the **Elk River,** a spawning stream for coho salmon that drains into Arcata Bay. Management plans are still being developed, but the emphasis is on habitat protection, not recreation. Hikers can take day trips into the north end of the reserve on the 5-mile **Elk River Trail** (via Elk River Rd. exit off US 101, 1 mile S of Eureka), where they can approach but not enter old-growth areas. Hikes at the south end are guided by BLM inter-preters (707-825-2300 for reservations, 20-person limit 4 days per week May–Nov.). The 4-mile round-trip (access from Newburg Rd. in Fortuna) travels the edge of an ancient forest along **Salmon Creek.**

■ 7,400 acres ■ Northern California ■ Best season summer ■ Hiking, walking, guided walks, bird-watching, wildlife viewing ■ Contact Arcata Field Office, Bureau of Land Management, 1695 Heindon Rd., Arcata, CA 95521; 707-825-2300

Humboldt Bay National Wildlife Refuge

50 miles south of Redwood

This is the largest natural bay north of San Francisco, once fringed by deep old-growth forests, marshes, and mudflats that provided a rest stop for thousands of birds on the Pacific flyway. The 14-mile-long bay, protected by a sandbar, formed 10,000 years ago, at the end of the last ice age. During Eureka's heyday as a busy port for the timber and logging industries, bird traffic plummeted. But since 1971 the U.S. Fish and Wildlife Service has begun acquiring lands and restoring the marshes, mudflats, willow groves, and open water sought by aquatic life and the migratory birds that are thickest from September to April.

Key to the refuge are the extensive beds of eelgrass in the mudflats. The eelgrass provides food and supports a large portion of the total world population of black brant, a small, black-headed goose, during winter and spring. Sandpipers, curlews, egrets, and herons are also among the 200 bird species seen here. There are dungeness crabs and clams in the mud, and at high tide ocean fish such as sanddabs and salmon enter the slough. Every first and third Saturday, interpreters guide visitors through the rare plant community of the **Lanphere Dunes,** where you'll see beach layia and Humboldt Bay wallflower.

Trails through the refuge include the 3-mile round-trip **Hookton Slough Trail** from the Hookton Road visitor contact point, and the 2-mile **Shorebird Loop,** a 0.75-mile trail with a 3-mile seasonal loop. The refuge is set to expand to more than 9,000 acres.

■ **3,000 acres** ■ **Northern California** ■ **Best months Nov.-Dec., March–April** ■ **Hiking, walking, sea kayaking, canoeing, bird-watching, wildlife viewing** ■ **Contact the refuge, 1020 Ranch Rd., Loleta, CA 95551; 707-733-5406. pacific.fws.gov/visitor/california.html**

Humboldt Redwoods State Park

70 miles south of Redwood

Since 1921, when the Save-the-Redwoods League purchased the first plot of land here, Humboldt Redwoods State Park has grown grove by grove to include 17,000 acres of old-growth redwoods and nearly all of the Bull Creek watershed. At the heart of the park is **Rockefeller Forest,** named for John D. Rockefeller, Jr., who gave two million dollars to help the league purchase 10,000 acres of redwoods along Bull Creek from a logging company. Here, trees rise from green pockets of redwood sorrel and lady fern on the forest floor. The largest remaining old-growth coast redwood forest in the world, Rockefeller Forest holds trees that are thousands of years old and have never been logged—a mesmerizing world as pristine as it was 100 years ago.

The main road through the park is the 32-mile **Avenue of the Giants** (from the N, take Weott exit off US 101 and turn right; go

1.5 miles to visitor center. From the S, take Myers Flat exit and turn right; go 4.4 miles to visitor center). Various groves with distinctively big redwoods are within easy walks of the roadway.

Probably the best popular is **Founders Grove** *(4 miles N of visitor center, off Avenue of the Giants on Dyerville Loop Rd.),* home to the ancient **Dyerville Giant,** a mammoth specimen more than a thousand years old. It stood 362 feet tall—57 feet higher than the Statue of Liberty—before it toppled in 1991. At 17 feet in diameter, the tree still dwarfs mere humans, even on its side. Or take the short trail from the **Big Trees Area** parking lot on Mattole Road *(8 miles W of visitor center)* to the **Giant Tree.** At 359 feet, it is the

Founders Grove, Humboldt Redwoods State Park

park's champion redwood since the Dyerville Giant went down.

The park is laced with trails where you can hike, backpack, ride horses (your own), or mountain bike. While the redwoods congregate along the stream valleys, the backcountry mostly embraces prairies, sunny uplands, and steep ridges. Most of the mountain bike routes are located in the **Bull Creek** area of the park *(8 miles NW of visitor center).* Note that mountain bikes are restricted to the park fire roads and are not allowed on the many hiking trails.

For more ambitious hikers, a strenuous trail heads out from the Big Trees Area to 3,379-foot **Grasshopper Mountain,** the park's highest point, with panoramic views of the landscape and the redwoods. About a 7-mile trek one way, it's a good choice for an all-day or overnight hike.

■ **53,000 acres** ■ **Northern California** ■ **Best season summer** ■ **Hiking, backpacking, orienteering, canoeing, swimming, fishing, biking, mountain biking, bird-watching, wildlife viewing** ■ **Contact the park, P.O. Box 100, Weott, CA 95571; 707-946-2409. www.humboldtredwoods.org**

Rocky Mountain

Nowhere else in the United States can a visitor see so much alpine country with such ease. A mere 2-hour drive from Denver, Trail Ridge Road takes visitors into the heart of Rocky Mountain National Park, traversing a ridge above 11,000 feet for 10 miles. Along the way, tiny tundra flowers and other wild blooms contrast with sweeping vistas of towering summits; 78 of them exceed 12,000 feet. Alpine lakes reflect the grandeur.

The summits form at least the third generation of mountains to rise in this region. The first probably protruded as islands above a shallow sea more than 135 million years ago, when dinosaurs reigned. Another range grew out of a later sea some 75 million years ago. Over the eons these summits eroded to rolling hills, which rose once again, although unevenly: Some portions sank along fault lines, helping create the striking texture of the current scenery.

Rock as old as that at the bottom of the Grand Canyon—nearly two billion years—caps the summits in Rocky Mountain. Within the last million years, glaciers, grinding boulders beneath them, carved deep canyons. Erosion later scoured the more jagged summits into their present profiles.

Although it is only about an eighth the size of Yellowstone, Rocky Mountain accommodates nearly as many visitors—2.9 million or more a year. That's quite a change from 1917, when a superintendent felt he had to boost park visitation by hiring a young woman to live off the land, clad in a leopard skin. It worked: People flocked to the park. But today overcrowding worries park officials and conservationists, who cite distressed animals, trodden plants, and eroded trails. Condominium development is crowding the park's borders also, shrinking the habitats of elk and other wildlife and threatening to turn the park into an isolated patch of protected land.

- Northern Colorado
- 265,828 acres
- Established 1915
- Best seasons early summer–fall
- Camping, hiking, bird-watching, wildlife viewing, scenic drives
- Information: 970-586-1206 www.nps.gov/romo

Front Range peaks looming over parkland meadow, Rocky Mountain NP

How to Get There
Take I-25 north from Denver
or south from Cheyenne, Wyo.;
then US 34 west at Loveland.
From the west, pick up US 34
at Granby. Airports: Denver,
Colo., and Cheyenne, Wyo.

When to Go
Summer and fall. To avoid
crowds, visit popular areas
early or late, and hike.

How to Visit
On a 1-day blitz, drive **Trail
Ridge Road** to **Farview Curve**
for classic vistas and an assortment of short hikes, including
the **Tundra Communities Trail.**
Then double back and take
Bear Lake Road to Bear Lake
and pick a day hike, perhaps
to **Emerald Lake.**

What Not to Miss

- **Drive Trail Ridge Road**

- **Stop at Milner Pass and
  stand on Continental Divide**

- **Take short stroll to
  Forest Canyon Overlook**

- **Visit Toll Memorial Mountain Index for 360-degree
  panorama**

- **Hike Colorado River Trail
  to old mining settlement
  of Lulu City**

- **Drive Bear Lake Road
  and walk nature trail to
  Dream Lake**

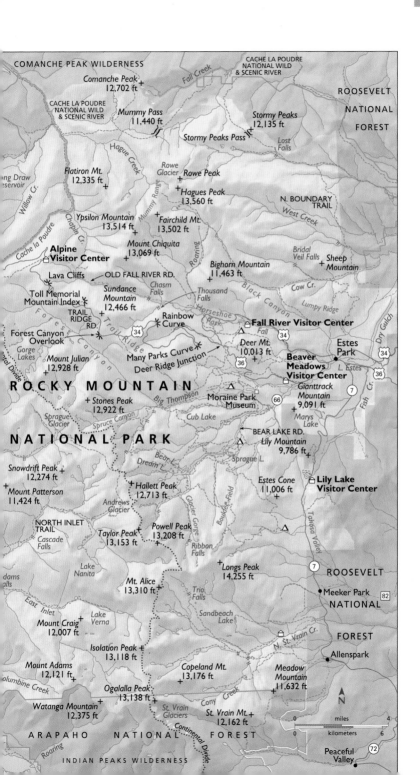

EXPLORING THE PARK

Trail Ridge Road: 50 miles; at least a full day

This spectacular highway crosses the broad back of Colorado's Front Range and winds through the scenic heart of Rocky Mountain National Park. It climbs to 12,183 feet—well above tree line—and then bounds along over a gentle landscape akin to the world's Arctic regions. Along the way, tremendous views open up of peaks, deep glacially carved valleys, and, often, the churning violence of approaching thunderstorms. Expect to be pelted by hail one moment, baked by sunshine the next.

You get more than stunning vistas on this drive. You also skirt wide meadows where bighorn sheep, elk, and deer browse. You follow streams and rivers—including the meek headwaters of the Colorado—and plunge through dense forests of subalpine fir and Englemann spruce. The route also roughly follows a 10,000-year-old trail that linked western valleys with the Great Plains.

Start in **Estes Park,** a growing resort town in a wide basin first homesteaded in 1860 by Joel Estes. At nearly every turn, the flat summit of **Longs Peak,** elevation 14,255 feet, and its companion peaks loom over the rooftops. Enter the park on US 36 and stop by the **visitor center,** where a short film offers a useful overview of the park and where you can buy books and maps.

Continue straight on US 36 after the entrance station. The road leads through Beaver Meadows, a classic ponderosa parkland setting. Here, large ponderosa pines spread their branches over a broad expanse of prairie grasses and nodding wildflowers. Various rodents thrive among the plants: mice, voles, shrews, and golden-mantled ground squirrels. These in turn attract such predators as badgers, coyotes, owls, and hawks. Among the trees, you might spot a few of the silent, elusive tassel-eared squirrels called Abert's squirrels. They live exclusively among ponderosa pine forests and depend on the woods for food, nesting, and cover.

At **Deer Ridge Junction,** either bear left onto Trail Ridge Road or, if it's summer, detour to the right and circle through **Horseshoe Park,** a meadow at the bottom of the Mummy Range. As you pass

Sheep Lakes, look for bighorn sheep, which sometimes stump out of the forest and cross the road to visit a natural mineral lick. During the autumn, the meadow often fills with herds of elk.

Horseshoe Park once lay beneath the tail end of one of Rocky's biggest glaciers. The ice reached depths of 1,500 feet and extended from Fall River Pass to the east end of Horseshoe Park. As the glacier retreated, it left a terminal moraine, which dammed a small lake. The lake was eventually filled in with fine-grained soils which discourage tree growth.

If you made the detour, either continue on Old Fall River Road to Fall River Pass, or double back to Deer Ridge Junction and turn west. This is the official start of Trail Ridge Road, which soon climbs into deeper forest.

Calypso Cascades

After about 2 miles, look for the boardwalk on the right that marks a short **interpretive trail** that leads through the trees to an overlook of a wetlands meadow. Just a decade ago, this area held a network of large beaver ponds, dikes, and canals. For about 50 years, the beavers maintained their dams, and the ponds collected a deep layer of silt and organic debris that washed down from Hidden Valley. Then, in the late 1990s, the beavers abandoned their work here. The dams decayed and the ponds drained, leaving a layer of fertile soil 20 feet deep.

Back on the road, you soon climb to **Many Parks Curve,** elevation 9,640 feet, which offers a panoramic vista to the east of forested ridges, knobby mountains, and expansive meadows. French trappers called the prairie meadows *parques,* and the term

Plant Adaptation in a Ferocious Climate

The stunning array of midsummer flowers is a big attraction of alpine tundra—a beautiful reminder of the plants' need to bloom and reproduce within the span of an extremely short growing season. The biggest challenge to plant life on the tundra is the fierce, bitter cold. Even in summer the average temperature here is only 50° F; the year-round average is below freezing. In addition, these highlands are buffeted by fantastic winds.

Tundra plants have adapted to both conditions by staying low to the ground, nearer the sun-warmed surface and less exposed to big blows. Some plants—such as moss campion, with its glorious pink blossoms—grow in dense mats.

What you see on the surface, however, is just that: a cover story. A plant such as claytonia may poke but a few inches above the ground; its root system, meanwhile, plunges 2 feet or more down into the ground, yielding stability and nutrients.

stuck. From the boardwalk, you see **Moraine Park** to the right of **Beaver Meadows.** Stroll down to the lower parking area to see Horseshoe Park. All three were carved out by glaciers. Estes Valley, just visible beyond Deer Mountain, looks glaciated but wasn't.

Many Parks Curve lies high in the Montane Ecosystem, the second major ecosystem you encounter in Rocky as you gain elevation. Here, the predominant tree species are Douglas fir, limber pine, and lodgepole pine.

Four miles and 1,200 vertical feet up the road, stop at **Rainbow Curve,** named for the spectacular rainbows often seen from this point after thunderstorms. New tree species, better adapted to cold weather, surround you here, thanks to the change in elevation. Englemann spruce and subalpine fir join limber pine in the forests around this point, all denizens of the Subalpine Ecosystem. More snow collects in this ecosystem than in any other in mountain zone: between 10 and 15 feet from the clouds, with more raked in by fierce winds from the treeless back of Trail Ridge.

The last turnout before tree line, Rainbow Curve showcases the effects of an increasingly harsh climate on trees. Some wind-blasted trunks grow branches only to leeward, and 100-year-old, sapling-size dwarfs grow horizontally, protected by boulders.

As you continue along Trail Ridge Road, the trees give out completely as you traverse a knife-edged ridgeline. Soon, you've arrived in the wide, rolling meadows of the Alpine Tundra Ecosystem, home to hardy plants that cope with a ferocious climate. Temperatures here average 20 degrees cooler than in Estes Park. Wind speeds often exceed 100 mph, and sometimes reach 200 mph. Conditions are also very dry. Despite the heavy snowfall and summer thunderstorms, there is less effective precipitation here than anywhere else in the park. Water evaporates faster. The sun shines with greater intensity. Winds blow away much of the snow that falls, and porous soils quickly drain moisture from the surface.

To the left, a deep glacial canyon drops away toward an incredible panorama of the park's major peaks. Stop at **Forest Canyon Overlook,** 11,716 feet, and take the footpath down to the platform perched along the rim. A peaks-finder chart identifies the summits, which run across your field of vision for 20 miles. Glaciers carved the bowls and basins, spires and ridges that make this ragged mass of gneiss and granite such a pleasure to look at. A valley glacier also gouged out **Forest Canyon,** 2,500 feet below.

Back in your car, drive on 2 miles, crossing smooth mountaintops that are part of a plain formed when an ancestral mountain range eroded. The plain was uplifted largely intact and remained above the Ice Age glaciers.

Stop at **Rock Cut,** 12,110 feet, where a steep, self-guided, 1-mile round-trip nature trail climbs a hill. Worth every gasping breath, the **Tundra Communities Trail** offers more than views of mountains rising over colorful wildflower meadows. You'll also learn about the adaptations plants and animals make to survive the harsh climate. *(High altitude can cause dizziness and nausea, so walk slowly and don't overdo. If you feel ill, you'll most likely recover as soon as you reach lower elevations.)* The trail leads from a parking lot to the **Toll Memorial Mountain Index,** a peak-finder atop a rock pile. The 360-degree views of mountain, tundra, and weird rocks are splendid.

Farther along, pull over at **Lava Cliffs,** 12,085 feet. These walls of welded volcanic ash, called tuff, formed 28 million years ago as a volcano erupted to the west in the Never Summer Mountains. Molten ash flowed east roughly to this spot, where it stopped and hardened. During the ice ages, snow accumulated beneath the cliffs and eventually formed an immense glacier. Scan the meadow some 400 feet below the cliff for elk. Trail Ridge Road reaches its highest point, 12,183 feet, between the Lava Cliffs and the turnoff for the Gore Range overlook.

Stop at the **Alpine Visitor Center,** 11,796 feet, for more about the alpine tundra. The roof of the building itself, secured with a heavy log frame, testifies to the intensity of the weather. Behind the building, a viewing platform overlooks a broad, glacially carved basin covered with thick mats of sedges, grass, wildflowers, low shrubs, and islands of dwarf subalpine fir. If you've brought binoculars, you can often see a dozen or more elk.

The road descends quickly to **Medicine Bow Curve,** 11,640 feet, a hairpin with a view of the Medicine Bow Mountains, 20 miles north. On clear days, you can see Wyoming's Snowy Range, 44 miles to the north. The site also overlooks the headwaters of the Cache la Poudre River, a silver thread meandering over the treeless floor of a long valley.

The river flows northeast, out of **Poudre Lake,** which nestles along the Continental Divide, just a few miles down the road. At the northeast end of the lake, you might consider a steep, 1-mile hike on the **Crater Trail,** which climbs through a subalpine forest on Specimen Mountain to the rim of a broad, semicircular valley where bighorn sheep are often seen. The trail remains closed until mid-July so the sheep can lamb in peace.

The Continental Divide cuts along the southwest shore of the lake, at **Milner Pass,** 10,758 feet, named for the surveyor of a never built railway route through the Rockies. Water flowing east of the divide will eventually find its way to the Atlantic, and water wending west will flow to the Pacific.

The overlook at **Farview Curve,** 10,120 feet, about 2 miles farther, provides a riveting view of the Never Summer Mountains and glacier-carved Kawuneeche Valley. Through this valley winds the infant Colorado River, whose headwaters lie just 5 miles north. About halfway up on the western part of the Never Summer Mountains, you can see a horizontal scar. It is the 14-mile-long **Grand Ditch,** built between 1890 and 1932 to divert water from the wetter western side of the Continental Divide to the drier Great Plains to the east.

If short of time, turn back now. Otherwise continue the 14 miles remaining on Trail Ridge Road, descending to the beaver ponds, willows, conifer forests, and broad meadows of the valley floor. You might spot moose, reintroduced in 1978 after settlers

Marmots & Pikas: Whistling Watchmen

Most walks on talus slopes near timberline have a certain lyrical quality to them—an almost steady pattern of whistles and teeth-chattering trills, each announcing your approach. The whistling watchmen are marmots and pikas, ever on the lookout for intruders.

The pika is especially fleet of foot, scurrying about the rocks with great energy. Also known as a haymaker, this tiny member of the hare family spends its long summer days gathering plants for winter. Before storing this stash (which may grow to four bushels), the pika drapes the plants on rocks to dry—a tactic that obviates mold damage. Walk the high country often enough, and time and again you'll come upon these minuscule haystacks of grasses and stems, laid out in the sun. Just as we might race to get laundry off the line before it rains, so do pikas scamper about the boulders when a storm threatens, carrying their collections to shelter.

The much larger yellow-bellied marmot seems to have it easier here in the highlands. Sometimes called the "rock-chuck" because of its preference for the rockier areas of western North America, it leads a simple life: Eat, sleep, sun. During the tough winter months, rather than cache food stores as the pika does, the "whistle pig" (as it is also known) snoozes the season away. With the first snows of September, the marmot retreats to an underground den.

Yellow-bellied marmot

eliminated them in this area. Hunters also killed off wolves, grizzly bears, and bison in the region.

In the late 19th century, smatterings of silver and gold lured miners by the hundreds to the valley. Resulting boomtowns vanished as quickly as they arose when mining claims proved unprofitable. From the **Colorado River Trailhead,** about 4 miles past Farview Curve, an easy 1.8-mile hike brings you to the decaying 1870s cabins of miner Joe Shipler. About 2.5 miles farther up the trail lies the site of **Lulu City,** once a bustling mining camp.

Stop again 2 miles down the road at the **Holzwarth Historic Site,** where you'll find a miner's cabin beside the parking area. Stroll the easy half mile across the meadow and over the Colorado River, to **Never Summer Ranch** *(for tours check hours of operation at visitor centers)*, a restored dude ranch dating from the 1920s. John Holzwarth moved his family there when Prohibition closed down his Denver saloon. They started as ranchers, but soon found they could make more money by charging guests $11 a week for room, board, and a horse. Some of the buildings still retain their original furnishings.

As you continue southwest along the Kawuneeche Valley, look for the **Coyote Valley Trail,** an interpretive trail that follows the Colorado River upstream for a half mile. Suitable for strollers or wheelchairs, the trail offers excellent exhibits on streamside ecology, glaciation, wildlife, and other interesting topics. A branch of the trail leads to a pleasant picnic area along the forest fringe.

Displays at the **Kawuneeche Visitor Center,** about 6 miles beyond the Coyote Valley Trail, focus on animals and plants that live on the colder, wetter west side of the park. A self-guided trail runs along the outside of the building and identifies common wildflowers, shrubs, and trees.

Farther along the road, you might take the turnoff for the **Historic Grand Lake Lodge** *(970-627-3967)*, which perches on a mountain slope overlooking Grand and Shadow Mountain Lakes.

Old Fall River Road: 9.4 miles; a half day

This winding gravel road provides a leisurely (15 mph) climb from Horseshoe Park to the Alpine Visitor Center atop Trail Ridge. It is also a self-guided auto tour, with flyers for sale at the visitor center, about 4 miles from the Fall River Entrance Station *(no RVs or vehicles over 25 feet long)*.

En route you'll emerge from dense conifer forests, climb into high mountain meadows and see evidence of ancient glaciers, recent rockslides, flash floods, and avalanches.

Begin the tour at **Endovalley Road,** in Horseshoe Park where US 34 bends around the west side of Sheep Lakes. The huge ramp of boulders the road crosses is a reminder of the 1982 Lawn Lake flash flood. A dam, built prior to the creation of the park, burst one July morning, releasing a flood that turned the Roaring River into a tree-ripping torrent and deposited boulders, mud, and debris as far as the main street of Estes Park.

Pull over at the **Alluvial Fan Trail** and take a few minutes to stroll the short paved pathway over the debris—up to 44 feet thick—and observe how nature recovers: Young aspens and conifers and dozens of species of willows and grasses are reclaiming the area, as are a wide variety of birds and other animals. Walk back to your car along the trail, not the road.

As you drive on, note the scars on the aspens: Elk and other animals gnaw the bark, which then becomes infected with the black fungus you see; given enough damage, the aspens eventually die. Some observers cite the extent of aspen damage within the park as evidence that elk have reached or exceeded their population limit here. At Endovalley, continue on to the one-way Old Fall River Road with your self-guiding leaflet. Join Trail Ridge Road at Fall River Pass.

Bear Lake Road: 10 miles; at least a half day

Popular especially for its trails, wildflowers, and fall foliage, Bear Lake Road starts off US 36 just past the Beaver Meadows Entrance Station. Make your first stop the **Moraine Park Museum,** near the homestead of pioneer and resort owner Abner Sprague. Buy a pamphlet for the nature trail, an easy stroll that starts in front of the building. Along the trail, be sure to smell the ponderosa pine bark; its vanilla scent is luscious.

The road between Sprague Lake and Bear Lake is extremely busy, and parking at Bear Lake is limited. Leave early, or plan to take one of the convenient shuttle buses that operate during high season. The bus comes frequently, and its schedule is in the park newspaper.

The road tunnels through stands of lodgepole pine and aspen—dazzling in fall. At **Sprague Lake** awaits one of the park's wheelchair-accessible trails. Sprague Lake is a fishing pond created by

Abner Sprague. An easy, half-mile self-guided **nature walk** loops around the pond and offers views of peaks along the Continental Divide, including Flattop Mountain and Hallett Peak.

At **Bear Lake,** buy a pamphlet and stroll the half-mile **Bear Lake Nature Walk,** enjoying this dramatic, often photographed scenery while you learn about forest ecology. Nearby, you'll find the start of the 1.8-mile **Emerald Lake Trail,** which includes the park's most popular short hike: a stroll to **Dream Lake,** over which towers Hallett and Flattop.

For a somewhat less crowded walk to another spectacular lake, start from the **Glacier Gorge Junction Trailhead,** about 0.75 mile back down the road. The **Loch Trail** passes **Alberta Falls** in half a mile, and reaches the rocky shoreline of **The Loch** after a moderately steep climb of 2.7 miles.

More Hikes

The park's excellent 355-mile trail system presents you with endless possibilities, just a few of which are listed below. See a ranger for details and ideas on less crowded walks.

■ **Wild Basin:** This corner of the park—14 miles south of Estes Park off Colo. 7—offers fine day hikes, including those to **Calypso Cascades** (1.8 miles) and **Ouzel Falls** (2.7 miles) through spruce-fir and mixed conifer forests along North Saint Vrain Creek and its tributaries. Pick up a nature booklet to learn how the forest has been making a comeback since a major fire in 1978.

■ **Longs Peak, Chasm Lake:** More than 800 people have been counted climbing Longs Peak on a single summer's day. The predawn climb (8 miles one way) to the park's tallest peak requires planning—check with a ranger, especially about lightning. Some

Hikers resting along shore of Emerald Lake

consider the challenging trail to Chasm Lake (4.2 miles one way) the park's most beautiful and rewarding hike. Both hikes begin at Longs Peak Ranger Station, a mile off Colo. 7, about 10 miles south of Estes Park. Note that parking is limited.

■ **Cub Lake:** The less traveled **Cub Lake Trail** (an easy 4.6-mile round-trip) is known for birding and wildflowers, including the yellow water lilies afloat on Cub Lake in summer. The trail begins from a spur road off Bear Lake Road at Moraine Park.

■ **Green Mountain Trail to Big Meadows:** This easy trail (3.6 miles round-trip) passes through woods, marsh, and meadows. It starts from Trail Ridge Road, 3 miles north of the Grand Lake Entrance.

INFORMATION & ACTIVITIES

Headquarters
1000 Hwy. 36
Estes Park, CO 80517
970-586-1206
www.nps.gov/romo

Visitor & Information Centers
Beaver Meadows Visitor Center, on US 36 at east entrance to park, and Kawuneeche Visitor Center, on US 34, all year. Alpine Visitor Center, June to mid-October. Fall River Visitor Center, on US 34 west of Estes Park near Fall River entrance, May through October. Moraine Park Museum and Visitor Center, May to mid-October.

Seasons & Accessibility
Park open year-round. Trail Ridge Road closes mid-October to late May. In summer, free shuttle bus service operates on Bear Lake Road.

Entrance Fees
$15 per car; $30 annual fee.

Pets
Prohibited from trails and backcountry; leashed elsewhere.

Facilities for Disabled
Visitor centers, museum, campground amphitheaters, but not all rest rooms. Also accessible: the Lily Lake, Bear Lake, and Sprague Lake nature walks.

Handicamp, at Sprague Lake, accommodates wheelchair backcountry campers. Call 970-586-1242.

Things to Do
Free naturalist-led activities: nature and history walks, hikes, campfire talks, slide shows, arts programs, snowshoe walks. Also, hiking, horseback trail rides (303-627-3514), bicycling, fishing, ice fishing, rock climbing, mountain climbing, cross-country skiing.

Special Advisories
■ Stay on trails to prevent erosion and damage to fragile alpine plants.
■ Filter or chemically treat surface water before drinking.
■ Permits (fee) required for backcountry camping; available by mail or in person at headquarters and the Kawuneeche Visitor Center (970-586-1242).

Campgrounds
Five campgrounds. Longs Peak, 3-day limit; others, 7-day limit June through September. Additional days permitted other times of year. Glacier Basin and Moraine Park open June through September; reservations suggested, call 877-444-6777, or visit www.Reserve USA.com. Other campgrounds

Forest Canyon Overlook, Rocky Mountain National Park

open all year—first come, first served. $18 in summer; $12 in winter, when water is not available. No showers. RV sites at all campgrounds except Longs Peak; no hookups. Reservations required for group sites at Glacier Basin Campground.

Hotels, Motels, & Inns

(Unless otherwise noted, rates are for two persons in a double room, high season.)

In Estes Park, CO 80517:

■ **Aspen Lodge Ranch Resort** 6120 Hwy. 7. 970-586-8133, or 800-332-6867. 59 units. From $129 per person, all inclusive. 3-day minimum. Open April through November.

■ **Romantic RiverSong Bed & Breakfast Inn** P.O. Box 1910. 970-586-4666. 10 units.

$150-$295, includes breakfast.

■ **The Stanley Hotel** 333 Wonderview Ave. 970-586-3371 or 800-976-1377. 136 units. $159-$299. Pool, restaurant.

■ **Winding River Ranch** 5770 Hwy. 7. 970-586-4212. 11 units. $1,500 per person per week, includes meals. Pool. Open June through August.

In Grand Lake, CO 80447:

■ **Bighorn Lodge** 613 Grand Ave. 970-627-8101 or 800-341-8000. 20 units. $50-$140.

■ **Blackbear Lodge** 12255 Hwy. 34. 970-627-3654. 17 units, 9 kitchenettes. From $70. Pool.

■ **Western Riviera Motel** 419 Garfield. 970-627-3580. 20 rooms, 4 cabins, 2-bedroom condo, 3-bedroom house with dock. $110-$175.

Excursions from Rocky Mountain

Arapaho & Roosevelt National Forests

Several tracts adjoining Rocky Mountain Encircling the magnificent peaks of Rocky Mountain National Park, Arapaho and Roosevelt National Forests boast qualities similar to those of the more famous park—as well as similar problems. These national forests contain a string of beautiful wilderness areas, and though their status protects them from man-made development, the more accessible areas can leave many visitors with a sense that the Colorado wilderness is being loved to death. Many trailhead parking lots fill early, most campgrounds ask for reservations, and certain wilderness areas require camping permits. Hiking and camping options abound in this vast area, however, so it is possible to leave most of the crowd behind.

Three scenic drives offer a taste of the forests' widely varying terrain. The northernmost, **Cache la Poudre-North Park Scenic Byway,** runs 101 miles between Fort Collins and Walden, following the **Cache la Poudre National Wild and Scenic River** and offering access to wilderness areas and hiking trails.

From Fort Collins, head north on US 287 and turn west on Colo. 14. The road climbs out of juniper and cottonwood country into gorgeous stands of aspen mixed with ponderosa and, at higher elevations, lodgepole and spruce. At some points along the river, the cliffs rise 3,000 feet high. The **Cache la Poudre Wilderness** flanks the river's south side. Near the Mountain Park Campground, look for the **Mount McConnell Trail,** which makes a 2-mile loop through shady clusters of ponderosa and Douglas-fir and sun-baked slopes of prickly pear, yucca, and juniper. Beyond the small town of Gould, the road emerges from the dense forests and crosses the wide open spaces of North Park, where local ranchers have joined with state and federal agencies to improve riparian habitat along the Michigan River.

Along the eastern flank of the Front Range, the **Peak to Peak Scenic Byway** runs north-south for 55 miles between Estes Park and Black Hawk on Colo. 7, Colo. 72, and Colo. 119. Rising steadily out of the Big Thompson Valley, it offers access to several destinations, including **Twin Sisters Peaks, Longs Peak,** and the **Wild Basin** area. Along the way, a pleasant, well-groomed but unspectacular gravel trail circles grassy-sided **Lily Lake,** with views of Twin Sisters and Longs Peaks. The road south of here, a popular biking route,

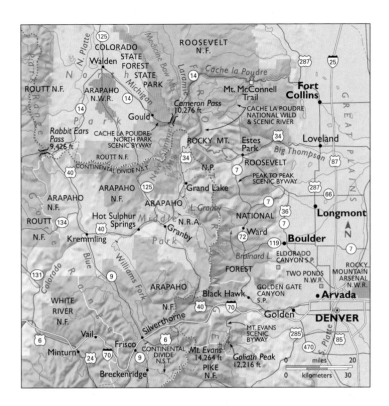

dips and rolls through foothills of aspen and ponderosa pine. Farther south and high above the town of Ward, you might explore **Brainard Lake Recreational Area** which accesses the **Indian Peaks Wilderness.** Here, trails start at 10,300 feet. One, the 2-mile loop around **Long Lake,** is so popular with families and dogs that some of the meadows have boardwalks to lessen impacts. Tree line is not far away, and the more ambitious, somewhat less populated, jaunt to **Lake Isabelle** gets you even closer.

Farther south, you'll find the **Mount Evans Scenic Byway,** a 28-mile, high-altitude drive that starts from Idaho Springs and climbs to the summit of the 14,264-foot peak. This is one of the nation's first roads designed primarily as a scenic drive, created in 1912 by Frederick Law Olmsted, Jr., son of the landscape architect who planned New York's Central Park. The route slowly circles to showcase outstanding vistas in all directions. Viewing scopes at the summit are good for spotting area wildlife, including marmots, pikas, bighorn sheep, and mountain goats.

Kayaking Grand Lake, Arapaho NRA

Along the way, **Echo Lake** offers fishing, camping, and trails into the **Mount Evans Wilderness.** These include **Chicago Lakes Trail,** a 9-mile round-trip to a glacial valley. Another (13 miles round-trip) leads to **Resthouse Meadows** and a gorgeous chain of lakes.

On summer afternoons **Mount Goliath Natural Area** (also called Mount Evans Information Center) offers a variety of programs. Among its interesting trails is a quarter-mile wheelchair-accessible tour of an alpine garden with plants from a variety of elevations. Another loop trail visits a grove of bristlecone pines. Keep a lookout, too, for stunted, nearly prostrate trees that have been affected by the severe weather of the high country.

Located west of Rocky Mountain National Park, the **Arapaho National Recreation Area** takes in a series of lakes along the Colorado River drainage and includes campgrounds, picnic areas, and trailheads into the **Indian Peaks Wilderness.** Motorboats and Jet Skis dominate weekend recreation on **Lake Granby,** but motors are prohibited from **Monarch Lake,** reached via a short portage from the southeast end of Lake Granby. The islands at the south end of **Shadow Mountain Lake** *(also closed to motors)* offer another option for paddlers. If you're on foot, you might consider taking the 4-mile **Monarch Lake Trail** around that body of water, or use this as a jumping-off point to the Indian Peaks Wilderness, popular for wintering bald eagles.

■ **1.5 million acres** ■ **Northern Colorado** ■ **Year-round** ■ **Camping, hiking, climbing, boating, fishing, hunting, biking, horseback riding, skiing, bird-watching, wildlife viewing, scenic drives** ■ **Fee for Mount Evans toll road and some parking areas** ■ **Contact the national forests, 1311 S. College Ave., Fort Collins, CO 80524; 970-498-2770. www.fs.fed.us/arnf**

Arapaho National Wildlife Refuge

30 miles NW of Rocky Mountain An important stopover for migratory waterfowl and geese, this refuge offers visitors a 6-mile self-guided **auto tour** through uplands, grassy meadows, past several ponds. Also, a half-mile interpretive **boardwalk trail** wanders along the **Illinois River** through willows and wet meadows—good habitat for gadwalls, lesser scaup, and mallard. In addition to supporting birdlife, Arapaho is also an outstanding place to see moose, reintroduced to the mountains southeast of here by the state in the late 1970s. The new arrivals have thrived. Though they often prefer the mountains in summer, moose have shown up in the river here in the middle of August.

■ **24,804 acres** ■ **Northern Colorado, near Walden** ■ **Best months May–Oct.; peak waterfowl migrations in late May and late Sept. or early Oct.** ■ **Hiking, bird-watching, wildlife viewing, auto tour** ■ **Contact the refuge, 953 Co. Rd. 32, Walden, CO 80480; 970-723-8202. www.r6.fws.gov/refuges/arapaho/**

Eldorado Canyon State Park

35 miles SE of Rocky Mountain South of Boulder, a tiny creek wends its way through a narrow canyon in this small park, exposing 1.7 billion years of Rocky Mountain geology—from tilted layers of red sandstone to ancient granite. A popular picnicking and rock-climbing destination, the park fills to capacity on summer Sundays. A handful of hiking trails are far less crowded than the number of cars might suggest. From South Boulder Creek, the 0.7-mile **Fowler Trail** is relatively flat, wheelchair accessible, and cuts along the side of the canyon, penetrating a huge slab of the Fountain formation at a place called the Bastille. **Rattlesnake Gulch Trail** climbs more than 800 feet in 1.4 miles, leading to the ruins of an old hotel. Though the ruins themselves are unremarkable, the high vantage point provides views of the canyon and eastern plains that are anything but.

■ **1,442 acres** ■ **Colo. 170 near Boulder, west of Eldorado Springs** ■ **Year-round** ■ **Hiking, rock climbing, fishing, biking, horseback riding, bird-watching,** ■ **Adm. fee** ■ **Contact the park, P.O. Box B, Eldorado Springs, CO 80025; 303-494-3943. www.parks. state.co.us/eldorado**

Of Quaking & Cloning

The most prevalent tree in North America is anything but ordinary. Of the many far-flung corners of the continent in which the aspen grows, nowhere does it seem more glorious—nowhere does it possess more power to revive the spirit of the weary traveler—than in the highlands of Utah and Colorado.

True, these are not the complex, highly diverse hardwood forests of the East and Middle West. Yet be it in summer, when larkspur and columbine gather at their feet, or in autumn, when their leaves flash gold in the long, clean light, walking through a mature aspen forest remains one of America's transcendent outdoor experiences.

Aspens typically grow 40 to 100 feet tall, with a trunk diameter of 23 inches or more. The full common name of this tree, quaking aspen, refers to the fact that its heart-shaped leaves tremble at the slightest hint of a breeze. The sound of this distinct flutter is a comforting whisper; along with the characteristic tang of tannin, it often betrays the tree's identity.

A naturalist would tell you that the quaking occurs because the aspen's long leafstalks, or petioles, are flattened contrary to the plane of its leaves. Other, more fanciful explanations abound: According to the voyageurs of Canada, aspen furnished the wood for the Cross, and the tree has not stopped quaking since.

Besides boasting a broad geographical distribution—from California to Alaska, from Minnesota to Maine to Mexico—aspen is the only tree that grows in every mountain ecozone except the tundra. Indeed, the tree's most significant deterrents are heat and drought, not cold. Aspen grows best in middle- to upper-mountain zones, where winters are fairly cold but summers are warm, and moisture—either rain or snow—comes in annual quantities of at least 25 inches.

Aspen, a pioneer species, quickly overtakes areas disturbed by fire, blowdown, or avalanche. Key to this rapid advance is the aspen's ability to regenerate through clonal growth—in other words, by sprouting new trees (so-called suckers) from a parent root system. This is why the aspen forest you see sprawling across a mountainside is usually a collection of clone groups. To find where one clone group ends and another begins, examine leaf development: The leaves of a single clone group have the same shape and size, and they with enough chloroplasts in its bark (hence the sometimes greenish tint observed on its trunk) to carry on a lower but still productive level of respiration.

In many areas but not all, aspen is a temporary resident. It will be replaced one day by more shade-tolerant species such as Engelmann and Colorado blue spruce, Douglas-fir and subalpine fir—members of the so-called climax community. On the other hand, an aspen woods containing little understory but grass or shrubs—no conifers and no young aspen trees—could be a place where suckers are being heavily browsed by cattle or wildlife, a condition that will eventually deplete the vigor of the rootstock.

The list of species supported by this tree reads like Who's Who in the Wildlife World. The buds and bark are an important food for everything from moose to bears, rabbits to elk, deer to grouse. And don't forget the beaver: It finds the inner bark of aspen more appealing than any other food, including willow, cottonwood, or alder.

Birds, too, are at home in aspens. Woodpeckers excavate nests in the trunks, creating cozy homes later used by swallows, nuthatches, or bluebirds.

A grove of mature aspen trees

all change color at the same time in the fall; they even turn an identical shade of gold, or yellow, or orange.

When it comes to survival, aspens have some interesting tricks up their trunks. The bole and branches store prodigious amounts of water, enabling the leaves to draw on this moisture in times of drought. Should the leaves be killed by a late freeze—or should the canopy be devastated by insects— aspen is one of the few trees

Sequoia & Kings Canyon

Bigness—big trees and big canyons—inspired the separate founding of each of these parks. In 1943 Sequoia and Kings Canyon National Parks began to be jointly administered. The two contiguous parks form one superpark 66 miles long and 36 miles at its widest point.

Nearly every square mile of this vast park is wilderness. A backpacker here can hike to a spot that is farther from a road than any other place in the 48 contiguous states. But visitors can easily reach Sequoia's famed attraction, the Giant Forest of sequoias.

The survival of California's ancient sequoias is one of the conservation movement's greatest triumphs. The trees themselves have been coveted by loggers since the 1800s, and the area in which they grow has faced other threats. Many of the region's rivers have been dammed and diverted by farmers in the valley below. Thanks to federal protection, bighorn sheep still roam the cliffs, California condors still soar on thermal air currents, and the big trees live on.

Relatively few visitors hike any of the parks' hundreds of miles of trails. Still, there are enough backpackers to worry officials, who protect the backcountry by regulating the number of people entering it.

Mount Whitney, at 14,494 feet the highest peak in the United States south of Alaska, rises at the border. Backpackers coming in from the east can get to Whitney in 1 or 2 days. From the park's western trailheads, backpackers reach it by a 70-mile, 8-day trek across the park's snow-swept, glacier-dotted heights.

Both parks have sequoia groves, dramatic rock formations, and untamed rivers. The former is more accessible to the casual visitor; Kings Canyon, on the other hand, is primarily a wilderness park, although some of the most thrilling sections of the canyon actually lie outside the boundaries of the park in Sequoia National Forest.

- Eastern California
- 868,000 acres
- Established 1890 (Sequoia); 1940 (Kings Canyon)
- Best seasons late spring–early fall
- Hiking, horseback riding, wildlife viewing, cave tours
- Information: 559-565-3341 www.nps.gov/seki

Old-growth sequoia

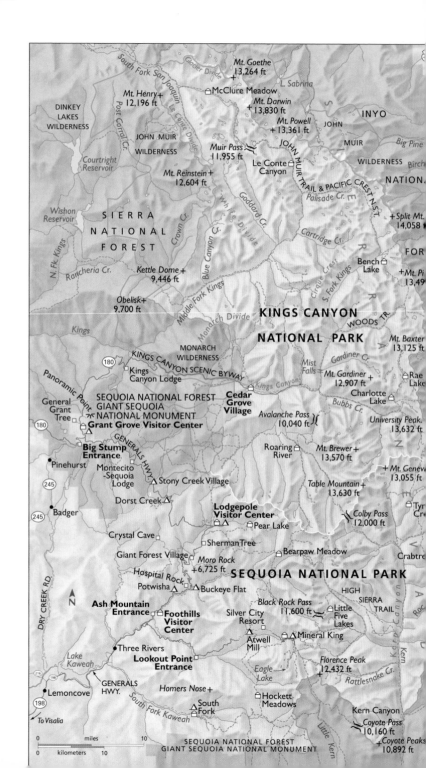

DINKEY
LAKES
WILDERNESS

South Fork San Joaquin

Glacier Divide

Mt. Goethe
+13,264 ft

McClure Meadow

L. Sabrina

Mt. Henry+
12,196 ft

Mt. Darwin
+13,830 ft

Mt. Powell
+13,361 ft

INYO

JOHN

JOHN MUIR
WILDERNESS

Post Corral Cr.

Le Conte Divide

Muir Pass
11,955 ft

Le Conte
Canyon

MUIR

WILDERNESS

Big Pine

Courtright
Reservoir

Mt. Reinstein+
12,604 ft

JOHN MUIR TRAIL & PACIFIC CREST N.S.T.

Palisade Cr.

Birch

NATION.

Wishon
Reservoir

SIERRA

NATIONAL

FOREST

N. Fk. Kings

Rancheria Cr.

Crown Cr.

Goddard Cr.

White Divide

Blue Canyon Cr.

Cartridge Cr.

Cirque Crest

S. Fork Kings

+Split Mt.
14,058

FOR

Bench
Lake

+Mt. Pi
13,49

Kettle Dome+
9,446 ft

Obelisk+
9,700 ft

Middle Fork Kings

Monarch Divide

KINGS CANYON

NATIONAL PARK

WOODS TR.

Mt. Baxter
13,125 ft

Kings

MONARCH
WILDERNESS

Mist
Falls

Gardiner Cr.

Mt. Gardiner+
12,907 ft

Rae
Lake

180

KINGS CANYON SCENIC BYWAY

Kings
Canyon Lodge

Cedar
Grove
Village

Kings Canyon

Charlotte
Lake

Bubbs Cr.

University Peak.
13,632 ft

Panoramic Point

General
Grant
Tree

SEQUOIA NATIONAL FOREST
GIANT SEQUOIA
NATIONAL MONUMENT

Avalanche Pass
10,040 ft

180

Grant Grove Visitor Center

Big Stump
Entrance

GENERALS HWY.

Roaring
River

Mt. Brewer+
13,570 ft

+ Mt. Genev
13,055 ft

Pinehurst

Montecito
-Sequoia
Lodge

Stony Creek Village

Table Mountain+
13,630 ft

245

Dorst Creek

Lodgepole
Visitor Center

Colby Pass
12,000 ft

Tyr
Cre

245

Badger

Crystal Cave

Pear Lake

Sherman Tree

Giant Forest Village

Bearpaw Meadow

Crabtre

DRY CREEK RD.

N

Hospital Rock

Potwisha

Moro Rock
+6,725 ft

Buckeye Flat

SEQUOIA NATIONAL PARK

HIGH

Ash Mountain
Entrance

Foothills
Visitor
Center

Black Rock Pass
11,600 ft

Silver City
Resort

SIERRA

TRAIL

Little
Five
Lakes

Atwell
Mill

Mineral King

Lake
Kaweah

Three Rivers

Lookout Point
Entrance

Eagle
Lake

Florence Peak
+12,432 ft

Rattlesnake Cr.

Kern Canyon

216

198

Lemoncove

GENERALS
HWY.

Homers Nose+

South Fork Kaweah

South
Fork

Hockett
Meadows

Kern

198

To Visalia

Little Kern

Coyote Pass
10,160 ft

Coyote Peaks
10,892 ft

0   miles   10

0   kilometers   10

SEQUOIA NATIONAL FOREST
GIANT SEQUOIA NATIONAL MONUMENT

What Not to Miss

- **Congress Trail and General Sherman Tree**
- **Generals Highway through Redwood Forest**
- **Panoramic Point at Grant Grove**
- **River Trail and Zumwalt Meadow Trail**
- **Crystal Cave tour**
- **Moro Rock Trail to Hanging Rock**
- **Hiking Eagle Lake Trail in Mineral King area**

How to Get There

From Visalia (about 35 miles west), take Calif. 198 to Sequoia's Ash Mountain Entrance. From Fresno, take Calif. 180 to Kings Canyon's Big Stump Entrance. The only road entrance into the main part of Kings Canyon is a dead-end, summer-only extension of Calif. 180 into Cedar Grove. Airport: Fresno.

When to Go

Spring through fall is the best time for sequoia gazing. Generals Highway, which connects Sequoia and Kings Canyon, is open year-round except during heavy snows. From December to April, there is cross-country skiing and snowshoeing in the Giant Forest area and at Grant Grove.

How to Visit

The two immense parks challenge anyone planning a 1-day visit. To appreciate the rugged splendor, you must hike a trail. No east-west road crosses either park. But a drive-in visitor, in a day, can see sequoias in **Giant Forest,** along the **Generals Highway,** and in **Grant Grove.** A quiet walk in a grove of sequoias will give you more than a drive to named trees and other busy areas.

EXPLORING THE PARKS

Giant Forest & Grant Grove: 48 miles; a full day

From the Ash Mountain Entrance, on **Generals Highway,** drive 17 miles to Giant Forest, home of the General Sherman Tree, the world's largest tree. About 6 miles along the road from the Ash Mountain Entrance, stop to see the Native American exhibit at **Hospital Rock.** Native Americans lived here from prehistoric times until the 1870s, when the white man's diseases killed them off. The Western Mono made flour from acorns—the most important staple food of California Indians. They crushed the acorns in small hollows gouged into bedrock; you can see several such rock mortars at the exhibit.

The **Four Guardsmen,** a quartet of sequoias, stand as sentinels near the entrance to Giant Forest. Trails radiate from the star attraction, the **General Sherman Tree,** about 2,100 years old, 274.9 feet tall, and 102.6 feet in circumference, with a volume of 52,500 cubic feet. (In board feet, this is the equivalent of 119.3 miles of 1-by-12-inch planks.) A 13-story building would fit beneath its first large branch. The tree was named by a pioneer cattleman who had served in the Civil War under Gen. William Tecumseh Sherman.

The easy 2-mile **Congress Trail** (the name honors the institution that gave legal protection to the sequoias) takes 1 to 2 hours and begins at the base of the champion tree, where you can buy a self-guiding pamphlet. At stops along the way, you will see young sequoias (a mere 140 or so years old); sequoias scarred by fire but standing tall because their bark, thick and lacking resin, protects them; and fallen sequoias, not rotting because they contain tannin, which helps them resist decay. Sequoias have the greatest trunk circumference of any tree species—up to 102 feet around—but their tops are often stumpy and jagged from lightning strikes. The trees attain their full height after about 800 years; after that they only grow stouter, much like aging humans.

Return to Generals Highway and begin the 30-mile drive to **Grant Grove** in Kings Canyon by heading northwest to Calif. 180. Turn east on Calif. 180. On your right a road loops in and out of Wilsonia, a private community.

Just beyond the Grant Grove Visitor Center, take the road on your left to **General Grant Tree Trail,** a half-mile loop leading to the **General Grant Tree** (267.4 feet tall, 107.6 feet in circumference at the ground). The name of the tree recalls the original 1890 name of the park, created to preserve General Grant Grove. To counteract

Black bear at Giant Forest, Sequoia National Park

lumbering, champions of the sequoias bought more and more land to expand the 4-square-mile grove. When Kings Canyon and its trees were added to the park system in 1940, sequoias within the boundaries were forever protected from logging.

On the trail are many giants saved by the park, along with a reminder of the years of casual havoc: **Centennial Stump,** a sequoia cut down for exhibition at the 1875 Centennial in Philadelphia. Near the park entrance is **Big Stump Trail** (1-mile loop), where stumps, logs, downed trees, and a pile of sawdust help you imagine the sequoia logging of the past.

Drive back to the visitor center and head east on the steep, narrow, 2.5-mile road to **Panoramic Point** (*no trailers or large vehicles allowed*). From the parking lot, take the quarter-mile **trail** to the 7,520-foot ridge. Before you stretches the Sierra Nevada. A trailside diagram of the landscape names the mountains. You won't see Mount Whitney; the Great Western Divide blocks the view.

Cedar Grove: 36 miles; a full day

Follow Calif. 180 for 30 miles north and east of Grant Grove through Sequoia National Forest. The road winds into the canyon of the **South Fork Kings River.** Stop at **Junction View** to gaze down on a wild river flanked by sheer canyon walls glistening in the sun. The road dead-ends at Cedar Grove, a mile-deep valley. Scouring streams began the carving of the valley, which got its U-shape from subsequent glaciers that pushed into the canyon and widened out the floor.

Incense cedar, ponderosa pine, black oak, live oak, white fir, and sugar pine grow in the valley's flats. In the 1870s the area attracted stockmen as well as gold and silver prospectors. Even so, John Muir, who explored here in 1873, would still recognize this well-preserved high-country valley. Decades of protection, and a remote location, have kept the area wild.

The **Cedar Grove Motor Nature Trail,** just beyond Cedar Grove Village, gives the drive-in visitor a tame tour on what had been a livestock trail. Better to park, get out, and walk, even for a short distance, to savor this beautiful hidden valley. The easy half-mile **River Trail** takes you from the South Fork Kings River to **Roaring River Falls.** Back at the parking lot you can return to your car or continue on for a hike along the curves of the river. Cross a suspension bridge and climb a slight rise for a view of the valley.

Sequoia Reproduction

Giant sequoias—sometimes called Sierra redwoods—are ancient forest survivors, resistant to fire and disease. Tree fossils indicate their ancestors grew in Nevada and California millions of years ago. But climate changes in modern times have limited these giants to a narrow band of elevation on the western slope of the Sierra, and they need certain conditions in order to reproduce.

A sequoia can weigh 1,000 tons and rise 250 feet tall, but the seeds that drop from its cones are so small that 90,000 of them weigh a pound. Beetles and squirrels gnaw at the cones, releasing the seeds. Heat from fire does the same thing.

But to take root, the seeds need to fall on bare ground. Fire, which clears away underbrush, has generally been suppressed for the last century in American forests to preserve commercial timber. Current park policy allowing natural and prescribed fires in the Sierra Nevada, though controversial, does lead to a healthier forest and more young sequoias sprouting in the shadows of their huge relatives.

Retrace your steps to the bridge and take the **Zumwalt Meadow Trail,** a 1-mile loop.

Crystal Cave: **18 miles; a half day**

The cave temperature is a constant 48° F, so bring a jacket. Tickets must be purchased at either the Lodgepole or Foothills Visitor Centers. Take the Generals Highway south from Lodgepole Visitor Center. Turn right down the rough, summer-only road *(no trailers or large vehicles)* to Crystal Cave. The twisting 9-mile trip consumes about 45 dusty minutes. From the parking lot you walk a paved, steep path along a canyon wall, down to the entrance. Don't expect multicolored lights or tales of goblins; the 1-hour tours *(mid-May–Sept.),* conducted from 11 a.m. to 4 p.m., introduce you to a cave that got its name from an unusual geological phenomenon. The cave is formed of marble—instead of limestone—that underground water slowly dissolved and then redeposited as dazzling stalactites, stalagmites, columns, and flowstone. For more information contact the Sequoia Natural History Association *(559-565-3759).*

Moro Rock: **4.6 miles round-trip; a half day**

Although you can drive to Moro Rock, a huge granite monolith, via the 2-mile **Moro Rock-Crescent Meadow Road** from Giant Forest Village, you get a better perception of its setting by hiking to it. Either way, try to be there at sunset when the view is spectacular. The 2-mile **Moro Rock Trail** begins near Giant Forest Museum and quickly leads you away from the throngs. About 1.3 miles along the trail, a short path veers off to **Hanging Rock,** a high granite stage for viewing Sierra Nevada scenery.

Return to the trail and continue to the base of Moro Rock. Here you start climbing a stone stairway of nearly 400 steps (and several welcome spots for resting). Your 300-foot ascent takes you to an elevation of 6,725 feet, about 4,000 feet above the canyon floor. From here you can look down on the tops of the sequoias you craned at from the ground. On clear days you can see the Coast Ranges, more than 100 miles west.

When you return from the summit, you can retrace your steps on the Moro Rock Trail or return to the Generals Highway via the 2.3-mile **Soldiers Trail,** named for the U.S. Cavalry troopers who patrolled the sequoias before the Park Service's rangers took over the task.

Mineral King: **50 miles round-trip; at least a full day**

Three miles north of the town of Three Rivers, near the Ash Mountain Entrance, is the sign for Mineral King, in 1978 Sequoia's last major addition. It was named in the 1870s by gold miners who gained little more than unfulfilled dreams from it. In the 1960s dreams of a ski resort also failed to come true because of public opposition.

Turn off Calif. 198 onto a narrow, twisting, 25-mile road. (One driver counted 29 turns in a single mile.) To avoid driving it twice in one grueling day, plan your schedule so that you'll be able to stay at least a night. But, if you must do it in a single day, start early. Mineral King is a hiker's paradise. And the road is the secret to the paradise's solitude. "The road is terrible," one grinning hiker said. "And we hope it stays that way."

During the summer, stop at the Mineral King Ranger Station and check to see whether a ranger-guided walk is scheduled that day. Or take a hike on your own. Get a map at the station, find a legal parking place, and select a trail. Remember that all trails here begin at altitudes of at least 7,500 feet and climb steeply. If you are not acclimated to the high elevations here, you may suffer altitude sickness.

A good hike for beginners just getting their legs in shape is **Eagle Lake Trail,** which starts at the Eagle-Mosquito parking area. This trail starts gently, then begins to get steep near **Spring Creek,** which sprouts from the mountainside. Every switchback treats visitors to an overlook with a stunning view. If you keep your eyes open, you may catch sight of marmots, which sometimes stand up and watch back, and tiny pikas, which whistle and scurry around. After a 2-mile climb, you reach the **Eagle Sink Holes,** where water disappears just as suddenly as the creek appeared. Here you can turn around and start down or continue up another 1.5 miles to **Eagle Lake,** a tarn.

Along the park's southeastern edge looms **Mount Whitney,** the tallest mountain in the continental U.S. (14,494 feet). It is also the Sierra Nevada's most frequently climbed peak. Although Whitney lies within Sequoia, it is generally climbed from the east side, through **Inyo National Forest** *(see pp. 260–61),* with the most direct trail (10.7 miles) leaving from Whitney Portal. Other, less traveled, routes include the **High Sierra Trail,** which leaves from Giant Forest on Sequoia's west side and takes at least six days. All hikers entering the Mount Whitney zone, including day-hikers, are required to obtain a permit *(Eastern Sierra Inter-Agency Visitor Center 760-876-6222).* Note that from mid-May through October there is a daily maximum of 50 overnight climbers and 150 day-hikers.

Horse packers, Kings Canyon National Park

INFORMATION & ACTIVITIES

Headquarters
Ash Mountain
47050 Generals Hwy.
Three Rivers, CA 93271
559-565-3341.
www.nps.gov/seki

Visitor & Information Centers
Sequoia: Lodgepole Visitor
Center and Giant Forest
Museum, both in the Giant
Forest area; Foothills Visitor
Center in Ash Mountain, where
Calif. 198 enters park; Mineral
King Ranger Station in south of
park. Foothills open daily all
year; others open in winter,
reduced hours.
Kings Canyon: Grant Grove
Visitor Center open daily all
year; Cedar Grove, on Calif.
180, open daily in summer.
For visitor information call
559-565-3341.

Seasons & Accessibility
Park open year-round. Roads to
Mineral King (Sequoia) and to
Cedar Grove (Kings Canyon)
closed winter; Generals Highway from Lodgepole to Grant
Grove may close after heavy
snowstorms; also at night in
winter. Call 559-565-3341
for current weather and
road information.

Entrance Fees
$10 per vehicle per week, good
for multiple entries. $5 per
person on bus, foot, bicycle,
motorcycle.

Facilities for Disabled
Visitor centers are wheelchair
accessible, as are some trails in
Grant Grove and Giant Forest.

Things to Do
Free naturalist-led activities
(many offered in summer only):
nature walks and talks, night-
sky watches, children's programs, evening programs,
snowshoe walks. Also available,
Crystal Cave tours, nature center, fishing *(license required),*
horseback trail rides, pack trips,
cross-country skiing.

Overnight Backpacking
Free permits required. Reservations for specific trails and
dates must be made by mail.
(Fee for reservations.) A few
permits issued on departure
day, first come, first served.
Call 559-565-3341.

Campgrounds
Sequoia: 7 campgrounds,
14-day limit mid-June to
mid-September. Lodgepole,
Potwisha, and South Fork open
all year. Others open spring to
fall, depending on weather.
First come, first served, except
Lodgepole and Dorst, which

require reservations in advance through the National Parks Reservation Service *(800-365-2267)* mid-May to mid-October. Fees $12-$20 per night. Showers near Lodgepole, closed in winter. RV sites at Dorst, Lodgepole, and Potwisha; no hookups. Food services available in park.

Kings Canyon: 7 campgrounds, 14-day summer limit. Azalea open all year, others late April to mid-September. First come, first served. Fees $14 per night. Showers nearby. Tent and RV sites; no hookups. Reservations required for group campsites; write Sunset/Canyon View Group Sites, P.O. Box 926, Kings Canyon National Park, CA 93633. Food services available in park.

Hotels, Motels, & Inns
(Unless otherwise noted, rates are for two persons in a double room, high season.)

INSIDE THE PARKS:
For the following lodges in Sequoia, call 888-252-5757:
■ **Bearpaw Meadow Camp** 6 group tent cabins, central showers. $320, includes meals. Open mid-June to mid-September.
■ **Wuksachi Village** 102 units. $155-$189. Restaurant, gift shop.

For the following lodges in Kings Canyon, call 559-335-5500:
■ **Cedar Grove Lodge** 21 units. $105. AC, restaurant. Open May through October.
■ **Grant Grove Lodge** 24 lodge rooms $110-117; 8 bath cabins $105; 27 rustic cabins $69; 15 tent cabins $45. Restaurant.
■ **Stoney Creek Lodge** 11 units. $125. Restaurant. Open mid-May to mid-October.

OUTSIDE THE PARKS
In Three Rivers, CA 93271:
■ **Best Western Holiday Lodge** 40105 Sierra Dr., P.O. Box 129. 559-561-4119. 54 units. $99. AC, pool.
■ **Holiday Inn Express** 40820 Sierra Dr. 559-561-9000. 103 units. $67-99. AC, pool.
■ **Lazy J Ranch Motel** 39625 Sierra Dr. 559-561-4449 or 800-341-8000. 18 units, 7 with kitchenettes. $60-$190. AC, pool.
■ **The River Inn** 45176 Sierra Dr. 559-561-4367. 10 units. $89-$129. AC.

Excursions from Sequoia & Kings Canyon

Kern Wild & Scenic River

Inside Sequoia

In Sequoia National Park, the southern end of the Sierra massif splits, forming two lines of peaks running on either side of the Kern River's dramatic gorge. The Sierra Nevada has many rivers tumbling down its steep sides, but only the Kern runs in a southerly direction. Along its banks are some of the finest remaining virgin riparian woodlands in California, and the river itself boasts some great white water.

The Kern begins among alpine lakes along the Kings-Kern Divide, surrounded by huge peaks, including Mount Whitney. Over the eons, rainwater dug into a "soft" spot here, where a long geological fault had fragmented the underlying rock. Glaciers gouged the U-shaped upper valley, which becomes more V-shaped as the river makes its wild descent. On its journey south, the Kern offers lengthy sections of rough-and-tumble river.

Only the most intrepid hikers and paddlers make it to the upper section of the Kern's **North Fork.** It isn't just the unremitting Class V and VI rapids, it's the long wilderness trek, 21 miles carrying boats and gear. Capable kayakers can get plenty of challenges downstream near Kernville, often putting in at the **Forks.**

Just upstream from Isabella Lake, the National Audubon Society's **Kern River Preserve** (760-378-3044) protects crucial riverbank woodlands of red willow, Fremont cottonwood, and the largest contiguous stand of Great Valley cottonwood in the country. Every fall 25,000 to 30,000 vultures—the largest documented sightings north of Mexico—gather in the preserve over a six-week period.

■ **151 miles long** ■ **Eastern California** ■ **Best seasons summer–early fall** ■ **Hiking, boating, white-water rafting and kayaking, bird-watching, wildlife viewing, river boat tours (fee)** ■ **Contact Kern River, Cannell Ranger District, Sequoia National Forest, P.O. Box 9, Kernville, CA 93238; 760-376-3781. www.r5.fs.fed.us/sequoia/Kernriver**

Ancient Bristlecone Pine Forest

60 miles northeast of Sequoia

The oldest living thing on the planet looks like a giant, gnarled piece of driftwood that somehow got cast ashore high in the White Mountains of the **Inyo**

National Forest along the California-Nevada border. It's an ancient bristlecone pine called Methuselah, after the Old Testament patriarch who lived to be nearly a thousand. In fact, the Methuselah tree is much older, about 4,700 years, meaning it was already more than two centuries old when the Great Pyramid of Khufu was built.

Bristlecones grow stunted and twisted in harsh environments at over 9,500 feet above sea level. Hammered by wind, scorched by lightning, they survive freezing winters and prolonged drought. Their thick, resinous wood grows as little as an inch in diameter over the course of a century.

Forest rangers claim that this area has the best view of the Sierra Nevada anywhere. To see this stunning vista take White Mountain Road 8 miles north of Calif. 168. Here you will also find **Schulman Grove,** the best place to see the trees and learn about the forest at a seasonal visitor center. Then hike the 4.5-mile **Methuselah Trail,** which drops down into a canyon full of wildflowers.

■ **28,000 acres** ■ **East-central California** ■ **Best seasons late spring–fall** ■ **Hiking, mountain biking, cross-country skiing** ■ **Adm. fee** ■ **Contact White Mountain Ranger Station, Inyo National Forest, 798 N. Main St., Bishop, CA 93514; 760-873-2503. www.r5.fs.fed.us/inyo**

Bristlecone pines in Shulman Grove, Inyo National Forest

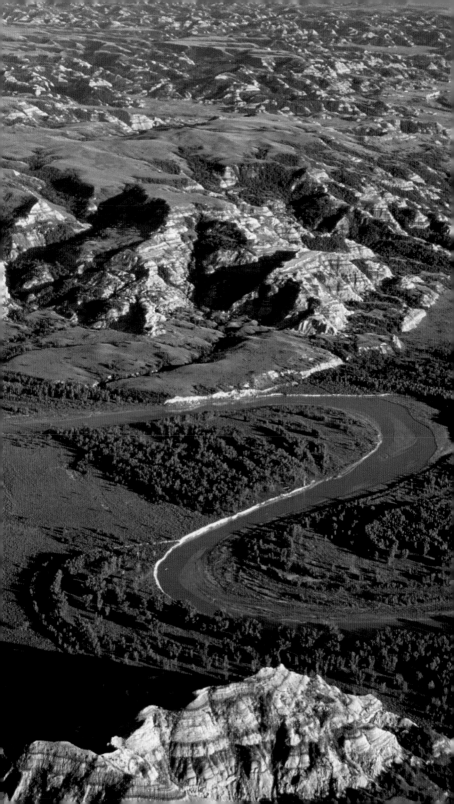

Theodore Roosevelt

Theodore Roosevelt is unique among the scenic parks in that it preserves an extraordinary landscape as well as the memory of an extraordinary man. It honors the president who probably did more for the National Park System than anyone before or since.

Theodore Roosevelt, who would later establish five national parks and help found the Forest Service, first came to Dakota Territory as a young man in 1883 to "bag a buffalo." He tried cattle ranching with no luck, but returned many times over the next 13 years and became a confirmed conservationist. It was the rugged badlands that taught him a healthy respect for nature while toughening him physically and mentally. "I would not have been president," he would later say, "had it not been for my experience in North Dakota."

The history of the North Dakota badlands, however, goes back long before Roosevelt—65 million years, to be exact. It was then that streams flowing from the newly arisen Rockies began depositing sediments here that would later be carved by the Little Missouri River and its tributaries. The results of this ongoing process of deposition and erosion are spectacular: wildly corrugated cliffs; steep, convoluted gullies; and dome-shaped hills, their layers of rock and sediment forming multicolored horizontal stripes that run for miles.

This austere landscape is home to a surprisingly dense population of wildlife. Bison, pronghorn, elk, white-tailed and mule deer, wild horses, and bighorn sheep inhabit the park, as do numerous smaller mammals, amphibians, and reptiles. After a rainy spring, wildflowers color the river bottomlands and prairie flats. And perhaps best of all is the shortage of one particular mammal: human beings. This park is hardly ever crowded, so you can experience the gorgeous loneliness of the badlands much the way Roosevelt did.

- Western North Dakota
- 70,447 acres
- Established 1978
- Best seasons spring–summer
- Hiking, backpacking, riding
- Information: 701-842-2333 (North Unit); 701-623-4466 (South Unit) www.nps.gov/thro

Oxbow Bend of the Little Missouri River, Theodore Roosevelt National Park

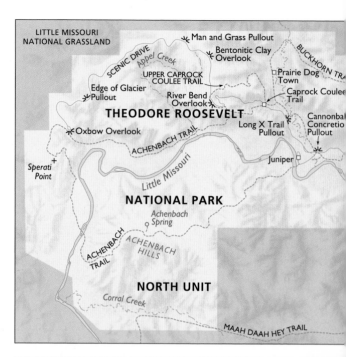

LITTLE MISSOURI
NATIONAL GRASSLAND

Man and Grass Pullout
Bentonitic Clay
Overlook

BUCKHORN TR.

SCENIC DRIVE
Appel Creek

UPPER CAPROCK
COULEE TRAIL

Prairie Dog
Town

Edge of Glacier
Pullout

River Bend
Overlook

Caprock Coulee
Trail

THEODORE ROOSEVELT

Long X Trail
Pullout

Cannonba
Concretio
Pullout

Oxbow Overlook

ACHENBACH TRAIL

ACHENBACH TRAIL

Little Missouri

Juniper

Sperati
Point

NATIONAL PARK

Achenbach
Spring

ACHENBACH
TRAIL

ACHENBACH
HILLS

NORTH UNIT

Corral Creek

MAAH DAAH HEY TRAIL

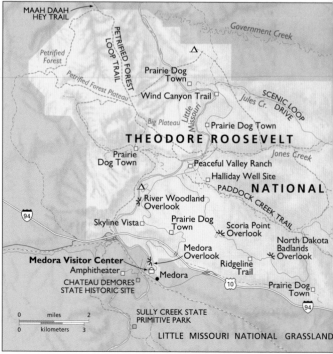

MAAH DAAH
HEY TRAIL

Government Creek

PETRIFIED FOREST LOOP TRAIL

Petrified
Forest

Petrified Forest Plateau

Prairie Dog
Town

Wind Canyon Trail

SCENIC LOOP DRIVE

Jules Cr.

Big Plateau

Little Missouri

Prairie Dog Town

THEODORE ROOSEVELT

Jones Creek

Prairie
Dog Town

Peaceful Valley Ranch

Halliday Well Site

PADDOCK CREEK TRAIL

NATIONAL

River Woodland
Overlook

94

Skyline Vista

Prairie Dog
Town

Scoria Point
Overlook

North Dakota
Badlands
Overlook

Medora
Overlook

Ridgeline
Trail

Medora Visitor Center
Amphitheater

Medora

10

Prairie Dog
Town

CHATEAU DEMORES
STATE HISTORIC SITE

94

0   miles   2

0   kilometers   3

SULLY CREEK STATE
PRIMITIVE PARK

LITTLE MISSOURI NATIONAL GRASSLAND

What Not to Miss

- Canoeing or kayaking on Little Missouri River

- In North Unit, hike Buckhorn Trail Loop

- Visit Wind Canyon and hike trail there

- A visit to Maltese Cross Cabin and hike short trail to Medora Overlook

- Skyline Vista for great view across the badlands

- Drive to Buck Hill Summit for 360-degree view of park's east side

How to Get There

South Unit: From Bismarck, 130 miles east, take I-94 west to the entrance near Medora. From points south, take US 85 north to Belfield, then I-94 west 17 miles to Medora. **North Unit:** US 85 north from Belfield goes to the North Unit entrance. Airport: Bismarck.

When to Go

Although this is an all-year park, portions may close in winter.

How to Visit

If you have only a day, take the **Scenic Loop Drive** in the **South Unit.** Spend a second day on **Scenic Drive** in the **North Unit,** 70 miles away.

EXPLORING THE PARK

South Unit: Scenic Loop Drive: 36 miles: a half to full day

Start at the visitor center near Medora, where you can visit the relocated **Maltese Cross Cabin.** The rustic headquarters of Roosevelt's first ranch contains period furnishings, ranching equipment, and some of Roosevelt's personal belongings.

Then follow the road up the side of the eroded cliff to the **Medora Overlook.** Here you get a good view of the rough little town that epitomized the Wild West back in Roosevelt's day.

Continue on, making sure to stop at the roadside prairie dog town (they bark warnings to each other as you approach). A little farther along is the **Skyline Vista,** a high plateau that overlooks the broken badlands. Actually, you are not so much "up" as the badlands are "down." The plateau is just a remnant of the original prairie before erosion took its toll, scooping out the bewildering landscape below.

The road descends again to the **River Woodland Overlook.** Beyond the row of cottonwood trees on the left lies the **Little Missouri River.** Notice how, in this arid environment, the vegetation is rigidly stratified according to the availability of water. There are tall cottonwoods near the river, and dark green junipers on the relatively moist northern hillsides and in places where water-bearing layers are exposed. On the dry southern slopes, where the sun quickly evaporates rainwater, little grows except grasses.

Turn right at the T-intersection to begin the Scenic Loop Drive. When you reach **Scoria Point,** you are deep into classic badlands territory. The material around you that looks like it's made of brick provides the brightest color in the badlands palette. It was formed when a layer of black coal ignited and baked the gray clay above, turning it into the reddish material known locally (but inaccurately) as scoria.

Along the next 6 miles of road, you encounter two self-guided nature trails that are well worth taking. The **Ridgeline Nature Trail,** while only 0.6 mile long, involves some strenuous climbing; a pamphlet at the trailhead introduces the complex interaction of wind, fire, water, and vegetation in this harsh environment. The **Coal Vein Trail,** at the end of the short unpaved road branching off at Mile 15.6 (there's a sign), is a full mile but less difficult; look for the manifold effects of a lignite bed that burned here from 1951 until early 1977. Between these two trails, pull off at the **North Dakota**

Dakota grasslands, Theodore Roosevelt National Park

Badlands Overlook for an exceptional view of the surroundings.

A mile and a half past the turnoff for Coal Vein is the short road to **Buck Hill.** Take the 100-yard path to the summit for a 360-degree panorama of the eastern end of the park and beyond. Those oil wells on the horizon remind you that, although the badlands stretch for hundreds of miles, the park does not.

Return to the main road and turn right. The backstretch of the loop, running from Buck Hill to **Wind Canyon,** offers several possibilities for longer hikes. The **Talkington Trail** can be followed to the east or to the west, but even better is the **Jones Creek Trail** at Mile 21. This trail follows a deeply eroded creek bed for about 3.5 miles, bisecting the loop road and offering good opportunities to see wildlife *(including prairie rattlesnakes, so be careful).* Since this trail is not a loop, you'll want to turn back at the halfway point or arrange to be picked up at the other end.

Back in the car, continue to the **Wind Canyon Trail.** This short but steep path offers a magnificent vista of a long oxbow curve in the Little Missouri River. You also get a glimpse of how wind plays a part in shaping this unique landscape. The prevailing winds pick up sand from the riverbed and elsewhere and blow it into the canyon to your left that faces northwest, sandblasting the rock into smooth, bizarre shapes.

On the road again, you pass another prairie dog town and then the **Peaceful Valley Ranch** on your right. These historic buildings have had a number of incarnations over the years, from working cattle ranch to park headquarters. These days the ranch is a private saddle horse concession, so you can stop for a ride *(May–Sept.)* before driving back to the visitor center.

North Unit: Scenic Drive: **30 miles round-trip; a half to full day**

Many people regard the North Unit as the more attractive of the two major portions of the park. Certainly the canyons seem steeper here, the river bottomlands lusher, and the blue, black, red, and beige stripes on every butte more pronounced. Located about 52 miles north of I-94, the North Unit is also more isolated and, consequently, less visited.

Starting at the visitor center, take the Scenic Drive west into the park. Stop at the **Longhorn Pullout** to catch a glimpse of the park's herd of longhorn steers, kept here to commemorate the historic Long-X Trail that was a major conduit for longhorns traveling from Texas to the Long-X Ranch just north of the park. If you hike the 11-mile **Buckhorn Trail Loop,** you'll travel along a part of this Old West highway.

Stop at the **Slump Block Pullout** to see badlands erosion in action. The small hill to your right was once part of the higher cliff beyond until unstable underlying sediments caused this piece to slump away. Try matching the diagonal layers of the slump block to the horizontal layers on the cliff to see how the block once fit in.

Pull off at the **Cannonball Concretions Pullout** to see how weathering agents have carved out sandstone spheres formed when the minerals in groundwater came together. Opposite the pullout, look for the **Little Mo Nature Trail.** This easy half-mile loop takes you through typical river woodlands, and a guide leaflet *(available at trailhead)* allows you to identify many of the native plants the Plains Indians used for medicine, food, and raw materials. Watch for beavers and white-tailed deer.

Follow the road to the **Caprock Coulee Pullout,** where you can pick up the nature trail of the same name. Take this easy trail 0.75 mile up a dry canyon, called a coulee, to a grove of pedestal rocks, called caprocks. The harder caprocks protect the sediments below while the surrounding sediments erode and leave the mushroom-shaped formations around you. At the end of the nature trail, you can either turn back or make a 5-mile loop by continuing to the **Upper Caprock Coulee Trail.** Tackling the trail involves climbing some steep terrain, but it offers lots of opportunities to see wildlife.

Beyond the Caprock parking lot, the road climbs steeply to the level of the original prairie. At the top, the **River Bend Overlook** offers an absolutely stunning vista of the deep Little Missouri Valley and the extensive badlands on either side.

A bit farther along, the **Bentonitic Clay Overlook** offers a less dramatic but perhaps more instructive view. The blue-colored bentonite layer visible for miles is made of an extremely absorbent volcanic ash that flows when wet. The plasticity of this layer accounts for much of the dynamism of the badlands landscape.

The road now traces the edge of a grassy plateau. This is prime bison territory; you may even have to wait while a herd crosses the road. At the **Man and Grass Pullout,** you can get some idea of the extensive grasslands that made this part of Dakota worth the trip up the Long-X Trail.

Finally, the road ends at the **Oxbow Overlook.** After enjoying the visual banquet of badlands, return along the same road to the visitor center.

Prairie Potholes

Prairie potholes are small depressions in the landscape that were created 12,000 years ago when glaciers were gouged. Over time, these holes have filled with rain and snowmelt, creating wetland oases for birds and bird-watchers alike.

Often billed as the "duck factory of North America," the 300,000-square-mile prairie pothole region spreads from central Iowa to Alberta, Canada. It serves as a breeding ground for about half of all wild ducklings bred on the continent and as nesting grounds for hundreds of migratory bird species on the central flyway. While the area has millions of basins—from 0.2 acre to a square mile in size—they are not always filled with water. Occasionally drought cycles and agricultural draining have forced these small ecosystems to adapt. During dry spells, plant seeds lie dormant and nesting decreases. Once the water returns, so does the resilient habitat.

INFORMATION & ACTIVITIES

Headquarters
P.O. Box 7
Medora, ND 58645
701-623-4466
www.nps.gov/thro

Visitor & Information Centers
Medora Visitor Center and the
Maltese Cross Cabin, at the
entrance to the South Unit,
open daily all year. Painted
Canyon Visitor Center, in the
southeastern part of the South
Unit off I-94, open from April
to mid-November.

North Unit Visitor Center,
open daily April through September, and weekends in winter. Call headquarters for visitor
information.

Seasons & Accessibility
Park open all year, but access
may be limited in winter
because of snow. The South
Unit road from Medora Visitor
Center through Wind Canyon
to the north boundary is kept
plowed, but the Scenic Loop
Drive is not. The North Unit
road is plowed from the
entrance to the Caprock Coulee
Trailhead. Call headquarters for
weather and road information.

Entrance Fees
$5 per person, maximum of
$10 per vehicle per week;
$20 annually.

Pets
Pets are permitted on leashes
except on trails and in buildings. Horses are prohibited in
campgrounds, picnic areas, and
on self-guided trails.

Facilities for Disabled
Visitor centers, rest rooms,
campground sites, and some
trails are wheelchair accessible.

Things to Do
Free naturalist-led activities:
nature walks and talks, tours of
Roosevelt's Maltese Cross
Cabin (mid-June–mid-Sept.),
evening campfire programs.

Also available, hiking, horseback riding (call Peaceful Valley
Ranch, in South Unit. 701-623-
4568), interpretive exhibits,
auto tours, limited canoeing
and float trips, fishing (license
required), and cross-country
skiing.

Special Advisories
■ View bison from a distance;
they might attack if provoked.
■ Rattlesnakes and black widow
spiders often live in prairie dog
burrows; watch for them when
hiking.
■ Do not feed the prairie dogs;
they bite and may carry disease.
■ Be prepared for extremes of
temperatures and sudden violent thunderstorms.

Bison herd, Theodore Roosevelt National Park

Overnight Backpacking

Permits required. They are free and can be obtained at visitor centers.

Campgrounds

Two campgrounds, both with 14-day limit. Cottonwood and Juniper open all year, first-come, first-served. Fees $10 per night. No showers. Tent and RV sites; no hookups. Three group campgrounds, Cottonwood, Juniper, and Roundup (horses); reservations required; contact park headquarters.

Hotels, Motels, & Inns

(Unless otherwise noted, rates are for two persons in a double room, high season.)

OUTSIDE THE PARK
In Dickinson, ND 58601:
■ **Comfort Inn** 493 Elk Dr. 701-264-7300 or 800-228-5150. 117 units. $75-$140. AC, pool.

■ **Hospitality Inn** 532 15th St. W. 701-227-1853 or 800-422-0949. 149 units. $60-$80. AC, pool, restaurant.
■ **Oasis Motel** 1000 W. Villerd St. 701-225-6703. 27 units, 6 with kitchenettes. From $39. AC, pool.

In Medora, ND 58645:
■ **Badlands Motel** 501 Pacific Ave. 701-623-4444 or 800-633-6721. 116 units. $85. AC, pool. Open May to October.
■ **Medora Motel** 1 Main St. (mailing address: 400 E. River Rd. S). 701-623-4444 or 800-633-6721. 208 units. $64. AC, pool. Open June to Labor Day.
■ **Rough Riders Hotel** 301 Third Ave. 701-623-4444 or 800-633-6721. 10 units. $85. AC, restaurant. Open June to Labor Day.

Excursions from Theodore Roosevelt

Sakakawea Trail

30 miles northeast of Roosevelt

109 miles; half a day This 2-hour, east-west drive traverses the open ranges and rolling fields of grain between US 83 and US 85, south of Lake Sakakawea. From the unspoiled banks of the Missouri River to the striking mesas and buttes of the badlands, the road runs through scenic western North Dakota. En route, a handful of historic forts and Native American sites attract motorists hypnotized by the highway. Anchoring the drive's east end, the agricultural town of **Washburn** occupies a bluff on the Missouri, an ideal site for riverboat trade in the late 1800s.

Head 3 miles west of town on N. Dak. 17 to **Fort Mandan** *(701-462-8535. www.fortmandan.org)*, which commemorates the 1804–05 winter quarters of Meriweather Lewis and William Clark. The site has a reproduction of the wooden fort the explorers stayed in on their way up the Missouri. Their Native American guide, Sakakawea (commonly spelled Sacagawea), joined them at the fort.

Back in Washburn on N. Dak. 200A, take the bridge across the broad Missouri and go west past rolling ranches and fields of corn, wheat, and hay. Soon you begin to see the kinds of mesas and buttes that typify the landscape of the American West.

About 3 miles after the Arroda Lakes, turn right to the **Fort Clark Historic Site** *(701-794-8832)*. Nothing remains of the fort and surrounding village on this windswept prairie. Brochures and plaques detail the history of the fur-trading post that operated here from 1832 to 1860. Steamboat passengers brought smallpox, wiping out 90 percent of the local Mandan Tribe in 1837.

To learn more about the area's Native Americans, go 8 miles west to the **Knife River Indian Villages and National Historic Site** *(701-745-3309)*. An interpretive center traces the life of the Hidatsa through artifacts and a full-size reproduction of an earth lodge. Ground depressions offer evidence of the Mandan and Hidatsa villages that thrived here between the 16th and 19th centuries.

Drive 1.5 miles west of Dunn Center to see waterfowl on their semiannual layovers at the **Lake Ilo National Wildlife Refuge** *(701-548-8110)*. There are picnic areas within the 4,043-acre refuge.

■ **109 miles long** ■ **Western North Dakota** ■ **Best seasons spring—fall**
■ **Bird-watching, auto tour, historic sites**

Little Missouri State Park

20 miles southeast of Roosevelt

Like its national park neighbor, Little Missouri State Park encompasses a maze of mesas, buttes, coulees, and narrow arroyos, all carved by the **Little Missouri River** and its ephemeral feeder streams. Some 30 miles of trails are reserved for hikers and equestrians *(call Badlands Trail Rides 701-764-5219)*. They meander through the park's erosional wonderland, where you might glimpse mule deer, coyotes, wild turkeys, maybe even a bobcat.

The park's pleasant, primitive camping area is especially popular for those traveling with horses in tow. If you are camping, try to claim the secluded, somewhat shaded site found at the north end of the park. Adjacent to the site is the trailhead for an outstanding 4-mile hike, a clockwise loop made by following the **Travois Trail** (signed T) and the **Indian Trail** (signed I).

Begin by dropping down a very steep pitch, then walking beneath a canopy of green ash along a narrow, grass-covered rim that skirts a major coulee sloping down toward the Little Missouri. After 0.75 a mile, descend into a confusion of canyons and flats where dwarf juniper, yucca, and prickly pear cactus all proliferate. At 1.25 miles, where a left goes toward a horse-watering tank, bear right on the main trail, investigating the fantastic display of vertical veins corrugating the steep side slopes to your right. At just shy of 2 miles you'll pass through a gate. At 2.5 miles, veer right to stay on the Travois Trail or go left to get on the **TX Trail** to the Little Missouri; beefy cottonwood trees mark its course.

Many of the unpaved roads in the surrounding uplands are surfaced in scoria, making them appear like red ribbons wrapping across much a drabber, mellow green to brown landscape. As you head back toward Killdeer, you'll see one such road going west toward the Killdeer Mountains, which are hills actually, where elk, mule deer, pronghorn, white-tailed deer, and bighorn sheep run wild. You'll have a terrific chance of spotting some of them if you explore the road around dawn or dusk.

■ **5,749 acres** ■ **West-central North Dakota, 17 miles north of Killdeer**
■ **Best seasons spring and fall** ■ **Camping, hiking, horseback riding, wildlife viewing** ■ **Contact the park, c/o Cross Ranch State Park, 1403 River Rd., Center, ND 58504; 701-794-3731 or 701-260-1753. www.state.nd.us/ndparks/parks/Little_Mo/Home.htm**

Wind Cave

Too many visitors leave Wind Cave National Park knowing only half of its charms. Ironically, the half they know is the half that's not visible from the surface.

Above the spectacular underground labyrinth for which the park is named lies an unusual ecosystem, one that marks the boundary between the mixed-grass prairie of the western Great Plains and the ponderosa pine forests of the Black Hills. Thus, the park plays host to plant and animal species from several distinct geographical areas—prairie falcons and meadowlarks from the grasslands coexist here with nuthatches and wild turkeys from the pine forests.

Wildlife should be a major draw here. Because of the park's small size and relatively large bison population, the chances of seeing bison—the so-called American buffalo—are probably better at this park than at almost any other; indeed it's often difficult to avoid the great beasts. Pronghorn, mule deer, and prairie dogs are present in large numbers—and highly visible since 75 percent of the park is open grassland. Elk live in the forest fringes; you probably won't see many of them, but if you have the good luck to come in the autumn you'll hear their eerie bugling.

Below ground lies Wind Cave, where more than 104 miles of explored passages make it one of the world's longest caves. Because the cave is relatively dry, it contains few of the stalactites and stalagmites you see in other caves. But it has many unusual mineral formations, including perhaps the world's best collection of boxwork, a calcite formation resembling irregular honeycombs created from erosion around gypsum-filled cracks. The most distinctive feature of the cave may be the strong winds that alternately rush in and out of its mouth, equalizing air pressure between the passages inside and the atmosphere outside.

■ Southwestern South Dakota

■ 28,295 acres

■ Established 1903

■ Best seasons summer–early fall

■ Camping, hiking, biking, wildlife viewing, scenic drive, cave tours

■ Information: 605-745-4600 www.nps.gov/wica

Bison, Wind Cave National Park

How to Get There

For the scenic route from Rapid City (74 miles away), take US 16 to US 16A south, detouring for a glimpse of Mount Rushmore, to S. Dak. 87 south. This route—not open to RVs and trailers—takes you along the Needles Highway and through Custer State Park to Wind Cave's north entrance. The faster route is to follow S. Dak. 79 south from Rapid City to Hot Springs and then turn north onto US 385 to the south entrance. From the west, take US 16 east to Custer and US 385 south from there. Airport: Rapid City.

When to Go

All-year park. Although the cave and visitor center are open daily, the park offers far fewer cave tours off-season *(late Sept.–May)*. Late spring to midsummer are best for wildflowers. The campground is rarely, if ever, full.

How to Visit

A good plan of action for a single-day visit would be to spend the morning in **Wind Cave** on one of the shorter introductory tours and the afternoon exploring the park's prairies and forests

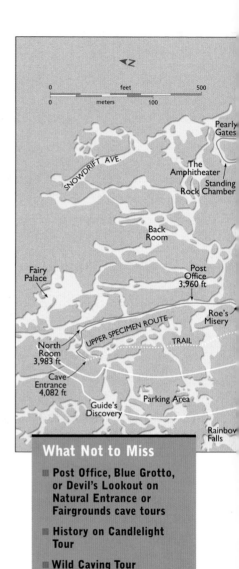

What Not to Miss

- **Post Office, Blue Grotto, or Devil's Lookout on Natural Entrance or Fairgrounds cave tours**

- **History on Candlelight Tour**

- **Wild Caving Tour**

- **Bison off Scenic Drive**

- **Rankin Ridge Trail**

- **Prairie Dog Pullout**

- **Wind Canyon Cave Trail for bird-watching**

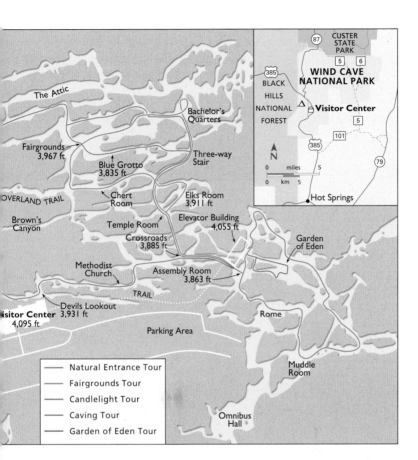

The Attic

Bachelor's
Quarters

Fairgrounds
3,967 ft

Blue Grotto
3,835 ft

Three-way
Stair

OVERLAND TRAIL

Chert
Room

Elks Room
3,911 ft

Brown's
Canyon

Temple Room

Elevator Building
4,055 ft

Crossroads
3,885 ft

Garden
of Eden

Methodist
Church

Assembly Room
3,863 ft

TRAIL

Devils Lookout

Rome

Visitor Center 3,931 ft
4,095 ft

Parking Area

Muddle
Room

Natural Entrance Tour
Fairgrounds Tour
Candlelight Tour
Caving Tour
Garden of Eden Tour

Omnibus
Hall

CUSTER
STATE
PARK
87

5   6

385
BLACK
HILLS
NATIONAL
FOREST

WIND CAVE
NATIONAL PARK

Visitor Center

5

101

N

385

79

0   miles   5
0   km   5

Hot Springs

on the **Scenic Drive.** A second day would be the time for one of the longer **Candlelight** or **Caving Tours.**

People with physical limitations will want to stick to the shorter, less strenuous tours, although even the shortest involves climbing up and down about 150 steps. *(If claustrophobia is a problem, think twice about entering the cave at all.)* Wear good walking shoes, and, since the cave temperature is a constant 53° F, take a jacket even on hot summer days. Reservations for tours are recommended.

EXPLORING THE PARK

Wind Cave: Guided Tours: 1 hour to a half day

All tours begin at the **visitor center,** where several exhibits provide important background information. A video explains the connection between the park's subsurface world and the above-ground prairie. The same forces that lifted the nearby Black Hills created cracks in the limestone layers beneath the present-day park. Water seeped into these cracks and, over millions of years, gradually dissolved the rock, creating the fascinating maze of passages and tunnels we see today.

Most first-timers will choose to take either the **Natural Entrance Tour,** which lasts an hour and 15 minutes, or the **Fairgrounds Tour,** which is 15 minutes longer. These tours introduce you to the underground world, stressing basic information about caves and cave formations; they take you through such colorfully named places as the **Post Office** (named for the extensive boxwork on the walls), the **Devil's Lookout,** and the **Blue Grotto.**

The **Garden of Eden Tour** is a loop around from the elevator to the Garden of Eden lasting 1 hour; it is recommended for people with time or physical limitations.

Sunflowers, Wind Cave National Park

If you are a history buff, by all means take the **Candlelight Tour** (*summer only*). Conducted by the light of candle lanterns, this 2-hour tour harkens back to the 1890s, when Wind Cave was owned by the Wonderful Wind Cave Improvement Company and tours were measured by the number of candles needed to complete them. The tour goes past the Blue Grotto to the Pearly Gates and beyond; it stresses the cave's ambience and exploration. The tour involves some stooping and stair-climbing.

For those in good physical condition with a keen interest in caves, the park offers a 4-hour **Wild Caving Tour,** designed to simulate a cave exploration trip. Rangers lead participants into the ghostly far reaches of the cave. You crawl through narrow openings, squeeze into tight passages, and make a glorious mess of yourself (*take a change of clothes*). The guide's commentary focuses on recreational caving and its impact on cave ecology over the years.

Scenic Drive: 13 miles; at least a half day

Begin on US 385 at the southern boundary of the park, about 11 miles north of Hot Springs. At the **Bison Pullout** you get the first of many excellent views of the prairie, much as it existed before the plows of the white man drastically changed it. You may see bison and pronghorn grazing side by side on the grassy hillsides. The **Mineral Lick Pullout** a little farther on overlooks a site where bison lick salt from the soil.

From the visitor center, drive out to the campground for the self-guided **Elk Mountain Nature Trail.** This easy 1-mile hike takes you through a transitional prairie-and-pine-forest environment, where you'll see the grasses and trees encroaching on each other's domain. An accompanying trail guide points out some of the plant life around you, including prickly pear cactus and yucca.

Back on the road, continue to the junction with S. Dak. 87 and turn right, stopping at the **Prairie Dog Pullout** just after the turn. This is a good place to observe these once abundant rodents, who survive the predation of many natural enemies by their system of scanning territory and warning their fellows of eminent danger. Your approach will probably set off a cacophony of barks. If you stay in the car, you'll have more to watch; cars don't spook the prairie dogs but people do. At dawn or dusk, watch the outskirts of the prairie dog town for patrolling coyotes.

The road now climbs from the prairie into the higher ponderosa pine forests that cover much of the Black Hills. Stop at the **Ancient Foundations Pullout** to learn about the granite core of the Black Hills. Other pullouts show how various kinds of plants and animals coexist in this dynamic prairie-forest border area.

Turn right at the **Rankin Ridge Pullout** and follow the half-mile road to the trailhead. The **Rankin Ridge Trail,** a 1-mile loop,

Black-tailed prairie dogs with bison, Wind Cave National Park

climbs up among the pines to a fire tower. In summer, you can climb the tower for a great view.

Back in the car, return to the main road and continue to the park's north entrance to complete the tour. Those with maneuverable vehicles may wish to make a loop by turning right on unpaved Park Rd. 5. This road connects with Park Rd. 6 and then Co. Rd. 101; it takes you through pronghorn and bison territory. Turn right on Co. Rd. 101 to return to US 385 south of the park.

INFORMATION & ACTIVITIES

Headquarters
Hot Springs, SD 57747
605-745-4600
www.nps.gov/wica

Visitor & Information Centers
Visitor center located 11 miles from Hot Springs on US 385; both it and the cave open all year. A variety of tours are offered daily year-round, though less often in the off-season.

Seasons & Accessibility
Open year-round.

Entrance Fees
None. Fees for cave tours: $6–$20 for adults; ages 6–16, $3.

Facilities for Disabled
The visitor center and a cave tour are wheelchair accessible.

Things to Do
Naturalist-led activities: a variety of cave tours, nature walks, campfire talks. Also, interpretive exhibits, scenic drive, nature trails, hiking, bicycling, wildlife-watching. Note: Children must be 8 years old for the Candlelight Tour and 16 years for the Wild Caving Tour.

Overnight Backpacking
Permits required; free at visitor center.

Campgrounds
One campground, 14-day limit. Fees $10 per night mid-May to mid-September; $5 per night April to mid-May and mid-September to late October, with reduced services. Closed remainder of year. First come, first served. Tent and RV sites; no hookups or showers.

Hotels, Motels, & Inns
(Unless otherwise noted, rates are for two persons in a double room, high season.)

In Custer, SD 57730:
- **Bavarian Inn Motel** P.O. Box 152. 605-673-2802 or 800-657-4312. 65 units, 1 condo. $70-$120. AC, pool, restaurant.
- **Best Western Buffalo Ridge Inn** 224 W. Mt. Rushmore Rd. 605-673-2275. 87 units. $89. Pool, restaurant.
- **Comfort Inn & Suites** 301 W. Mt. Rushmore Rd. 605-673-3221. 83 units. $69-$235. AC, pool.
- **Custer Days Inn** 519 Crook St. 605-673-4500. 48 units. $65-$129. Restaurant.
- **Dakota Cowboy Inn** 208 W. Mt. Rushmore Rd. 605-673-4659 or 800-279-5079. 48 units. $70-$155. AC, pool, restaurant. Open May to early October.

Pronghorn, Wind Cave National Park

In Hot Springs, SD 57747:
■ **Best Value Inn by the River**
602 W. River St. 605-745-4292
or 888-605-4292. 31 units. $35-
$109. AC, pool.
■ **Comfort Inn Hot Springs** 737
S, Sixth St. 605-745-7378.
51 units. $59-$209. AC, pool.
■ **Historic Braun Hotel** 902
N. River St. 605-745-3187.
11 units. $85. AC, restaurant.
■ **Super 8 Motel** 415 W. Mt.
Rushmore Rd. 605-673-2200.
54 units. $50-$79. Restaurant.

In Rapid City, SD 57701:
■ **Holiday In Rushmore Plaza**
505 N. Fifth St. 605-348-4000.
205 units. $79-$250. AC, pool,
tennis courts.
■ **Radisson Hotel Rapid City**
445 Mt. Rushmore Rd. 605-
348-8300. 177 units. $114-$144.
AC, pool, restaurant.

Also, write or phone adjacent
Custer State Park for information about its lodges: HC 83
Box 70, Custer, SD 57730. 605-
255-4515 or 800-710-2267.

Excursions from Wind Cave

Black Hills National Forest

10 miles
west of
Wind Cave

The Black Hills earned their name—originally Paha Sapa, Lakota for "hills that are black"—from the way that they appear so intensely dark from a distance. Considering that this is due primarily to the abundant cover of pine trees, which after a century-plus of fire suppression are more abundant than they were in the 1800s, the hills are probably "blacker" today than they've ever been.

Most folks associate the Black Hills with popular tourist attractions like **Mount Rushmore National Memorial;** indeed, the main roads of the Black Hills National Forest are often clogged in summer nearly bumper to bumper with vehicles. Those main arteries of pavement, however, provide access to a terrific network of low-traffic, all-weather gravel roads, the "veins" of the national forest, which in turn link up with a system of "capillaries": literally hundreds of miles of rarely used unimproved roads and old four-wheel-drive tracks. It's a fact that most people tend to go where everyone else goes when visiting destinations such as this, and total solitude can often be found merely a few hundred yards away from a main road.

The climate of the Black Hills is like a blend of the moist, warm upper Midwest, the hotter and drier western plains, and the relatively cool Rocky Mountains. Plant and animal species common to regions both east and west of here can be found in the Hills' mosaic of mixed-grass prairie, wet prairie, northern coniferous forest, Rocky Mountain coniferous forest, and eastern deciduous forest. Of South Dakota's nearly 1,600 plant species, all but around 300 are at home in the Black Hills. In the mix of habitats thrive large animals like pronghorn, white-tailed and mule deer, elk, mountain goats, and bighorn sheep. A few of the winged things that live in the Black Hills year-round include mallard, northern goshawks, golden eagles, and owls such as the great horned, eastern screech-, and northern saw-whet.

A complete book could be dedicated to the recreational opportunities of the immense Black Hills National Forest. Consider the statistics: 30 campgrounds, a dozen reservoirs (no natural lakes), over 13,000 acres of wilderness, and several hundred miles of trails. Regard the following as a primer, then, a recipe for getting your feet wet and helping you to discover further adventures.

Mount Rushmore, Black Hills National Forest

The 18-mile **Spearfish Canyon Scenic Byway** is a scenic and recreational highlight at the northern end of the Black Hills National Forest. With its high walls of, from bottom to top, Deadwood shale (it's brown and multilayered), Englewood limestone (pink to reddish), and the thickest layer of all, Paha Sapa limestone (buff colored to weathered gray), the canyon is nothing short of spectacular. That's particularly true in the fall, when the canyon floor and high ledges are embellished with rainbows of turning aspen trees and colorful shrubs such as red-osier dogwood.

To get there, take US 14A exit off I-90 at Spearfish, then go west and turn left after 1.5 miles, near the golf course. After a mile-plus you'll see a kiosk on the right where you can obtain information on the byway.

Continuing south, you'll enter the Black Hills National Forest in a couple of miles; then, 10 miles from there, turn west at Savoy to enter Little Spearfish Canyon. From the parking area of tidy **Roughlock Falls picnic area,** located a mile up the canyon, you can stroll about 100 yards to an impressive overlook on the falls, a lovely, lushly vegetated scene of water tumbling over bedrock.

After returning to US 14A and driving another 5.5 miles, you'll come to Cheyenne Crossing and the southern terminus of the scenic byway—but not the end of the scenery, by any means. To explore a sampling of the previously mentioned all-weather gravel roads, go about 4 miles east and turn south onto FR 17.

After about 6 miles on FR 17 you'll see the **Dumont Trailhead,** the highest point on the **Mickelson Trail** *(see feature pp. 288–89).* The open hay country you're traversing, embraced as it is by quaking aspen groves, is evocative of the high-elevation "parks" of Colorado. At about 10 miles you'll part ways with the Mickelson Trail as it follows a separate drainage, then rejoin it some 5 miles later after you're spit out of Irish Gulch and into the intriguing little settlement of Rochford.

Rochford, established 1878, as well as some of the colorful encampments you'll pass over the next few miles, are more like what you'd to see in Appalachia, perhaps, than in the Black Hills. After crossing a watershed divide, you'll again rejoin the Mickelson Trail at the spot on the map known as Mystic, then more or less parallel the trail the rest of the way to Hill City. Not far south of Mystic you'll see **Deerfield Trail No. 40** on the right. It's a top-notch, 18-mile-long trail that connects Deerfield Lake *(6 miles W of this point)* and Pactola Reservoir, and also makes possible a link between the Mickelson Trail and the **Centennial Trail** *(see feature pp. 288–89).* Veer left a little less than 6 miles beyond that trailhead, then proceed another 5.5 miles to Hill City.

Jewel Cave National Monument *(605-673-2288. www.nps.gov/jeca)* is entirely surrounded by Black Hills National Forest lands. To find it, from Hill City travel south to Custer, en route passing the immense **Crazy Horse Memorial,** which one day will rival Mount Rushmore as an impressive sculpture and tourist attraction. From Custer go 13 miles west on US 16 to the monument entrance and stop first at the visitor center *(open year-round).* After getting oriented, you can take either a 1.25-hour scenic tour of **Jewel Cave,** a 1.75-hour lantern tour, or a more intensive and involved, 4-hour spelunking tour into an undeveloped part of the cave. *(Call to make tour reservation before arriving. Fee)* The third longest known cave in the world, Jewel's name stems from its chambers brimming with calcite crystals, which glimmer like gems when light is shone on them.

The area around **Sylvan Lake** *(about 6 miles N of Custer)* holds one of the best concentrations of foot trails in the Black Hills National Forest. From here, paths lead into the forest's 13,426-acre **Black Elk Wilderness,** where destinations include the lookout tower atop **Harney Peak,** the highest point in the contiguous United States east of the Rockies, at 7,242 feet.

A 4-mile outing beginning at the picnic area on the northeast side of Sylvan Lake combines the **Lakeshore Trail** and the **Sunday Gulch National Recreation Trail.** It takes in some of the most fantastic terrain in the entire national forest. Parts of the trail are mellow, but other stretches are potentially treacherous, so the hike is not for everyone. Adding to the steep, boulder-strewn character of the trail, creek crossings may be difficult during high water, and ice can be present in shaded areas into late May or even early June. You may find it amazing that those responsible were able to construct a trail through such an impossible tangle of boulders, trees, and roots.

Begin by strolling onto the Lakeshore Trail, winding amid granite outcrops and passing the back of the dam holding Sylvan Lake in place. After half a mile you'll walk onto the Sunday Gulch trail, dropping steeply for nearly half a mile through an area of tricky footing; although handrails are provided for stability, some are broken or missing altogether. The rocks can be slick, too, in this wild setting of rock and ferns and the occasional deep trailside pool.

You'll enter a healthy looking forest supporting some huge conifers. Where you encounter a flight of 15 cement stairs, check for small trout in the pool to the left. You'll then cross under a power line, a rather unwelcome intruder in a setting that feels so wild. If you're lucky enough to be doing the hike on a sunny fall day, you'll see aspen leaves fluttering downward, glittering golden as they rock to and fro; meanwhile, the bubbling brook's sweet music somewhat compensates for the dearth of bird songs in the late season.

■ **1.2 million acres** ■ **Western South Dakota and northeastern Wyoming** ■ **Year-round** ■ **Hiking, canoeing, horseback riding, rock climbing, fishing, mountain biking, cross-country skiing, caving** ■ **Contact the national forest, 25041 N. Hwy. 16, Custer, SD 57730; 605-673-9200. www.fs.fed.us/r2/blackhills/**

World-class Trails

The Black Hills are home to two of America's preeminent long-distance trails: the George S. Mickelson Trail and the Centennial Trail.

George S. Mickelson Trail

A gently graded path running the length of the rugged Black Hills sounds at first like an oxymoron, but the 114-mile Mickelson Trail is just that. The secret to finding a relatively flat route—it never exceeds a 4 percent grade—was to follow the former right-of-way of the Burlington Northern rail line that ran from Deadwood to Edgemont, at the south end of the Black Hills.

South Dakota's first rails-to-trails project, the Mickelson Trail is named for the state's late governor, a big supporter of the trail who died in a 1993 plane crash while still in office. Completed in autumn 1998, this showpiece passes through four hard-rock tunnels and over more than a hundred revamped railroad bridges. Its 14 trailheads are equipped with parking areas, toilets, picnic tables, and self-service trail-pass stations. The crushed-stone surface makes it suitable for hiking, horseback riding, and mountain biking; additionally, cross-country skiing is popular in winter. Ranging in elevation from around 3,500 feet to over 6,000 feet, the trail is closed to motorized use, except for a short stretch between Deadwood and Dumont where snowmobiles are permitted in winter. Information: 605-584-3896 or www.mickelsontrail.com/.

Centennial Trail

At 111 miles in length, the Centennial Trail is much more rugged than the Mickelson Trail. From Bear Butte State Park, it winds southward through mixed-grass prairie before climbing into the heart of the Black Hills and terminating at Wind Cave National Park.

Hiking is permitted on the entire trail; horses are excluded only from the extreme northern part in Bear Butte State Park and the extreme south, within Wind Cave National Park; mountain biking is permitted everywhere except where horses are excluded and on the section of the trail passing through the Black Elk Wilderness. Motorized vehicles are banned, with one exception: a brief stretch between the Pilot Knob and Dalton Trailheads. Tent camping is available at many locations along the trail, making it

Cathedral Spires, Custer State Park

popular for multiday backpacking and horsepacking trips.

The Centennial is also known as Trail No. 89, a reference to South Dakota's centennial year of 1989, which the trail commemorates. A trip along its length, where you'll encounter elevations ranging from 3,200 feet to 5,600 feet, reveals up close and personal the Black Hills' surprising diversity, from hidden canyons and tall granite towers to open grasslands, wet meadows, and old-growth forests. Information (Wind Cave National Park): 605-745-4600.

Custer State Park

Adjacent to Wind Cave National Park

Nestled within and adjacent to the southeastern Black Hills, Custer State Park (adjoining Wind Cave National Park) presents a panoply of opportunities for exploring, both inside the car and well out of sight of any roads. The park is an appealing mix of the wild and the civilized, with 71,000 acres of largely undeveloped lands, but also featuring four resorts with amenities such as cabins, lodges, and fine dining. The park's bison herd of nearly 1,500 animals is one of the largest in existence. Elk, bighorn sheep, mountain goats, and pronghorn are a few of the other large animals found in the park, along with the irresistibly cute burros descending from a herd that was brought in to carry visitors of an earlier day up Harney Peak.

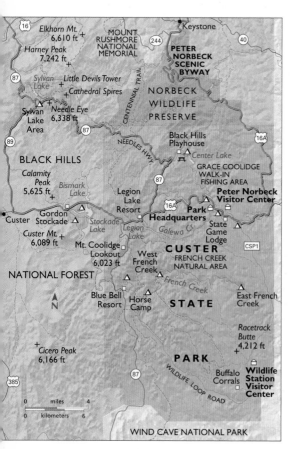

Beginning at Sylvan Lake in the extreme northwest corner of Custer State Park, drive southeast on S. Dak. 87. The next 14 miles of highway known as the **Needles Highway** make up part of the longer **Peter Norbeck Scenic Byway,** named for the South Dakota governor and U.S. senator who spearheaded the 1919 establishment of Custer State Park, and who traveled by foot and horseback to survey the routes now bearing his name. The Needles Highway is the epitome of a winding mountain road, with countless tight turns and some tiny, steering-wheel-gripping, hard-rock tunnels (as low as 11.5 feet and as narrow as 8.5 feet).

About 1 mile after leaving Sylvan Lake, just before tunnel number one, pull off to the right to take in the overlook encompassing the Needles Eye formation and a portion of the greater Precambrian heart of the Black Hills. Just up the road to the left you'll see a small pullout for a trailhead; from here, by way of the awesome **Cathedral Spires,** a strenuous 1.5-mile (one way) route gaining 1,000 feet of elevation. The trail, along which you might see some of the park's all-white mountain goats, also passes through the mile-square **Limber Pine Natural Area,** which holds the only known stand of limber pine in the Black Hills.

At the junction with US 16A, a westerly turn will take you past Legion Lake Resort *(camping, lodging, mountain bike rentals. 605-255-4521),* then to a junction where you can turn south to continue on S. Dak. 87. On this road you'll crest a high divide separating the Galena Creek and French Creek watersheds; you'll see that quite a lot of logging has taken place in the recent past in the vicinity of the pass. Nearby you can leave the highway to drive about a mile on gravel to the **Mount Coolidge Lookout,** a Civilian Conservation Corps-built rock beauty that stands 6,023 feet above sea level and proffers a panorama taking in, among much else, the Badlands nearly 100 miles to the east. The road then descends from the summit and continues to the Blue Bell Resort (camping, lodging), where guided horseback trail rides, including overnight pack trips, are an option *(605-255-4531).* Watch for bighorn sheep on and around the road as you drive.

Alternatively, an easterly turn at the above-mentioned S. Dak. 87/US 16A junction takes you past the grand and venerable State Game Lodge (camping, lodging) and the nearby Peter Norbeck Visitor Center *(April–Nov.).* Among the many activities available at the State Game Lodge is the popular **Buffalo Safari** *(605-255-4541),* a Serengeti-like Jeep tour hosted by an interpretive guide. Just east of there, turn south onto CSP 1, the **Wildlife Loop Road,** along which you can expect to encounter bison, pronghorn, and many other critters. After about 4 miles on the CSP 1, a quarter mile up a gravel road to the right is the trailhead for the **French Creek Natural Area.** The trail running westerly from here to a point 3 miles from the Blue Bell Resort passes through a rugged and relatively undisturbed swatch of the Black Hills with steep gorge walls.

Prairie Dog Primer

The quintessential rodent of the plains, the heavy-bodied prairie dog, with its large eyes and small tails, always gets smiles as it pokes its head up through the ground, taking a look around. But they're more than cute—they contribute much to their prairie home.

Their simple act of burrowing holes, for example, provides homes to many other creatures, including burrowing owls, rabbits, snakes, and insects. Burrowing also loosens the soil, priming it for plant growth.

Prairie dogs are part of the greater prairie food chain, providing nourishment for coyotes, prairie falcons, rattlesnakes, black-footed ferrets, and badgers.

A sociable group, prairie dogs live in prairie dog towns, or colonies, which can range from one to more than 1,000 acres. Each town is subdivided into neighborhoods called "wards." Wards are further broken down into family groups, or "coteries." Each coterie is made up of an adult male, between one and four adult females, and any offspring younger than two years old.

Prairie dogs take advantage of the cool hours of the day to visit and groom, as well as to feed on grass and herbs. When they are out and about, a sentry perches on the ring around the burrow and watches for predators. If danger is spotted, he emits a "take heed" bark; when danger is cleared, he sends out the all-clear bark.

Black-tailed prairie dog, Custer State Park

■ 71,000 acres ■ Southwestern South Dakota ■ Year-round ■ Camping,
hiking, horseback riding, biking, cross-country skiing, caving ■ Adm. fee
■ Contact the park, HC 83 Box 70, Custer, SD 57730; 605-255-4515 or
605-255-4464. www.sdgf.info/parks/regions/custer/index

Bear Butte State Park

50 miles north of Wind Cave

Long before nearby Sturgis became a destination for hordes of leather-clad pilgrims riding Harleys, Bear Butte was a sacred place to Plains Indians, large numbers of whom still travel here to hold ceremonies, seek visions, and gather plants for food and medicine. The isolated rhyolite mountain, an igneous intrusion that was uncovered by the erosion of overlying shales, was known to the Lakota Sioux as Mato Paha, or "bear mountain." With its trio of subpeaks, Bear Butte appears like an entire mini-mountain range.

Beginning from the trailhead located above the small interpretive center *(May–Sept.)* are a pair of **hiking trails,** one leading to an American Indian ceremonial area and the other winding 1,000 vertical feet to the butte's 4,426-foot summit. On a clear day, the view from the top is nearly infinite, taking in the plains of four states and, to the south, the Black Hills, which ripple away in ever higher ridges. Watch as you climb for critters like badgers, yellow-bellied marmots, and 13-lined ground squirrels; and for birds such as evening grosbeaks, western Meadowlarks, and northern harriers. Far below, a small bison herd grazes at the base of the mountain. Star lily and prairie rose are among the wildflowers that brighten things up in summer, competing with the hundreds of colorful ceremonial offerings—corn, tobacco ties, prayer cloths, and more—that Indians have hung from tree limbs and shrubbery.

Bear Butte State Park is also the northern trailhead for the 111-mile **Centennial Trail** *(see feature pp. 288–89),* one of the country's preeminent long-distance hiking trails. The rugged trail delves into the heart of the Black Hills before surfacing at Wind Cave National Park.

■ 2,000 acres ■ West-central South Dakota ■ Hiking ■ Best seasons
spring and fall ■ Adm. fee ■ Contact the park, P.O. Box 688, Sturgis, SD
57785; 605-347-5240. www.state.sd.us/gfp/sdparks/bearbutt/bearbutt.htm

Yellowstone

A geological smoking gun, Yellowstone reminds us of how violent the Earth can be. One event overshadows all others: Some 600,000 years ago, an area many miles square at what is now the center of the park suddenly exploded. In minutes the landscape was devastated. Fast-moving ash flows covered thousands of square miles. At the center there remained only a smoldering caldera, a collapsed crater 28 by 47 miles. At least two other cataclysmic events preceded this one. Boiling hot springs, fumaroles, and geysers serve as reminders that another could occur.

Yellowstone, however, is much more than hot ground and gushing steam. Located astride the Continental Divide, most of the park occupies a high plateau surrounded by mountains and drained by several rivers. Park boundaries enclose craggy peaks, alpine lakes, deep canyons, and vast forests. In 1872, Yellowstone became the world's first national park, the result of great foresight about our eventual need for the solace and beauty of wild places.

In early years, what made Yellowstone stand out was the extravaganza of geysers and hot springs. As the West was settled, however, Yellowstone's importance as a wildlife sanctuary grew. The list of park animals is a compendium of Rocky Mountain fauna: elk, bison, mule deer, bighorn sheep, grizzly bear, black bear, moose, pronghorn, coyote, mountain lion, beaver, trumpeter swan, eagle, osprey, white pelican, and many more.

During the summer of 1988, fire touched many sections of the park, in some areas dramatically changing the appearance of the landscape. Yet not one major feature was destroyed. The geysers, waterfalls, and herds of wildlife are still here. Many places show no impact at all, while those that are regenerating benefit both vegetation and animal life. Side by side, burned areas and nonburned areas provide an intriguing study in the causes and effects of fire in wild places.

- Wyoming, Idaho, and Montana
- 2.2 million acres
- Established 1872
- Best seasons spring–fall
- Camping, hiking, geyser walks, wolf- and bear-watching
- Information: 307-344-7381 www.nps.gov/yell

Great Fountain Geyser, along Yellowstone's Firehole Lake Drive

How to Get There

There are five entrances: from the west, West Yellowstone (Montana); from the north and northeast, Gardiner and Cooke City (Montana); from the east on US 14/16/20, Cody (Wyoming); and from the south, Flagg Ranch (Wyoming), which is north of Grand Teton National Park and Jackson (64 miles away). Airports: West Yellowstone (*summer only*), Bozeman, and Billings, Mont.; Cody and Jackson, Wyo.

When to Go

More than half of the three million annual visitors come in July and August. In September and early October, the weather is good, the visitors

What Not to Miss

- Watch Old Faithful Geyser, then walk into Upper Geyser Basin

- Visit Excelsior Geyser at Midway Geyser Basin

- Drive north through park and visit Mammoth Hot Springs' steaming terraces

- Check out great views of Yellowstone River and Falls on Canyon Rim Drive

- Spot wildlife on Hayden Valley Road. A good picnic spot is Gull Point.

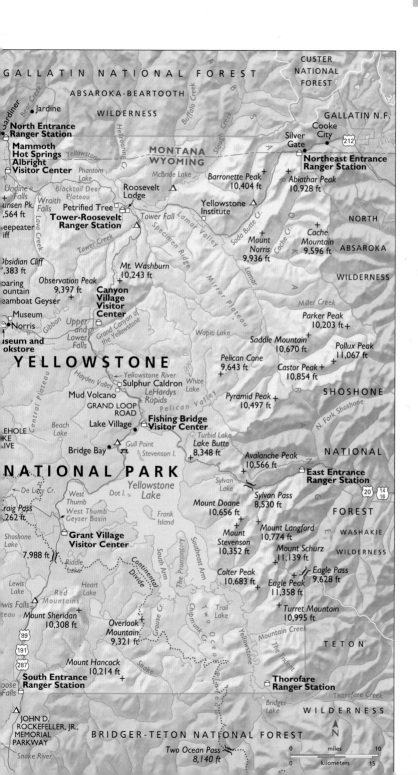

GALLATIN NATIONAL FOREST

CUSTER NATIONAL FOREST

ABSAROKA-BEARTOOTH

WILDERNESS

Jardine

North Entrance Ranger Station

Mammoth Hot Springs
Albright Visitor Center

MONTANA
WYOMING

Silver Gate

Cooke City

GALLATIN N.F.

212

Northeast Entrance Ranger Station

Phantom Lake

McBride Lake

Barronette Peak 10,404 ft

Abiathar Peak 10,928 ft

Undine Falls
Wraith Falls
Bunsen Pk.
,564 ft
Undine
,iff

Blacktail Deer Plateau

Roosevelt Lodge

Yellowstone Institute

NORTH

Petrified Tree

Tower-Roosevelt Ranger Station

Tower Fall

Lamar Valley

Soda Butte Cr.

Mount Norris 9,936 ft

Cache Mountain 9,596 ft

ABSAROKA

Obsidian Cliff
,383 ft

Roaring Mountain
Steamboat Geyser

Observation Peak 9,397 ft

Mt. Washburn 10,243 ft

Canyon Village Visitor Center

Specimen Ridge

Tower Creek

Mirror Plateau

Miller Creek

WILDERNESS

Parker Peak 10,203 ft

Museum
Norris

Gibbon

Upper and Lower Falls

Grand Canyon of the Yellowstone

Wapiti Lake

Saddle Mountain 10,670 ft

Pollux Peak 11,067 ft

useum and okstore

YELLOWSTONE

Hayden Valley

Yellowstone River

Pelican Cone 9,643 ft

Castor Peak 10,854 ft

SHOSHONE

Sulphur Caldron
LeHardys Rapids

White Lake

Pelican Valley

Pyramid Peak 10,497 ft

Mud Volcano

GRAND LOOP ROAD

Lake Village

Fishing Bridge Visitor Center

Turbid Lake

Lake Butte 8,348 ft

N. Fork Shoshone

EHOLE KE IVE

Beach Lake

Bridge Bay

Gull Point

Stevenson I.

Avalanche Peak 10,566 ft

NATIONAL

NATIONAL PARK

Yellowstone Lake

Sylvan Lake

East Entrance Ranger Station

De Lacy Cr.

West Thumb

Dot I.

20

14 16

raig Pass
,262 ft

West Thumb Geyser Basin

Frank Island

Mount Doane 10,656 ft

Sylvan Pass 8,530 ft

FOREST

Shoshone Lake
7,988 ft

Grant Village Visitor Center

Riddle Lake

Mount Stevenson 10,352 ft

Mount Langford 10,774 ft

Mount Schurz 11,139 ft

WASHAKIE

WILDERNESS

Lewis Lake

Red Mountains

Heart Lake

Continental Divide

South Arm

The Promontory

Southeast Arm

Colter Peak 10,683 ft

Eagle Peak 11,358 ft

Eagle Pass 9,628 ft

wis Falls
teau

Mount Sheridan 10,308 ft

Overlook Mountain 9,321 ft

Grouse Cr.

Trail Lake

Turret Mountain 10,995 ft

Chipmunk Cr.

Two Ocean Plateau

89

191

287

Mount Hancock 10,214 ft

South Entrance Ranger Station

Snake River

Yellowstone

Mountain Creek

The Trident

TETON

Thorofare Ranger Station

Thorofare Creek

oose Falls

JOHN D. ROCKEFELLER, JR., MEMORIAL PARKWAY

Snake River

BRIDGER-TETON NATIONAL FOREST

Two Ocean Pass 8,140 ft

Bridger Lake

WILDERNESS

N

miles
0   10

kilometers
0   15

few, and the wildlife abundant. In May and June, you can see newborn animals, but the weather may be cold, wet, and even snowy. From about November through April most park roads are closed to vehicles. During the winter season, mid-December to mid-March, Yellowstone becomes a fantasy of steam and ice; facilities are limited but sufficient. Only the road between the North and Northeast Entrances stays open to cars, but snowmobiling is permitted on unplowed roads. Heated snow coaches offer tours and give cross-country skiers access to about 50 miles of groomed trails.

How to Visit

The 142-mile **Grand Loop Road** forms a figure eight, with connecting spurs to the five entrances. In early years, visitors took a week going around the loop—still a good idea. On any visit, start with the geyser basins and **Mammoth Hot Springs** to see wildlife and thermal features. On the second day, travel to the **Grand Canyon of the Yellowstone, Hayden Valley,** and **Yellowstone Lake.**

On a longer stay, visit the **Northern Range,** or consider a boating or fishing trip on Yellowstone Lake; a backcountry excursion on foot or horse; or any of the easy nature trails.

Bison crossing a stream of hot springs water

EXPLORING THE PARK

Old Faithful to Mammoth: 51 miles; a full day

Begin by leaving your car in the parking lot at **Old Faithful.** Check at the visitor center for predicted eruption times of the major geysers. While there, pick up an Upper Geyser Basin map *(also available from area dispensers).* Wait on benches near the visitor center for the eruption of Old Faithful (named and celebrated for its steadiness rather than a predictable schedule of eruptions) or walk the path that circles it. Almost any point along the path offers a good view of the eruption, so don't worry if you're not at the benches when it happens.

You can see from here that Old Faithful is not alone. The mile-long **Upper Geyser Basin** contains the world's greatest concentration of hot springs and geysers. Try to allow a minimum of 2 hours to see more of it. This must be done on foot, but trails are easy and diversions many. The best choice is to start from the back side of Old Faithful, on the trail that crosses the **Firehole River** to **Geyser Hill,** and follow the map (or your nose; you can't get lost here). You can cross the river at several points and return on the other side, making the walk as long or short as you like. You'll pass dozens of colorful boiling springs and delicate formations of geyserite, a silicate mineral deposited by hot water. Chances are good to see one or more geysers erupt at short range. Keep an eye out for elk and bison. **Morning Glory Pool,** named for its resemblance to the flower, marks the far end of the basin.

Back in your car, drive north. **Black Sand Basin** is worth a quick stop, but bypass Biscuit Basin. The road follows the Firehole River several miles to **Midway Geyser Basin,** where a 20-minute stroll on the boardwalk takes you past the enormous crater of **Excelsior Geyser.** It erupted for 2 days in 1985. A huge boiling vat, it produces about 4,000 gallons of scalding water each minute. The boardwalk continues across the delicate terraces of **Grand Prismatic Spring,** 370 feet wide, the largest and most beautiful hot spring in the park. The bright colors are caused by algae and bacteria, different types of which thrive in different water temperatures.

Two miles farther, turn right on the one-way **Firehole Lake Drive** to **Great Fountain Geyser.** Check the prediction board for the estimated time of eruption. Great Fountain goes off every 11 hours or so. If you have the time, wait. This eruption is one of the best. A bit farther along is **White Dome Geyser.** Its cone may be massive, but its eruption is a thin spray. Perhaps centuries ago it had more power. Yellowstone is always changing.

Rejoin the main road at **Fountain Paint Pot,** a cauldron of hot reddish-pinkish mud, blooping and spitting—always entertaining. Any hot spring could become a mud pot with the right balance of acidity, moisture, and clay; however, a constant flow of water keeps most springs clear.

For the next few miles, rest your eyes on meadows and forest. Look for bison on **Fountain Flat;** also for purple-colored western fringed gentian, the park flower. **Fountain Flat Drive** is closed to vehicles 1 mile from the main road. But it's open to visitors walking to **Goose Lake,** a peaceful picnic site. The Firehole River, warmed by hot water from springs and geysers along its course, flows through the meadows and along the main road before dropping into a canyon with nice waterfalls; to see them, turn left on **Firehole Canyon Drive** just before Madison Junction.

At Madison, a left turn follows the Madison River to the West Entrance, but stay on the road to **Norris.** In this area, the fires of 1988 burned extensively. Their effects—the jagged sweeps of charred lodgepole pine forest—will be visible for a long time. However, millions of new lodgepole pines have since grown back (the fires' heat released seedlings from cones on the forest floor). And, because the fires moved erratically, the burned areas are not far from unburned areas, another source of seeds for regrowth.

The road climbs beside the **Gibbon River** to **Gibbon Falls** and continues through the **Gibbon Canyon** and large meadows, where elk are commonly seen, to Norris.

Norris Geyser Basin contains the hottest ground in the park, as well as the world's tallest geyser, **Steamboat.** The geyser's eruptions are infrequent and unpredictable; it may stay quiet for years at a time. Steamboat last erupted on April 26, 2002, the second time since October 2, 1991. Contrast its sleepy behavior with that of **Echinus,** which goes off about every 40 to 80 minutes, an easy show to witness.

Highlights of the drive north include the steamy fumaroles of **Roaring Mountain** that snore rather than roar and **Obsidian Cliff,** an outcrop containing black volcanic glass that was valued for arrowpoints by Native Americans throughout the area. The road crosses **Gardners Hole,** with nice views of the Gallatin Range to the west, and drops toward Mammoth through **Golden Gate,**

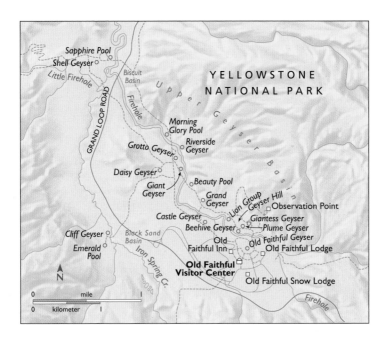

Sapphire Pool
Shell Geyser
Biscuit Basin
Little Firehole
Firehole
GRAND LOOP ROAD
YELLOWSTONE
NATIONAL PARK
Upper
Geyser
Basin
Morning Glory Pool
Riverside Geyser
Grotto Geyser
Daisy Geyser
Giant Geyser
Beauty Pool
Grand Geyser
Lion Group
Geyser Hill
Observation Point
Castle Geyser
Giantess Geyser
Beehive Geyser
Plume Geyser
Cliff Geyser
Black Sand Basin
Old Faithful Geyser
Old Faithful Inn
Old Faithful Lodge
Emerald Pool
Iron Spring Cr.
Old Faithful Visitor Center
N
Old Faithful Snow Lodge
Firehole
0   mile   1
0   kilometer   1

cliffs gilded with the bright yellow lichen that grows on them.

At **Mammoth Hot Springs** you can drive or walk around the dozens of colorful steaming terraces. They are made of travertine—calcium carbonate—which the hot water brings to the surface from beds of limestone. The formations look quite different from the silica-based geyserite deposits seen elsewhere in the park. The park's headquarters and largest visitor center are at Mammoth. The North Entrance is located 5 miles down the Gardiner River Canyon.

Canyon to West Thumb: 37 miles; at least a half day

From the Canyon Village Visitor Center, follow the one-way **Canyon Rim Drive** to lookout points for great views of the canyon and the Yellowstone River's 308-foot **Lower Falls,** nearly twice as high as Niagara. The bright yellow, orange, and red of the canyon walls are caused by heat and chemical action on gray or brown rhyolite rock.

Walk the rim trail from **Inspiration Point** to **Grandview Point** for the best look at the canyon's natural grandeur. Also consider the paved but strenuous **Brink of the Lower Falls Trail,** which descends several hundred feet through steep forest. Standing beside the

Hayden Valley, one of Yellowstone's most promising sites for spotting wildlife

green river where it suddenly drops into space is one of the most exciting experiences in the park.

Continue south on the main road. The **Upper Falls** are, at 109 feet, almost as impressive as the Lower Falls and easier to reach. A short trail leads to **Upper Falls View.** Half a mile farther south, a side road crosses the river to **Artist Point,** the best overall view of the canyon.

Upriver, the Yellowstone flows gently through the sage-covered hills of **Hayden Valley.** Go slowly and stop often in the roadside parking areas; this is prime wildlife country. American white pelicans and trumpeter swans share the river with Canada geese, gulls, and ducks. Bison are visible most of the year. Keep your distance. Use binoculars to check meadows across the river for grizzlies digging for roots or rodents. Grizzlies are often seen in the open; black bears, their smaller, shier relations, rarely. But be careful not to surprise one; both are dangerous.

Well-named **Mud Volcano** and **Black Dragon's Caldron** are not pretty to look at, but they are impressive. Springs in this area have been known to hurl football-size blobs of mud tens of feet. From here to the lake, the Yellowstone River provides excellent catch-and-release fishing for cutthroat trout. At **Lehardys Rapids** in June you can watch cutthroat jumping on their way to spawning grounds *(no fishing allowed)*. Look for trout also at **Fishing Bridge** *(no fishing allowed)* where the river flows out of the lake. Two miles farther east is **Pelican Valley,** a lush lakeside meadow where you might find moose or white pelicans.

Return to the loop road, following the shore of **Yellowstone Lake** most of the next 21 miles. This is the largest lake in North America above 7,000 feet. The volcanic **Absaroka Range,** visible across the blue waters, define the park's eastern boundary.

Bison frequent the meadows near **Bridge Bay,** while moose favor ponds along the **Gull Point Road.** Gull Point is a good picnic site.

West Thumb, almost a separate lake, is a water-filled caldera created by an eruption about 150,000 years ago, a smaller version of the great Yellowstone caldera. A boardwalk leads around the **West Thumb Geyser Basin,** a modest group of thermal features made charming by its location beside the lake.

Northern Range: 47 miles; a half to a full day

Between Mammoth Hot Springs and Cooke City, Yellowstone is warmer and drier than the interior. Called the Northern Range for its importance as wintering ground for large animals, this area is characterized by sagebrush and grassy valleys. Open all year, the

Life among Algae Mats and Hot Springs

A self-contained life system exists in the steamy warmth of hot spring outflow channels. Filamentous bacteria, growing in long, hairlike strands, join with mats of colored algae to provide food for brine flies. If you look close, you'll see little orange spots on some of the flies; these are parasitic mites. The flies are also preyed upon by fast-moving spiders and avian invaders such as killdeer. Even in winter, temperatures near the ground stay warm enough to support what is in effect a natural terrarium. Nearby, in steam-heated hollows, leafy plants stay green, sometimes blooming even in January. Look for yellow monkey flowers that hug the edges of hot streams.

To Tower Fall ↑

GRAND LOOP
ROAD

OLD CHITTENDEN ROAD

N

Trailhead 8,753 ft

Y E L L O W S T O N E

N A T I O N A L

MOUNT
WASHBURN
TRAIL

P A R K

MOUNT
WASHBURN
10,243 ft

To
Grand
Canyon
of the
Yellowstone

Dunraven
Pass
8,859 ft

To
Canyon
Village

0   mile   0.5
0   kilometer   0.5

road from Mammoth starts with a drive through mixed meadows and forests above the **Black Canyon of the Yellowstone River;** look for trumpeter swans in seasonal wetlands. Take the **Blacktail Plateau Drive,** stopping often to scan the hills for wildlife, including grizzly bears and elk.

Turn left at Tower-Roosevelt, cross the Yellowstone, and continue east around the northern end of **Specimen Ridge,** which contains the world's largest fossil forest. More than a hundred plant species, including redwoods, are found in 27 layers of volcanic ash from repeated eruptions 50 million years ago. Today, its slopes and the wide-open grasslands of the **Lamar Valley** provide some of the best wildlife viewing in Yellowstone, especially during spring when grizzly bears and wolves concentrate in the area to prey on elk calves. Drive slowly through the Lamar Valley from the Slough Creek turnoff to Soda Butte Creek, stopping often at roadside turnouts to scan the hillsides. The park's most easily spotted wolves, the Druid pack, live in and around the Lamar Valley. At dawn and dusk, they are often seen from the road. But if you miss the wolves, you are almost certain to see pronghorn and herds of bison, and, in winter and spring, large herds of elk. Here, too: coyotes, bald eagles, ospreys, black bears, and grizzlies.

Hiking, Fishing, & Boating

More than 1,000 miles of trails lead to wilderness valleys, mountaintops, lakes, and thermal basins. Take horses and a guide for a week-long trip, or go on foot for an hour or 2. Even a short walk can put you in a wilderness setting beyond roads and crowds. Ask for recommended hikes at any visitor center.

The best single overview of Yellowstone awaits atop **Mount Washburn,** south of the Tower Fall area. Two moderate trails, each about 3 miles long, reach the summit via abandoned roads *(see map, opposite);* one starts from **Dunraven Pass,** the other from the **Old Chittenden Road,** 5 miles farther north.

Yellowstone offers fine trout fishing, especially for those carrying fly rods. A fishing permit is required *(fee),* available at visitor centers and ranger stations. Regulations are complicated and are often different for separate sections of any given stream. Guide services are available at fishing shops in surrounding communities.

Motorboating is permitted on most of Yellowstone Lake and Lewis Lake; passenger boats operate from **Bridge Bay Marina** for sightseeing and fishing. Other lakes are limited to hand-propelled craft. Rivers and streams are closed to all boating to avoid disturbing wildlife; an exception is the channel between **Lewis** and **Shoshone Lakes,** where paddlers are permitted.

Canoeing into remote Shoshone Lake

INFORMATION & ACTIVITIES

Headquarters
P.O. Box 168
Yellowstone NP, WY 82190
307-344-7381
www.nps.gov/yell

Visitor & Information Centers
Albright Visitor Center at
Mammoth Hot Springs open
daily all year. Old Faithful Visitor Center open May through
October and mid-December to
mid-March. Canyon Village
Visitor Center and visitor
centers at Fishing Bridge and
Grant Village open May
through September.

Seasons & Accessibility
Park open year-round. Road
from North Entrance to Northeast Entrance open all year;
most other park roads closed to
cars November through April.
Call headquarters for latest
weather and road conditions.

Entrance Fees
$20 per vehicle, good for one
week at both Yellowstone and
Grand Teton. $40 annual.

Facilities for Disabled
Visitor centers; exhibits; Madison Canyon; Bridge Bay; Grant,
Lewis Lake, and Fishing Bridge
Campgrounds; most rest
rooms; amphitheaters; and
numerous ranger-led activities
and walks are wheelchair accessible. Free brochure available.

Things to Do
Free naturalist-led activities:
nature walks, camera walks,
evening programs. Also available: hiking, boating, fishing
(permit required), horseback
riding (stables at Roosevelt,
Canyon, and Mammoth), bicycling, stagecoach rides, courses
in natural history and photography, art exhibits, children's
activities, bus and boat tours,
snow-coach tours, cross-country skiing, ice-skating, snowshoeing, and snowmobiling.

Special Advisories
■ View large animals from a distance, or from inside your car.
■ Grizzly bears and bison are
particularly unpredictable and
very dangerous. Read and obey
all regulations.
■ Never hike alone. Make noise
when rounding blind curves or
topping hills, especially on
backcountry trails.
■ Stay on trails, especially in
thermal areas, where thin surfaces often cover scalding water.
■ Permits required for backcountry camping; free at visitor
centers and ranger stations,
apply in person within 48
hours of setting out, advance
reservations $15.

Campgrounds

Twelve campgrounds, all with 14-day limit (except Fishing Bridge RV Park) from May through October; other times 30-day limit. Mammoth open all year, others open late spring to mid-fall. Reservations accepted for Fishing Bridge RV Park, Madison, Grant Village, Canyon Village, and Bridge Bay; contact Xanterra Parks & Resorts, P.O. Box 165, Yellowstone NP, WY 82190. 307-344-7311. All others first come, first served. $10-$15. Fishing Bridge RV Park $29. Pay showers near several campgrounds. Both tent and RV sites at most campgrounds; at Fishing Bridge RV Park hard-sided units only. Hookups at Fishing Bridge RV Park only. For group campgrounds, reserve through Xanterra Parks & Resorts. Food services in park.

Hotels, Motels, & Inns

(Unless otherwise noted, rates are for two persons in a double room, high season.)

INSIDE THE PARK:
The following are operated by Xanterra Parks & Resorts, P.O. Box 165, Yellowstone NP, WY 82190. For reservations call 307-344-7311.

■ **Canyon Lodge** 613 cabins, 81 rooms. $44-$140. Restaurant.
■ **Grant Village** 300 units. $79-$112. Restaurant. Open May through September.
■ **Lake Lodge & Cabins** 186 units. $59-$119. Restaurant. Open June to mid-September.
■ **Lake Yellowstone Hotel & Cabins** 296 units. Hotel $109-$186; cabins $80-$99. Restaurant. Open mid-May through September.
■ **Mammoth Hot Springs Hotel & Cabins** 212 units. Hotel $49-$96; cabins $64-$91. Restaurant. Open May to October; December to early March.
■ **Old Faithful Inn** 327 units. $78-$185. Restaurant. Open early May to late October.
■ **Old Faithful Lodge & Cabins** 134 cabins. $55-$81. Open mid-May to late September.
■ **Old Faithful Snow Lodge & Cabins** 134 units. Lodge $156; cabins $80-$119. Restaurant. Open May to early November; December to March.
■ **Roosevelt Lodge & Cabins** 80 cabins. $156-$191. Restaurant. Open June to late August.

See also listings for Grand Teton National Park, p. 95.

Excursions from Yellowstone

Island Park Area

30 miles west of Yellowstone

Located along the western fringe of Yellowstone, the Island Park area encompasses a broad, nearly flat-floored volcanic crater, or caldera, cut from rim to rim by the handsome, trout-laden waters of the Henrys Fork River. It's a region of mostly gentle landscapes—restful, low-key, subtle yet seductive. Crystalline water bends across the wide sagebrush flats, passing shady copses of lodgepole pine. Marshy ponds nestle among the hollows and depressions, drawing moose, trumpeter swans, geese, and flotillas of young mergansers that dive in unison. Rolling hills and steep ridges, dark with evergreens, rise on all sides, and the distant but unmistakable crest of the **Teton Range** cuts across the southeastern skyline.

Through the caldera's heart flows the **Henrys Fork River,** a tributary of the Snake. It begins as a small stream flowing out of Henrys Lake (to the north of the caldera), surges to true river status after mingling with a huge freshwater spring, glides across the calderic floor, then breaks through masses of basalt along the caldera's south rim. Beyond, the river cuts through the rim of an older caldera, where it thunders over two major waterfalls.

Trumpeter swan

For a half-day outing, start 4 miles east of Macks Inn at **Big Springs,** a large, crystal clear pool tucked against a forested hillside. The springs puts out 120 million gallons of water a day. All that water flows as wide and as swift as a river over thick beds of monkey flower and watercress. An **interpretive trail** follows the glassy water downstream for at least a mile through lodgepole pine forests carpeted with grass and dotted with lupine, Indian paintbrush, and larkspur.

You can float over this luscious aquatic environment on the **Big Springs National Water Trail,** an easy, 4-mile trip that starts a mile below the springs and takes out just above Macks Inn. Traffic is limited to hand-operated light craft; you can rent a canoe or arrange a shuttle in town.

At the caldera's center, **Harriman State Park** takes in some of the most enticing stretches of the Henrys Fork and offers a tremendous variety of habitat and wildlife. Hiking, biking, and horseback riding trails, which loop through forest, meadow, and sagebrush flat, climb to the caldera's western rim, and hug the riverbank. At the end of the entrance road, an interpretive trail provides an overview of the region's geology and the park's major habitats: forest, marshes, wetlands, sagebrush flats, ponds, lakes, and riverbanks. Look for moose, elk, deer, pronghorn, beavers, muskrat, ospreys, bald eagles, and great blue herons.

A mile or so north of the Harriman entrance, pick up the **Mesa Falls Scenic Byway** (Idaho 47), a terrific 28-mile detour to Ashton that threads along the eastern slopes of the caldera and takes in Upper and Lower Mesa Falls—two of Idaho's few remaining undisturbed waterfalls. Separated by just a couple of miles and linked by a hiking trail, the two falls spill through a narrow gorge lined with colonnaded basalt walls. At **Upper Mesa Falls,** a network of walkways and viewing platforms zigzags down the cliffs to the very brink of the cascade, a wide curtain of concussive white water plunging 114 feet. **Lower Mesa Falls** is quite different, more of a funnel, with the full force of the river converging from three directions and dropping 70 feet through a narrow cleft.

■ **Eastern Idaho, main access at Harriman State Park off US 20, near town of Island Park** ■ **Camping, hiking, boating, fishing, mountain biking, horseback riding, bird-watching, wildlife viewing** ■ **Adm. fee for Harriman State Park** ■ **Contact Harriman State Park, HC66 Box 500, Island Park, ID 83429; 208-558-7368**

Madison River Canyon Earthquake Area

30 miles west of Yellowstone

A vivid reminder of Yellowstone's jittery seismic status, this deep, forested canyon still bears distinct scars from a 1959 earthquake that killed at least 28 people, stranded 250 more, and lifted the southern lobe of the Madison Range roughly 15 feet. The magnitude 7.5 quake triggered an immense landslide at the canyon's west end that peeled away the entire flank of a mountain and sent it crashing down into the bed of the Madison River. The rubble dammed the river and created **Earthquake Lake,** a small, serpentine body of water ringed with a band of dead trees that were killed as the lake level rose. Also during the quake, the northern bed of **Hebgen Lake** dropped 19 feet. Huge waves lurched back and forth across the lake and cracked the 1915 earthen dam.

Drop by the **visitor center,** which stands atop the massive heap of slide debris overlooking Earthquake Lake, and take in the landslide scree on the mountain across the road. An excellent film tells the story, and ties the quake to volcanism throughout the region.

Next, pick up a tour brochure and head east through the canyon, stopping at various quake landmarks. At the **Cabin Creek Scarp Area,** walk along the the steep, gravelly embankment that marks the quake's fault line. Farther east, you can see a section of the old highway dipping down into Hebgen Lake.

■ **38,000 acres** ■ **Southwest Montana on US 287** ■ **Camping, hiking, boating, fishing** ■ **Contact Hebgen Lake Ranger District, Gallatin National Forest, P.O. Box 520, West Yellowstone, MT 59758; 406-646-7369**

Shaky Ground

Earthquake Lake and the Hebgen Lake are impressive indicators of Yellowstone's seismic instability. Major quakes periodically rock the region, the most recent being the 1983 Borah Peak Earthquake in Idaho, which measured magnitude 7.3. Lesser tremors too small to be felt occur frequently—sometimes many tiny shakes in a day. See the results on seismographs at several area visitor centers, including the one at Old Faithful. The activity is tied to the Yellowstone hot spot, whose movements and pressure have built dramatic landscapes for miles around.

Red Rock Lakes National Wildlife Refuge

40 miles west of Yellowstone Remote but rewarding, this sprawling refuge for trumpeter swans and other birds stretches across a broad, open valley at the foot of the Centennial Mountains. Speckled with shallow lakes and crystal-clear ponds, carpeted with lush grasses and prairie wildflowers, the land was set aside in 1935 to help boost the trumpeter population, which had dwindled nearly to extinction. Thanks in large part to this refuge, the magnificent birds are making a comeback. Wander by foot, drive the roads, or launch a canoe. Besides swans, you'll see sandhill cranes and perhaps a moose or two.

To reach the refuge, go 5 miles north of Macks Inn on US 20 to a well-marked dirt road; take this west for 30 miles.

■ **44,963 acres** ■ **Southwest Montana, northwest of Macks Inn**
■ **Access road usually passable June–Oct.** ■ **Camping, canoeing, bird-watching** ■ **Contact U.S. Fish and Wildlife Service, Monida Star Rte., P.O. Box 15, Lima, MT 59739; 406-276-3536**

Centennial Mountains rising above Red Rock Lakes NWR

Lewis & Clark Caverns State Park

90 miles northwest of Yellowstone

Cool, damp, alien, this fascinating series of roomy chambers and crooked passageways lies within the crest of Cave Mountain, high above the Jefferson River west of Three Forks. Overgrown by slick dripstone formations, the cave system meanders for roughly 2 miles and descends approximately 500 feet. Stalagmites, stalactites, and other globular masses of dripstone crowd the caverns, and long, translucent ruffles of flowstone drape the walls.

Cave tours *(adm. fee)* begin at the historic stone-and-timber **visitor center,** which stands at the end of a winding 3-mile road. The trip lasts about 2 hours and leads through some 0.75 of a mile of winding passageways. A short, downward slide on your backside is necessary at one point, along with much bobbing and weaving. But there is no crawling or squirming through the muck. Interpretation is excellent, covering the formation of the caverns and their beautiful structures as well as their history.

■ 3,304 acres ■ Southwest Montana, 20 miles east of Whitehall off Mont. 2 ■ Cave tours mid-May–mid-Sept. ■ Adm. fee ■ Contact the park, Box 949, Three Forks, MT 59752; 406-287-3541

Missouri Headwaters State Park

100 miles northwest of Yellowstone

Within this small state park, three muscular rivers join to form the Missouri amid a seductive landscape of lush bottomlands, low cliffs, semiarid grasslands, and shady cottonwood groves. Stroll the short **Headwaters Trail** to the confluence of the Jefferson and Madison Rivers—the official start of the Missouri. Next, hike the 1-mile trail circling **Fort Rock,** a promontory of limestone topped with sagebrush, prickly pear, and wildflowers. Its southern end offers the park's finest vista of the converging river courses and surrounding mountains. At the north end, there's a small exhibit on Lewis and Clark, who passed this way in late July 1805.

■ 560 acres ■ Southwest Montana, off I-90 near Three Forks ■ Camping, hiking, boating, biking, horseback riding, bird-watching, wildlife viewing ■ Adm. fee ■ Contact the park, 1400 S. 19th St., Bozeman, MT 59718; 406-994-4042

Absaroka & Beartooth Ranges

40 miles north of Yellowstone From its starting point near Livingston, Montana, the Absaroka Range marches south to Yellowstone, curves around its east side, and continues southward to Wyoming's Wind River Canyon—a total distance of some 150 high and scenic miles. Stuck like a wedge into the Absarokas where they cross the Wyoming-Montana border is a smaller but strikingly beautiful range called the Beartooths. The two ranges merge so tightly that they seem one continuous chain. However, they are distinctly different in appearance and geology.

The Absarokas are volcanic in origin, made of ash and lava spewed out in periodic eruptions 40 million to 50 million years ago. Layer upon layer, the raw material of the Absarokas piled up to form a smooth plateau. At the south end of the range that old plateau surface is still present but for most of their winding length, the Absarokas have been deeply eroded, their rubbly volcanic rocks carved into sharp crests, steep slopes, and narrow valleys.

Before the Absarokas erupted, the Beartooths pushed up as a solid block of Precambrian metamorphics—the ancient bedrock of the Rocky Mountains, some 3.2 billion years old. The southern

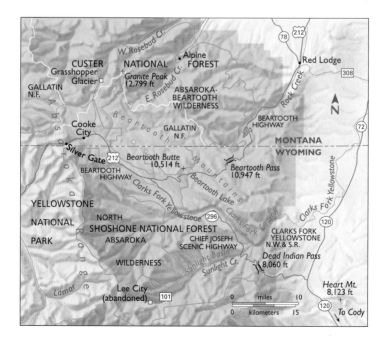

aspect of the range is a relatively gentle slope, often nearly flat, strewn with lakes, and blanketed with tundra plants. In contrast, the northern side lurches above the rolling ranchlands of Montana in near vertical ramparts 6,000 to 7,000 feet high. Carved and polished by glaciers, the old granite forms soaring cliffs, rounded knobs, and deep canyons reminiscent of Yosemite.

For such a large area, road access is good: US 26/287 passes the Absaroka Range at its south end, providing access to trailheads and recreation areas, notably the **Brooks Lake** area and **Togwotee Pass.** US 14/16/20 between Cody and Yellowstone parallels the **North Fork Shoshone River,** climbing from near desert on the edge of the Bighorn Basin to 8,530-foot Sylvan Pass. It's a famously beautiful drive through some of the Yellowstone ecosystem's best wildlife country. Two other highways, described below, magnificently showcase the region's rugged beauty.

Beginning a few miles north of Cody, the **Chief Joseph Scenic Highway** (Wyo. 120/296) is one of the world's great alpine drives. It is a less traveled route to Yellowstone's northeast entrance and to the old mining towns of Cooke City and Silver Gate. Toward the beginning, look for **Heart Mountain,** a chunk of paleozoic sediment that slid off the Beartooth Plateau. Then, on Wyo. 120, the road climbs through steep grassy ranchland to a jaw-dropping view at **Dead Indian Pass,** then dives to a crossing of the black-rock chasm of **Sunlight Creek,** a good place to stop and gawk. Continuing northward, the highway parallels the deep gorge of the Clarks Fork Yellowstone River, skirting its nearly inaccessible, rapids-filled canyon, heading toward the Beartooths. The river itself is hidden until you near the junction with US 212, the end of the drive.

At the junction of US 212 and the Chief Joseph highway, a left turn leads to Yellowstone; to the right, the **Beartooth Highway** (US 212) begins its long spectacular ascent. This improbable, audacious route teeters across the high tundra. There are numerous campgrounds and stopping points along the way, which are popular jumping-off places for day hikes, backpacking, or climbing expeditions. The weather can be ferocious even in July, but generally summer is a fine time for rambling (*road closed in winter and during storms even in summer*).

In the first mile of this spectacular road, the Absaroka panorama opens to the south. Next comes **Beartooth Lake,** shimmering at the base of Beartooth Butte. A bit farther, trees give way to the rarified zone of alpine tundra, where lakes and open meadows stretch to the 10,947-foot-high pass. The last stage is a brake-stomping descent to Red Lodge, a vertical mile below.

In contrast to the high-altitude experience atop the Beartooths, a number of access roads penetrate from the north, ending deep in the shadows of towering glacially smoothed walls. The drainages of **West Rosebud, East Rosebud,** and **Rock Creeks** are noteworthy, offering pleasant forested campgrounds and fishing in lakes and streams. The trails that start here climb all the way to the top of the plateau past waterfalls and chains of trout-filled lakes. The hiking is demanding, but the scenery is worth the effort. Any length hike is possible, from day trips to overnight loops and week-long treks across the range.

North of Yellowstone, the Absarokas are cut by a central drainage, the **Boulder River Valley,** which essentially divides the mountains in two. FR 6639, a cherry-stem road with wilderness on both sides, provides access to campgrounds, trailheads, and good trout fishing. At **Natural Bridge State Park** *(25 miles S of Big Timber. 406-932-5131),* footpaths lead to views of a 100-foot waterfall and natural bridge.

■ Southwest Montana and northwest Wyoming ■ Winter closes the Chief Joseph and Beartooth roads ■ Camping, hiking, fishing, wildlife viewing, scenic drives ■ Bear-country precautions pertain while camping and hiking ■ Contact Wapiti Ranger District, Shoshone National Forest, 203A Yellowstone Ave., Cody, WY 82414; 307-527-6921. www.fs.fed.us/r2/shoshone

Alpine Tundra

Alpine tundra is a world of miniature plants and hardy animals where winter is never far off. Survival means coping with ferocious conditions—high winds, severe temperatures, a short growing season, intense sunlight. Plants that in lower elevations grow tall are only inches high here. It's a place to explore gently on hands and knees, to see tiny flowers and dwarf shrubs, some of which are decades or even centuries old. Despite its toughness, tundra life is surprisingly fragile and slow to recover from damage. Thoughtless foot traffic can cause injury lasting many years.

Yosemite

I n a high-country meadow, two hikers crouch near the edge of a lake and watch a pika as it harvests blades of grass for a nest deep within a huge rock pile. When they resume walking, there is no other person in sight for as far as they can see. And on this sparkling summer's day, the view seems endless.

In the same valley, in a crowded mall, families stroll by, eating ice cream and dodging bicycles. People pile in and out of buses. Shoppers hunt for souvenirs. Children hang around a pizza place. Rock climbers, coils of rope slung over their shoulders, swap stories over beers on a patio. On this summer's day about 14,000 people are in Yosemite Village.

Both the solitude of the alpine meadow and the throngs of the valley are part of the experience when you visit Yosemite National Park. "No temple made with hands can compare with Yosemite," wrote naturalist John Muir, whose crusading led to the creation of the park. Three and a half million visitors come here a year. And about 90 percent of them go to the valley, a mile-wide, 7-mile-long canyon cut by a river, then widened and deepened by glaciers over the centuries. Surrounded by massive domes and soaring pinnacles, it covers about one percent of the park.

Beyond the valley, some 800 miles of marked trails offer hikers easy jaunts or grueling tests of endurance in the High Sierra wilderness. Even the casual visitor can explore this solitude without getting outfitted for a backpack expedition.

The park, roughly the size of Rhode Island, is a United Nations World Heritage site. In four of the seven continental life zones live the mule deer and chipmunks of the valley and the marmots and pikas of the heights; the brush rabbit and chaparral of the near desert; the warblers of mid-elevation forests; and the dwarf willow and matted flowers of the majestic mountains.

- Central California
- 761,266 acres
- Established 1890
- Best seasons spring and fall. Summer can get very crowded.
- Camping, hiking, kayaking, fishing, cross-country skiing, bird-watching
- Information: 209-372-0200 www.nps.gov/grca

Half Dome, Yosemite National Park

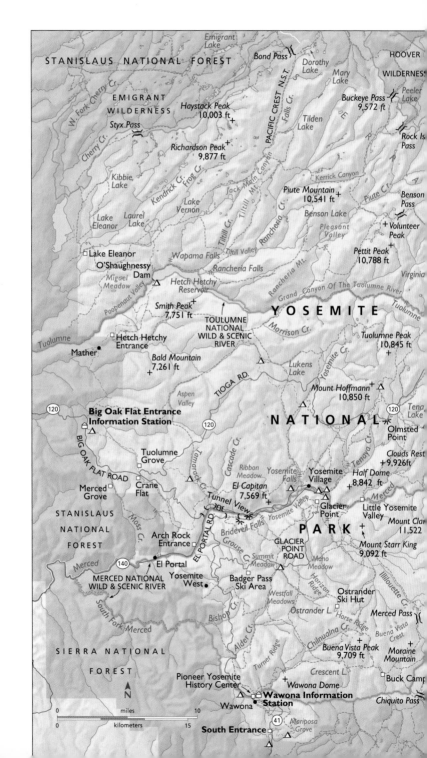

STANISLAUS NATIONAL FOREST

Emigrant Lake

Bond Pass

HOOVER

Dorothy Lake

Mary Lake

WILDERNESS

Peeler Lake

EMIGRANT WILDERNESS

Haystack Peak 10,003 ft

Buckeye Pass 9,572 ft

Rock Is Pass

Styx Pass

Tilden Lake

W. Fork Cherry Cr.

Cherry Cr.

Richardson Peak 9,877 ft

Kendrick Cr.

Frog Cr.

Jack Main Canyon

Falls Cr.

PACIFIC CREST N.S.T.

Tiltill Cr.

Kerrick Canyon

Piute Mountain 10,541 ft

Piute Cr.

Benson Pass

Kibbie Lake

Lake Vernon

Rancheria Cr.

Benson Lake

Volunteer Peak

Lake Eleanor

Laurel Lake

Tiltill Valley

Pleasant Valley

Pettit Peak 10,788 ft

Miguel Meadow

Wapama Falls

Rancheria Falls

Rancheria Mt.

Virginia

Lake Eleanor

O'Shaughnessy Dam

Hetch Hetchy Reservoir

Grand Canyon Of The Tuolumne River

Tuolumne

Poopenaut Valley

Smith Peak 7,751 ft

Morrison Cr.

YOSEMITE

Tuolumne

Hetch Hetchy Entrance

TOULUMNE NATIONAL WILD & SCENIC RIVER

Tuolumne Peak 10,845 ft

Mather

Bald Mountain 7,261 ft

Lukens Lake

Yosemite Cr.

TIOGA RD.

Mount Hoffmann 10,850 ft

120

Aspen Valley

Tena Lake

120

Big Oak Flat Entrance Information Station

120

Olmsted Point

BIG OAK FLAT ROAD

Tuolumne Grove

Cascade Cr.

Tenaya Cr.

Clouds Rest 9,926 ft

Merced

Merced Grove

Crane Flat

Tamarack Cr.

Ribbon Meadow

Yosemite Falls

Yosemite Village

Half Dome 8,842 ft

STANISLAUS NATIONAL FOREST

El Capitan 7,569 ft

Yosemite Valley

Little Yosemite Valley

Mount Clark 11,522

Moss Cr.

Tunnel View

Glacier Point

Arch Rock Entrance

EL PORTAL RD.

Bridveil Falls

Yosemite Valley

Grouse Cr.

PARK

Mount Starr King 9,092 ft

Merced

El Portal

GLACIER POINT ROAD

Mono Meadow

140

MERCED NATIONAL WILD & SCENIC RIVER

Yosemite West

Summit Meadow

Badger Pass Ski Area

Horizon Ridge

Ostrander Ski Hut

Merced Pass

South Fork Merced

Westfall Meadows

Ostrander L.

Horse Ridge

Buena Vista Crest

SIERRA NATIONAL FOREST

Bishop Cr.

Alder Cr.

Chilnualna Cr.

Buena Vista Peak 9,709 ft

Moraine Mountain

Turner Ridge

Crescent L.

Buck Camp

N

Pioneer Yosemite History Center

Wawona Dome

Wawona Information Station

Chiquito Pass

miles 10

Wawona

kilometers 15

South Entrance

41

Mariposa Grove

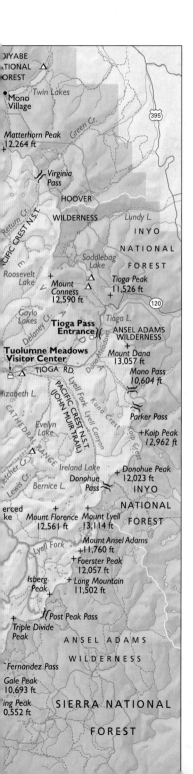

How to Get There

From Merced (about 70 miles west), follow Calif. 140 to the Arch Rock Entrance. Also from the west, take Calif. 120 to the Big Oak Flat Entrance.

From the south, via Fresno, Calif. 41 takes you to the South Entrance.

From the northeast, via Lee Vining, follow Calif. 120 to the Tioga Pass Entrance (*closed mid-Nov.–late May, depending on weather*).

Trains stop at Merced; check with Amtrak about connecting buses to Yosemite. Airports: Fresno and Merced.

When to Go

All-year park. Avoid holiday weekends. Expect crowded campgrounds from June through August and some crowding in late spring and early fall. Be sure you have reserved accommodations before attempting an overnight visit. You will find skiing and other winter activities in the Badger Pass Ski Area from about Thanksgiving to mid-April.

How to Visit

When a visitor asked a Yosemite ranger what he would do if he had only a day to visit the park, the ranger answered, "I'd weep."

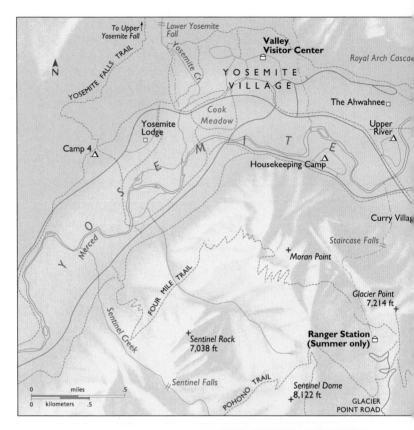

If you must zip through this huge park in a day, begin with **Yosemite Valley.** Yet even a dawn-to-dusk, 1-day visit hardly allows enough time for more than a tour of the valley plus a look at one or two of the park's other major areas, such as the vistas from **Glacier Point** *(in winter, road closed beyond the ski area)* and the sequoias of the **Mariposa Grove.**

As an alternative or on another day between late May and early November, take the

What Not to Miss

- A visit to Yosemite Falls, world's second highest waterfall

- Hiking Mist Trail to Vernal Fall and Nevada Fall

- A hike to Mirror Lake

- Mariposa Grove for a hike or tram tour around giant sequoias

- Tioga/Tuolumne Meadows Road to reach uncrowded alpine trails

- Kayaking on Merced River

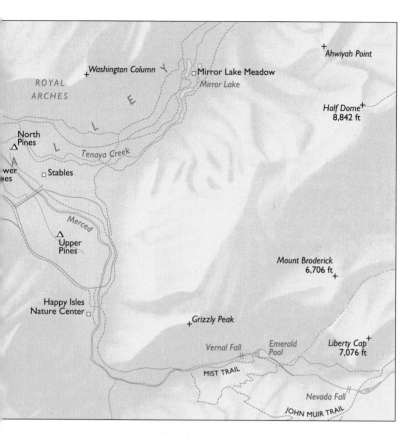

Map labels: Ahwiyah Point; Washington Column; Mirror Lake Meadow; Mirror Lake; ROYAL ARCHES; Half Dome 8,842 ft; North Pines; Tenaya Creek; Stables; Merced; Upper Pines; Mount Broderick 6,706 ft; Happy Isles Nature Center; Grizzly Peak; Vernal Fall; Emerald Pool; Liberty Cap 7,076 ft; MIST TRAIL; Nevada Fall; JOHN MUIR TRAIL

Tioga Road to see the park's alpine country.

Better still, stay long enough to get beyond the crowds and discover the sense of seclusion this park can give you along one of its trails. Several easy hikes begin from the valley floor including the 0.5-mile **Lower Yosemite Fall Trail,** the 1-mile **Mirror Lake Trail,** and the very scenic 0.5-mile **Bridalveil Fall Trail.**

For a more strenuous trek, try the 2-mile **Upper Yosemite Fall Trail** to **Columbia Rock,** where you'll get a terrific view of the valley.

Cyclists might want to devote an extra day to the paved, 12-mile **loop road** that begins at the Valley Visitor Center. The path gains very little elevation en route to **Mirror Lake** in the east and goes downhill to the swinging bridge in the west. Cyclists then share the roads with vehicles to visit sights farther afield, such as **El Capitan.**

EXPLORING THE PARK

Yosemite Valley: **12 miles; at least a half to full day**

Don't add to the traffic congestion by driving the one-way valley roads. Park at one of the lots along the shuttle bus route and take the free bus, which loops through the east end of the valley.

You can also explore the valley on a rented bike or on foot. Or, buy a ticket for a 2-hour guided tram tour. In addition to the day-time tours, the open-air trams venture out on moonlit nights and glide through the ghostly light that bathes the valley.

If you're traveling by shuttle bus, get off at the **Valley Visitor Center** in **Yosemite Village,** where an award-winning film introduces the valley's history, grandeur, and geology. For an easy stroll in an oasis of quiet, look for **Cook's Meadow** just south of the visitor center. The trail begins at the west end of the mall; pick up a brochure for a self-guided tour. This is one of the loveliest meadows in the park.

Bridalveil Fall

From here, the entire pantheon of Yosemite icons loom upward like great granite sentries. Look for Half Dome, Glacier Point, Sentinel Rock, and Cathedral Rock.

The meadows here are often alive with red-wing blackbirds, robins, and Stellar's jays. In the sky above soar predatory birds such as peregrines and golden eagles.

If you have time to spare, continue your walk and keep the Merced River to your left. Soon you'll come to **Leidig Meadow.** This is named after Charles Leidig, the first white man born in the valley. Follow the bike path to the meadow's edge and to the river, where you'll see stunning reflections of **Sentinel Falls.**

Keep along the north side of the meadow to Rocky Point, which is easy to recognize by the rubble at its base. Continue to the river and a large wooded area. Now stick to the trail along the river to an area known as Indian Swamp. In spring, the meadow here

Two hikers on the Mist Trail at Vernal Fall

floods, giving amazing reflections of **Cathedral Rocks** and **Spires.**

At this point, backtrack to the visitor center. Meander through the nearby **Indian Village of Ahwahnee,** where exhibits and bark houses evoke the life of the valley's earlier dwellers. Visit the **Indian Cultural Exhibit** to see the baskets and other works of art that tribes here produced.

At the bustling village shops you can find just about what you would find in any resort-town mall. But if you want to see the park, don't tarry here.

Get back on the bus and go to the Yosemite Falls shuttle bus stop. The upper, middle, and lower falls form the highest waterfall in North America (2,425 feet) and the second highest in the world. A quarter-mile walk takes you to the base of **Lower Yosemite Fall.**

If you have the stamina and another full day, take the strenuous 3.5-mile hike to **Upper Yosemite Fall,** where you will be rewarded with spectacular valley views away from the crowds *(trailhead behind Camp Four parking lot).*

Get back on the bus, and crane your neck for other scenic wonders. And get off when you want to absorb them; you will not have to wait long for another bus.

On the 3,593-foot vertical wall of **El Capitan** you may spot the tiny figures of climbers. During their ascent, which may take days, they sleep in slings hanging from the cliff.

After looping east you'll pass **Sentinel Rock** and then **Glacier Point.** (An arduous hike up **Four Mile Trail** takes you in 3 or 4 hours to Glacier Point's breathtaking vistas; for the trailhead, get off the bus at Yosemite Lodge and walk behind it to Southside Drive, then west a quarter mile to road marker V18.)

If you're still on the shuttle bus, get off at the stop near the Happy Isles Nature Center. After a walk around these two bridge-linked river islands, consider hiking the moderately strenuous 1.5-mile **Mist Trail** to the top of 317-foot **Vernal Fall.** From higher up this trail, you can also see **Nevada Fall** with its 594-foot cascade. Massive **Half Dome,** a cracked block of gray granite gnawed by a glacier, soars 4,733 feet above the valley floor, its sheer face dominating this part of the valley.

A gentle hike from the next shuttle bus stop takes you to lovely **Mirror Lake** a mile away; there's a 3-mile trail that goes around and above it. In spring and early summer, the lake's serene surface reflects stunning mountain scenery; during the summer, most of its contents evaporate.

As the shuttle turns back toward Yosemite Village, you'll pass the **Royal Arch Cascade,** glacier-carved granite shells. You will pass the full spectrum of Yosemite accommodations along the shuttle bus route, from tents, trailer hookups, and clusters of concrete shelters to comfortable lodges, cabins, and the luxurious Ahwahnee hotel.

Glacier Point & Mariposa Grove: 52 miles one way; a half to full day

Leave the valley by taking Calif. 41 (Wawona Road) to the Wawona Tunnel. Park at the turnout at the tunnel's eastern end and walk over to the **Tunnel View Overlook** to see what has been called the most photographed vista on Earth. Spread before you is a granite panorama encompassing El Capitan, Half Dome, Sentinel Rock, Cathedral Rocks, and 620-foot **Bridalveil Fall,** in the late afternoon a scrim of shimmering rainbows.

About 7 miles beyond the tunnel, turn left on the Glacier Point Road *(in winter, closed beyond ski area).* The 16-mile road, flanked by fir-and-pine forests, ends in a parking lot. Walk about 300 yards to the first of several overlooks on Glacier Point, which thrusts 3,214 feet above the valley, providing an enormous stage for a scenic spectacular of lights and shadows. Mirror Lake lies below; Half Dome looms across; and Vernal Fall and Nevada Fall hang like white tassels in the distance.

Return to the intersection of Calif. 41 and drive south 13 miles to Wawona, site of a hotel, golf course, and other facilities. Stop at the Pioneer Yosemite History Center, where, in summer, visitors enter restored buildings and chat about the past with costumed interpreters who portray a cavalry trooper, a 19th-century home-steader, and a mountaineer. From conversations with these players

Giant sequoias, Mariposa Grove

you learn Yosemite Valley's recent history, which, according to legend, began in 1851 when members of the Mariposa Battalion were tracking down Native Americans accused of raiding nearby trading posts. The Miwok Tribe that lived in the foothills called their counterparts in the valley *Yohemite*, which means "some of them are killers." Thinking that this was the tribe's name, the white settlers gave an approximation of that word to the valley.

Word of the beautiful valley spread quickly, and the first tourists arrived in 1855. Homesteaders and innkeepers soon followed. Next came the nation's early conservationists, who campaigned to protect the valley.

On June 30, 1864, President Abraham Lincoln took time out

from the Civil War to sign a bill granting both the valley and this grove to the state of California. This was the first time that any nation set aside land as a wilderness preserve. Yosemite became a national park in 1890, although not until 1906 did California formally give the original grants back to the federal government. More land was added to the park in 1913.

Return to Calif. 41 and continue south. Near the South Entrance continue straight to Yosemite's other long-cherished feature, the Mariposa Grove. From early May to late October you can take a guided tram tour *(fee)* of the grove's giant sequoias. Or, you can walk among them at any time of year.

The best known of the grove's more than 200 giant sequoias is the **Grizzly Giant,** whose estimated age of 2,700 years makes it one of the oldest living sequoias. A trail takes you past the **Fallen Monarch;** its shallow roots help explain why winds sometimes topple these giant trees.

Another fallen star, the **Wawona Tunnel Tree,** recalls another era. The living sequoia, gutted in 1881 to make a drive-through tree for horse-drawn wagons, became a photogenic attraction for generations of automobile travelers. The tree toppled in 1969. *(continued p. 330)*

Savior of the Sierras

John Muir was a vigorous advocate for the preservation of the Sierra Nevada Mountains. He was also a tireless backcountry explorer whose methods were decidedly low tech. If you tire of carrying a 75-pound pack in the mountains, try it Muir's way, which was to be "the free mountaineer with a sack of bread on his shoulder and an ax to cut steps in the ice."

At 11,000 feet in Yosemite, Muir made his bed without bag or blanket in a pine thicket, crawling out now and then to warm by a fire. He rarely seemed to consume anything but bread and tea, and welcomed the solitude of the wilderness. "Few places in the world are more dangerous than home. Fear not, therefore, to try the mountain-passes. They will kill care, save you from apathy, set you free."

Born in Scotland and raised in Wisconsin, Muir planned to study medicine at the University of Michigan until the outbreak of the Civil War convinced him to move to Canada. There, he invented a machine to mill broom handles that would have made him rich but for a fire in 1866 that burned the Canadian factory to the ground.

He then went on a vagabond botanical expedition south to Florida and Cuba. A bout of malaria led him to abandon the tropics for the cooler climes of the American West.

Though his name is now forever linked to the Sierra Nevada, his early love of the outdoors was rambunctious and indiscriminate: When he arrived in San Francisco by steamer and was asked where he wanted to go, he replied, "Any place that is wild."

He fell in love with the entire state of California. Looking from Pacheco Pass "one shining morning" for the first time at the Central Valley—so tamed by human ingenuity today—he dubbed it "flowery, like a lake of pure sunshine." Then he gazed upward and saw a towering mountain range "so gloriously colored and so radiant, it seemed not clothed with light, but wholly composed of it, like the wall of a celestial city.

Along the top and extending a good way down, was a rich pearly-gray belt of snow; below it a belt of blue and dark purple, marking the extension of the forests; and stretching along the base of the range a broad belt of rose-purple; all these colors, from the blue sky to the yellow valley smoothly blending as they do in a rainbow."

Rich, flowing brush strokes

Yosemite Valley in the 1860s

nent California geologist Josiah Whitney, who had theorized that Yosemite was the product of an earthquake cataclysm. Muir, however, correctly concluded that the deep valley had been sculpted by glaciers. His articulate treatise convinced the scientific community.

Muir was also an engaging raconteur, whether it was by a park campfire or in the corridors of power. When legislators were wrestling over whether to make Yosemite a national park, Muir contacted the powerful president of the Southern Pacific Railroad, with whom he had traveled in Alaska, and had him line up the votes.

He didn't always win; the construction of Hetch Hetchy Dam was his most heartbreaking failure. Yet he never shied away from a fight.

Still in the end, Muir was more mountaineer than politician, philosopher, writer, and scientist combined. Ralph Waldo Emerson, who visited him at Yosemite, urged Muir to end his lonely mountain "probation" and live among his circle of intellectuals in Boston.

But Muir was too imbued with the wilderness ever to retire from it. "I never saw a discontented tree," he wrote.

of words came easily to Muir when he was describing natural wonders. Such was not the case, however, when he tried to write about himself. Struggling with an autobiography he never finished, Muir confided to friends that "my life on the whole has been level and uneventful," and he found he had little to say to the "moiling, squirming, fog-breathing public."

Muir produced his best work when he was investigating geological or botanical riddles, such as the origins of Yosemite Valley. He challenged the emi-

The decision not to cut a hole in another tree symbolized the dawning of an ecologically enlightened age.

Tioga Road & Tuolumne Meadows: 124 miles round-trip; at least a full day

Take the Big Oak Flat Road, a modern version of an old mining town road, west out of the valley for 9 miles to 6,200-foot Crane Flat (a local term for "meadow"). Turn right onto Tioga Road, which climbs into an alpine world of snowy peaks, crystal lakes, wind-tousled meadows, and relatively few people. The road (closed in winter) crosses the park. Even in July you may see snow alongside the road. Stop at the frequent turnouts for magnificent views and interpretive signs that explain the geology behind the splendor.

Gauge your time and gasoline. Beyond Crane Flat, the nearest gas station on this winding, climbing mountain road is a mile east of the Tuolumne Meadows Visitor Center, which is 55 miles from Yosemite Valley.

Millions of years ago, the Tuolumne Meadows were under a sea of ice more than 2,000 feet deep. Wildflowers such as Jeffrey shooting stars, Lewis paintbrushes, and marsh marigolds carpet this High Sierra realm in spring and summer.

Trails of varying difficulty branch out along the road. Some trails link five commercially run High Sierra camps with showers and dining halls (reservations required; see pp. 332–333).

One of the trails you can pick up here is a segment of the **Pacific Crest National Scenic Trail** north of the meadows. This goes down into the steep, dramatic **Grand Canyon of the Tuolumne River.**

Back on Tioga Road, you'll climb to 9,945-foot **Tioga Pass,** the highest automobile pass in California, at the park's eastern boundary. At a trailhead here you can take a half-day **alpine hike** that rewards you with glimpses of both beauty and history. The 2.5-mile trail climbs sharply from 9,945 feet to about 10,500, then descends to **Middle Gaylor Lake,** a gem set in a broad meadow prowled by marmots and Belding ground squirrels.

The trail again winds upward, first to **Upper Gaylor Lake,** then to a surprise: the ruins of a stone cabin, rusting bits of machinery, and half-filled shafts, relics of a failed 19th-century silver mine.

June Lake Loop

On this drive you'll see five lakes and fascinating evidence of the passage of glaciers. This part of the eastern Sierra, having been raked by glacial ice, appears raw and rocky, but its aspect is softened when spring brings wild irises. In late September, the leaves on the aspens turn gold.

Turn west from US 395 onto Calif. 158 at the southern access point for the June Lake Loop. You climb a glacial moraine to its summit, called Oh! Ridge for its exclamation inducing view of June Lake and Carson Peak (10,909 feet).

Take the campground road to the right for a side trip to the sandy swimming beach at June Lake.

Now continue to **June Lake village,** where on your right rest two glacial erratics. These 30-ton boulders, amazingly balanced one atop the other, were left by retreating glaciers.

Soon you glimpse **Gull Lake,** offering good trout fishing. Next the highway flanks the geologically unusual **Reversed Creek;** glacial debris blocked its course and made it reverse direction. On your right, aspens hide **Silver Lake** until it edges the road. The vegetation starts thinning as you reach **Grant Lake,** where you may see great blue herons.

Leaving the lake, you drive over another glacial moraine and descend toward **Mono Lake.** On your right rise the **Mono Craters,** plug-dome volcanoes formed of pumice and obsidian and explained on a sign nearby.

You will rejoin US 395 at the northern entrance to the June Lake Loop.

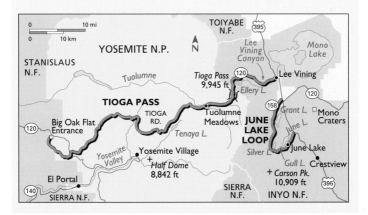

INFORMATION & ACTIVITIES

Headquarters
P.O. Box 577
Yosemite National Park,
CA 95389
209-372-0200
www.nps.gov/yose

Visitor & Information Centers
Valley Visitor Center open all
year. Tuolumne Meadows Visitor Center near Tioga Pass
Entrance open summer only.
Information also available at
Happy Isles Nature Center, in
valley, and at Big Oak Flat
Entrance on Calif. 120 at
western edge of park, both
open spring through fall; and
at Wawona Information
Station, open summer through
fall. For information, call 209-
372-0200.

Seasons & Accessibility
Park open year-round. Tioga
(Calif. 120 east) and Glacier
Point Roads closed by snow
from about mid-November to
late May. Call 209-372-0200 for
recorded conditions. In winter,
call 209-372-1000 for more
information.

   Free shuttle buses operate in
the valley year-round and at
Wawona and Tuolumne Mead-
ows in summer.

Entrance Fee
$20 per car per week.

Pets
Not permitted in buildings,
backcountry, or trails.

Facilities for Disabled
Visitor centers, art and nature
centers are accessible for people
in wheelchairs. Free brochure.

Things to Do
Free naturalist-led activities:
day and evening walks and
talks, hikes, camera walks,
children's and evening programs, living history; Native
American cultural interpretation. Also, auto tours, bus and
tram tours, films, plays, con-
certs, art and photography
classes, museums, horseback
riding, climbing, fishing, swimming, ice skating, downhill and
cross-country skiing.

Overnight Backpacking
Free permit required; issued
first come, first served; apply
up to 24 hours in advance of
trip to a park wilderness permit
station. Advance reservations
available by mail for a service
fee. Write wilderness office at
park address. Call 209-372-
0200 for more information.

Campgrounds
Thirteen campgrounds; in
summer, 7-day to 14-day limits;
other times some have 30-day

The Ahwahnee

limit. Four open all year; others
open mid-spring to mid-fall or
summer only. You must make
reservations through the
National Parks Reservation
Service (800-365-2267) year-
round for all in the valley,
except Camp Four, Hodgdon
Meadow from spring through
fall, and Crane Flat and half
of Tuolumne Meadows in
summer. Fees $5-$18 per
night. Most have RV sites,
without hookups. Four
group campgrounds.

Hotels, Motels, & Inns
(Unless otherwise noted, rates are
for two persons in a double room,
high season.)

INSIDE THE PARK:
Yosemite Concession Services
Corp., 5410 E. Home Ave.,
Fresno, CA 93727, operates the
following accommodations (for
reservations, call 559-252-4848
or go online at http://yosemite
park.com.)

■ **The Ahwahnee** (Yosemite Valley). 123 units. $373. AC, pool,
restaurant.

■ **Curry Village** (Yosemite Valley). 18 rooms. 80 cabins. 427
tent-cabins. $60-$110. Pool,
restaurant.

■ **High Sierra Camps** Five camps
with tent-cabins. Accessible by
hiking trail only. Guided trips
available. $47-$112 per person
includes breakfast, dinner. Late
June to Labor Day. Reserve by
mail September through
November.

■ **Tuolumne Meadows Lodge**
(8,600 feet, at Tuolumne Meadows). 69 tent-cabins, central
showers. $67. Restaurant. Open
summer.

■ **Wawona Hotel** (Calif. 41, 27
miles south of valley). 209-375-
6556. 104 rooms, 50 with private baths. $113-$166. Pool,
restaurant.

Excursions from Yosemite

Devils Postpile National Monument

20 miles southeast of Yosemite

A half-mad artist might have hallucinated the Devils Postpile as a comment on modern urban design; the close-packed vertical staves of gray stone are reminiscent of a cubist cityscape. This sculpture, though, hangs on the high crest of the Sierra, at the portal to Ansel Adams Wilderness. You'll find lush meadows and a beautiful waterfall close by.

It took a tricky combination of lava, glaciers, and time to make this rampart of columns on the mountains' western slope. About 100,000 years ago, basalt lava flowed from a vent on the side of the Mammoth volcano into the San Joaquin Valley, where it cooled, shrank, and cracked vertically. During the last ice age 10,000 years ago, a glacier flowed over the postpile, smoothing the tops and sheering off a wall 60 feet high.

To get there, pass through the resort area of Mammoth Lakes and take a shuttle bus from the Mammoth Inn on Minaret Road to the monument's visitor center. Due to snow, the road is open only from mid-June to Labor Day. A **loop trail** takes visitors atop the postpile to examine the smooth floor of the sheared hexagonal rocks that resembles a tiled floor. Climbing the face is prohibited. There is a huge talus field at the base, evidence that these pillars now and then break off.

The 2-mile **Rainbow Falls Trail,** which starts downstream from the postpile, leads to the spot where the **Middle Fork San Joaquin** tumbles 101 feet over a wall of volcanic rock. The falls are actually dropping over what was once a canyon bank cut at an earlier time by the river when it followed a different course. At the edge of the river, you might see a black bear or mule deer.

There are also mineral springs and two other falls within the monument; a trailhead at the visitor center accesses the wilderness to the west.

■ **798 acres** ■ **Central California, 11 miles west of US 395 via Calif. 203**
■ **Best season summer (closed in winter)** ■ **Camping, hiking, backpacking, guided walks, mountain climbing, fishing (license required)** ■ **Shuttle required (fee) except for campers and hikers with reservations** ■ **Contact the monument, P.O. Box 501, Mammoth Lakes, CA 93546; 760-934-2289 (summer); or Sequoia & Kings Canyon National Park (fall to spring). www.nps.gov/depo**

Mammoth Lakes Area

10 miles southeast of Yosemite

The beautiful lakes and peaks of the Mammoth region and Inyo National Forest lie just around the corner of the eastern Sierra foothills from the dry floor of Owens Valley and the sagebrush ranges that edge the Great Basin. Though somewhat compromised by resort development, the area is still an alluring portal to the wilderness along the Sierra Crest. The forest itself covers more than two million acres.

Mammoth Mountain—a dormant volcano that harbors a bustling ski resort—is on the western edge of the huge Long Valley Caldera. In May 1980 four major tremors in the Mammoth area prompted geologists to take a closer look at the caldera, which is almost unnoticeable from ground level because of its tremendous size, 20 miles long by 10 miles wide. Small earthquakes in the valley and the mountains to the west continue, but there's no indication an eruption is imminent.

That should leave you plenty of time to hike around and above the glacier-carved **Mammoth Lakes Basin.** You can hang around the five lakes in the basin, surrounded by pine forest and some

Cross-country skier in Mammoth Lakes area

private development, or take day hikes from Lake George to the Crystal Crags, which rise abruptly above Crystal Lake, or from Lake Mary up over Duck Pass. On the other side of the Sierra Crest you'll join the **John Muir Trail,** a good way to begin a much longer backcountry wilderness trip.

If the traffic around Mammoth is too much, drive 20 miles north on US 395 to the **June Lake Loop,** which takes you around lakes and creeks as stunning as the Mammoth Basin, but with smaller crowds *(see sidebar p. 331).*

There are several wilderness trailheads along this loop road, including those for the **Yost Lake, Fern/Yost, Rush Creek, Parker Lake,** and **Walker Lake Trails.** Information about these and other trails within **Inyo National Forest** can be obtained at the Mammoth Ranger and Visitor Center. Except for Rush Creek, these trails are less than 5 miles with moderate-to-steep elevation gain. The **Rush Creek Trail** goes farther into the wilderness and eventually connects with the **Pacific Coast Trail** and John Muir Trail.

Mountain bike trails throughout the Inyo offer long cross-country rides through Jeffrey pines and along the tops of the ridges. One popular one is the 5.5-mile (one way) **Mountain View Trail,** a single-track descent from Minaret Summit. Rent a bike from the sporting goods stores in the town of Mammoth Lakes and at the Adventure Center at Mammoth Mountain Ski Area *(800-626-6684).*

Many species of mammals can be found here, including black bears, mule deer, coyotes, red and gray foxes, and pine marten. Bighorn sheep spend the majority of the year on precipitous slopes at high elevations and are harder to spot. Avian species range from songbirds such as the colorful western tanager to large raptors including red-tail hawks, northern goshawks, and ospreys.

To see a decidedly less verdant side of the forest, head to the basin's western edge, where dry sagebrush plains unfold. This section is most prized for its stands of red fir, lodgepole pines, and quaking aspens. It also has some of the nation's largest grove of old-growth Jeffrey pines, some of which are several feet wide.

■ 35 square miles ■ Central California, near Mammoth Mountain Ski Area ■ Best seasons summer–fall ■ Hiking, backpacking, cross-country skiing, bird-watching ■ Contact Mammoth Ranger and Visitor Center, P.O. Box 148, Mammoth Lakes, CA 93546; 760- 924-5500. www.fs.fed.us/r5/inyo/

Mono Basin National Forest Scenic Area

15 miles east of Yosemite

After you've visited Mono Lake, you may never again take a sip of water in Los Angeles without feeling a twinge of guilt. Once much larger than its current size of 70 square miles, **Mono Lake** began dropping in 1941 when the Los Angeles Department of Water and Power diverted its feeder streams to slake the thirst of southern California. The shoreline marshes and stream habitats vital to wildlife began to disappear; the salinity of the lake doubled to about 10 percent.

One unanticipated side effect of this was the appearance of unusual, gnarly white rock formations above the surface. These tufa towers form underwater as mineral-rich springs rise into the lake carrying calcium carbonate, or limestone. The material is carried up through the porous rock toward the surface, adding layers to the top of the towers.

While the surface of the basin is placid, there is a lot of activity underground. **Black Point,** on the lake's northern perimeter, was once an underwater volcano. The **Mono Craters** to the south of the lake and the islands at its center only popped up recently, geologically speaking. There is no volcanic activity at present, but seismic records indicate that these newborn mountains have not yet finished growing. You can hike up and around its plug dome.

A Conservation Success Story

Anyone who has seen the movie *Chinatown* knows it's not healthy to mess with Los Angeles when it comes to water. But David Gaines, an ecology graduate student who fell in love with Mono Lake in 1978, worked extremely hard to draw attention to its plight.

In 1983—a year of heavy rains—the state legislature responded by directing water back into the streams that feed Mono Lake. The fish population grew, and Gaines found a new ally in the private organization, CALTrout. With grassroots pressure increasing, the state's Department of Fish and Game declared that future diversions from the lake would hurt Mono's rebounding fishery and, therefore, violate state law.

Sadly, Gaines died in 1988 before seeing the full effect of his campaign.

Tufa towers along the shore of Mono Lake

Start with a visit to the small town of **Lee Vining** on the west shore, where there is a national forest visitor center; here, too, are the informative displays at the the **Mono Lake Committee Information Center** *(760-647-6595)*, an advocacy group that defended the lake against L.A.'s water grab. Begin a tour of Mono Lake at the south end, where a veritable city of tufa towers rises both onshore and in the water.

Five miles east of US 395 on Calif. 120 lies a dirt road to the **South Tufa Area** on the southern lakeshore, with a 1-mile interpretive nature trail. Also at this end of the lake is **Navy Beach,** a considered the youngest mountain range in North America because they began forming only 40,000 years ago. You can hike up and around its plug dome. Take Panum Crater Road from Calif. 120 to the parking area at road's end where the **Panum Crater Trail** begins.

■ **120,000 acres** ■ **Central California, at Lee Vining** ■ **Best seasons spring–summer** ■ **Camping, hiking, boating, kayaking, canoeing, swimming, fishing, mountain biking** ■ **Contact the national forest, P.O. Box 429, Lee Vining, CA 93541, 760-647-3044; or Mono Lake Tufa State Reserve, P.O. Box 99, Lee Vining, CA, 760-647-6331. http://parks.ca.gov**

Calaveras Big Trees State Park

40 miles northwest of Yosemite

Established in 1931, this state park harbors more than a thousand old-growth giant sequoias in two large groves. More than 60 million years ago these trees covered large areas of North America, but climate change reduced the sequoia forests to a few isolated pockets on wet mountain slopes.

California's forests today are predominantly pine, making preserves like Calaveras all the more rare and delightful. From the visitor center head south on the **main park road,** a scenic drive that will take you over the Stanislaus River Bridge. In 9 miles you'll come to a parking area for the **South Grove.** Here is the largest sequoia in the park, called the **Agassiz Tree,** standing more than 250 feet tall and located midway along the 5-mile **South Grove Loop Trail.**

The **North Grove** gets more visitors because it's next to the visitor center, and the **loop trail** is only a mile long. With a brochure in hand, you can identify the rich plant life of the redwood understory, including monkey flowers, lilies, and the Pacific yew.

The park has two main campgrounds, six picnic areas and hundreds of miles of trails.

■ 6,500 acres ■ Central California, 75 miles east of Stockton on Calif. 4
■ Best seasons spring—summer ■ Camping, hiking, kayaking, fishing, cross-country skiing ■ Contact the park, P.O. Box 120, Arnold, CA 95223; 209-795-2334. www.sierra.parks.state.ca.us/cbt/cbt.htm

Fallen Giants

When a giant sequoia keels over, the earth shakes and people tremble.

This happened in April 2000 in the North Grove at Calaveras when visitors reported hearing a huge crash. Rangers found that tree No. 115, a sequoia with a 17-foot diameter, had fallen to the ground.

The tree was nicknamed "Anna Mehlig" after a European pianist whose U.S. tour was a big hit more than a hundred years ago.

The tree made a big hit, too, toppling several smaller sequoias. Once down, though, the fallen tree became a nurse log, providing a home for ferns and insects and a bed for new sequoia seedlings. So out of tragedy, something positive does happen in the forest.

Lake Tahoe Basin

70 miles northwest of Yosemite

You might say that Lake Tahoe has a split personality: a clear, blue mountain lake of enormous size and depth in a forested, peak-rimmed basin pervaded by logging, condominiums, casinos, and speedboats. If you come upon the lake from a high ridge in the Desolation Wilderness early on a fall morning, you see almost none of the surrounding development. The resilient lake lives, and there are steps under way that may make it healthier still in the future.

Tahoe is the second largest alpine lake in North America, after Oregon's Crater Lake, 22 miles long with a depth as great as 1,643 feet and 122,000 miles of surface.

Wedged between the Sierra Nevada and the Carson Range right on the California-Nevada border, the Lake Tahoe Basin is the product of volcanism and plate tectonics. It lies in a depression between two active faults; in fact, the steep-sided Sierra Nevada Crustal block on the west side of the lake is still moving toward the northwest. Lava from Mount Pluto blocked the basin's northern outlet two million years ago, and the lake began to fill. More recently, glaciers carved deep gouges in the surrounding land and the growing lake flowed into them as well. **Emerald Bay** is among the more scenic of these flooded valleys.

You can take a 72-mile **scenic drive** around the lake, but this means navigating the clots of overbuilt commerce at the south and north shores. You can rent various types and sizes of boats in the towns along the shoreline and explore by water, remaining watchful for sudden weather changes. Or you can stop at one of the state parks on the lakeshore for a swim, hike, or picnic.

On the California side, Calif. 89 passes above Emerald Bay, a deep sheltered cove flanked by forested peninsulas. Several breathtaking pullouts along here include one where you can take a short walk to **Eagle Falls** as it drops down to the bay; another accesses a moderate switchback drop to **Vikingsholm,** a 1920s mansion on the shore in **Emerald Bay State Park.** A little farther north is **D. L. Bliss State Park.** Here you can pick up the scenic 3-mile **Rubicon Trail,** which follows the shoreline south to Emerald Point.

If the lake seems too crowded or too commercial, head up into Lake Tahoe's surrounding backcountry. One of the most accessible areas is **Eldorado National Forest's Desolation Wilderness,** a 63,475-acre collection of alpine meadows, granite cliffs, and a few peaks that are almost 10,000 feet high.

A 12-mile segment of the **Tahoe Rim Trail** crosses Desolation Wilderness. The 150-mile loop follows ridges and mountaintops past alpine lakes and through dense red fir woods. This section of the trail surpasses most other stretches for the stark beauty of its alpine terrain with a mixture of high alpine meadows. The best way to reach the segment is to take US 50 to the Echo Summit exit and follow the signs to the parking lot.

On the Nevada side, **Lake Tahoe Nevada State Park** is a 14,242-acre preserve that includes some pretty shorelines and forests.

■ **72 miles of shoreline** ■ **On eastern border of California and western border of Nevada** ■ **Best seasons spring—fall** ■ **Camping, hiking, boating, swimming, waterskiing, fishing, biking** ■ **Contact Forest Service Lake Tahoe Basin Management Unit, 870 Emerald Bay Rd., Suite 1, South Lake Tahoe, CA 96150; 530-573-2600. www.r5.fs.fed.us/ltbmu**

Sailboat race on Lake Tahoe

Resources

USDA Forest Service Regional Offices

Pacific Northwest Region
(Oregon, Washington)
P.O. Box 3623
333 S.W. 1st Ave.
Portland, OR 97208
503-808-2468
www.fs.fed.us/r6

Pacific Southwest Region
(California, Hawaii)
1323 Club Dr.
Vallejo, CA 94592
707-562-8737
www.fs.fed.us/r5

Northern Region
(Montana, North Dakota, South Dakota)
Federal Building
200 E. Broadway
P.O. Box 7669
Missoula, MT 59807
406-329-3511
www.fs.fed.us/r1

Rocky Mountain Region
(Colorado, South Dakota, Wyoming)
740 Simms St.
Golden, CO 80401
303-275-5350
www.fs.fed.us/r2

For information on recreation and camping opportunities within the national forests visit:
www.recreation.gov or
www.reserveusa.com

California
Road Conditions
800-427-7623 (in California)
916-445-7623 (outside California)
www.dot.ca.gov/hq/roadinfo

California Tourism
California Travel
and Tourism
800-462-2543
http://gocalif.ca.gov
Information and maps on lodging, activities, wildlife, theme parks, state/national parks, and driving tours

State Parks
California Department
of Parks & Recreation
P.O. Box 942896
Sacramento, CA 94296
916-653-6995
http://parks.ca.gov
Information on camping, tour reservations, park passes, children's interactive learning programs, and public notices

Fishing and Hunting Licences
California Department
of Fish and Game
1416 9th St.
Sacramento, CA 95814
916-227-2245
www.dfg.ca.gov

Bureau of Land Management
BLM/California
2800 Cottage Way, Suite W1834
Sacramento, CA 95825
916-978-4400
www.ca.blm.gov/index.html

BLM Redding Field Office
355 Hemsted Dr.
Redding, CA 96002
530-224-2100
www.ca.blm.gov/redding

BLM Southern California
California Desert District Office
6221 Box Springs Blvd.
Riverside, CA 92507
909-697-5200
www.ca.blm.gov/cdd

Colorado

Road Conditions

877-315-7623 (in Colorado),
303-639-1234, or 303-573-ROAD
303-757-9228 (construction)
www.co.blm.gov/
conditions.htm

Colorado Tourism

Colorado Tourism Office
1625 Broadway, Suite 1700
Denver, CO 80202
303-892-3885
800-265-6732
www.Colorado.com
Maps of roads, activity, scenic
byways; information on lodging,
camping, shopping, dining, recreation, and events

State Parks

Colorado State Parks
1313 Sherman St., Room 618
Denver, CO 80203
303-866-3437
www.parks.state.co.us
Information on public programs,
cabins, camping, dining, events,
and tour reservations

State Park Camping

Reserve America
Reservations
800-444-7275
www.reserve america.com

Private Campgrounds

Colorado Association
of Campgrounds,
Cabins and Lodges
303-499-9343 or 888-222-4641

Bureau of Land Management

BLM Colorado Office
2850 Youngfield St.
Lakewood, CO 80215
303-329-3600
www.co.blm.gov/

Hawaii

Road Conditions

808-536-6566

Hawaii Tourism

Hawaii Visitors & Convention
Bureau
2270 Kalakaua Ave., Suite 801
Honolulu, HI 96815
808-923-1811
www.gohawaii.com
Information on travel tips, events,
hotels, campgrounds, resorts, hos-
tels; and land, sea, sky activities

Hawaii Tourism Authority

Hawaii Convention Center
1801 Kalakaua Ave.
Honolulu, HI 96815
808-973-2255
www.hawaii.gov/tourism/main.html
Information on tourism development and policy in Hawaii

State Parks and Licenses

State of Hawaii, Department of
Land and Natural Resources
Kalanimoku Bldg.
1151 Punchbowl St.
Honolulu, HI 96813
808-587-0400
www.hawaii.gov/dlnr/dsp/dsp.html
Information on camping, hiking
trails, safety, fees, licenses, permits

Montana

Road Conditions

406-444-6339, 800-226-7623,
or 511
www.mdt.state.mt.us/travinfo

Montana Tourism

Travel Montana
800-847-4868
www.visitmt.com
General travel information,
including camping and hotels

State Parks

Montana Fish, Wildlife and Parks
1420 E. 6th Ave.
Helena, MT 59620
406-444-2535
State park information and hunting licenses. For a list of recreational activities, call 900-225-5397.

Camping and Fishing Licenses

Montana Department of Natural Resources and Conservation
1625 11th Ave.
Helena, MT 59620
406-444-2074
Licenses and permits for stream fishing; camping information

Bureau of Land Management

P.O. Box 36800
Billings, MT 59107
406-896-5000

Montana Department of Transportation Bicycle Program

Box 201001
Helena, MT 59620
406-444-9273
Information on biking trails and tours in Montana

North Dakota

Road Conditions

All numbers listed provide state road conditions, as well as local conditions
701-328-7623 (Bismarck area)
701-857-7623 (Minot area)
701-795-3880 (Grand Forks area)
701-227-7460 (Dickinson area)
701-239-8950 (Fargo area)
701-845-8630 (Valley City area)
701-857-7623 (outside all other areas)
www.state.nd.us/dot/road.html

North Dakota Tourism

North Dakota Tourism Division
Century Center
1600 E. Century Ave., Suite 2
P.O. Box 2057
Bismarck, ND 58503
701-328-2525 or 800-435-5663
www.ndtourism.com
Maps and information on camping, canoeing, forests/refuges, historic sites, lakes/rivers, parks, preserves, and scenic routes

State Parks

North Dakota Parks & Recreation Department
1600 E. Century Ave., Suite 3
Bismarck, ND 58503-0649
701-328-5357
www.ndparks.com
Information on state parks, including outdoor activities, cabins and shelters, fees, maps, reservations; links to state's scenic byways

Fishing and Hunting Licenses

North Dakota Game and Fish Department
100 N. Bismarck Expressway
Bismarck, ND 58501
701-328-6300 (general information)
701-328-6335 (licensing)
www.state.nd.us/gnf

Bureau of Land Management

5001 Southgate Dr.
Billings, MT 59101
406-896-5000
www.mt.blm.gov

Oregon

Road Conditions

800-977-6368
503-588-2941 (outside Oregon)
www.tripcheck.com

Oregon Tourism

Oregon Tourism Commission
775 Summer St. N.E.
Salem, OR 97310
800-547-7842
www.traveloregon.com
Information on camping, lodging,
outdoor activities, sites, events,
and more

State Parks

Oregon Parks and
Recreation Department
1115 Commercial St. N.E.
Salem, OR 97310
800-551-6949 for information
800-452-5687 reservations
www.prd.state.or.us
Information on camping, reservations, safety, and events

Fishing and Hunting Licenses

Oregon Department of Fish and
Wildlife
P.O. Box 59
Portland, OR 97207
503-872-5268
www.dfw.state.or.us

Camping, Forest Service, and Bureau of Land Management

Nature of the Northwest
800 N.E. Oregon St., Suite 177
Portland, OR 97232
503-872-2750
www.naturenw.org
Maps and books; informa-
tion on campgrounds, cabin rentals,
national forests, and Bureau of
Land Management lands

Forest Service Fall Color Hotline

800-354-4595 (only in fall)

Portland Oregon Bicycle Program

1120 S.W. 5th St., Room 730
Portland, OR 97204
503-823-2925
State bike trails information, maps

South Dakota

Road Conditions

South Dakota Department of
Transportation
Becker-Hansen Building
700 E. Broadway Ave.
Pierre, SD 57501
605-773-3265 or 511
www.sddot.com

South Dakota Tourism

Department of Tourism and State
Development
711 E. Wells Ave.
Pierre, SD 57501
605-773-3301
www.travelsd.com
Information on history, events/
activities, and destinations

Parks, and Hunting and Fishing Licenses

South Dakota Game Fish and Parks
523 East Capitol Ave.
Pierre, SD 57501
605-773-3485 (hunting and fishing)
605-773-3391 (parks and
recreation)
800-710-2267 (state campground
reservations)
www.sdgfp.info/Index.htm

Bureau of Land Management

5001 Southgate Dr.
Billings, MT 59101
406-896-5000

Washington

Road Conditions

800-695-7623
http://wsdot.wa.gov

Washington Tourism

Washington State Tourism Division
P.O. Box 42500
Olympia, WA 98504
800-890-5493
www.tourism.wa.gov
Variety of travel and recreational
information, including lodging,
camping, and whale-watching

State Parks

Washington State Parks
& Recreation Commission
Information Center
P.O. Box 42662
Olympia, WA 98504
800-233-0321
www.parks.wa.gov
Information on services, amenities, campgrounds, and activities, including winter recreation

Fishing and Hunting Licenses

Washington Department
of Fish and Wildlife
600 Capitol Way N.
Olympia, WA 98501
360-902-2200
www.wa.gov/wdfw
Variety of information, including regulations and licensing for fishing and hunting. Call the Recreational Fishery Regulation Hotline at 360-796-3215.

Washington State Ferries

2911 2nd Ave.
Seattle, WA 98121
206-464-6400
888-808-7977
800-843-3779 (automated information only)
www.wsdot.wa.gov/ferries

Wyoming

Road Conditions

307-772-0824
888-996-7623
www.wyoroad.info/index.html

Wyoming Tourism

Wyoming Division of Tourism
I-25 at College Dr.
Cheyenne, WY 82002
307-777-7777
www.wyomingtourism.org
Travel information and guidance, including camping and hotel information

State Parks

Wyoming State Parks and Historic Sites
122 W. 25th St.
Herschler Building 1-E
Cheyenne, WY 82002
307-777-6323
Visitor guidance, including camping

Wyoming Recreation and Parks Association
P.O. Box 953
Rawlins, WY 82301
307-328-4570
General information and brochures on the state parks, trails, and lakes

Fishing and Hunting Licesnes

Wyoming Fish and Game
Department
5400 Bishop Blvd.
Cheyenne, WY 82006
307-777-4600
www.gf.state.wy.us

Bureau of Land Management

5353 Yellowstone Ave.
Cheyenne, WY 82009
307-775-6256
Maps and information on BLM-managed land. Recreational guide and small pamphlet includes camping information.

INDEX

Illustrations Credits

Cover Galen Rowell/CORBIS. Back Cover George H. H. Huey.
1 Barry Bishop. 2-3 Sam Abell. 6 William Allen, NGS. 9 David Alan Harvey. 14-24 (all) Annie Griffiths Belt. 29 Phil Schermeister/NGS Image Collection. 30, 35 Phil Schermeister. 38 James D. Balog. 44 Phil Schermeister. 47, 50 Phil Schermeister/NGS Image Collection. 55 Joel Sartore/NGS Image Collection. 56 Raymond Gehman. 60 Joel Sartore/www.joelsartore.com. 62 Erwin & Peggy Bauer. 65 Raymond Gehman. 68, 71 Paul Chesley. 73 Raymond Gehman. 75 J.C. Leacock. 78 Dewitt Jones. 82-89 (all) Raymond Gehman. 90 Paul Chesley. 93, 97 Raymond Gehman. 101 Paul Chesley. 104 William Allen, NGS. 109 Bill Losh/Getty Images. 110 William Allen, NGS. 116 Ralph Lee Hopkins. 122-123 Richard A. Cooke III. 126-127 Robert W. Madden. 128 Phil Schermeister. 132, 134-135 Jim Richardson. 137-145 (all) Phil Schermeister. 146 James P. Blair. 152-153 Sam Abell. 156 James P. Blair. 159 Tomasz Tomaszewski. 160 Peter Essick. 164 Jim Richardson. 166-174 (all) James P. Blair. 177 Bruce Dale. 183 James P. Blair. 184, 189 Sam Abell. 190 James P. Blair. 193 Sam Abell. 194 Art Wolfe. 198 Bates Littlehales. 202 Raymond Gehman/NGS Image Collection. 206 Melissa Farlow/NGS Image Collection. 212-225 (all) Phil Schermeister. 226-239 (all) George H. H. Huey. 241 Alan Briere. 244, 247 George H. H. Huey. 248-261 (all) Phil Schermeister. 262, 267 Michael Melford. 271 Thomas J. Abercrombie. 274 Sarah Leen. 278 Jim Brandenburg/Minden Pictures. 280-281, 283 Raymond Gehman. 285, 289 Kent Dannen. 292, 294 Raymond Gehman. 298 Paul Chesley. 302-311 (all) Raymond Gehman. 316-324 (all) Phil Schermeister. 326 Charles Cramer. 329 Photographer Unknown. 333 John Poimiroo. 335-341 (all) Phil Schermeister.

Staff Credits

National Geographic Guide to the National Parks: West
Published by the National Geographic Society

John M. Fahey, Jr., *President and Chief Executive Officer;* Gilbert M. Grosvenor, *Chairman of the Board;* Nina D. Hoffman, *Executive Vice President, President, Books and School Publishing;* Kevin Mulroy, *Vice-President and Editor-in-Chief;* Marianne Koszorus, *Design Director;* Elizabeth L. Newhouse, *Director of Travel Publishing;* Barbara A. Noe, *Project Director;* Robin Reid, Thomas Schmidt, John Thompson, *Editors;* Cinda Rose, *Art Director and Designer;* Carl Mehler, *Director of Maps;* Matt Chwastyk, Thomas L. Gray, Melissa Hunsiker, Joseph F. Ochlak, Nicholas P. Rosenbach, Gregory Ugiansky, Martin S. Walz, and The M Factory, *Map Research and Production;* Lise Sajewski, *Style/Copy Editor;* Lewis Bassford, *Production Project Manager;* Barbara A. Noe, *Photo Editor;* Meredith Wilcox, *Illustrations Assistant;* Robert Swanson, *Indexer;* Ben Archambault, Ben Bodurian, Caroline Hickey, Cindy Kittner, Lawrence Porges, John Thompson, Ruth Ann Thompson, Mel White, Simon Williams, Jordan Zappala, *Contributors*

Copyright © 2005 National Geographic Society. All rights reserved. Reproduction of the whole or any part of the contents without permission is prohibited. Library of Congress Cataloging-in-Publication Data

National Geographic guide to national parks. West.
p. cm.
Includes index.
ISBN 0-7922-9538-2 (alk. paper)
1. National parks and reserves--West (U.S.)--Guidebooks. 2. West (U.S.)--Guidebooks.
I. National Geographic Society (U.S.)
F590.3N37 2005
917.804'34--dc22

2004022726

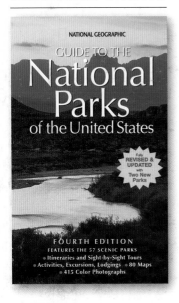
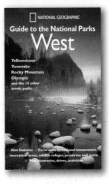
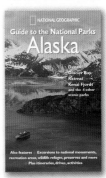